DATE DUE

1/2/99			

Between Profit and State

For Murray and Rita Zelin
and Peggy Harris

Between Profit and State

Intermediate Organizations in Britain and the United States

ALAN WARE

Princeton University Press
Princeton, New Jersey

Published by Princeton University Press, 41 William Street,
Princeton, New Jersey 08540

Library of Congress Cataloging-in-Publication Data

Ware, Alan.
Between profit and state : intermediate organizations in Britain and the United States / Alan Ware.
p. cm.
Bibliography: p.
Includes index.
ISBN 0-691-07818-1
1. Corporations, Nonprofit—Great Britain. 2. Corporations, Nonprofit—United States. 3. Charities—Great Britain. 4. Charities—United States. I. Title.
HD2769.2.G7W37 1989
338.7′4′0941—dc19 88-34148

Printed in Great Britain

Contents

List of Figures and Tables

Figures

Tables

Preface

During the 1980s social scientists have started to devote increasing attention to a wide range of organizations which were previously the subject of remarkably little research. These organizations fall outside the immediate domain of the state, yet they are not part of the profit-making sector of the economy. In this book they are referred to as intermediate organizations. There is much empirical research still to be undertaken on intermediate organizations, for there are many aspects of their relations with both the market system and the state which have yet to be examined. However, when I first became interested in these organizations, it seemed to me that there were no satisfactory analytic frameworks in political theory into which the now-burgeoning empirical studies could be fitted. *Between Profit and State* is an attempt to synthesize much of our new understanding of intermediate organizations within such a framework.

In the three years or so in which I have been engaged in writing this book I have become indebted to several organizations and to a great many individuals. During 1984–5 I received a grant from the University of Warwick's Research and Innovation Fund which enabled me to spend a term's sabbatical leave in the United States. As a result I could attend research seminars at Princeton and Yale, and I benefited enormously from the help I received then from Stanley Katz and John Simon. In 1986–7 I was fortunate to be awarded a Research Fellowship by the Nuffield Foundation; this freed me from teaching and administrative responsibilities at Warwick, and allowed me to concentrate on research and writing – both in Britain and in the United States. Having the fellowship also enabled me to interview government officials, legislative aides and lobbyists in London, Ottawa and Washington. My time in America was made more rewarding by my being made a Research

Affiliate at the Program on Non-Profit Organizations (PONPO) of Yale University's Institution for Social and Policy Studies. For the help I received at Yale that year, I am especially grateful to Paul DiMaggio and John Simon, but there were many other participants at the seminars at PONPO from whom I was able to learn a great deal.

Early drafts of various chapters were presented at seminars at the Universities of Edinburgh and Manchester, as well as at the Political Theory Workshop in my own department, and I am grateful for the helpful criticisms I received from the participants at these seminars. I have also been very fortunate in that several academic friends and colleagues have been willing to read, and comment on, the manuscript. In particular I wish to thank Peter Burnell, Tom Deans, Des King, Andy Reeve and Madeleine Zelin, all of whom commented on the entire manuscript. The extensive help I have received from them has much improved the book, although, of course, responsibility for the errors that remain is mine alone.

In addition, I have received much encouragement, once again, from David Held, Polity Press and Princeton University Press. But my final debt, as always, is to my family: as well as commenting on the manuscript, Matti encouraged me to 'keep going on with it', and Iain has been exceptional in understanding that there were times when I had to work and could not play with him.

Alan Ware, Warwick

1

Introduction

The development of liberal democracy is intimately bound up with the rise of capitalist economies. To say this is not to deny that democracy, and possibly far more complete forms of democracy than liberal democracy, could be established under very different economic arrangements. But there is no denying that the kind of democracy which emerged in North America and western Europe in the nineteenth century was heavily influenced by a profit-orientated economic system based on private ownership. And just as for-profit organizations have shaped the structure and operations of the liberal democratic state, so the state has affected the *modus operandi* of business enterprises. Nevertheless, as virtually every citizen is aware, not every organization found in a liberal democracy is either a profit-making concern or a branch of government. There are a wide variety of institutions which are not part of the state nor engaged in earning profits for owners. Indeed, many democratic theorists, and not just those who defend the liberal democratic form, have argued that non-state, non-profit-distributing organizations can play a crucial role in advancing democracy within a society. This book is about this broad category of organizations, which we shall refer to as intermediate organizations (IOs). The term IO is used in this book to refer to organizations which in law are private institutions but which take a legal status that prevents the distribution of any profits they might make.[1] They lie between the state and the profit-making sector. Among the kinds of organizations which can be classified as intermediate organizations are churches, non-profit-making hospitals and social welfare agencies, famine relief agencies, 'private' universities, consumer co-operatives, credit unions and social clubs.

One consequence of identifying IOs in terms of their being legally private, non-profit-distributing organizations is that it enables us to circumvent, at least initially, some major problems in classifying organizations. As many studies by political scientists have shown, the boundaries between the modern state and private institutions are difficult to draw. There are numerous institutions that may be described as merely semi-private; some of the organizations that are the subject of this book are semi-private.[2] One example, though it is not discussed explicitly here, is the Medical Research Council in Britain. It has the legal status of a charity, and hence is non-governmental, but it derives nearly all its funds from central government and, indeed, does not advertise for donations, although it does accept gifts. This kind of organization is one of many types to be found in the increasingly blurred penumbra of the state. The advantage of identifying IOs in the way that I have here is that, in avoiding at the beginning the issue of 'how far the state extends', we can look at the more interesting, and less discussed, question of the nature of the 'private' (and the 'semi-private').

The idea of there being organizations which lie between the state and the market is one which is partly related to an older argument – that of the role of associations and organizations which lie intermediate to the state and the individual. It was, of course, only after the effects of the industrial revolution became apparent that political theorists woke up to the problem of the power of economic *organizations*; for at least the first half of the nineteenth century it was the potential power of the state which was the concern of most writers. Consequently, as in the case of Tocqueville, the intermediate associations with which they were concerned usually included for-profit enterprises as well as the sorts of organizations which form the subject of this book. Moreover, many of the writers who were interested in the relation of the individual to the state regarded other institutions, like the family, as much as a part of the 'intermediate universe' as the IOs which we are discussing. Yet the context of modern debates about the role of IOs, in which the for-profit economy is seen as an incomplete mechanism for distributing goods, cannot be understood fully except by reference to a few aspects of the older argument. However, the primary focus of the book remains that of IOs as we have just identified them.

At the risk of some over-simplification, we may suggest that controversy about intermediate entities in a society has tended to focus on two main debates. The first is whether in the modern state IOs are threatened by other institutions, and, indeed, two radically different traditions have held that there is such a threat. On the one side, there is a major strand of modern conservatism, which can be traced back through nineteenth century liberal thought, and which has seen the state as undermining IOs unless tight constraints are placed on state power. A modern version of this thesis is outlined by Nisbet who argues that:

> The real conflict in modern political history has not been, as is so often stated, between State and individual but, between State and social group. What Maitland once called the 'pulverizing and macadamizing tendecy of modern history' has been one of the most vivid aspects of the social history of the West, and it has been inseparable from the momentous conflicts of jurisdiction between the political State and the social associations lying intermediate to it and the individual.[3]

From the general proposition that the state will take over activities previously within the domain of IOs, a number of more specific hypotheses about the threat posed by the state have been identified by other writers. For example, it has often been claimed by those who today would be described as conservatives that extensive state provision of welfare would not simply lead to the replacement of private agencies, but would actually discourage philanthropy. State intervention would transform attitudes as well as institutions. Some anarchist writers too have argued that the presence of the state discourages altruism.[4]

But there are also lines of argument more worrying to socialists who have expressed concern about the undermining of IOs. One set of arguments about the dangers posed by the modern state were provided by the early English pluralists, including Cole and Laski, who were major contributors to the social democratic tradition in Britain.[5] The English pluralists argued that freedom was best preserved through the dispersion of power in a society.[6] A more directly socialist argument, though, has been that the threat to IOs comes from the market. As the market extends to more areas of social life, so institutions based on co-operation between individuals, and those founded on altruism, will be undermined. The introduction of a market transaction depresses notions of community and impersonal reciprocity, and the more social practices become open to these transactions, the greater will be the pursuit of individual self-interest. Many non-Marxist socialists have drawn on the opposition of *Gemeinschaft* (community) and *Gesellschaft* (society) identified by Tönnies, but arguments derived from liberal economics have also been used to explain the conflict between the two.[7] One of the most well known modern statements of the opposition of the market-place to community and altruism is that of Hirsch, while Titmuss has also drawn attention to their opposition in his study of the market in blood.[8]

The second debate about intermediate bodies on which attention has been focused has been their role in a *democratic* state. In particular, IOs have been seen as being capable of performing a number of functions in a democracy, although there has been considerable disagreement between democratic theorists as to which of these functions can actually be performed and exactly how important each of them is for the sustenance of a democratic state.

This book is concerned with issues arising from this second debate and is an attempt to fill what seems to be a major gap in our understanding of the working of representative democracy. It focuses on the distinctiveness of IOs and examines the boundaries between these organizations and the liberal democratic state, on the one hand, and the market system, on the other. We shall see that the 'real world' of IOs is rather different from the idealized account of them that appears in many theoretical discussions about democracy. The boundaries with the market are difficult to define, and many organizations that pass as IOs are, partly or wholly, commercial enterprises operating under a legal framework which was not intended originally for such enterprises. Similarly, the boundaries with the state are often imprecise. Ultimately our purpose is to examine whether this rather more accurate account of IOs has important consequences for some of the arguments about their contribution to democracy.

The study is largely confined to Britain and the US, and it is necessary to explain both why it has been restricted in this way and why these two particular states have been selected. The variety of IOs to be found in all western states, and the complex relations between them, would make a fully comparative study impossibly cumbrous. Legal and institutional structures vary so much, even within western Europe, that in a book of this length more limited comparisons must be undertaken. Although there is a long-standing tradition of Anglo-American comparisons in political science, the justification for them is not always obvious; this is especially true in relation to their respective legislatures and executives, where intra-European comparisons drawing on similar parliamentary structures are often far more illuminating. Nevertheless, in the case of IOs there are three reasons for believing that an Anglo-American comparative study might well be revealing. Firstly, the legal frameworks within which many IOs have operated are remarkably similar, so that, even though major differences can be traced back to the early years of the Republic, the relevant legal structures in Britain and the US have far more in common than either does with those in continental Europe. Secondly, many of the institutions have been transplanted or copied within a few years of their becoming established in one country; among the examples in the nineteenth century (of exports from Britain to the US) were Building Societies and the Charity Organization Societies. Thirdly, in both countries the state, as an institution and as an analytic construct, has been developed weakly, although there are some significant dissimilarities here that should not be overlooked. While there are instances of some of the Anglo-American IOs developing in other countries, a comparative study involving other regimes would be much more difficult to operate, and any conclusions drawn about the role of IOs in a democracy would necessarily be even more tentative than those we might draw from an Anglo-American comparison.

There is, admittedly, one problem which arises in most comparative studies involving Britain and the US – the unitary nature of the British state in contrast to the federalism of the US. In the context of this study this poses no particular problems in analysis, although, as we shall see, federalism has had a major impact on the financial dependence of many IOs on the state. It must be remembered, of course, that many laws affecting the formation and activities of IOs in the US are those of the individual states, and there are variations between them.

The transformation of Britain and the US in the twentieth century from merely industrial to post-industrial societies has had important consequences for IOs, but it is necessary to distinguish the effects on IOs that were most apparent a few years ago from those which are regarded as significant today. Until quite recently three developments seemed to be crucial. The first was that some of the working-class mutual-benefit organizations established in the nineteenth century had become major components of national economies, and were now largely indistinguishable from for-profit enterprises, both in respect of their business practices and their internal control. The second was the growth of the welfare state which had resulted in many IOs in the field of social welfare becoming supplementary to the state – their purpose was to 'fill gaps' by providing services which the state could not, or would not. The third development was that while it was recognized that there were unclear boundaries involving both the state and the market, IOs were generally seen as independent from both. Some were highly political in character, some liaised closely with government departments, others were engaged in economic activities, but for the most part they constituted a distinctive arena of activity. The popular image of most of these organizations was that they depended neither on market activity nor on the state for their funding; whenever they had to deal with the state, they did so as autonomous actors, and overtly political activity tended to be sporadic. At the core of this group of organizations were charities – bodies which seemed to exemplify the distinctiveness of this set of organizations. Indeed, in recent years it has become fashionable in the US to refer to them as constituting a separate *sector* of capitalist democracies – sometimes it is referred to as the 'third sector', sometimes 'the independent sector', sometimes the 'non-profit sector', and sometimes the 'the voluntary sector'.[9] Many of the organizations themselves have fostered propaganda of this sort because of the favourable publicity it engenders.

However, there is another side to IOs in Britain, and most especially in the US, which has been recognized only during the last few years – at the same time as the view of an independent *sector* has been propagated. This does not completely change our understanding of these bodies, but it does suggest that their relations with the market and the state are far more complex, and far less 'independent', than the 'third sector' image suggests. Far from economic activity being confined to the fringes of the 'sector', it became increasingly obvious that trading activities of various kinds constituted a major aspect of the operations of many IOs, and in the US there were areas of extensive competition between for-profit enterprises and IOs, and between IOs themselves. In addition, many organizations had also become heavily dependent on funding from the state, which both raises questions about their independence and suggests that patterns of influence involving IOs and the state are highly complicated. Furthermore, the supposed non-political character of much of the 'sector' has been cast into doubt not merely by the issue of dependence on state resources, but also by evidence that the activities of even those IOs with charitable status draw them regularly into the political arena. In brief, the lines of demarcation between IOs and both the market and the state seem more blurred than a simple model of a 'third sector' would suggest. Undoubtedly, there are many organizations that conform to this model, but it would seem that there are fewer than the simple model suggests.

This book is an attempt to provide a general overview of IOs in relation to both the market and the state. It raises questions as to why the boundaries with the other 'sectors' should have become more blurred and about the problems this raises for the state. As I have said, its purpose is to re-examine the claims that have been made for IOs in democratic theory in the light of this more complex picture we now have of these organizations. It seeks to provide an analysis and synthesis of information that is already available about IOs, rather than presenting wholly new data about particular IOs.

The remainder of this chapter is concerned with three aspects of analysis that are central to an understanding of the subsequent discussion of IOs in Britain and the US. In the next section we outline the ways in which IOs have been seen as contributing to the advancement of democracy; then we consider a relatively new development in American social science – attempts to account for the existence of certain kinds of IOs, known as non-profit organizations, in market economies; finally, there is a brief introduction to the development of IOs in the two countries. The subsequent chapters cover three broad themes in sequence – the economic activities of IOs, the supposedly distinguishing features of many IOs (the independence of their income and their use of volunteer labour), and state involvement with IOs.

Both chapters 2 and 3 are about the economic activities of IOs, but each deals with organizations of a particular legal form. Chapter 2 examines one of the main points of contact of IOs with the market system – the activities of mutual-benefit organizations. In the past organizations based on the principle of co-operation have provided the main challenge to for-profit enterprise, and chapter 2 traces the development and transformation of co-operativism when it comes into competition with overtly commercial organizations. Chapter 3 is concerned with the other main legal form that IOs can take – namely charities. It is about competition between for-profit enterprises and the state, on the one hand, and charities on the other. It examines the issue of why competition, and also co-operation, between charities and for-profit businesses should develop in capitalist economies as well as the impact this can have on the state.

In chapters 4 and 5 we discuss the features that many people believe distinguish several kinds of IO from both the state and for-profit enterprises – the autonomy which their sources of income provide and their heavy reliance on volunteer labour. Following on from the discussion in the previous chapter, chapter 4 is also about charities and consists of an examination of the role of donations in the funding of these organizations. It considers how much independence is provided for charities by both donations and other sources of income, as well as the impact this has on their ability to respond autonomously to social needs. Chapter 5 examines an aspect of many IOs, and not just charities, that is often regarded as one their distinguishing features – the use of volunteer labour. In particular it considers changes in the pattern of volunteerism in Britain and the US and their effects on the state.

Both chapters 6 and 7 are about the interaction of the state with IOs. Chapter 6 considers three areas of activity where the provision of services either by the state or on a market basis is widely regarded as undermining the value of the activities themselves – religion, basic research and the arts. In chapter 7 we examine the problem of how the state in both Britain and the US has attempted to regulate IOs.

Finally, in chapter 8, we draw together the discussion in the previous chapters and reconsider whether IOs do indeed contribute to the advancement of democracy in some of the ways identified in section 1 below.

1 Intermediate Organizations and the Advancement of Democracy

Broadly speaking the legal forms which IOs might take are of four kinds; this is illustrated in figure 1.1. Firstly, there are organizations which can qualify for charitable status – a status which embraces several types of organization which the general public does not normally consider to be 'charities' while it also excludes others which are widely perceived to be 'charities'. Secondly, there is a diversity of legal forms which organizations established to promote the mutual benefit of their members may take. Thirdly, there are bodies which are simply associations. In some cases they are neither charitable in law nor covered specifically by regulations relating to mutual-benefit organizations. In many instances, though, the body is simply not large to make it worth operating as anything other than an association. Finally, there are overtly political organizations – some categories of which may be regulated by laws unique to themselves, while others may be very similar in their legal position to non-political associations. In this respect, the classification presented in figure 1.1 is a little misleading, since in the interest of simplicity *all* political organizations have been shown as separate from other kinds of association.

However, the complexities involved in identifying IOs do not end here. In many US states there are legal provisions for a variety of kinds of IO to register as 'non-profit corporations', and the distinction between this category and other organizations cross-cuts the schema we have presented. In figure 1.1 non-profit corporations are indicated within the area embraced by the dotted line. We consider these organizations more fully in section 2.

Why, it might be asked, has the subject matter been defined in quite this way? One of the difficulties which must be faced in any analysis of IOs is that of defining the boundaries between these sorts of organizations and those in the for-profit sector and in the state sector. In part, as we have already noted, the difficulties reflect complexities involved in separating 'private' and 'public'. As Lane has pointed out, there are a number of different dimensions along which we may seek to distinguish 'private' from 'public' – including ownership and allocation mechanism (market versus public budget).[10] There are a great many organizations which, in relation to these dimensions, might be thought of as *intermediate* bodies. Examples might include some of the quasi-governmental agencies which proliferated in post-war Britain, and upon which the first Thatcher administration launched a policy of 'quangocide'. But the organizations which are the focus of attention in this book are not just a collection of

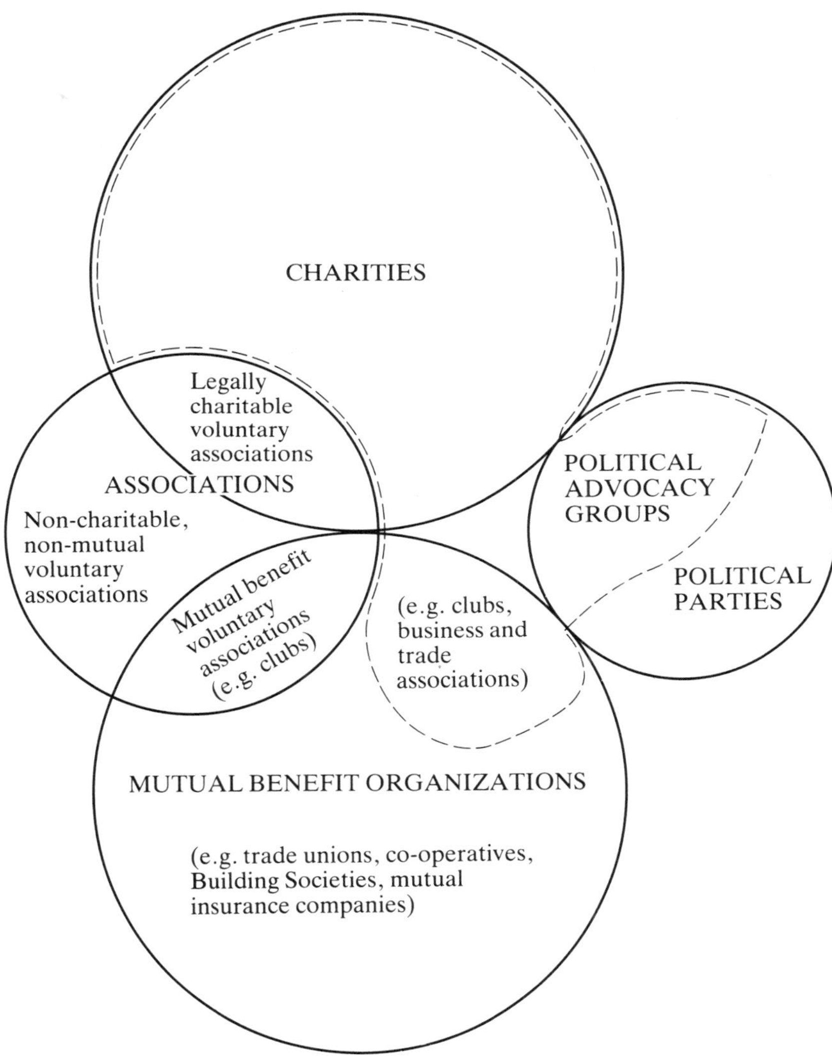

Figure 1.1 Intermediate organizations: a typology

agencies which fall into a 'no-man's land' in the uncertain area outlined by attempts to separate 'private' from 'public'. If they were, they would surely constitute a disparate collection of organizations about which few general conclusions could be drawn.

The key feature of IOs, as the term is used in this book, is that they are unambiguously private institutions with respect to their legal status. Unlike, for example, the Milk Marketing Board they are not agencies which have 'special chartered or statutory powers to punish offenders or to raise licences or levies for specified purposes'.[11] But that they are legally private institutions does not entail either that all of them have autonomy with respect to their own policies or that the state is not a causal factor in their formation. As we shall see, some IOs like British universities have lost much of their autonomy while in the US there are many instances of federal government funding being responsible for the formation of IOs. IOs are not state agencies, or agencies established by the state to exercise authority *in lieu* of state intervention, yet they are bodies possessing a legal status separate from organizations established to earn profits for their owners.

Thus, in relation to the ownership dimension, we may say of IOs that they are not owned by the state, that many are not *owned* at all, and where (as in the case of consumer co-operatives) it is possible to talk about their having owners these owners cannot distribute profits to themselves. It is in this sense that we can speak of IOs as being between profit and state; this is illustrated in the horizontal axis of the typology presented in figure 1.2. But how do IOs fit into other dimensions of the dimensions of the 'public' – 'private' distinction? For example, consider the often cited distinction between market and taxation as sources of income. One conception of IOs, a conception we consider later, is that IOs have distinctive forms of funding – they rely neither on commercial transactions to generate income nor on the imposition of taxes for this purpose. Rather, they rely on such sources as donations and subscriptions and other contributions from their members. In fact, as we shall see, if this were to count as a distinctive aspect of IOs, IOs would be a rather small category of organizations – for a vast number of IOs (as defined in relation to the 'ownership' dimension) now depend on either the market or the public budget, and frequently on both. If we were to define IOs in terms of both the ownership and the income-source dimensions, then the shaded area in figure 1.2 would omit many kinds of organizations (including universities and 'charitable' hospitals) which are usually thought of as typifying organizations that lie between the market sector and the state.

Lane has observed that: 'It is often argued that the distinction between the public and the private sectors has become more diffuse in the rich

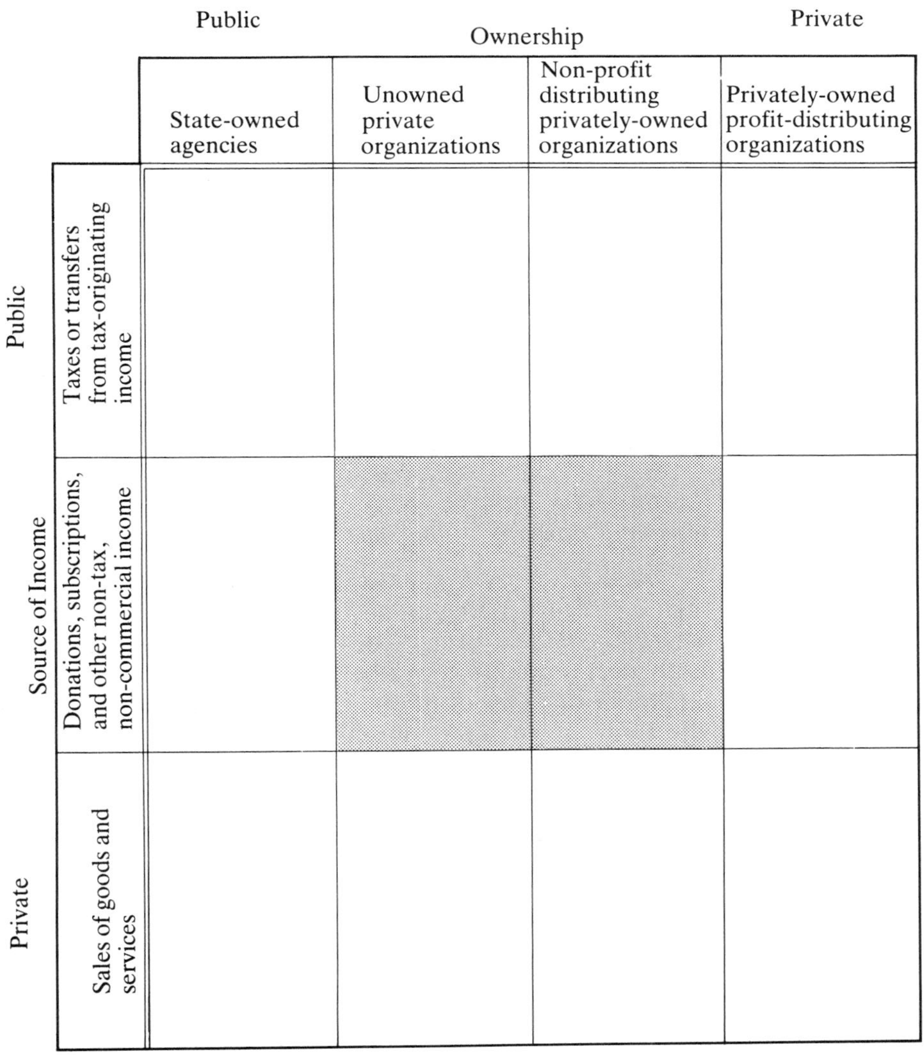

Source of Income ↓ / Ownership →	Public: State-owned agencies	Unowned private organizations	Non-profit distributing privately-owned organizations	Private: Privately-owned profit-distributing organizations
Public: Taxes or transfers from tax-originating income				
Donations, subscriptions, and other non-tax, non-commercial income		(shaded)	(shaded)	
Private: Sales of goods and services				

Figure 1.2 Typology of the distinction between 'public' and 'private' in relation to two dimensions – ownership and sources of income

countries with representative governments.'[12] What should become apparent in this book is that, in many respects, the distinctions between IOs and both the private, for-profit economy and the state have become more diffuse too. This has caused peculiar problems for state supervision and regulation of certain kinds of IOs, because their legal forms have their origins in the early developments of economy and state when the distinctiveness of IOs was more evident.

If we accept that, at least for our purposes, IOs are most usefully defined with respect to their legal forms, we must now turn to the issue that lies at the heart of this book: the role played by IOs in advancing democracy. Our discussion focuses on both descriptive and normative considerations: how IOs have been involved in its advancement and how they should be used to further democratization. This reflects the close relationship in democratic theory between normative and positive arguments. It is, perhaps, most useful to begin by identifying nine principal ways in which these organizations have been seen as agents of democracy; we will return to consider these arguments again in chapter 8.

A Countervailing power – to the state and/or the market

One contention is that IOs act as a countervailing force either to the state or to the market. This argument has been accepted by many democratic theorists who could be broadly described as pluralists, but it is important to distinguish a number of rather different arguments that have been propounded in this general form. First, there are some IOs, and most especially trade unions and consumers' organizations, which have been established directly to counteract the power of particular business interests. Disputes among democrats here tend to focus on the ability of these bodies to effect control over for-profit enterprises, and on disagreements about the need for countervailing power of this kind in a market economy. Many conservative writers regard the market itself as the best regulatory mechanism governing for-profit enterprises, so that unions and consumer groups merely tend to distort the market. On the other hand, many non-conservatives have been far more sceptical about the self-regulatory potential of markets, and have argued the case for checking corporate power.

Second, some democrats have seen many other kinds of IO as capable of performing a more general checking role to counteract the power of for-profit concerns. In a variety of complex ways, churches, social-welfare agencies, and universities, among others, can help to temper the remorseless pursuit of profit that might otherwise develop in a market economy. The 'unacceptable faces of capitalism' are indirectly kept in check by institutions that create and mould public opinion and which can act as centres of opposition to the policies of business firms that would seriously disadvantage those without economic power.

Third, there are democrats who see IOs as a valuable check not on the market system, but on the state. Most usually today this is associated with conservatism, but the English pluralists of the early twentieth century, who constituted an important strand of liberal and social democratic thought in Britain, were worried by state power: 'The pluralist writings of Maitland, Figgis, Laski, Cole, Russell, Lindsay and others certainly amounted to a vigorous attack upon the sovereignty of the state, and on the wide claims for the state that were being made in many liberal and socialist circles.'[13]

For the conservatives it is state power which is most dangerous and intermediate organizations can be useful in two ways in counteracting it. Like the second group of democratic theorists, they argue that indirectly, through opinion and value formation, IOs can help to develop a political culture that is hostile to excessive state power. But, because many of the organizations themselves can provide the services that the modern state does, such as education, health care and so on, there is a more direct way for them to counteract state power. Many services, they claim, could be supplied by these organizations, even if the state is ultimately responsible for funding them, and even if the state has to provide some services directly, the availability of other suppliers helps to prevent the state from abusing its powers.

B Arenas of participation

With the exception of those conservative democrats, like Schumpeter, who regard democracy at the level of the state as consisting of no more than a mechanism for removing elected elites, there has been agreement that widespread participation in policy making in the state is an important component of democracy.[14] By some, participation has been seen as crucial for citizen control of the state, while for others it is its developmental aspects which are more valuable. However, there are two problems in realizing greater mass participation in the state – it is difficult to decentralize many areas of state decision making to provide for genuine input by citizens to the policy process, and citizens may lack the skills and values necessary for this kind of participation. Some democratic theorists have seen in at least some IOs a remedy for these problems. In organizations where members undertake much of the work of the organization, participants can acquire the skills necessary for other kinds of participation and can also be involved in making decisions affecting themselves and others. This is true for organizations based on the principle of self-help, as well as for those providing services for others.

Controversy about this possible role for IOs has tended to centre on two main issues. One is the extent of membership involvement in these organizations. Critics have pointed out that many of them are not of the membership kind, and even those that are often give relatively little power to their members. The other issue has been the relevance of participation in these bodies to participation in a democratic state. While critics have usually not denied that participatory IOs may contribute to the growth of a democratic culture in a state, they have often rejected the view that these sorts of organizations give people very much control over their own lives or over the affairs of their communities.

C Provision of 'non-market goods'

There are some goods which people want that can be supplied by for-profit enterprises only at the cost of the possibility of distorting or devaluing the good itself – facilities for religious observance, basic research, and works of art are perhaps the most important of them. At the same time, however, there has been considerable agreement among many democrats that these goods should also not be supplied directly by the state, because once again there is the likelihood that much of what is valued might be undermined by state provision. Instead it has been widely argued that non-market organizations should be free to establish themselves in the state to practise religious values, promote basic research and create works of art and give artistic performances. This idea that there are special kinds of 'non-market goods' which are best provided by non-profit-distributing, non-state agencies has developed as the liberal democratic state has grown. While freedom of religious observance, freedom to develop new theories, and freedom of artistic expression are now accepted as essential conditions of liberal democracy, these freedoms were only slowly recognized as the pre-democratic states of the sixteenth and seventeenth centuries were transformed into mass democracies by the early years of twentieth century. Thus, in place of the private patron (in the arts) and state intervention to suppress dangerous tendencies (in churches and in colleges), the liberal democratic ideal has been to develop institutional structures to allow these activities to be practised extensively and to protect more fully unorthodox practitioners.

Disagreements between democrats have not so much focused on whether certain activities should remain beyond either interference or support from the state, but on the issue of how state interests in other activities in which the organizations engage might undermine the 'protected' activities. Thus while some have defended virtual autonomy for the organizations, others have claimed that extensive co-operation with, and regulation by, the state does not weaken the independence necessary for the practice of the valued activity.

D Provision of goods not supplied by the state or the market

Both the market and the state may fail to provide certain goods for which there is a demand in society, and supply by IOs may be the only means by which they can be supplied at all. But why should both market and state fail in this way? The problem with markets is two-fold. First, they do not tend to operate well in supplying public goods – loosely, goods which cannot be confined to those who have helped pay for them. Moreover, where the level of demand is uncertain, where entrepreneurs believe the market is too small to sustain profitable activity and where they believe they cannot realize normal profits, for-profit suppliers are unlikely to emerge. A second, very different, argument is that, as a mechanism for satisfying demands in society, the state is deficient, because in seeking an electoral majority governments will tend to meet the demand for goods of the median voter. There will then be some voters who want more of these goods, and in the case of public goods, these are unlikely to be supplied in the market. In addition, of course, there is the argument that, even in the case of non-public goods, states are often ill-equipped to perform all the functions of a market not least because of the difficulties in acquiring the relevant information about citizens' wants. IOs can provide for a greater diversity of services than can the state. This point has been expressed well by Douglas:

> The classic pluralist argument is that a voluntary nonprofit sector permits a greater diversity of social provisions than the state itself can achieve. Using Ylisaker's interesting suggestion that we can regard the voluntary sector as a private version of government, we can say that the voluntary sector enables us to achieve a sort of diversity that would require the impossible combination of a secular, Catholic, Protestant, Jewish, Moslem, rightist, leftist, and centrist government operating simultaneously in the same jurisdiction.[15]

When there are market failures, therefore, we should not expect a state to be able to rectify all of them, and thus some goods may not be supplied. Organizations which do not have to make a profit to continue their operations may be a means of remedying some of these failures – in some cases because they can operate even when profit margins are below normal, and in other cases because they can act as providers of public goods.

Controversy about this 'gap-filling' role for IOs has focused on several issues. There are those who deny that the relationship between citizen and government can be, or indeed should be, similar to that between purchaser and supplier in a market and claim, for example, that it should be based on notions of social obligations instead. On this view 'government failure' in a democracy is not a real problem but a misperception of the nature of democracy based on the false assumption that citizens articulate *wants* to which leaders should respond.[16] Again, some economists have argued that, while market failure may exist in the short term, in the longer term market solutions will emerge when there is a demand for a product. A very different disagreement centres on the ability of IOs to provide services which the state and market fail to supply. Writers who have seen IOs as comprising a 'third', and distinctive, sector in society, consider them to meet social needs more effectively than the state – needs which are distinct from the wants that are satisfied in the market. Others have rejected the idea that between them IOs can meet these needs – partly because of practical problems in transforming altruistic sympathies into a voluntary system for ameliorating complex patterns of needs, and partly because the 'logic of collective action' restricts the application of co-operation as a basis for meeting needs.[17]

E 'Safer' provision of goods or services

The arguments outlined in the last section have to be distinguished from a separate argument about the alleged failure of markets for which certain kinds of IOs, known as 'non-profit organizations', are thought, by some writers, to provide a solution. The claim is made that in some kinds of transaction it is very difficult for those providing the good or service to know whether it has been supplied at the expected level of quality or, indeed, has been supplied at all. This can lead to 'contract failure', with the supplier of the goods exploiting those who pay for them.[18] Failure of this sort is possible in two very different circumstances. The person paying the supplier of the good may be different from the person for whom the good is provided and, if there is little communication between the parties, the payer may have difficulty in controlling the self-interested behaviour of the supplier. An example of this is the person who wishes to contribute money for the purchase of food for the victims of famine in another country. Alternatively, 'contract failure' can occur when the good or service supplied is a complex one, and where, consequently, it is hard for the purchaser to make comparisons with other suppliers and determine if value for money has been obtained. Treatment in a hospital and private education might be examples where the purchaser is at a disadvantage with the supplier. Those who propound this argument claim that organizations which are prevented by law from distributing profits to their members or owners are a means of overcoming 'contract failure'. Because they lack the incentive to exploit those paying for the goods or services, these 'non-profit organizations' provide something resembling a guarantee to the purchasers, and, therefore, they are likely to operate in those transactions where 'contract failure' would be prevalent. A key dissimilarity between this 'failure' and the 'failure' discussed in the previous section is that in the present case it is acknowledged that the goods *could* be supplied by a for-profit enterprise; but the potentially exploitative relationship provides an advantage to 'non-profit organizations' in attracting customers or clients.

Once again, there have been disputes about this alleged role for IOs in a capitalist democracy. One argument is that, even if an inability to distribute profits does provide some kind of safeguard against the self-interested behaviour of those who control organizations that supply services, it does not constitute much of a safeguard. There are many other ways in which those who pay could fall victim to the pursuit of self-interest by those involved in supplying services. It is also unclear that the two kinds of 'contract failure' actually have that much in common. With the exception of cases like the sending of flowers through an agency to a person living elsewhere, 'contract failure' of the first kind is primarily a problem relating to donations. Here IOs largely serve as a device enabling those who are not self-interested to act as intermediaries between *donors* and *recipients*. The point of such organizations is to ensure that the provision of the good is not in the hands of those who are supplying it for the purpose of advancing their own interests. With the second kind of 'contract failure', the point of the non-profit-distribution constraint is a more limited one – to circumscribe the behaviour of individuals who are otherwise presumed to be advancing their own interests, by providing an organizational form that restricts an important element of that behaviour. This is an issue we consider more fully in section 2.

F More effective provision of goods and services

Another area where some democrats have argued that IOs are crucial for the effective working of a democracy is in providing certain goods and services that are ultimately paid for by the state. The claim is that, with some kinds of services and in some circumstances, state provision may be less effective in the organization and delivery of the services than non-state provision. Broadly speaking, there are two main approaches to this issue. On the one hand, emphasis may be placed on the alleged ability of IOs to deliver services more cheaply; because they have to sustain smaller bureaucratic structures, because they can rely partly on volunteers to help in service delivery or because their employees are less likely to be unionized and hence will tend to have lower wage rates. On the other hand, there are those who stress that IOs are more likely to be interested in meeting the actual needs of those to whom services are provided, are less likely to be concerned with formal bureaucratic guidelines, and, because of their greater desire to understand the position of the recipients, are more likely than the state to retain the confidence of their clients. While these views are often propounded by those who argue for a restricted state role in funding social services, they are, of course, compatible with the view that the state should finance a wide range of welfare services.

The first claim – that of the cost-effectiveness of non-state service delivery – tends to pit conservative democrats against those more influenced by social democracy. At the heart of the latter's suspicion of the lower cost argument usually lies the contention that the co-ordination necessary in supplying a complex range of services necessitates overall state direction, and that the cost of this is often ignored by proponents of IOs. But, especially since the advent of welfare states in western democracies, even social democrats often accept that in some areas service provision by IOs may be cheaper than direct state provision. The same is true in relation to the arguments from 'care for the recipient'. However, social democrats remain opposed to provision by private agencies (as in the case of private education), where advantages accruing to those served by them necessarily conflict with the ethic of universalism embodied in state provision.

Allowing for these exceptions, private welfare agencies are no longer rejected, as they tended to be by socialists at the turn of the twentieth century, as mere fronts for the propagation of bourgeois ideology. The model of 'partnership' between state and IOs which has been widely accepted in the welfare state recognizes that there can be advantages in IOs supplying services, irrespective of the original source of funding. These can include a greater capacity to experiment in service provision and a different operating perspective which enables IOs to recognize, and fill, gaps in that provision.[19] Like many other widely proclaimed assertions, though, the argument from experimentation certainly does not hold in all circumstances, and may not hold in most of them. (Tendler, for example, has concluded that private voluntary organizations (PVOs) involved in third world development 'as a group are *not* innovative but that some PVOs, or PVO projects, have made important innovations in certain areas').[20] Debate usually focuses, therefore, on the question as to which sorts of services arguments about experimentation and gap-filling most readily apply. For example, socialists generally oppose the decentralization of schooling to state-financed, non-state agencies but often favour community development schemes being left in the hands of locally-based organizations.

G Facilitators of social and political integration

Another argument is that which holds that IOs provide a kind of 'social glue' – that they facilitate the integration of groups into both the polity and the wider society. At one level there are arguments about the ability of groups to actually provide foci of loyalty for individuals, while at another level there is debate about the impact of group loyalty on the political system.

Critics of the claim that integration into state and society is enhanced by IOs have tended to concentrate on two issues. First, it has been said that citizen interaction with formal organizations is often far less, and the loyalties to many of these bodies are weaker, than many pluralists imagined. Here an important distinction is drawn between states, such as the Netherlands, where IOs do play a major role in linking citizens to society and polity, and states like the US and Britain where these links are much looser. Second, the precise connection between loyalties to organized groups and loyalty to the state needs specifying. Many of the organizations in which the British working class of the nineteenth century were active were only partly supportive of the pre-democratic regime even though most were not anti-regime in character. Clearly, the conditions in which membership of an organization fosters group solidarity rather than identification with the state have to be specified if the 'integration' argument is to have plausibility.

But what of the argument that group solidarity provides a source of stability for the political system? Those who propound this argument claim that in ethnically divided societies, service provision by IOs provides essential diversity although there are limits to its integrating effects. Hence Douglas argues:

> . . . such comparative data as we do possess suggest that there are limits to the extent to which a voluntary sector can heal the breaches caused by a seriously fractionalized society. . . . James's careful analysis of the nonprofit sector in Sri Lanka (1980) does not suggest that voluntary organizations have succeeded in greatly reducing ethnic tension. The same is true of Northern Ireland, where voluntary organizations have been unable to bridge the gulf between the two communities. On the other hand, where tensions are less severe and less violent, a voluntary sector seems to provide the desired diversity.[21]

The argument about integration into the polity was most associated with the analytical pluralism of American political science in the 1950s, which saw group attachments in the US as especially important in building support for the political system.

However, it can be argued that there are not merely limits to the ability of IO service provision to produce political stability, but that it actually plays little part in stabilizing a political system. Critics contend that it is the willingness of elites to compromise with each other that generates this stability. In the consociational democratic system of mid-twentieth century Netherlands elites were prepared to accommodate themselves to each other.[22] But in post-war Italy, where there was also a high degree of organizational encapsulation by the political parties this was absent. The Italian political system appeared always to be in crisis. It is far from obvious that a plurality of IOs providing services in stable, but fractionalized, societies like the Netherlands, itself contributes anything to binding the state together.

H Facilitators of diversity of opinion in society

While democrats have recognized that too much conflict of interest within a state, and too little agreement on the legitimacy of a particular state, destabilizes a democracy, there is a democratic tradition which goes back at least as far as J. S. Mill which values some degree of diversity of opinion within the state. The argument is that consensus can be stultifying, and Mill himself argued that '... society has now fairly got the better of individuality; and the danger which threatens human nature is not the excess, but the deficiency of personal impulses and preferences.'[23] But how is individuality to be cultivated? One argument, even if it was not Mill's, is that IOs in a society can play a central role in encouraging individuality and the growth of diverse opinions. The claim is that, when there are multiple organizations to which citizens belong, different opinions and interests in society will become apparent to them, and they will be less willing to defer automatically to the received opinion of any one group. Clearly, such an argument assumes that the organizations are separate from one another and not, as in the Netherlands, linked to each other as parts of 'pillars' in society.[24]

But not all democrats have been convinced by the idea that a high degree of diversity of opinion is necessarily valuable in a democracy. The 'personal impulses and preferences' which Mill wished to sustain might well be satisfied at the expense of broader, shared, interests in the community: individualism is often the enemy of public-regardingness. IOs which encourage the former may well restrict the latter. There are also disagreements among democrats on the issue of whether, for a society in which there is sufficient consensus to provide for regime stability, IOs do actually stimulate diversity of opinion. One argument is that people are most likely to join bodies whose members hold views very similar to their own, and the extent of their involvement in formal organizations, when compared with other aspects of their lives, is also rather limited. This is true, at least, in Britain and the US. The person who starts to develop unconventional opinions will probably 'exit' from an organization, rather than stay to argue for his/her point of view. Moreover, there are many aspects of social life for which membership of formal bodies is just not needed. Indeed, it has been argued that changes in leisure activities available to people in the twentieth century, together with changes in social values, have meant that people today have even less need for the facilities of formal organizations than their counterparts did two or three generations ago.

I Mobilization of interests and demands in a society

Of all the claims that have been made about IOs, perhaps the best known is one associated with American analytic pluralism: it is through IOs and other groups that the demands of citizens can be articulated, and it is by responding to the pressure put on them by these groups, in proportion to their strength in society, that governments can provide for political equality.[25] On this view IOs are rather like for-profit firms in an economy: competition between them leads to demands within society being satisfied optimally. Political parties are merely one kind of IO in a complex process of demand and response.

The debate about this analysis of the contribution of IOs to democracy is too well known to summarize here. Suffice to say, there are two main flaws in the pluralist argument to which critics quickly drew attention. It was abundantly clear from the evidence of the operations of actual states that the way they responded to demands from groups was not related in any direct way to some amalgam of their size and the intensity of their members' opinions. Factors such as the resources available to groups, pre-existing political agendas and limitations in the electoral mechanism as a constraint on government were just some of the causes of 'non-optimal' responses by governments. Moreover, it was argued that the 'collective action' problem was a major barrier to the mobilization of groups with potentially large memberships: there was little incentive for anyone to join out of self-interest alone, and 'free riding' was usually the best strategy even for an individual with an important interest at stake.

2 Non-profit Organizations and Market Economies

It should be clear from the preceding discussion that a wide and varying contribution to democracy has been accorded to IOs. How much attention, then, has political science devoted to them? Given the important functions many democrats have attributed to IOs in the working of a democracy, we might expect that they would have constituted one of the principal areas of research. And, in a sense, they have. A brief glance at any publisher's list of political books, or at the catalogue in an academic library, reveals a large number of books on particular kinds of IOs – such as on relations between trade unions and the state, or on the role of voluntary organizations in the provision of social services in a welfare state. Again, at the macro-level of political analysis, there is a long tradition of studying the role of pressure groups in the democratic state, and more recently of studies focusing on the intermediation of groups in neo-corporatist democratic states.[26] Where political science has been deficient, however, is in looking beyond the most *directly* political aspects of IOs at this set of organizations as a whole; even studies of major sub-categories of IOs have been noticeably lacking. Nor is this surprising. The sheer variety of IOs makes it difficult to structure empirical studies so as to provide a broad coverage of the range of organizations involved. There is thus a considerable gap between the importance often accorded to IOs in democratic theory and our knowledge of the ways these institutions actually operate. Consider in this regard the concept of *voluntary association*, which characterizes a large sub-category of IOs; many IOs are voluntary associations, in that they are bodies which individuals are free to set up and free to join and which do not exist simply to make profits for the membership. Many of the arguments we have just outlined, about the value of IOs in a democracy, have been made specifically in relation to voluntary associations – they facilitate participation and social integration, they channel demands from citizens to the state and so on. While political theorists have sought to explicate the role of voluntary associations, as for example in the *Nomos* volume published in 1969, the range of empirical studies on which theorists can draw is extremely limited – as the *Nomos* essays also indicate only too well.[27] Moreover, of course, many IOs are not overtly involved in politics, or are involved only intermittently. Quite naturally, in pressure group studies, the inclination of political scientists has been to focus on how groups become politicized, or how they operate when they are politicized. They have not looked more generally at how groups' 'everyday' activities contribute to (or fail to contribue to) the working of democracy.

Recently, though, the situation has been changing, and in part this book is a response to these developments. In the US a few economists, and social scientists who have been influenced by economic analysis, have sought to develop theories as to why a large sub-category of IOs – non-profit organizations (NPOs) – should exist in capitalist democracies.[28] The growing popularity of the concept of the NPO has stimulated empirical studies ranging from those focused on organizations operating in specific policy areas to broader studies of an alleged 'non-profit sector' as a whole. For reasons that will become apparent shortly, I do not agree with either the arguments NPO theorists have outlined to explain the existence of NPOs in market economies, or the idea that the NPO is the most useful concept to employ when examining IOs. Nevertheless, the significance of the contribution of these scholars in drawing attention to the need for analysing IOs cannot be overstated.

What are NPOs? One unfortunate feature of the term, as those studying them nearly always point out, is that it is misleading – NPOs are prohibited from *distributing* profits; but many NPOs do try to *earn* profits. Moreover, the term is used in at least three different ways. Sometimes American social scientists use it similarly to the way I use 'IO' – to refer to all non-state organizations that are prohibited from distributing profits to their members. Often it refers to organizations that are entitled to form under the non-profit corporation laws which every US state has; this is a less inclusive category than the first, because a number of large organizations, including co-operatives and Savings and Loan Associations (the American equivalent to Building Societies) are not covered by these statutes. In addition, many small voluntary associations may not bother to incorporate themselves. In this, the most common usage of the term, NPO is a less inclusive concept than that of IO – as indicated in figure 1.1. Then, again, the term is used in a yet more restrictive way to refer to those non-profit corporations which are entitled to receive donations which are tax-deductible for the donors under the Internal Revenue Service's 501(c)(3) classification. This last usage of the term NPO makes it more like that of a 'charity' under British law, although the British category is more restricted in a number of ways. One reason for avoiding the term 'non-profit', whenever possible, therefore, is simply that it is so ambiguous.

Further ambiguity arises, of course, from the number of different meanings given to the term 'profit' by accountants, economists and other specialists, in addition to its 'everyday' meaning, so that the concept of 'non-profit' is itself likely to be contentious. The simplest way of looking at profit is to regard it as a 'reward' for entrepreneurship – the benefits that accrue to risk-taking. Without probing the issue very far, however, it can be seen that even the 'everyday' notion of profit is problematic.

Not only do some profit-making ventures not involve much (if any) risk for owners of capital, but there are some financial benefits which individuals may receive that are not profits. For example, a newly-formed consumer co-operative may well involve risk for its members, but if they are able to issue a dividend on their trading at the end of the year, such a reward would not usually be regarded as profit. This is an issue which we examine rather more closely in chapter 2 in relation to mutual benefit organizations.

A more serious problem in using NPO as a concept around which to organize a comparative study of IOs is that the second and third usages identified above derive entirely from a category in American law. Even in Britain there is no precise counterpart, and the recent introduction of the term 'non-profit organization' into Britain indicates that it is being employed in a rather different way than in any of its usages in the US.[29] Certainly, as many NPO theorists have pointed out, institutions similar to many kinds of American non-profit corporations do exist in other countries, and this is not surprising given similarities in state development. But there have been significant differences. As James notes, making a contrast with the US, 'In Sweden ... private philanthropy is actually frowned upon as a source of undesired status differentials.'[30] But it should be added that this does not simply reflect dissimilar cultures, but also a very different tradition of the role of the state. We are less likely to be misled in a comparative study if we do not organize our research around a concept that has its origins in a specific legal system, and reflects a particular cultural and institutional history. One of the dangers of the NPO as a concept is that it fosters the belief that certain institutional forms, most especially those found in the US, are somehow 'natural' to market economies, rather than being artefacts of its cultural and institutional history. Even among the western states, these histories are only partly shared, so that in a comparative study it is perhaps better to start with a more all-embracing category, such as intermediate organization.

This brings us to NPO theorists' explanations of the existence of NPOs in capitalist democracies. Broadly speaking, there are two main kinds of theory, although, as in Douglas's *Why Charity?*, arguments have been combined to produce variations on these accounts of the existence of 'third sectors' under liberal democracy.[31]

The first type of argument is most closely associated with Weisbrod and is best characterized as a kind of 'government failure' argument.[32] The second type was first put forward by Hansmann and concerns contract failure. The essence of the first argument is that it is highly unlikely that the state will supply all the public goods in a society for which there is a demand. Both with regard to the total quantity of public goods, and with regard to the quality of public goods made available in cases where there are diverse tastes about the kind of good wanted, the state will make inadequate provision. It will provide too few public goods and an insufficient range of them. As we noted in sub-section 1(D), the cause of this shortfall in supply is that, to stay in office, a government must satisfy the demand for public goods of the median voter; it will raise taxes to cover this amount of public goods, but just as there will be people who will be paying taxes for more public goods than they want, so there will be others for whom there are insufficient public goods of various kinds. Similarly, there will be a shortfall in the supply of private goods from government, and here, according to Weisbrod, the unsatisfied demand will meet a response in the private sector. In the case of public goods, though, it will be NPOs which meet the demand. Now, for our purpose, it is not necessary to challenge Weisbrod's argument about how a shortfall in public goods comes about, although it should be noted that even rational-choice theorists, including Anthony Downs, have made plausible assumptions about voter perceptions of public goods and taxes which make Weisbrod's asssumption seem very crude.[33] Instead, attention should be drawn to three other difficulties with his analysis.

The first is the free-rider problem. Where a single person with an unsatiated demand for public goods has the personal resources to supply them, then, at the intersecting point of his/her demand curve and the supply curve of the good, a certain quantity of the public good will be produced. Weisbrod's analysis, therefore, might be able to account for the wealthy philanthropists and for the philanthropic foundations they establish. Unfortunately, this does not get us very far in providing a rationale for 'the non-profit sector', even in the US. As we will see later, foundations account for only a tiny proportion of the total income of NPOs, even though many, like the Ford Foundation, are highly visible and well known. Furthermore, especially from the 1930s onwards, many foundations were not established by the classic philanthropist of the Andrew Carnegie kind, but as devices for controlling private resources. This was the case with the Ford Foundation. Although it did provide funds for charitable causes, it was created as a means by which family control of the car company could be maintained.

Leaving aside the single philanthropist, how is the free-rider problem to be overcome? Weisbrod mentions three resources which are relevant. One is the selective incentive – the private good given to those who make donations, and he cites one organization which gives a free road atlas to those who contribute a certain sum. But such instances are comparatively infrequent and, more importantly, on grounds of *economic self-interest* at least, no one would bother to make a donation if they could buy the atlas for less elsewhere. So the two resources on which the Weisbrod argument must rely are peer group pressure to make donations and the sense of satisfaction people get from making a contribution to a cause of which they approve. Of course, invoking psychological rewards in rational-choice models has been denounced frequently by critics as a device for 'squaring the circle' in the argument. However, even if we ignore this point, Weisbrod has still left himself a major problem. Whether there will be peer group pressure to make donations for public goods, and whether individuals will 'feel good' by making donations, will depend on the particular set of social values dominant in his/her community, or in the wider society. Obviously, among rational egoists there would be no such donations on grounds of economic self-interest. But even in a society where certain forms of altruism were valued, this might be much more supportive of help to specific individuals than to the promotion of public goods. Clearly, there are differences between societies in this regard, as James's comment about attitudes to private philanthropy in Sweden quoted above indicates. In other words, to overcome the free-rider problem Weisbrod would have to make specific assumptions about the other-regarding attitudes of the people involved, and this would detract from any general explanatory value his model may have by undermining the rational-choice assumptions.

The second difficulty with the Weisbrod argument is that, even if it could explain why individuals would contribute towards the provision of public goods, this would not explain much of the activity of NPOs. In many areas in which non-profits operate in the US (including higher education, health care, and others) the goods they are supplying are largely private goods not public goods. This is why, as we see later, fees and charges constitute such a large proportion of the income of American non-profits. Of course, between them the activities of non-profit hospitals, say, in treating fee-paying patients may provide public goods – through creating a generally healthier population and in subsidizing medical research – but then the activities of some for-profit enterprises also generate public goods. The commercial theatres in London make that city more exciting to live in than Coventry. Now it is true that some NPOs are engaged primarily in the production of public goods. Many of the organizations that initially come to mind when we are asked, 'what is a charity?', are suppliers of public goods. Examples include Oxfam's aid to third world economic development, and in its capacity to preserve open countryside, the National Trust in Britain. But what this suggests is that the attempt to provide a theory of a 'non-profit sector' as a whole may be radically misdirected. Indeed, Weisbrod himself seems to have come to recognize the problem. While his original essay continues to be reprinted in collections of essays on NPOs, in an essay written in 1980 he acknowledged that different models of NPOs might have to be developed depending on the 'degree of collectiveness' of the good they were producing.[34]

The third difficulty is one related to an argument we raise shortly in connection with the second group of theories of NPOs. It is that, while the Weisbrod argument might be able to explain why the legal form of the NPO would be utilized by suppliers of certain kinds of goods, it cannot explain why such a legal form should exist in the first place, or why it is necessary if public goods are to be supplied on a private basis at all. In a world of individuals who attempted rationally to employ efficient means to given ends, and assuming the free-rider problem could be overcome, public goods could be supplied by for-profit enterprises. Even if the only existing private organizational forms were for-profit bodies, public goods would be supplied. Individuals, like the founders of the National Trust, who wanted to preserve places of beauty would pay money to firms that would buy up and manage endangered parts of the countryside. Competition between these firms would play much the same role as it does in the provision of other services. Making this argument does not, of course, indicate support for a minimal state, because the free-rider problems do seem more or less insuperable. But, leaving aside the free-rider issue, the argument can be made that markets could provide public goods if there were no NPOs. This is not to say, necessarily, that as many would be provided as at present, because in the real world many of the institutions have been able to develop reputations which allow people to donate with confidence to the supply of public goods, in the knowledge that these goods will actually be produced. There may well be aspects of the way these institutions are run which inspire greater confidence among donors than would for-profit enterprises. However, this is precisely the kind of argument which falls outside the framework of Weisbrod's analysis. He tried to demonstrate that a 'non-profit sector' is logically entailed by the assumptions he makes about individual and governmental behaviour, and he failed to do so.

Despite its obvious limitations, Weisbrod's model was significant in stimulating the development of further rational-choice models of NPOs. In 1980 Hansmann was the first to develop a theory which took account of the problem of how those wanting a good could have confidence in its being produced either at all, or at the quality level wanted by those paying for it. Since then similar theories have been developed by other researchers.[35] These theories differ from Weisbrod's in postulating that the rationale for NPOs lies not in government failure but in 'contract failure'.

The starting point for Hansmann is the recognition that, in the case of certain kinds of goods, it is difficult for those paying for them to know whether they have been supplied, or supplied at the desired level of quality. As we saw earlier, generally there can be two reasons for this: the person who pays for the good is not the same as the person who consumes it, and there are certain kinds of complex personal services (including, according to Hansmann, nursing-home facilities and day-care centres for children) where it is difficult to evaluate the quality of a service, even when that service is experienced in a direct way. Both of these are instances of 'contract failure' – of the inability, in Hansmann's words 'to police producers by ordinary contractual devices'.[36]

If the pursuit of self-interest by for-profit enterprises leads to the exploitation of those paying for the good or service, then it is in the self-interest of those with whom they have contracted to utilize means of controlling this. Hansmann argues that the non-profit corporation provides a kind of guarantee against the exploitation of those who have made the contract, along with other devices such as government regulation of rates of profit, co-operatives, cost-plus contracting and so on. Each of these devices has disadvantages as well as advantages, so that for some industries it is the non-profit form which offers the best guarantee and will, therefore, be adopted. For Hansmann, donative charities of the Oxfam kind are as much an industry as hospitals.

As with Weisbrod's model, there are a number of serious problems. The first is that Hansmann's model assumes that potential users of the services of NPOs, or donors to them, can readily distinguish them from for-profit concerns. But it is far from clear that this condition is usually met, and the limited empirical evidence available suggests it is not.[37] Nor is this surprising. While, for example, the major charities soliciting donations from the public are household names, many NPOs are not and the periodic instances of outright fraud testify to the limited information available to many donors. Even when the name of an organization is well known, its legal status may not be. Moreover, in the case of many American NPOs selling services, such as hospitals, the user is often not the ultimate source of payment. Instead, it is 'third parties' (insurance schemes) which meet most of the costs, and this gives less of an incentive to the user to acquire information about the organizational form of the service provider. S/he relies more on the fact that the third party will actually pay bills proffered by a particular organization as the guarantee against exploitation. Again, as we see later, with other American NPOs selling services, such as research and analytic testing organizations, the precise legal status of an organization may be unclear to the purchaser, because it is part of a complex which includes non-profit and for-profit concerns. In brief, it is far from evident that the conditions in which many transactions with NPOs occur facilitate great awareness on the part of the consumer or donor of the guarantee against exploitation NPO status supposedly offers.

The second problem is that non-profit status does not provide much of a guarantee to the consumer who is worried about the possibility of contract failure. It is true that he does not have to worry about his/her money being used to create excess profits, but there are many other ways in which s/he might fail to get value for money. Those who run an NPO might be able to use any surplus to increase managerial salaries, or give themselves perks to supplement salaries; in the absence of a profit motive, the consumer cannot be sure what pressures there are on managers to provide the goods efficiently and without waste; nor can s/he be sure that a desire to 'empire build' will not lead to profit maximizing behaviour, with the profits then being ploughed back into the organization.

A third problem is that, arguably, Hansmann's model is of little value in explaining the behaviour of those who contribute money to many kinds of NPOs that solicit donations for the promotion of their activities. Let us suppose that a commercial, for-profit company demonstrated conclusively that it could provide famine relief to third world countries more efficiently than conventional relief agencies such as Oxfam. It might use particular sources of donations on specific projects and, by providing accounts for every project, it could demonstrate to contributors how effectively their donations were being used. The 'contract failure' problem would have been solved. Yet, it can be argued, that even with clear-cut evidence of greater efficiency, many people would not donate to such a for-profit concern, but would prefer to continue contributing to the traditional relief agencies. The reason is simply that many of the activities undertaken by such bodies are widely regarded as the sort of activities from which profits should not be made. In other words, there is a strong antithesis to the market ethos in certain activities, and in these cases models which treat donors as merely being concerned with 'utilities', whether their own or someone else's, are of limited value. Obviously, it is difficult to specify exactly which activities are widely regarded as properly lying beyond the market system, but the relief of poverty is probably one clear example, as is the relief of distress among the disabled or the terminally ill. By contrast, the present argument probably has little applicability to the types of activities supported by, say, the National Trust.

A fourth problem is that it may be doubted whether there is a *general* tendency for complex personal services to be an area in which NPOs have a good opportunity to compete with for-profit concerns. Many people have great difficulty in knowing how to go about evaluating someone engaged to advise them on their financial affairs – how to handle investments for retirement and so on. Like evaluating nursing homes or day-care centres, choosing someone to perform these services involves making decisions when there is no direct way of comparing the performance of competing firms. With accountants and financial analysts there is no equivalent to consumer guides like *Which?*, and yet we do not find non-profit enterprises competing here either. Now it is true that a bad financial advisor can merely lose you money – s/he won't beat up your grandparents or molest your children, which might be your relatives' fate in the hands of unscrupulous nursing homes or day-care centres. But, even if we restrict attention to services where people can be physically or emotionally harmed, there are still many instances where only for-profit concerns operate. To my knowledge, there are no non-profit car body repair shops, for example. This suggests that legal and institutional history may play as great a part in explaining the success of NPOs in those areas where they do operate, as an explanation based on 'contract failure'.

Finally, it is important to point out that the central mistake Hansmann (among others) makes is in confusing the importance of the *reputation* an organization has for providing a service, where there is a danger of 'contract failure', with the guarantee non-profit status allegedly provides. Generally, people give to those charities which have a good reputation for doing what they claim to do, and in the case of complex services they tend to employ organizations that have a reputation for performing them well. But what gives an organization a good reputation? Obviously, this is far too complex a question to answer here, but I want to suggest that, for the most part, NPOs operate in areas of activity where they have always been strong, or in related areas – areas where they now have a *history* of good performance. However, if we then ask why, in areas like higher education, hospitals, and some aspects of the arts, NPOs were in a position to get this reputation, we must turn to *institutional explanations*. The real limitation of most of the attempts to derive a theory of the 'non-profit sector' is that attention has been focused almost exclusively on deriving conclusions from 'rational-choice' premises, and too little consideration has been given to the institutional history of economic and quasi-economic organizations.[38] Nor is it that surprising that in this case 'rational-choice' premises have generated rather less insight than some of those who utilize them seem to believe. As Simon has argued, many economic analyses are based on loose notions of rationality that are akin to those employed in functional analyses in other social sciences; they are not based on the narrower notion of rationality – of the person as a utility *maximizer* – which is the distinctive contribution of liberal economics to the social sciences. While the looser notion of rationality can generate important hypotheses about institutions, its limitation is that it does not identify *unique* explanations of institutional behaviour. Simon puts the point this way:

all that can be concluded from a functional argument is that certain characteristics (the satisfaction of certain functional requirements in a particular way) are consistent with the survival and further development of the system, not that these same requirements could not be satisfied in some other way.[39]

One of the main arguments being propounded in this book, then, is that the kinds of IOs to be found in a liberal democracy are influenced greatly by the interaction of state and economy at various stages of economic development. There is no reason to suppose that the pattern of organizations found in, say, Britain or the US would be the one to emerge in a very different historical context. Nevertheless, those who try to understand IOs outside the US in terms of an NPO framework can point to two features of IOs elsewhere which might seem to justify this. Colonization has meant that a number of organizations and practices in the Anglo-American tradition are to be found in many other countries, and, indeed, Britain's first empire provides good evidence of the 'export potential' of certain native institutions. To India, which was to become the 'jewel in the crown' of the second empire, the British exported the idea of philanthropy. As Haynes has noted, before the nineteenth century gifts by wealthy merchants were most commonly viewed as 'acts of propitiation or service to their deities', and the western notion of humanitarian service was largely absent.[40] Even 'mature' states copy legal and institutional structures from elsewhere – as the British did when introducing the Parliamentary Commissioner (Ombudsman). In Canada too some legal structures have been influenced by the US – for example, we find laws relating to non-profit organizations rather similar to those in the US, and markedly different from British law. Moreover, there are problems common to all states which are likely to find solutions in institutions that fall outside the state and commercial sectors. For example, in Qing China lineages engaged in a range of charitable activities for their members – including support for the poor, unemployed, disabled and widowed, as well as providing for schooling, illness, weddings and burials.[41] Although trade guilds in both medieval Europe and China provided some services to their members, in China there was a more diverse institutional structure engaged in providing services that state and market did not.[42] Because the form that social institutions took there, as well as their subsequent development, was very different, comparative studies drawing on these radically different historical experiences are unlikely to be very fruitful. But what have been the main factors influencing the growth of IOs in Britain and the US? In the remainder of this chapter, we attempt to provide a brief account of the background to the development of IOs in the British, and later the American, state, so that we can try to answer this question in the next few chapters. We will then be in a better position to assess the contribution of IOs to the advance of democracy.

First, however, we must first draw attention to one possible source of confusion, which is difficult to deal with in an entirely satisfactory way and which will have been apparent in the preceding discussion. In Britain there is no single set of laws pertaining to IOs, and while many apply to the whole of Britain, there is one important body of law, that relating to charities, which applies only to England and Wales. The laws on charity in Scotland and Northern Ireland are different, and neither of these cases is discussed directly here.[43] Unfortunately, this requires that sometimes reference is made to Britain, and sometimes to England (including Wales), and variations in this, arising from a need not to complicate a discussion, inevitably occur.

3 The Development of Intermediate Organizations

In pre-capitalist societies one of the central difficulties facing both the state and many of its individual members is how to cope with the exigencies of life, when, even in the best of circumstances, total production is insufficient to yield much of an economic surplus. For the individual, wars, natural disasters and so on are life threatening, and while the state lacks the resources to do much to alleviate such conditions it has an interest in preventing the social disruption emanating from them. Excluding repression, the two obvious solutions to this are for individuals to join together to provide mechanisms and institutions that can provide for their mutual benefit in times of need, and for the state (and individuals) to encourage the wealthy to make provision from their own resources for those adversely affected.

To take the second solution first. Nearly all societies have recognized the need to encourage some forms of altruism to prevent disaster for the entire community. For obvious reasons, religious groups are often among the main institutions encouraging altruism; in China, for example, Buddhist temples and monasteries provided social services including 'hospitals and dispensaries for the sick, feeding stations for the hungry and havens for the aged and decrepit', as well as sometimes engaging in community projects such as road building.[44] Pre-capitalist societies lacked the necessary tax bases to provide many of these services themselves, so that provision often fell on the shoulders of religious organizations usually with continuing state encouragement to extend their work. But the weakness of European states for over a thousand years after the collapse of the Roman empire made it especially difficult for them to provide for the alleviation of disaster at all. In contrast, at various levels of administration the Chinese state maintained permanent granaries to provide for famine relief and to stablise grain prices after poor harvests. In all pre-capitalist societies, though, there was no question of medical care being provided on a for-profit basis, except for the relatively small social and economic elites. Provision on a philanthropic basis was required because provision on a mutual-benefit basis was so difficult to establish. The very circumstances which meant that starvation and death were never far from most people's lives also made it difficult for them to organize against this – there were simply not enough resources to 'insure against' future disasters. The mutual-benefit principle starts to emerge in the form of institutionalized co-operation, therefore, in more affluent groups, such as Chinese lineages and commercial guilds, and also among tradesmen and craftsmen in early medieval European towns. For peasants, informal co-operation based on traditional norms and practices of reciprocity remained an insecure basis for combatting the adversity which regularly affected their lives.

A distinctive feature of western Europe from the late Roman empire onwards was the role of the Catholic church in both encouraging philanthropy, and in providing institutions through which many kinds of philanthropy could be channelled. The church encouraged the rich not just to provide doles for the poor in times of extreme hardship, but also, for instance, to found monasteries which were supposed to be instruments for charitable dispensation. One peculiarity of western Europe, in comparison with, say, China, was that philanthropy was directed through a large, politically powerful, international institution which claimed extensive rights even *vis-à-vis* political elites. The English pluralist Figgis noted that 'the Church was not a State, it was the State; the state or rather the civil authority (for a separate society was not recognized) was merely the police department of the Church.'[45] The medieval church was not an entirely autonomous entity, however, and nor were the institutions functioning 'under its umbrella'. English kings worried about the power that ecclesiastial bodies might accumulate and sought through a variety of devices, such as legislation on mortmain, to restrict this power.

The Reformation required Protestant states to devise ways to ensure that the wealthy continued to make some provision for the poor. In England social dislocation in the sixteenth century created problems of social instability for the Tudor state – problems which could not be overcome by Poor Laws designed to discourage both mobility on the part of the poor and pauperization. (Although the Chinese imperial state sometimes encouraged internal migration, to areas of underpopulation, this was not an option for the sixteenth-century English state. The lack of a large state administration which could control some of the consequences of a mobile population forced the Tudor state to opt for keeping the poor in their place of origin.) The Tudor state sought to encourage philanthropy by the wealthy, and the culmination of this was the codification of laws on charity in 1601 in the Statute of Charitable Uses. Even today this remains the basis of law on charity in England and the US. In Tudor England, then, charity became secularized in the sense that the (now reformed) church no longer provided the only framework within which charity was practised. The main kinds of bodies which might rank as IOs in Tudor England would include on the one side organizations like guilds, with their close interaction with the for-profit economy, and on the other side philanthropic foundations, such as colleges, schools and hospitals, many of which predated the Reformation. The significance of the break with Rome was not that it led to the creation of new kinds of IOs in England (it did not), but that it forced the state to regulate the activities of some IOs, and in doing so it created a legal structure which had a major influence on the future development of IOs – in both England and, later, America.

The growth of commercial society and the subsequent transformation to an industrial economy greatly increased the variety of IOs. There was an expansion of organized mutual benefit activity – not only did new organizational forms develop, but subsequently these could embrace a much larger population than were covered by the guilds in pre-capitalist society. In proving a model for future mutual benefit organizations, the key institutions were:

> Friendly Societies, whose rise coincided almost exactly with the guilds' decline around 1700. Not unlike the protection guilds of the Dark Ages, they provided members with insurance against sickness, poverty and bereavement, and met the expenses of a decent funeral . . . In the late eighteenth and early nineteenth centuries, Friendly Societies afforded a cover for trade union activity, and some actually evolved into trade unions.[46]

And as Thompson notes, Friendly Societies provide an important link between trade unionism and early forms of mutual benefit activity:

> there is a sense in which the friendly societies helped to pick up and carry into the trade union movement the love of ceremony and the high sense of status of the craftsman's guild. These traditions, indeed, still had a remarkable vigour in the early 19th century, in some of the old Chartered Companies or guilds of the masters and master-craftsmen, whose periodical ceremonies expressed the pride of both the masters and of the journeymen in 'The Trade'.[47]

At the same time there was a diversification of charitable institutions and practices; of special importance later was the growth of the idea that giving money to the poor and disadvantaged was insufficient, and might well encourage pauperism. Instead, at the end of the nineteenth century, the middle class were encouraged to devote time to meeting those they might help – interactions that supposedly were of benefit to both parties.

Greater economic resources made activities possible among individuals whose time was no longer devoted entirely to making a living. Voluntary associations devoted to political, cultural, leisure and other activities expanded as the number of people with 'free time' grew: in the early eighteenth century such associations were largely the preserve of the relatively small middle class, but a century later working-class societies and unions were flourishing sufficiently for the British state to attempt to suppress them. In the nineteenth century several alternative structures to the for-profit firm developed (consumer co-operatives and Building Societies, for example) in working-class communities, further expanding the range of IOs. Indeed, the Victorian state is often regarded as the model against which subsequent relations between IOs and state must be judged: under *laissez-faire*, it is claimed, IOs were largely independent of the state, constituting a genuine 'third sector' in society. But this separation of the two is often overstated.[48] The Victorian state provided much of that legislation for regulating Friendly and other societies which still forms the basis of regulation today. More especially, in the reforms of the universities and charitable trusts in the middle of the century, the state adopted a highly interventionist policy. Moreover, in the nineteenth century much greater indulgence was given to lobbying and overt political activity by charities than in the twentieth century. The view that there is a distinct non-market, non-state 'sector' in capitalist countries is largely a twentieth century construct drawing selectively on some features of the nineteenth-century experience.

The US inherited much of the legal framework within which different kinds of IOs operated in eighteenth-century Britain, as well as some institutional forms. Some of these forms continued to be 'exported' during the nineteenth century. But there were significant differences in circumstance then that were to contribute to further divergence later. The ex-colonies faced rather different problems in co-operation between individuals because of the greater dispersion of their populations. Religious heterogeneity, and a tradition of religious independence ensured that very different kinds of relations between state and church from those in Britain, would develop. And there was diversity of opinion about the role both philanthropic and business corporations should play. Even in New England, which was to pioneer the development of the corporate form, eighteenth-century corporations (such as Harvard

College) were a curious mixture of elements from public and private institutions. Moreover:

Early business corporations such as the Massachusetts Bank (1783) were similarly ambiguous in their status: their capital often consisted of combinations of public and private subscriptions; public representatives sat on their boards; the state reserved a right to interefere with or abrograte their charters at will . . .[49]

But in the southern states there was open hostility to the private corporation. In Virginia, for example:

By 1806, the legislature had enacted a statute that provided that all property given for charitable purposes was to be turned over to the management of county overseers of the poor.[50]

Governmental aid to private charities persisted, however, in many parts of the US, as surveys from the late nineteenth and early twentieth centuries demonstrate.[51] Nevertheless, a key development by the mid-nineteenth century was the eventual triumph of the corporation as an organizational form, and this resulted in corporations (including philanthropic corporations) actually being freer of state intervention than their counterparts in Britain. The Registrar of Friendly Societies and the Charity Commission, both established in the nineteenth century, had no counterparts at either federal or state levels.

It is at this point that we need to examine the development of IOs in much more detail, and as noted earlier, we start by examining their economic activities. We begin, in chapter 2, by considering mutual-benefit organizations, and then in chapter 3 we focus attention on a central aspect of charitable IOs – the growth of competition between them and for-profit businesses.

2

Mutuals and the Supply of Goods and Services

In chapters 3 and 4 we will consider IOs that we might not expect, at least initially, to be closely involved in competition or co-operation with for-profit firms. First, though, we focus in this chapter on superficially very different kinds of IOs – ones where we might expect extensive interaction with the for-profit economy to develop. Our subject here is mutual-benefit organizations (mutuals) – organizations that are created to provide some kind of benefit to the members who establish the organization and to those who join it subsequently. Collective action is required to generate the benefit, and once available its supply can be restricted to those who have contributed to it. Life insurance schemes, for example, demand a large number of contributors, but the benefits will be received by all who have paid for them. In this particular case, and unlike some other mutual activities such as trade unionism, benefits granted to particular individuals can be related directly to the scale of their contributions.

The exercise in which we are engaged in this chapter is a rather complex one. In part, the chapter is concerned with tracing the growth and transformation of mutuals in the US and Britain. But the chapter also reviews some of the major issues in the debate about mutuals. More importantly perhaps, we attempt to reach some conclusions in relation to problems posed by two putative characteristics of mutuals.

The first relates to the distinction between profit-distributing and non-profit-distributing organizations. As we shall see, it is difficult to resolve the dilemma posed in the case of mutuals, and this indicates a more general problem in distinguishing the for-profit sector from IOs; mutuals seem to straddle the boundary between that sector and IOs. For the state this is significant in several ways, not least because the major tax base of the modern state, the income tax, must make assumptions about the nature of this distinction. For the democratic theorist, the distinction is important if we are to establish the boundaries of IOs in relation to the market as a preface to evaluating some of the claims that have been made about the role of IOs in a democracy, such as the countervailing power they can exert against either the market or the state.

The second set of problems relates to the fact that many mutuals have their origins in what may be described as 'marginal' areas of an economy. (As we shall see, there is an important distinction to be drawn between the factors which bring mutual-benefit organizations into existence and those which sustain them in competition with for-profit concerns once they have become established.) What happens to mutuals in areas of the economy which later become less 'marginal' than they were at the time of their founding? One consequence, of course, of greater market potential is that for-profit rivals are likely to emerge. But another effect of the growth of a mutual can be the virtual elimination of that distinctive feature of mutual organization, control by the membership. With this loss of control, and its replacement by control by professional managers, mutuals are likely to lose the social objectives and praçtices they may have had in their early years. Instead, financial objectives predominate. In later sections we consider these two issues in connection with the major kinds of mutual-benefit organizations that have developed in Britain and US.

The first question we must ask is: why are mutuals needed at all in a free-enterprise economy? In a perfectly competitive economy, it might be argued, there would surely be no need for any mutual-benefit IOs to form, because the market would respond to any demand within it. In fact, mutuals form because real-world capitalist economies do not conform to the model of perfect competition, and there are three kinds of 'failure' in these economies to which the mutual-benefit principle is a solution.

(i) In any economy there are areas of economic activity which are marginal – areas in which for-profit entrepreneurs fail to, or expect to fail to, realize a normal rate of return on their investment. Consequently, the good is not provided. In such circumstances, groups of individuals may decide to work together to provide the good for themselves – because they are able to utilize resources which cannot be otherwise sold or mobilized in an economic market. People who devote their labour to helping to turn a farmer's field into a village football pitch very often do not have the choice of doing this or working overtime at their job and using the extra income to pay someone else to help prepare the pitch. There are many resources, and not just labour, for which there is no market demand to compete with that of a potential organization, so that mutuals are often able to draw on resources at below what would otherwise be their market cost. These opportunities are usually not available to for-profit concerns, so that unless the latter obtain subsidies through philanthropy or from the state, there is no initial competition for a mutual from within the for-profit sector. Mutuals often arise, then, because there are limits to the market's penetration of societies.

(ii) Even when the possibility of for-profit supply exists, the market mechanism may be too insensitive to provide the consumers with exactly what they want. Consider the case of a social club. A for-profit supplier might well be sensitive to tastes regarding the type of club for which there is demand, and to the kinds of services his/her clients would want. But there are certain aspects of taste which are too complex for a market mechanism to deal with in the real world. Very often in a club people want to interact with 'their sort of people' and they want to exclude those who do not share their tastes or lifestyle. A club run on mutual lines typically gives its *members* the right to decide on such matters, and on a variety of other issues. The members participating in the making of a decision can readily bring information about their tastes to the attention of the club, while it is far more difficult for a for-profit supplier to do this, unless s/he embraces some of the aspects of the organization of mutuals. In addition, of course, members may value the *direct* exercise of control over activities in itself; part of the ethos of new kinds of self-help groups, usually community-orientated, established since the 1960s has been self-determination.[1]

(iii) Mutuals may also form when consumers are faced by a firm that 'is in a position of natural monopoly or otherwise faces very limited competition'.[2] Hansmann argues, and this is a point over which there is disagreement, that this is typically how consumer co-operatives originate. But he also points out that in order for the co-operative to actually form, the consumers must be in a position to take over supply without incurring excessive costs:

> Generally . . . consumer cooperatives arise in situations in which the consumers involved find it convenient to purchase goods or services repeatedly from the same firm over a substantial period of time, and the value of the purchases is relatively large; otherwise the transaction costs of registering, keeping track of, and communicating with members will be disproportionate to the value of goods consumed.[3]

Once they are supplying their members, co-operative ventures can usually supply them with lower prices than those offered by the monopolist or the supplier operating under imperfect competition. Typically, for example, the price of drinks in working men's clubs in Britain is much lower than in nearby pubs.

In commencing our discussion with the idea that mutuals are a response to market failure, we are not ignoring the fact that, in the formation of many mutuals, major elements have been non-economic objectives. Comradeship, for example, was an important factor in the growth of Friendly Societies in the early nineteenth century. As Gosden notes:

> The monthly meeting of the societies was far more than a business meeting to facilitate the collection of premiums. This was, no doubt, the main reason for gathering if the societies are thought of simply as agencies of mutual insurance. But since the convivial quality of the meetings was such a powerful attraction for members, the inevitable home for the gatherings was the working man's social centre, the inn.[4]

Economic self-interest was not a sufficient condition for the creation of many mutuals though it may have become a powerful factor in preventing the 'exit' of members later. But here too factors like comradeship must not be ignored in accounting for the sustenance of mutuals. And, indeed, the discussion in section 8, which is concerned with newer, non-commercial, mutuals, indicates that in the late twentieth century the 'sharing of experience' provided by some mutuals has become an important force in mobilizing people around non-economic aspects of their welfare. But, in exploring the boundaries of the for-profit sector and IOs, we shall start by focusing on those features of mutuals which bear most directly on the *economic interests* of the members.

How significant are mutuals in the British and American economies? Tables 2.1 and 2.2 provide data on some of the large 'financial' mutuals, and an indication of the shares of their markets enjoyed by some of these mutuals is provided later in this chapter. There are many mutuals, though, for which such data cannot be provided, because they do not have to register with a particular governmental agency. In Britain, the Registrar of Friendly Societies is responsible for overseeing the activities of far fewer organizations than the Charity Commissioners (about one tenth the number), because there is no incentive for many small mutuals to acquire the legal status that would require registration. (For charities, even small ones, there are advantages in the form of tax repayments on covenants.) One result is that there is little data on the smaller mutuals. And, for example, while the Registrar has data on social clubs that are registered under the Friendly Societies Act of 1974, there is no data, to my knowledge, on clubs that are not registered; indeed, it is unclear whether the financial turnover of such organizations would be as useful a measure of their role as their total memberships. In areas where for-profit firms are not involved at all, assessing the level of economic activity becomes extremely difficult, except when a large element of the mutuals' activity is making sales to the members – as in sale of drinks

Table 2.1 Major mutual benefit organizations in the US (excluding mutual insurance companies)

(a) Financial Organizations	
	Assets ($B), 1984
Mutual savings banks	135.6
Savings and loan associations	902.4
Credit unions	99.0
Total	1,137.0
(b) Consumer Co-operatives and Farmer Co-operatives Selling Consumer Goods	
	Business ($B), 1981
Credit unions	50.4
Electric power co-operatives	7.4
Independent and self-insured health plans	9.4
Farmer co-operatives selling producer and consumer goods	17.1
Total	84.3

Source: *Statistical Abstracts of the United States 1985*

in working men's clubs. Nevertheless, it is evident that in both Britain and the US there are very large numbers of organizations catering to the shared interests of their members.

But what of the issue of membership control of mutuals? There is one kind of IO, the political party, which plays only a small part in the discussion within this book, about which there has been a long-standing debate on membership control. One of the early 'classics' of political science, Michels's *Political Parties*, purported to prove that mass control of a party was impossible: organization begat oligarchy.[5] In recent decades political scientists have started to re-evaluate Michels's claims and to examine the processes by which members can lose their control over a group once it moves from being a small face-to-face body to a large organization.[6] One of the main problems for members, which is especially relevant to our discussion, is that if the members have no reason to interact with each other except for 'business' purposes, then power is likely to accrue very quickly in the hands of managers because there is no forum in which opposition could possibly mobilize. This is what has happened to Building Societies. Where a sense of shared communal activity survives, the prospects for at least some input from the membership is greater. Moreover, when the tradition of membership input is lost, new organizations may enter the field and take on the

Table 2.2 Mutual benefit organizations in Britain (excluding mutual insurance companies)

(a) Societies Registered under Industrial and Provident Act, 1965		
	Assets, 1983 (£M)	Sales, 1983 (£M)
Retail	1,243	3,914
Wholesale and producer	761	2,642
Agricultural	409	1,670
Fishing	9	31
Clubs	248	
General service	2,343	
Housing	6,856	
Credit unions	2	
Total	11,871	8,257
(b) Building Societies		
	Assets, 1983 (£M)	
All societies	85,868	
(c) Friendly Societies		
	Total funds, 1980 (£M)	
Orders	104	
Collecting societies	877	
Other centralized societies	442	
Total	1,423	

Data taken from: *Report of the Chief Registrar of Friendly Societies for 1983–1984*

mutual form of the older organizations, but without any intention of treating their members as anything other than clients. Many of the more recently-established Building Societies, for example, were set up by local builders and estate agents, as a way of promoting the housing industry in their area.

This brings us to the further point that, while the mutual principle of membership control can be devalued by organizational growth, it remains the case that the idea of being a 'member' is an attractive one for potential clients, so organizations seeking to attract clients sometimes offer them 'membership'. The mutual form of organization has been imitated, therefore, by for-profit firms who do not give their clients any control, but who wish to suggest that they will be given greater attention and consideration. One of the best examples of this *ersatz* type of membership is that offered by the American Express Company with its credit cards. Its advertising in the US in 1987 was directed to persuading potential clients that it offered *membership* (and hence privileges) while other companies merely had 'card holders'.

In comparing Britain with the US, it becomes apparent that the kinds of mutual organizations which have developed are remarkably similar, but the legal framework in which they operate is rather different. In the US many kinds of mutuals, though not all, are covered by the non-profit corporation laws governing charities: co-operatives, however, are covered by separate statutes. In England, not only does 'self-help' preclude an organization from being charitable, but there are no general statutes embracing most kinds of mutual-benefit organizations. However, at the level of regulation the situation is very different. While most of the larger mutuals (Building Societies, Friendly Societies, co-operatives and even social clubs) have been subject to supervision from the Registrar of Friendly Societies, there is no single regulatory body at the federal level in the US, and usually none at the state level either. (In 1986, though, a separate Building Society Commission was 'hived off' from the Registry, as part of an expansion of the financial services which British Building Societies could provide.) Because of the similarity of the organizations found in the two countries, it is possible in this chapter to examine our main themes in relation to each of the principal types of organization. We begin with co-operatives because it is here that the problem of the distinction between profit-distributing and non-profit-distributing bodies is most evident.

1 Co-operatives

In its most basic form a consumers' co-operative consists of a small group of individuals coming together to provide funds for the purchasing of items for which there is widespread demand among the group. The incentive to form a consumers' co-operative usually derives from one of two kinds of market failure we have discussed earlier – the absence of commercial firms, on a long-term basis, in a particular area of economic activity or the tendency for supply to fall into the hands of monopolists. The members agree to act together in a co-operative for a fixed period of time, after which it will then be dissolved. Purchasing and other policies are determined democratically at meetings of the membership. The co-operative then holds the goods it purchases and sells them to members when they require them. It does not sell to non-members, so there is an identity between those who provide the capital for the initial purchasing, storage and so on, and those who buy the co-operative's goods. Any surplus accrued is then refunded to members, in proportion to their share of the goods bought from it, on its dissolution. The principal differences between this ideal model of a co-operative and the normal kind of for-profit enterprise are: (i) the former does not attempt to generate any profits, because it makes no sales to non-members; (ii) it is not hierarchical in structure, and it provides for democratic decision making among all members; (iii) it lasts for a pre-arranged period of time. Of these differences, the first would seem to be critical in separating a co-operative from a for-profit concern. While its decision-making arrangements do distinguish it from many for-profit enterprises, many smaller businesses, such as partnerships, also practise democratic decision-making among the partners; partners, however, do not extend democracy to customers, while in a primitive co-operative customers are also owners. It is with the larger, corporate forms of enterprise that co-operatives most differ in this respect. The third difference, a fixed term of operation, was typical of many early working-class mutual-benefit organizations, but perpetuation does not transform co-operativism.

The first successful modern co-operative, of course, was the one founded in Rochdale, Lancashire, in 1844 to sell domestic consumer goods to its members. Co-operative societies had been established before this, such as the one established in an Oxfordshire village for the benefit of the poor, but they had not survived long or been copied elsewhere.[7] The principle utilized at Rochdale was that members who paid to join the society could not only purchase goods from the co-operative's store, but were entitled to a refund from any trading surplus at the end of the year in proportion to the value of their purchases. Its viability led to the creation of more than 200 other co-operative societies during the 1840s. Co-operative business became financially sound in poor districts for two reasons: the stores did not give credit to their customers and they charged them market prices for goods. In effect, the early consumer co-operatives were overcharging their customers at the time of their purchases, but this overcharging enabled reserves to be built up and provided insurance against emergencies. This overcharging was partially corrected at the end of each year, when some of the trading surplus was redistributed to members in the form of the dividend (or 'divi' as it was popularly known). Until well into the twentieth century the ideology of the co-operative movement held that they were non-profit-making bodies, although the dividend was usually not the only form that the distribution of the surplus took. Along with its emphasis on non-profit-making, co-operatives continued the Friendly Society tradition of developing 'fraternal' elements in the pursuit of mutual interests.

Not surprisingly, co-ops tended to grow more in those countries where the ethic of communalism was strong, and that of individualism weak, among the working class. In western Europe they have been most successful in Scandinavia, where their development was further aided by the marginal nature of the retail trade in many of the sparsely populated rural areas. Even today co-operatives constitute a huge segment of the retail industry; Stolpe reports that 'between one third and one half of all families in the Nordic countries are involved in consumers' co-operatives'.[8] Throughout Europe, though, the debt to the Rochdale model is widely acknowledged: a few years ago I was puzzled to find bottles of table wine in a modern French supermarket which were being marketed under the label 'Rochdale', until it was pointed out that the store was a co-operative. The influence of the individualistic ethic in constricting co-operative ventures in marginal areas of the economy can be seen in the contrast between Britain and the US: relatively few consumer co-operatives developed in the latter. At the height of co-operative penetration of the retail trade in Britain, in the years immediately after the second world war, co-operatives accounted for more than 10 per cent of total retail sales, but US co-operatives held considerably less than one per cent of the retail market there.[9] This is not to say, though, that individualism was an insuperable barrier to mutual-benefit activities in the US: it was not. Agricultural producers' co-operatives were more successful, partly because they had a smaller number of more homogenous communities to draw on than did consumer co-operatives in the multi-ethnic cities.

In Britain the expansion of the consumers' co-operative movement was frustrated by the boom in consumer spending in the 1950s. The movement did possess several important advantages in meeting this challenge: a large share of the retail market, the backing of a huge wholesale organization, the Co-operative Wholesale Society, as well as its own bank and insurance business. In the hundred years since its founding, the movement had accumulated enormous resources from trading surpluses, by not declaring such large dividends as they could have, and this enabled it to compete with for-profit business in areas which were no longer marginal ones. The problem facing the societies in the 1950s was that, while they were still able to supply basic commodities quite efficiently, they lacked the willingness and expertise to market goods in an era of rapidly rising personal incomes that enabled most people to make purchases beyond basic necessities. The public image of the co-operatives, as carrying a relatively small range of lower-quality products, worked against them. By 1978 co-operatives accounted for only 6.8 per cent of total retail turnover in the UK, about two thirds of the share of the market they enjoyed just after the second world war.

Only in the 1960s had co-operatives tried to change their marketing strategies in an effort to recapture some of their former market share. And in attempting to modernize they eliminated two of the main characteristics of early co-operative practice: whatever vestiges of 'fraternalism' remained were lost as the societies concentrated on keeping their markets, and the 'divi' was replaced by a form of trading stamp.

That consumer co-operatives are not profit-making, and hence not profit-distributing, has been recognized in British and American law, in that the dividend paid out to members is not subject to income tax. It is treated as a refund to members who were overcharged at the time of their purchases. But what about the distinctiveness of co-operativism when it is extended beyond this basic model? As we have noted, permanent rather than fixed-term operations do not affect this distinctiveness. Growth in the number of members, so that they no longer all know each other, interact with each other, or take all decisions democratically, certainly alters co-operativism as a form of *social* organization, but the introduction of professional management does not undermine the distinction between co-operativism and for-profit enterprise. Sales to non-members, though, seem more problematic. Obviously, if the profits from them were to be distributed as part of a 'divi' the parallel with for-profit enterprise would be clear and, indeed, this would constitute taxable income in Britain and America. But does even the retention of profits from these sales turn co-operatives into profit-making enterprises? Like a commercial firm, and similarly like a charitable hospital or school, they could accumulate reserves from outside sales for the purpose of extending trading activity. And, what of the further step of acquiring some form of corporate status so that the individual member no longer has unlimited liability in respect of its activities? This last point is interesting because some observers have seen incorporation as the transformation which would undermine the mutual-benefit character of an organization. It was an argument propounded by the Royal Commission on the Taxation of Profits and Income in 1955. With respect to mutuals, the Commission was concerned with the problem that mutual trading surpluses were means by which capital assets could be built up at the expense of taxable income, and it is worth quoting at length its argument about the relevance of corporate status:

> We think that there is great force in the observation . . . that the incorporation of a mutual trading society is a factor of determining importance. It is the incorporation that makes possible large-scale business and turns the members of the society from a group of persons in genuine mutual association into an indeterminate number of persons whose real concern is to do business with the corporation. We recognize that it is not necessarily inconsistent with the continuance of genuine mutuality that a corporation should be employed by the

members of the association to act as a managing trustee on their behalf. Their rules may take a form which secures to every member a continuing and realizable share in the trading surplus of each year as it arises. But... we observe that this does not seem to be what has happened in practice once a corporation becomes the effective manager of the trading operations. The surpluses become more and more like the reserves of an ordinary trading corporation and the property interest of any individual member in the funds which are held on behalf of his society less and less distinguishable from the interest of a shareholder in the funds of a company in which he holds shares.[10]

The Commission was seeking a way of distinguishing commercial from non-commercial operations, and the solution it proposed was a pragmatic one. Incorporation did not mean that overtly commercial activities would result, but the Commission argued that it was a good predictor of this. Consequently, it recommended a change in British law, so that no corporation would be exempt from taxation on profits for the surpluses it accrued. Whatever the merits of the proposal in preventing tax evasion, on the Commission's own admission it did not resolve the issue of distinguishing genuinely co-operative ventures from for-profit ones.

We must now return to the point about sales to non-members. At first glance this might seem to be the key to the peculiar character of co-operativism. However, there are two problems in viewing 'outside' sales in this way. On the one hand, once they are established as organizations, co-operatives may find it possible to enroll most potential customers as members with a relatively low membership fee, so that the cost of doing business with a co-operative, even on a casual basis, may be relatively low for the new customer. That is, even organizations that do not make any sales to non-members (as is the case with many social clubs) could be highly entrepreneurial in their efforts to increase business. On the other hand, sales to non-members, even on a large scale, do not necessarily permit the building up of reserve capital which in turn would allow the co-operative to become entrepreneurial. The pricing policy may be such that the co-operative is attempting to make all its sales virtually 'at cost', and has no plan or intention of expanding into other markets even if it has the opportunity to do so.

Like incorporation, 'sales to non-members' is not quite the 'litmus test' of co-operativism that it might appear to be at first sight. The problem is a more fundamental one, which derives from the fact that profit-making is only one way that people can *advance their own interests* at the expense of others in an economy. And yet for many purposes, including taxation, profit-making is treated as either the only form or the most significant form of interest promotion. Consider again the basic model of a consumer co-operative. Traditionally it has been regarded as a 'coming together' of individuals for the purpose of joint purchasing;

on this view their activity is non-commercial because their intention is simply to make purchases for their own consumption more cheaply than they could as individuals. Yet viewed from another perspective there is a commercial element to this. The very act of association creates a supplier–seller relationship between the group and the individual; there is an intermediary involved in trading even though none of the human actors has any intention of engaging in business or in generating profits. On this view, even a three-person co-operative formed to buy goods from a wholesaler, because it is cheaper than individual purchases from a retailer, is engaged in trade. The distinction between the for-profit sector and mutual-benefit organizations seems to be in danger of collapsing.

We shall return to the question of whether this is the case, and its significance for our analysis of the role of IOs in a democracy, when we have considered the full range of mutual-benefit organizations found in Britain and America. For the moment, though, it is worth pointing out that the courts, like the Royal Commission, have sought a pragmatic solution to the problem of organizations using the advantages of co-operative status to advance their commercial activities. They have not tried to grapple with the Janus-faced characteristics of co-operativism, but in general have simply disallowed any co-operative arrangement which seemed to be too overtly commercial. The most illuminating instance of this is the *Assam Tea* case (1948).

This particular case involved the English and Scottish Joint Co-operative Society which owned a tea estate and sold the tea grown there exclusively to members of the society. The Privy Council held that this was not a mutual trading body on the ground that the kind of activity they were engaged in could not qualify as mutual trading:

> ...their lordships are of opinion that the principle [of mutual trading] cannot apply to an association, society or company which grows produce on its own land or manufactures goods in its own factories, using its own capital, or capital borrowed whether from its own members or from others, and sells its produce or goods to its members exclusively.[11]

In disallowing this society's claim to be exempt from tax, the Privy Council accepted that mutual insurance was properly considered mutual trading activity, and therefore exempt from tax. It took the view, though, that some kinds of purchasers could be formed into mutual-trading organizations, while those purchasing in other sectors of the economy were not eligible to be thus treated. The decision has the merit of preventing massive tax avoidance by organizations, but does so at the cost of introducing a wholly artificial distinction between those sectors of the economy where a mutual benefit form is permissible and those where it is not.

If, as we have argued, even relatively straightforward co-operative arrangements embrace elements of 'commerce', then the development of co-operatives since 1844 has brought many of them still closer to the for-profit sector in several respects. Firstly, many co-operatives (certainly those in Britain and most in the US) have had schemes for paying interest to those who have contributed capital. Often there are restrictions on the rate of interest that may be paid, just as the size of share capital does not determine voting power; but, while this practice differs from that in companies limited by shares, it scarcely makes them *non-profit-distributing* organizations. In Hansmann's words, they are 'limited profit' enterprises.[12] Secondly, consumer co-operatives have conducted increasing trade with non-members. Mid-twentieth-century prosperity, combined with much greater competition in poorer districts from large retail chains, has made the benefits of membership less apparent to potential members. Competition for sales with non-members has made many co-operatives more closely resemble for-profit firms in terms of how they conduct their business. Thirdly, the need to increase trade with non-members prompted the British retail co-operatives in 1968 to start to change their method of refunding the 'surplus' accrued from their trading. Subsequently they issued their own trading stamps, which were given on sales to members and non-members alike, although the stamps had a higher value to members who paid them into their share accounts. Fourthly, as a way of organizing economic transactions, the co-operative became more attractive as a device for producer enterprises than for consumers. This had always been a feature in the US, where the consumer co-operative movement was weak, and, as Ellman has said of the US, 'Although some large consumer co-operatives do exist, producer co-operatives dominate the field, and most co-operative laws appear to be written with them in mind'.[13] In Britain the slow decline of consumer co-operatives in the post-war years was accompanied by the use, though in a relatively small number of cases, of the producer co-operative form, especially where closure of plants or firms was being effected because they were deemed to be 'uneconomic'.[14] However, producers' co-operatives are not of direct interest to us, because they are not IOs: they seek to make profits for their members and to distribute these profits to them, even if these arrangements sometimes restrict the amount of profit that may be distributed in any one year.[15] This is not to deny that a polity dominated by producer co-operatives would differ in a number of important respects from liberal democracy as it has actually emerged under capitalism. But the focus of our attention is on organizations which at least have their origins in non-profit making ventures.

2 Building Societies

As with the later retail co-operatives, the incentive to form Building Societies emanated from market failure – in this case primarily from the absence of commercial enterprises which would finance building for the working class. Like co-operatives, Building Societies (or savings and loan associations, SLAs, as they are known in the United States) can trace their origins to the British Friendly Societies which emerged in the eighteenth century. In Britain the first Building Society was founded in Birmingham in 1775 and the movement soon spread. The principle employed was much the same as that for the 'basic' co-operative discussed in the last section. Members paid subscriptions to the society for the duration of its life. When sufficient money had been accumulated to buy or build one house, some form of selection procedure was adopted to decide which member would be allocated this house. This continued until all the members had houses, and at that point the society terminated. Unlike the later co-operative movement, which was a response to market failure in the form of high prices in working-class areas, Building Societies began to operate in a marginal area of the economy where for-profit firms had not entered at all. Mutuals were the only organizations which could provide housing finance to the working class. Initially most societies registered as Friendly Societies, and it was not until the Building Societies' Act of 1836 that they were first recognized as a distinct legal entity. By then the institution had been copied in the US. The first association, the Oxford Provident Building Association, was founded in Philadelphia in 1831. During the next twelve years only two further SLAs were started but after that growth was much more rapid.[16]

In the case of Britain the major problem with the early societies has been described by Boddy:

> Their financial structure discouraged members joining after the initial foundation, since back-payments would be required, and their capacity to accumulate funds was severely limited. Societies tended, therefore, increasingly to take in deposits from investors seeking interest rather than loans or houses, to increase the funds available for members wishing to borrow.[17]

In Britain this problem was first overcome in 1845 with the founding of a 'permanent' society – one that was not in existence merely for a fixed period of time. The growth of permanent societies over the next 29 years was one of the main reasons for further legislation, the Building Societies' Act of 1874, which granted corporate status to the societies. In the US the split between the role of investor and that of borrower occurred in two stages: first with the emergence of 'serial plans' (the issue of successive series of stock) in the 1850s, and then with the 'permanent share plan' in the 1870s. With this later development the SLAs once again closely resembled their British counterparts.

Government regulation of SLAs was also slower to develop than regulation of the British Building Societies. For example, New York, the first state to implement it, did not require annual reports to be submitted by SLAs until 1875.[18] By that date the British Act of 1874 was already in effect. This comprehensive Act, which followed the report of a Royal Commission set up in 1870, remained the basis of legal control of Building Societies until the major reforms of 1986. Its main provisions were to restrict the business which the societies could conduct to building and owning land in connection with their business, and to strengthen the powers of the Chief Registrar of Friendly Societies in relation to Building Societies.

From the late nineteenth century, both the British Building Societies and the American SLAs developed into some of the most powerful financial institutions in their respective countries. In 1980 Building Society assets in the UK amounted to nearly £54,000 million (nearly one quarter the size of the assets in the UK banking sector), with nearly five and a half million borrowers and with 48 per cent of the population having a Building Society account; by that year over 82 per cent of all mortgages issued in the UK were from Building Societies. In the US the growth of SLAs was great but not as spectacular. In 1983 SLAs insured through the Federal Savings and Loan Insurance Corporation (FSLIC) had a 26.5 per cent share of the domestic deposit market, compared with a 38 per cent share of the deposit holdings of UK residents Building Societies enjoyed in 1976. Moreover, while the SLAs held about 42 per cent of all first mortgages in the US in 1980, the largest share of the market, this was still only about half the share of the British market held by the Building Societies.

One of the most interesting aspects of these two sets of institutions is that their share of both the deposit market and the mortgage market increased dramatically in the mid-twentieth century. In both countries rapid growth was facilitated by vastly increased demand for home ownership and, of all the financial institutions, it was the Building Societies and SLAs that were best placed to take advantage of this. In Britain their near-complete domination of the housing finance market was facilitated by much greater specialization in the financial system. Generally the commercial banks had stayed out of the home mortgage market, although in the early 1980s this policy was reversed. In the two years after 1980 the commercial banks' share of mortgage lending rose from less than 6 per cent to 14 per cent of the total. However, their policy of rapid expansion was reversed again in 1983–4, and the policy has fluctuated further since then.

As with consumers' co-operatives, there are two features of Building Societies and SLAs which are important in understanding the relation of mutual-benefit organizations to the market. One point we have noted already: both had their origins in areas of marginal economic activity at the time of their formation. In the late eighteenth century the British banking system had not expanded into the potentially large market of the newly-emerging upper-working class; there were no sources of finance for house building or purchasing for this sector of the community, and mutual-benefit organizations were the obvious solution. It was a marginal area of the economy because there were inadequate means of insuring against the risk of default by borrowers, even though debtors could be imprisoned. In the case of co-operatives, the problem was that the retail trade was based on firms that were too small to absorb the risks associated with trading in districts which were especially exposed to the effects of the trade cycle; profit margins tended to be high, therefore, and this left scope for the growth of mutual-benefit organizations. The other feature, which is obvious but worth remembering, is that once these sectors of the economy were no longer marginal, Building Societies and SLAs did not collapse in the face of competition from for-profit organizations. Once established, mutuals were not a limited institutional form that could survive only in certain economic conditions. Nevertheless, the contrasting fortunes since the 1950s of Building Societies and SLAs on the one side, and consumer co-operatives, on the other, and the particular success of the British Building Societies, demands further explanation if we are to substantiate our claim that mutuals are not at a disadvantage in areas of an economy that are no longer marginal. The main reasons for the success of the Building Societies lay in their ability to operate in a specialized market that was expanding beyond its original base, while retail co-operatives were not so protected. However, in Britain especially, there were other factors which contributed to their dominance, and there are five main factors to which attention should be given in explaining the dominance of mutuals in the area of housing finance.

(i) An important advantage enjoyed by the Building Societies and the SLAs in competing with commercial banks (and other for-profit organizations) for the rapidly expanding housing market in the second half of the twentieth century was expertise in a potentially high-risk area of finance. Mortgages are assets which are redeemable only in the very long term, whereas the savings deposited with societies and associations are subject to withdrawal at short-notice. In both countries these dangers have been realized in the past, and contemporary expertise draws on this earlier experience. There were failures of major Building Societies in 1892 and 1911, and the aftermath of the 1929 'crash' included the collapse of SLAs as well as of American commercial banks. Consumer co-operatives did not enjoy the advantage of possessing specialized skills that potential for-profit competitors would have to acquire.

(ii) British Building Societies enjoyed a further advantage over their banking rivals. The societies themselves pay the income tax on savers' interest before the interest is paid to the depositors. This is disadvantageous for those seeking to conceal income from the Inland Revenue, but since 1894 a special system of calculating the amount of tax the societies should pay 'for the savers' has developed, and it was often alleged by the banks that this arrangement benefited the Building Societies in attracting savers. The arrangement:

> ... effectively averages out the basic rate liability of building society investors. The rate paid is a weighted average of a zero tax rate and the basic rate of tax. Both tax payers and non-tax payers receive the same net-of-tax return but the gross equivalents are very different ... Non-taxpaying investors are invariably able to obtain a higher return from one of the institutions able to pay interest gross such as a clearing bank or the National Savings Bank.[19]

This scheme gave the societies an advantage in competing for deposits from tax payers, and in 1985 a similar arrangement for taxing the interest of depositors was granted to the banks. However, there have not been any comparable special benefits available to consumer co-operatives.

(iii) The Building Societies and the SLAs expanded their activities into social classes who wanted to own their homes and were growing in size. From being institutions of the upper-working class, they have become the means by which the middle classes in both Britain and America have been able to acquire large subsidies on housing, through tax relief on mortgage interest payments. This subsidy is far greater than that acquired by those in public housing while, of course, those in the (now relatively small) private rental market have no subsidy at all. (In passing we might note that the best fictional exemplar of lower-middle-class life in the late Victorian period, Charles Pooter, rented the house he lived in; most of his modern equivalents would have a mortgage with a Building Society.)[20] Initially British co-operatives grew because they extended downwards from their original base in the upper-working class into the poorest communities. But in the mid-twentieth century this was a class in *relative* decline, and it was not until after the co-ops had lost part of their market to supermarkets, that they introduced newer retailing techniques, such as out-of-town shopping centres, to which wider sections of the community would be attracted.

(iv) Like all large mutuals, most members of consumer co-operatives are inactive and policy is primarily determined by professional managers. In the Building Societies, though, this separation of *de facto* from *de jure* control has been taken further. Managers have been able to pursue policies that have contributed to the expansion of their business without even having to explain them to members. The social objectives associated with early mutuals are virtually absent in the Building Societies who have been criticized, for example, for policies refusing to issue mortgages in inner-city areas (known in the US as 'red-lining' policies), thereby furthering their decay. Management autonomy is partly explained away by the managers in terms of the members not wishing to participate in the affairs of a society; Boléat, the Deputy Secretary-General of the Building Societies Association observed that 'in practice investing members tend to regard themselves as depositors rather than owners and seek to play no part in the management of the society'.[21] In fact, the societies have done little to encourage member participation and much to discourage it.[22] One example might be useful in illustrating the absence of the democratic culture in Building Societies.

In 1987 there was a contested election for the board of directors of the Abbey National Building Society. Three members of the board were seeking re-election, and they were challenged by another candidate. In the same envelope as their ballot forms the society's members received the annual report by the directors which featured statements about all the members of the board, including those seeking re-election, together with a photograph of them. The challenging candidate did not receive this publicity, and the only mention of her at all was a very brief statement on the ballot form itself indicating her profession. Not only did the Abbey National not bother to provide members with statements from the candidates as to the policies they might wish the society to pursue, but the candidates seeking re-election were provided with an advantage that would be regarded as unfair in most membership-based organizations. It is in this kind of non-democratic culture that the professional managers of societies have been able to exert their influence in pursuing policies of expansion to the exclusion of other objectives.

(v) Government policy toward the expansion of home ownership in the mid-twentieth century enabled the Building Societies to enjoy a privileged position in relation to the British state. Subsequent efforts in Britain to deregulate the financial sector have further worked to the advantage of Building Societies. Deregulation in the US has had a more mixed impact on the SLAs. While there have been a number of SLA failures as a result of it, many SLAs have expanded into other forms of banking – such as in the provision of chequing accounts. Before deregulation Building Society power in Britain was dependent partly on societies being organized in a cartel, the Building Societies Association

(BSA), which among its other functions set the rate of interest to be charged by all the societies. In 1973 rapidly rising mortgage rates, following a period of rising house prices, had led to the establishment of a Joint Advisory Committee bringing together the BSA and officials from the Department of the Environment. This reviewed mortgage finance throughout the 1970s, and was an acknowledgement of the privileged position of the Building Societies – as organizations which had been involved in implementing the policy of every post-war government in extending home ownership in Britain. By the 1980s strains in the BSA led to the breakdown of the cartel in the setting of interest rates, and several societies attempted to provide additional financial services through their links with other financial institutions. In any event, the policy of the incoming Thatcher government in 1979 was directed towards greater competition between financial institutions, and the result was the Building Societies Act of 1985 which enabled societies to diversify both their borrowing and lending arrangements, and to increase the range of financial services they offered. In some circumstances societies would even be able to transform their mutual status into corporate status with shareholders. Within a relatively specialized banking system, these reforms seemed to create even greater opportunities for the societies.

But what of the possible costs to the state, in terms of lost taxes, in having such a major economic activity as housing finance in the hands of mutuals? In both countries there have been strict limits to the tax privileges available to these mutuals. As Kendall points out in the American case, 'savings associations are subject to the same corporate income tax rates and the same general regulations applying to all major financial institutions'.[23] Profits retained by SLAs are taxable and thus, to the extent that SLAs want to expand their business or guard against future risks, they are corporate income tax payers. The same is true of Building Societies; in 1978 3 per cent of the societies' expenditures (£90 million) was paid as corporation tax.[24] Whatever the loss in income tax to the state resulting from their having no shareholders, Building Societies and SLAs have provided a number of significant advantages to the state in organizing a potentially risky market, that might otherwise require more extensive state regulation.

3 Mutual Savings Banks

These organizations have a rather different origin from the Friendly-Society inspired bodies we have considered so far. Indeed, in view of court decisions at the time the Trustee Savings Bank (TSB) was converted into a corporate firm in the mid 1980s, it is at least arguable that it was never a mutual-benefit organization. In both countries, mutual savings banks were introduced by paternalistic members of the upper and upper-middle classes. The idea was that the encouragement of saving among the poor would help to alleviate various social problems, and despite their paternalistic origins they did become popular in poorer districts. In the US they developed in only seventeen states, primarily in the north east, although in recent years *federal* savings banks have also been established throughout the country. In Britain they developed nationwide, and their significance stemmed partly from the fact that, along with the Post Office, they were the financial institution most willing to open up branches in poorer districts – in marginal areas of the economy. Although their growth in North America was confined to certain regions, the importance of savings banks in the two countries is remarkably similar. In 1978 the TSB had a 6.1 per cent share of the deposit holdings of UK residents,[25] while in 1983 the share of the domestic deposit market of American mutual savings banks was 7.1 per cent.[26]

Rather like the SLAs, American mutual savings banks have become good examples of mutual-benefit organizations where the formal powers held by the members are not exercised. There has been a high degree of managerial autonomy, with managers pursuing profit-maximization for the purpose of protecting institutional stability or for expansion. In fact, with federal deregulation in the financial sector, the former goal has usually been more important. Indeed, the pressure from deregulation has been sufficiently great that a number of savings banks have undertaken the complicated task of turning themselves into shareholder-owned organizations, so as to obtain the greater flexibility in operations which this form provides.

In the British case, however, there was an important difference between the Building Societies and the TSB in that the latter was not owned by the members. Curiously, the banks which were amalgamated to form the TSB were not owned by anyone; they had been set up for the benefit of depositors, but they were controlled by self-appointed boards of trustees, and not by the depositors. During the 1960s and 1970s the ability of the savings banks to attract funds was being threatened by, among other factors, the success of the Building Societies. Following the Page Committee Report in 1973, the banks were reorganized in 1976 under an Act initiated by the Labour government. There was a reduction in the number of banks, and in the long term it was planned that the banks' status would change so that they would become mutual-benefit organizations. But with a change in chairmanship in 1979, and with a Conservative government in power, this proposal was dropped in favour of conversion to a shareholder-owned corporation. This action was unprecedented in that the government did not claim to own the bank, nor did it intend to nationalize it first before privatization; it merely assumed the responsibility to act in the absence of owners. In fact, the argument that the banks were not owned by the depositors was itself far from clear; when the Treasury had sought legal advice in the 1970s, they were told that the banks 'did belong to' their depositors.[27] Despite legal challenges to this move, which delayed the transfer to a joint-stock company, the change was eventually effected.

4 Other Mutual Financial Organizations

Mutual-benefit organizations have developed in several other fields where, initially at least, the market could not sustain effective operations by for-profit firms. This kind of market failure provided an incentive for the formation of mutuals – providing, of course, the usual problems of co-ordinating collective action could be overcome. Of the mutual activities which can be described as broadly financial in character, there are three main types: insurance-related activities, credit-facilitation activities, and (non-mortgage) housing finance. We consider each in turn.

The obvious institutions with which to start a discussion of insurance-related activities are the British Friendly Societies. Although the first Friendly Societies appeared at the beginning of the eighteenth century, it was the social disruption of industrialization in the nineteenth century that prompted their emergence as the exemplars of working-class co-operation. In 1815 fewer than a million people were members of Friendly Societies. Sixty years later there were four million members – though the population of Britain had only doubled in size. To the extent that the ethos of self-help triumphed in the nineteenth century, it was the Friendly Societies that were the most significant vehicle for its realization. Yet they varied enormously in respect of the extent of insurance they provided. As Fraser has pointed out: 'Some of these mutual insurance schemes involved little more than burial funds to avoid a pauper's grave, others were far more ambitious with medical, accident and unemployment benefits, or widows' and old-age pensions.'[28]

Moreover, just as the Building Societies' later expansion was to facilitate the emergence of new entrepreneur-sponsored Societies, so too did growth encourage *ersatz* forms of Friendly Society. The outstanding examples of this were the large collecting Societies which were 'essentially commercial undertakings exploiting the contemporary abhorrence of the pauper's funeral and only incidentally encouraging anything that could be described as thrift or providence.'[29]

The Friendly Societies' success in the nineteenth century – in the late Victorian period they were often held up as displaying the advance of the working class – was followed by failure in the twentieth century. There were two stages to this collapse. In the negotiations between the Liberal government, the Friendly Societies, the medical profession, and the commercial insurance firms over the 1911 National Insurance Act, it was the societies' interests that were damaged most.[30] Thus, although they worked with the state in the operation of the new policy of social insurance, the rise of for-profit insurance companies had seriously affected the terms on which they became partners with the state. In the inter-war years the societies continued to oppose direct state intervention in social welfare and, given the very restricted coverage of the 1911 Act, this approach did not find favour with a Labour party committed to a massive expansion of welfare provision when it came to power.

In 1945, with the election of a Labour government possessing a parliamentary majority for the first time, direct provision of services by the state could be introduced. The use of intermediaries to supply services, irrespective of any state funding that might be involved in this, was ruled out by the Labour party, which sought to make the state primarily responsible for providing minimum standards of welfare. Where the state did not propose to intervene, at least initially, a role would be left for the IOs which had traditionally operated there. Consequently, many charities were to survive and become integrated into the welfare state. But the activities of the Friendly Societies, in providing insurance for the individual against adversity, lay at the heart of the new proposals for state provision of welfare. The societies could expect to play little part in the kind of welfare state the Labour party wanted to set up, and most clearly they were excluded from it. In Beveridge's words in 1949, the societies were first 'married to the State machine for social insurance in 1911, and now by unilateral action they have been divorced from the State. They have been sent back to live in their own homes and the State is undertaking the whole administration.'[31]

While the Friendly Societies actually survived the advent of the welfare state, they became relatively minor elements in the overall structure of social welfare in Britain. However, one feature of the eighteenth and nineteenth-century Societies has survived, at least in part. Unlike many other mutuals, some Friendly Societies have retained an ethos of being more than a commercial arrangement between individuals. The point is emphasized by the Registrar of Friendly Societies: 'An important feature of many traditional friendly societies is that [their] business activities are complemented by a more general care for individual members in ways which would normally be outside the practice of a purely commercial organization.'[32]

As we have said, one of the principal themes being developed in this chapter is that mutual-benefit organizations seem to straddle the boundary between the for-profit sector and IOs. In addition to our main argument, that trading and the pursuit of economic advantage lies at the centre of the activities of many mutuals, it must be pointed out that there are some organizational forms which are to be found among both mutual benefit and charitable activities. Friendly Societies are one example; the Registry distinguishes between those which exist to provide benefits to members alone and those providing certain benefits to non-members as well as, or instead of, the members. Some of this last group are 'charities' under English law.

As well as Friendly Societies there are, of course, other, long-established, insurance schemes operating on the principle of mutual benefit. There are mutual insurance companies – companies in which the policy-holders have the same relation to the company as do the members of a modern Building Society to their society. That is, it is a purely commercial relation. In Britain too there are Industrial Assurance Companies, which provide a particular kind of life insurance, and which are regulated under a 1923 Act: only certain companies are authorized to conduct this sort of business and all must be registered with the Registry of Friendly Societies. Then, again, in Britain there are also insurance and superannuation societies which are classified as Industrial and Provident Societies with the Registry. It is an area where there has been considerable organizational diversity. In America too the mutual form of organization has been prominent in insurance activities. For example, even in the 1960s 60 per cent of insurance in force, and 70 per cent of assets, were still held by mutual companies. So why have mutuals done so well in the insurance industry?

Hansmann explains that the first life insurance on the market in the US, in about 1810, was supplied by for-profit firms, and that it was not until 1843 that the first mutuals entered the market.[33] After that the latter became the dominant form, and indeed later, in this century, there were instances of for-profit companies converting to mutuals. He argues that mutuals were able to establish their place in the market because of the problems firms in the life insurance industry faced in dealing with long-term contracting under conditions of uncertainty:

> With the mutual form there is no class of shareholders with an interest adverse to that of the policyholders; consequently, the incentive for the company to behave opportunistically in setting the level or riskiness of reserves is substantially attentuated. A mutual company can set a nominal premium rate that is high enough to provide reserves adequate for the most pessimistic forecasts of mortality, market rate of return, and inflation; then, if and when events turn out better than a worst-case forecast, the excess reserves can be liquidated and returned to policyholders as dividends. The difficulty of market contracting

between companies and policyholders is eliminated simply by eliminating the market and replacing it with an ownership relationship.[34]

In this case, unlike the British Building Societies, for-profit firms tried and failed to establish a market before the entry of mutuals. They failed largely because of difficulties in accurately forecasting risks, so that the terms they could offer clients were unattractive. Once they dominated the market, the mutuals were able to maintain their position, even though advances in the calculation of risks made this no longer a marginal area of the economy.

Unlike the Friendly Societies, consumer co-operatives, savings banks, or the early Building Societies, the rise of the mutual form in areas like life and fire insurance was related to a 'technical' problem which obstructed the working of a market, rather than to the inability of financial institutions to extend themselves to embrace the working class. The provision of credit facilities on a mutual basis, though, reflects the more usual problem of the failure of for-profit firms to extend their operations to poorer sections of society. Credit unions are a means by which those who would normally be able to obtain loans only at very high rates of interest, if at all, are able to secure them at more competitive rates. They have long been established in Canada and the US, although they are still in their infancy in Britain, and they are rather similar in their operations to the original Building Societies. Members save with a credit union, and receive interest which is derived from that paid by members who take out loans. Unlike the loans obtained from Building Societies (at least originally), they can be spent on ordinary consumer purchases and not just on an immoveable asset. Credit unions are similar to the original Building Societies, however, in that members can expect to be net creditors some of the time and net debtors at other times. Their main problem, of course, is that of securing the loans they make, and this is overcome by forming unions within communities or places of work, so that there is peer group pressure to prevent borrowers from absconding. In the US there are over 20,000 credit unions with assets (in 1982) in excess of $81 billion; they account for about 14 per cent of the consumer instalment credit market, and about one American in five is a member of a credit union. This situation contrasts with that in Britain. There were no regulations governing such organizations in Britain until 1979 when the Credit Union Act was passed; by 1982 there were eighty-one such unions, with assets of £1.6 million, and they remain a tiny (if growing) type of mutual.

If Friendly Societies are one area where the boundaries between mutuals and charities is sometimes indistinct, another example is housing associations. In Britain housing associations are generally organizations which construct, manage, or improve housing on a non-profit basis. Many of them have the status of companies limited by guarantee, while others are registered as housing societies under the Industrial and Provident Societies Act of 1965. However, there are a number of kinds of housing association – for example, the Registrar of Friendly Societies employs a five-hold classification for the associations which fall within his/her purview. One category of association, the growth of which has been restricted by recent legislation, is those formed on a for-profit basis. Those registered under the 1965 Act must be co-operatives or conduct their business for the benefit of the community. There are also some housing associations which are charities, such as those providing housing for the poor, and only those which are charities or registered as Industrial and Provident Societies are eligible to receive funds under the 1974 Housing Act. Many of the latter are self-help groups, but not all are. Associations formed by firms to provide housing for their employees, for example, can be registered. Thus the Registry is responsible not only for genuinely mutual-benefit organizations in the housing field, but also for organizations set up by the beneficent employer to supply housing to his/her workforce and those established by the self-interested employer, who sees the provision of housing as a way of maintaining his/her workforce.

5 Trade and Professional Associations

For the most part the organizations discussed so far have arisen out of the first and third kinds of market failure identified at the beginning: the failure of markets to penetrate societies and failure due to monopoly or highly imperfect competition. We must now turn to consider organizations where one of the main problems of the market is that in the real world it cannot provide 'consumers' with the sensitive control that they want over those providing the service, so that, instead, they found an organization based on membership control. Trade and professional associations are formed to advance the interests of firms in a particular trade, industry or profession. In the case of chambers of commerce the organization is geographical. The aim in starting the organization is primarily to increase the income and profits of members, but the organizations themselves are usually non-profit distributing; in Britain they are usually companies limited by guarantee and in the US non-profit corporations.

Why is the market an insensitive mechanism of control? We may begin by assuming that, just as there has been no shortage of individuals willing to set up (for-profit) lobbying firms, so also there would be no shortage of entrepreneurs willing to take on the business of promoting an industry or the economic interests of a city. Nevertheless, there are three considerations that have an important bearing on how such ventures are best organized for their beneficiaries. One point is that, for the potential clients of an entrepreneurial lobbying firm, it is probably to their advantage for any association formed to be a monopoly: competition between themselves is likely to weaken, whether directly or indirectly, their bargaining power with respect to third parties. But, secondly, as Hansmann recognized, mutuals are a solution to the disadvantages of *facing* a monopolist; while unity is desirable in relation to others, only a mutual form of organization allows direct control over the organization providing that unity. The third point is that mutuals would still be a preferred form of organization, even if either there were no benefits to the association from having just one association or it was cost-free for the clients to terminate a contract with a monopolist and award it to someone else. To understand this, we must recognize that both mutuals and for-profit firms allow 'exit' (quitting the organization) and 'voice' (discussion, bargaining and complaints) to be exercised. Just as a client can complain about the quality of a lobbying firm's services, and seek to obtain the services elsewhere if it chooses, so a firm could complain about the activities of its trade association and quit it if necessary. The difference between the two kinds of organization is that a mutual is likely to have built into it decision-making mechanisms which allow for 'voice' from the membership. For-profit bodies have less well developed mechanisms for 'voice', and usually none for jointly expressed 'voice' by clients. The operating principle in the market is that the supplier will seek to provide what clients want and can best do so without seeking regular directives from them.

Now this distinction between the more 'voice'-orientated mutuals and the more 'exit'-orientated for-profit firms is less clear cut in practice than we have suggested here. As we have seen earlier, mutuals with large memberships can collapse into management-dominated bodies, and there are some market relationships between a for-profit supplier and a group of clients in which the supplier does take directives from them regularly. But often for-profits are reluctant to provide clients with a free hand in this regard for fear that they may commit themselves to policies that will involve losses. (Even a consulting firm that is paid just for its time will balk at the idea of implementing policies that it believes are disastrous, for fear that its own reputation will be undermined.) Consequently, the mutual form is more likely to be chosen when it is important to the individual member/client to have his/her own views listened to and taken into account.

That chambers of commerce, the American Medical Association, or the Food and Drinks Industries Council are important economic actors scarcely needs to be stated. But their purpose is to create conditions which will increase the income and profits of their constituent members, rather than to generate profits for themselves. British and American law take rather different approaches to the taxation of these sorts of bodies. In Britain any profits actually made by a trade association are taxable in just the same way that profits accrued by Building Societies are taxed. That the profits cannot be distributed to anyone is irrelevant. In the US, business leagues (of which trade associations are the most common type) have never been subject to federal income tax – they have 501(c)(6) status and are one of the categories of tax-exempt organizations. However, this category:

> exclude[s] organizations created by business competitors to co-ordinate or centralize their advertising or purchasing activities, engage in research for their exclusive benefit, furnish credit reports and collect delinquent accounts, or otherwise advance their special business interests.[35]

In other words, a distinction is drawn between improving the general conditions of business in a particular industry or trade and specific benefits generated for specifiable firms.

In addition to the usual kind of trade association, there are also various kinds of organization supplying services of benefit to firms in an industry. An example is an organization which accredits schools, and a curious feature of this particular case is that although its clients included privately-owned schools it was actually able to register as a 501(c)(3), charitable, organization.

6 Trade Unions

Of all the nineteenth century working-class mutual-benefit organizations, trade unions have made the greatest impact on social and economic life, and they have remained one of the few institutions in which control by the membership is still valued even if it is not always practised. Obviously, of all the mutuals they are the ones about which most has been written in relation to their impact on both the capitalist economy and their contribution to democratization in the capitalist state. It is because so much more is known about them that they are given considerably less attention here than some other mutuals. Nevertheless, there are several points about unions which it is useful to discuss in relation to other mutuals.

Unlike consumer co-operatives, Building Societies, or the other 'working-class' mutuals, unions do not establish a trading relationship between the organization and its members. Clearly, they promote their members' interests, with respect to rates of pay, working conditions and so on, but relations with members are not based on commercial transations. Of all the organizations considered so far, then, they seem to be the ones about which there is least doubt in excluding them from the for-profit sector. But, like trade associations, they are organizations that could, in theory, be organized on a for-profit basis. Indeed, some American unions, including the Teamsters, have some of the characteristics of a truly 'entrepreneurial' union.[36] Once again, arguments from the advantages of monopoly and from the desire to be able to exercise control over policy (through 'voice') give a clear edge to the mutual form. And there is a further point to consider here. The value of successful collective action for the members of a union, unlike many trade associations, is likely to be considerable in relation to their overall individual welfare. As with all collective benefits, though, there is the problem of free riding to be overcome, and (in the way suggested by Olson) there are selective benefits, as well as the closed shop, which can be provided to stimulate contributions from potential free riders. But an additional benefit that the mutual form of union can offer, which the for-profit form usually could not do directly, is control through democratic participation in the organization. Participation is an important resource for a union partly because, at the margin, it provides an incentive to join, and it can be a resource also in that participation in decision making can increase solidarity within the group.

Although British law has generally been more favourable to the activities of trade unions than American law, the reverse is true in regard to their liability to taxation. In Britain they are subject to the same tax laws as other associations, except that there are special provisions for money applied to provident purposes. But a union investing surplus funds in shares would be liable for tax on the interest and on any capital gains. In the US there is a special category of tax-exempt status for unions, 501(c)(5). Like all otherwise tax-exempt bodies they are taxed on unrelated earnings, under the 1969 Tax Reform Act, but interest on investments is taxable only on income acquired on borrowed funds.

7 Social and Recreational Clubs

Social clubs (and we include in this category sporting and other recreational clubs) can be provided on a for-profit basis. Indeed, there are examples of this type of business in both Britain and the US, but the mutual form is the more common. There are various reasons for this. Most obviously, some of them are so small that an entrepreneur could afford to supply them only by charging a relatively high price to clients. These clubs can operate on an informal mutual basis because members provide their labour for helping to organize them at well below the price they would normally obtain for their labour in the market. Sometimes labour is 'donated' out of a sense of communality; sometimes because the member cannot undertake paid labour at that time anyway and so does not even calculate his/her lost earnings, and often because people actually like organizing activities. (One of the standard characters in twentieth-century Anglo-American comedy is the person who faces competition from a rival in undertaking onerous organizing tasks, and who bitterly resents that competition.) People rarely contribute their labour to for-profit bodies. Again, with much larger and formally organized bodies, like working men's clubs, the absence of profits and taxes on profits significantly reduces the cost of membership and of goods and services provided by the club.

Moreover, members often value the control that a mutual seems to give them. Clubs are rather different, of course, from business associations and trade unions, in that there is usually no advantage to being a monopoly. On the contrary, members are often more worried about their club becoming too large and impersonal. Members want to be able to influence the kind of club it becomes and its other policies – such as the kind of music provided in the bar, the number of fixtures the team plays each season, and so on. 'Voice' exercised through general meetings provides some kind of control, and, at least in smaller clubs, leads to more frequent attending to the 'voice' of members, which is exercised informally to club officials. More especially 'voice' provides the illusion of individual control, while 'voice' in a proprietorial club would be more indirect and 'exit' would have to be used more frequently. The disadvantage of 'exit' for those who want to be in a club is that it is interaction with a particular set of people that is one of the attractions in joining.[37] In this sense participating in a club is unlike, say, eating in a restaurant where interaction with other diners is usually minimal; diners do often value the 'right atmosphere' in a restaurant, but 'exit' (not returning to a restaurant that lacks it) is not too costly.

This feature of mutual clubs, that they provide an opportunity for members to control the nature of their joint activity, makes it possible, of course, for members to exclude those with whom they do not want to interact. For the most part, this has been an uncontroversial feature of a mutual – members *may* include anyone who wishes to join them and *can* exclude anyone they wish to – and it has been thought of as embodying one of the prime virtues of the voluntary association. But clubs, and similar associations, may also be important points of access for individuals to the wider society; being excluded from clubs could affect the life-chances of particular individuals and of whole communities of people. Whether it does depends on how much clubs, rather than other institutions, serve as 'gatekeepers' to the wider society. Clearly, in some circumstances, clubs could be important institutions for social integration, and a tendency to exclude certain kinds of people might be a factor in their failure to become integrated into the society. It is for this reason that clubs have been a major source of contention in relation to legislation against racial and sexual discrimination.[38]

In the US, and in Britain prior to the 1976 Race Relations Act, legislation prohibiting discrimination has tended to focus on the *public* dimensions of actions by individuals and organizations. In a private capacity individuals and groups of individuals have generally remained free to discriminate. Clubs have often straddled this distinction between 'public' and 'private', and their discriminatory practices have been the subject of dispute. For example, in New York City a ban on men-only clubs has been pursued on the grounds that elite clubs excluding women provide dining facilities which are important for business contacts, and hence their private practices have serious effects for sections of the public.[39] At the federal level the Supreme Court has cast doubt on the right of those clubs which do not strictly *select* their members to exclude women. The Court has not so far attempted to define a private club, although an ordinance in New York City has done so.[40] In 1971 a British court (in *Charter* v. *Race Relations Board*) also drew a distinction between the public and private dimensions of clubs – it too related it to the way in which people became members. The Law Lords decided that a members' club was a private body if it employed rules which made for a genuine selection of members on the grounds of their acceptability. Lord Simon argued that:

> some so-called clubs – even some which purport to be private members' clubs – do in reality constitute merely a section of the public. The dividing line, in my view, lies in the personal selection of members with a view to their common acceptability . . . The essential feature is that there should be a genuine screening at some stage as a pledge of general acceptability to fellow members. It is this screening that determines that membership is a private role. Without it the association remains a section of the public.[41]

In the event, subsequent legislation removed this distinction as the basis of controlling racial discrimination in clubs. Under Section 25 of the *Race Relations Act* (1976) a club with more than 25 members may not discriminate against potential members on racial grounds.

The taxation of clubs in both countries also reflects an attempt to distinguish between the the public (and profit-making) role on the one side, and the private (and personal-interaction) role on the other. In the

US social clubs are tax exempt, under section 501(c)(7) of the Internal Revenue Service (IRS) code. However, to prevent tax evasion the courts have refused to grant this status to clubs, like automobile associations, where the amount of personal contact between members was insignificant. Furthermore, since the *Tax Reform Act* (1969), there have been further curbs on the ability of clubs to claim non-member-related income as tax exempt; in particular, the income clubs derive from investments or from sales to non-members is taxable. The tax position in Britain is broadly similar in practice but it is based on a totally different principle. Like other associations, British clubs, many of which are companies limited by guarantee, are liable to pay corporation tax. However, as co-operative-type organizations they do not pay tax on trade with members or on any surpluses returned to members; this is often effected every few months in clubs with licensed bars by having evenings when drinks are sold at a reduced price. In fact, social clubs provide a good illustration of the approaches by the British and US tax authorities to the problem posed by mutuals. The British approach is to make all associations liable for tax, but to make exceptions for certain kinds of mutual benefit activity. The American approach is to distinguish between those kinds of mutual benefit groups which qualify for exemption, and those which do not, and to place the latter in a broad tax category, 501(c), along with charitable organizations. Restrictions are then placed on the type of income that these groups are permitted to have without tax. In some cases, as with clubs, the overall tax position is very similar in the two countries, but generally the American arrangement works to the advantage of organizations that can claim tax-exempt status.

8 Mutuality and Non-economic Objectives

As we have seen, in many of the early mutual-benefit organizations, the pursuit of self-interest through co-operation was usually linked to notions of fraternity. The people who started Friendly Societies and Building Societies were as often concerned with other aspects of their relations with their fellows as they were with purely economic ones. If, for the most part, these other elements have now died out in the large working-class mutuals, other kinds of mutuals have developed in which intra-group relations form a key part of the group's *raison d'être*. Leaving aside some of the experiments in communal living (farming communes and so on) which started up in the 1960s, most of these mutuals have been concerned wholly with the pursuit of the non-economic affairs of their participants. These kinds of mutuals have expanded greatly in the last twenty years, and it is worth considering briefly why this should have occurred as well as the prospects for further expansion.

There are four main factors contributing to their growth. First, in the twentieth century, a number of social problems which had always existed either became more widely discussed or were subjected to redefinition. Groups of battered wives assisting each other, or the formation of Alcoholics Anonymous, were developments that required wife-beating to become recognized as assault and alcoholism to be distinguished from drunkenness. Second, the breakdown in support systems for individuals in industrial societies, especially because of changes in family structure, meant that either new social problems arose or that they became far more widespread. Third, it became clear in virtually every western society that the introduction of a welfare state did not provide for *all* the needs of its patients and clients. In Rose's words there was now a 'welfare mix', with households and the market continuing to provide for social welfare, and within such a system there were gaps in provision for which mutuality yielded the best 'private' solution.[42] Fourth, the ethos of participation and self-determination which became prominent in the 1960s gave rise to a whole range of groups devoted to improving aspects of their members' lives. Political radicalization, and the rise of new political movements such as the civil rights movement in the US, and more generally the women's movement, produced a myriad of new gatherings, associations and organizations. Sometimes, as in Germany, this could lead to the establishment of alternative services on a mutual basis (such as kindergartens) which traditionally had been provided by hierarchical bodies.

As with most IOs the boundaries of these new kinds of mutuals are often difficult to identify. At one end, as with some of the organizations involved in helping people to lose weight, mutual support in the groups may merely be a means of generating profits for the organizers. At the other extreme are organizations in which mutual effort is greatly supplemented by volunteers who themselves do not experience the particular problems involved. But in the 'core' groups it is the principle of 'helping yourself by interacting with others' that predominates. In its rigidity in sticking to this principle Alcoholics Anonymous still provides one of the best examples. Behind this rigidity lies the argument that the intrusion of both market relations and philanthropic volunteers undermines the determination to action, which mutual support can generate. Certainly the experience of the nineteenth-century working-class mutuals does not contradict this. Consequently, such organizations tend to regard their expansion beyond a certain size as being detrimental to their operations, and prefer to devise ways of creating new bodies to work with new would-be members.

With some social problems markets (and sometimes the state) provide alternative services to those offered by the mutuals. Because of the very different principles governing the policies of the latter, often they do not regard the former as direct competitors, and sometimes not as competitors at all. With other social problems (as with rape counselling) provision by commercial firms may be very limited or non-existent. But just as the approach of the mutuals restricts direct competition with the for-profit sector, so too does their style of organization tend to limit their interactions with the state. A decentralized system of small groups is poorly structured for regular and effective influence over state agencies, unless they provide services which these agencies need. But in any case, the very strict interpretation of the mutual aid principle may lead the organizations to eschew all contact with the state – again Alcoholics Anonymous provides an outstanding instance of this.

One of the main features of mutuals in the twentieth century, then, has been the separation of the two objectives which intertwined in the early mutuals – of providing for the direct economic well-being of members and providing for other aspects of their lives. While the older mutuals have tended to become integrated into the market system, and have shed their non-economic functions, many of the newer mutuals are not concerned directly with the economic well-being of their members, and may be antagonistic to the provision of the services they supply on a commercial basis.

In the longer term the prospects for the expansion of these kinds of organizations seem considerable, even though their ability to 'plug many of the gaps' in state welfare provision is probably very limited. Cutbacks in state welfare provision in the 1980s, together with a great increase in unemployment, has increased social need. The more successful of the small-group mutuals, though, may well be able to provide models for new organizations in related areas of deprivation and need.

9 Mutuals and the Boundaries of the For-profit Sector

In this chapter we have examined organizations which are alike in that they provide benefits for their members and do not have shareholders to whom profits could be distributed. If we continue to use the term 'profit' in the everyday sense, we find that there are three main kinds of non-profit-distributing mutuals:

i organizations engaged in trade, as this is recognized in law, which attempt to make some profits – either to facilitate future growth or to provide further security against future risks. Usually they have a large membership;

ii organizations engaged in the buying and selling of certain products and services, and which distribute any 'surplus' on sales back to the membership at regular intervals. Usually they have a relatively small membership;

iii organizations which do not trade at all, but which seek to promote the interests or well-being of their members in non-monetary ways or provide facilities for them.

Obviously, in practice, some organizations have elements of more than one of these types, and others change from being predominantly of one type to another. Building Societies began as type (ii) bodies but during the nineteenth century became type (i) organizations. A sports club is more like a type (iii) organization, if it is bringing people together just to play a sport, and more like type (ii) to the extent that it provides a bar, entertainment and so on.

The fact that mutuals range from small, type (iii) associations, to major financial institutions found among the type (i) organizations poses a number of problems for the state in their regulation, not least with regard to taxation. As we have seen, in both Britain and the US type (i) organizations are usually taxed on their profits. They are treated as being an alternative form of business structure to the joint stock company. On the other hand, primitive consumer co-operatives, of type (ii), which return all their 'surplus' to members in the form of a dividend, are regarded as having generated no profits even though there is trading between the organization and the members. Finally, organizations like trade associations or trade unions are not taxed directly on their income from membership dues. Now this pragmatic approach is appropriate for a state intent on maximizing tax revenues at a reasonable cost and with some regard to fairness. But if our concern is to understand how IOs can advance democracy, then it is necessary to consider whether the boundary between the for-profit economy and intermediate bodies has to be drawn rather differently. If, for example, we wish to examine whether IOs can be a source of countervailing power to the market, then it might not be very helpful to say that organizations like Building Societies are clearly not IOs but that trade associations are. One way of looking at the issue *might* be to identify profit in a rather different way from its everyday meaning.

Consider one example. The economist Lipsey defined profit as 'the excess of revenues over opportunity cost, whatever the source of excess',[43] where opportunity costs are the benefits foregone by not using the resources in their best alternative use.[44] Now with this definition of profit, it becomes possible to speak of the profit involved in ventures where the activity is not necessarily 'profit-making' (in the everyday sense), but where we can point to the benefits that would have accrued if the resources had been used differently. Thus we can distinguish between organizations whose ventures seek to generate benefits (net of opportunity costs) for their members and those which do not; trade unions, for example, would now be in the former category. The value of making a distinction between profit-distributing and non-profit-distributing organizations on these lines is that it overcomes the artificiality of the distinction that had to be introduced in the *Assam Tea* case. The problem with this revised way of understanding profit, though, is that the small football team, say, which rents a council pitch and has no club room, but which collects fees to pay for its pitch rental and other expenses, most certainly has revenues which could have been put to some other purpose. Yet it is precisely this kind of mutual which democrats have often had in mind when they have discussed the virtues of IOs in a democratic society. It is far from clear that any attempt at identifying profit in a different way is likely to be of much use.

This problem has a parallel when considering the boundary between charity and the economy. Using the Lipsey definition even a charity largely dependent on donations would be 'profit-making'. But this is not helpful in identifying the peculiar characteristics of IOs. As we see in the next chapter not only are some charities overtly trading institutions (like non-profit hospitals in the US) which most certainly attempt to make profits, but many other charities also have sections which seek to supplement other income by trading, even though they do not plan to use such income to expand their business activities. For the democratic theorist organizations like non-profit hospitals, because of their close resemblance to for-profit bodies, are often candidates for exclusion from the category of IO.

An alternative way of dealing with these difficulties is to accept that the boundary between organizations that are involved in the pursuit of self-interest and profit and other kinds of organization is very imprecise, and that mutuals are to be found throughout this 'border area'. In discussing the contribution of IOs to democracy we might initially consider all of them, but then focus attention mainly on those IOs which have one (or both) of the following features:

i like the traditional Friendly Societies, they have social aims or ideals as well as intentions to serve the economic self-interest of the individual members; and

ii members are involved in influencing the decision making of the organization.

The point of excluding mutuals which lack other objectives or member control is that, while there may be some differences between them and for-profit firms, these are not likely to be very significant when considering the distinctive role of IOs in advancing democracy in a capitalist economy. In fact, as we have seen, one of the main features of mutuals has been the transformation of early nineteenth-century socially-orientated, participatory working-class organizations into ones which are almost entirely commercially orienated and manager dominated. The kind of organization on which we will focus attention in chapter 8, therefore, is a much smaller group (though the overall number of organizations and associations is very great) than that, for example, over which the Registrar of Friendly Societies has had responsibility. If IOs are to be considered as instruments with potential to advance democracy, then commercial organizations like modern Building Societies, clearly do not present a distinctive path to democratization. The retail co-operatives constitute a more marginal case, though, because the tradition of member participation tends to have survived more strongly here. There is similar variation among other mutuals – some housing associations and Friendly Societies retain their member-orientation, while others are more commercial ventures. To approach the problem in this way is not to preclude the possibility that in some respects organizations like Building Societies might be better considered as IOs than as part of the for-profit economy, but it is to recognize that, for the most part, they are merely a different legal form that commercial enterprises may now take.

In this chapter we have seen that mutuals seem to straddle the boundary been IOs and the for-profit sector in two different ways. First, the pursuit of self-interest through mutuals may not generate profits as such, but the activity of these mutuals, even in their 'primitive' forms, is so like that of for-profit concerns that the distinction between the two is in danger of appearing an insignificant one. Second, as they have grown, many mutuals in Britain and the US have become virtually indistinguishable from business enterprises. These mutuals may have a different legal structure from for-profit businesses but they are no less a part of the commercial sector. In the next chapter we shall see that this transformation of IOs into more fully commercial enterprises is not confined to mutuals but is evident also among 'charities'.

3

Economic Competition Involving Charities

This chapter is concerned with competition and co-operation between organizations which are legally charities and organizations in the for-profit sector. In Britain the former comprise those bodies registered with the Charity Commissioners (and the small number of charities that do not have to register with the Commission). In the US they are those non-profits with 501(c)(3) status under the IRS Code. (This last status not only grants exemption from federal income taxes, but also allows an organization to receive donations which are tax-deductible for the donors.) At the outset, however, we must emphasize that our enquiry is a restricted one. Our focus is the cause of this interaction between the two kinds of organization and its possible consequences for the democratic state. There are several important issues relating to competition between charities and for-profit firms, such as whether too much commercial involvement by charities is sub-optimal for a capitalist economy, which fall outside this study.

Charities are large components of capitalist economies, although in relation to the entire for-profit sector they may appear rather small. Until recently, data on this was non-existent, and even today data relating to Britain is far from complete. Nevertheless, it is evident that in the US about 3.2 per cent of GNP originates among charities, compared with over 81 per cent which originates in the for-profit sector and 14 per cent which originates in government.[1] In Britain it seems that the position is broadly similar, with income originating in English charities constituting at least 3.7 per cent of GNP.[2]

The starting point for our discussion is the perhaps surprising fact that most of the income of charities is raised in the forms of fees and charges. It is surprising because, of all IOs, they are most closely associated in the popular imagination with income that is donated by members and

Table 3.1 Estimate of sources of income of non-religious charities in England, 1980

	£B	% of total
Fund-raising and donations	0.59	9
Sales, fees and charges	4.70	69
Rents and investment	0.79	12
Grants from governmental agencies	0.56	8
Other	0.13	2
Total	6.77	100

Data taken from: John Posnett, 'A profile of the charity sector', *Charity Statistics 1983–84*

supporters. However, as can be seen in tables 3.1 and 3.2, non-religious charities in both countries do not conform to the image of 'institutionalized altruism', because they receive only a relatively small proportion of their total income in the form of gifts. In the US 22 per cent of income comes from gifts and in England only 8.7 per cent. (Religious charities are heavily dependent on donations, and their inclusion raises the share of income provided by gifts to 35 per cent and 12.2 per cent of the totals respectively.) Far from being mainly dispensers of current donations, or of the investment income yielded by gifts in earlier years, the 'typical' charity in both countries obtains most of its money from fees and charges – 56 per cent of the total in the US and 69 per cent in England.[3] (Of

Table 3.2 Sources of income of non-religious charities in the US, 1980

	$B	% of total donations
Donations	22.1	22
Sales, fees and charges	61.5	63
(to households and businesses)	(35.2)	(36)
(to government)	(26.3)	(27)
Investment income	6.7	7
Grants from governmental agencies	7.6	8
Total	97.9	100

Data taken from: Gabriel Rudney, 'A quantitative profile of the nonprofit sector', *PONPO Working Paper No. 40* course, many charities are atypical, in that they do rely mainly on income from donations past and present, but the point is that in relation to *total* charity income this is a relatively small source.)

Obviously, not all fee income is indicative of a purely market relationship. Many social service organizations would be unable to provide a service at all if they did not make a charge (either to their clients or to the governmental agency that has responsibility for them) and they use their non-fee income to subsidize these services. In such cases competition, either with for-profit agencies or state agencies, may be wholly absent, and one of the main aims of the organization may be to reduce its level of charges as much as possible. On the other hand, some income which in effect is fee income may not appear as such in the accounts of a charity. In 1986 about a quarter of the income of the National Trust came from membership subscriptions, compared with about seven and a half per cent from admission fees to its properties. The Trust, which nearly doubled its membership to 1.4 million between 1977 and 1986, grants members free admission to its properties, so membership is often acquired largely because it provides what is really a 'season ticket' at a discount price. Though it does not usually admit it, the Trust operates in the same market as the owners of many private stately homes.

But rather than drawing a sharp contrast between subsidization and fee-maximizing behaviour that is indistinguishable from that of a for-profit firm's behaviour, we must recognize that there is a continuum of behaviour indicating the importance different charities give to generating fee income. The boundary between charity and commercial enterprise is necessarily a broad one, then, when income from fees is a significant part of the income of charitable organizations. Our concern is not with the intermediate cases but with those charities which actually face competition from for-profit suppliers But in which industries has competition actually developed and become extensive?

Table 3.3 indicates some of the most important areas of competition in the US, and shows the relative shares in the supply of the services held by non-profit organizations, for-profit firms and governmental agencies. This is not a complete list, however, and there are several smaller industries where competition is intense, such as Racquet Sports, which are excluded. Unfortunately, comparable data for Britain is not available, but for reasons which will become apparent shortly, it is clear that the extent of competition is much less here. In general, and there are some notable exceptions to this, competition has been confined primarily to two areas of economic activity. By far the more important is the service sector, and most especially in the US, health care. The second is in the retailing of goods. British charities such as Oxfam, with

Table 3.3 Major US industries with competition between non-profit and for-profit firms: share of industry held by non-profits, for-profits and government as a percentage of the total

	Measurement basis	Non-profit	For-profit	Government
Health Services				
Short-term and general hospitals	Facilities	53*	12	35
Psychiatric hospitals	Facilities	18	26	56
Chronic-care hospitals	Facilities	29	7	64
Nursing homes	Facilities	34	61	5
Education				
Secondary	Revenues	14	3	83
Post-secondary (excluding higher education)	Revenues	20	33	47
Social Services				
Day-care centres	Facilities	43	57	—
Individual and family services	Employment	96	4	—
Legal services	Employment	2	98	—
Culture and Entertainment				
Performing arts	Employment	26	74	—
Radio and TV broadcasting	Employment	5	95	—
Art museums	Revenues	65	3	30
Research				
Research and development	Expenditures	15	72	13
Basic research	Expenditures	67	18	15

* In this and in some subsequent tables figures in individual rows have not been rounded up, so that some may not add up to 100.

Data taken from: Richard Steinberg, 'Nonprofit organizations and the market', in Powell, (ed.), *The Nonprofit Sector*, p. 120

its second-hand shops, or the National Trust with its shops selling a variety of items are well-known examples of this. The direct impact of these ventures on for-profit enterprises is usually small. There are exceptions to this, however. From about the 1960s onwards the decision by many charities to sell their own Christmas cards had a considerable effect on the retailers of cards, as well as on manufacturers.[4] But it is in the service industries identified in table 3.3 (health, education, social services, culture and entertainment and research) that competition, at least in the US, is most evident. In Britain competition has been more restricted, but where it does occur it is in similar areas of the service sector.

While it is certainly the case that many charities, and many activities undertaken by charities, do not compete in any way with for-profit enterprises, the interesting point is that there should be any competition at all. Why, it might be asked, has the state in capitalist economies made possible, and indeed in some ways fostered, rival organizations to those found in the market economy? For whereas liberal economists have long argued that there is an important role for charity in market societies, until recently few have seen charitable institutions as being either competitors or collaborators with for-profit organizations. In this chapter we identify seven main reasons for the growth of competition, before turning to examine the related issue of co-operation between organizations from the two 'sectors'.

1 Charities and Economic Competition

A The continuing use of early seventeenth-century categories of charity

While there have been some changes in England and its ex-colonies as to the objects which are held to be legally charitable, the legal concept of charity is substantially the one established in the sixteenth century, and which was codified in the Statute of Charitable Uses (1601). Two of the features of this Statute were crucial in making possible subsequent provision of the same services by charities and non-charities. One of these was that it made *benefit to the public*, rather than, say, the needs of the recipients of a service, the principal criterion in determining whether a gift was charitable. With the exception of items like the repair of sea walls, though, most of the purposes listed in the 1601 Statute related in some way to assisting the poor. In the eighteenth century, however, after the passage of the Mortmain Act of 1736, courts gave a broader interpretation to the purposes which could be charitable. The other feature was that it identified certain purposes as charitable, and courts have held these to be a categorization of charities, rather than merely an illustration of the sorts of activities which would be charitable in the circumstances of the early seventeenth century. (Macnaghten's classification of charitable purposes in 1891 in the *Pemsel* decision formalized the (now modified) list of purposes originating in the 1601 Statute, and this constitutes the basis of charity law today.) Providing, therefore, that the purposes of an organization are those which have been recognized in law as providing public benefit, it can become a charity, irrespective of whether the goods or services are now ones that can be supplied for the recipients, and paid for by them, in a market system. In other words, although the purposes identified as charitable in 1601 referred to services that could not then be supplied by the market system, in changed socio-economic conditions it is possible that charity and the market may no longer be mutually exclusive.

To understand this point, it is useful to outline the conditions which, following the 1601 statute and Macnaghten's restatement, have to be met in England today for an organization to be deemed charitable. The position has been summarized well by Chesterman. He argues that for an organization to be charitable it must satisfy three criteria.

(i) Its purposes must fall within one (or more) of four categories – (I) relief of poverty, (II) advancement of education, (III) advancement of religion, (IV) other purposes beneficial to the community which the law recognizes as charitable. Generally the organization 'must entail benefit of tangible nature for the public at large or of a sufficient section thereof'.

(ii) It must not be disqualified on one of the following grounds: it (I) contains 'an overt element of self-help', or (II) involves 'profit distribution', or (III) is 'substantially political'.

(iii) With some exceptions, it 'must be exclusively charitable'.[5]

The position in America is broadly similar, though two important differences from English law have developed. Some purposes which courts have recognized as having public benefit in England are specifically classified as charitable in the statutes of many American states. This is apparent in the following account of the concept of charitable purposes presented by Fisch et al.:

> Today the six part Restatement of charitable purposes into 1) relief of poverty; 2) advancement of education; 3) advancement of religion; 4) promotion of health; 5) governmental or municipal purposes; and 6) other purposes the accomplishment of which are beneficial to the community, is gaining increasing judicial acceptance.[6]

In addition, in many states a much narrower interpretation is given to the types of political activity which would render an organization non-charitable. This last point is not relevant here, but it is taken up again in chapter 7.

Among its other social objectives, the sixteenth-century English state wished to encourage the endowment of schools and hospitals in communities. The provision of such services was not recognized, of course, as a function of the state, nor would the market provide education and health care for more than a tiny proportion of the population. The law relating to charity, therefore, was a means of increasing the supply of some services to social groups who would not otherwise afford them, as well as a means of supplying certain public goods. Although there were potential problems in making benefit to the public, or to a large section of the public, an important criterion in determining which purposes were charitable, English law might still have avoided subsequent overlap in provision by charities and for-profit businesses, if decisions about what constituted public benefit had been subject to regular legislative review. Instead, the courts in England and the US have clarified and modified the objectives deemed to be charitable, but there have been hardly any attempts to change this through legislation. Certain purposes remained charitable long after they ceased to yield much benefit to the public, and after provision for the beneficiaries became possible through the market. The best-known examples of this are English so-called public schools. Education, of course, had been mentioned specifically as a charitable purpose in the 1601 Statute, yet even by the late eighteenth century many schools originally established for the poor had become more interested in recruiting fee-paying pupils. Today many public schools use their endowments to reduce the level of fees paid by their (predominantly) middle-class clients, rather than as support for genuinely poor scholars. That the market is now capable of providing education outside the state sector is indicated by the fact that, among all independent schools, 44 per cent are not charities. Virtually all the older, *public*, schools are charities, however – indicating changes in the viability of the market in this area in the last two centuries.[7]

Because the charitable status of independent schools in England has been so controversial, it might be thought that this is a highly exceptional effect of the fossilization of English charity law. In fact, it is not. There are numerous other examples of services where for-profit provision has been able to develop since the seventeenth century, but where the activity has also remained a charitable one, so that the result is competition between two kinds of organization. This development has been especially important in the US, and one of the best examples there is health care, as is evident in table 3.3. In the hospital industry, 'charitable' hospitals remain the dominant form (except among psychiatric hospitals) but for-profit chains of hospitals, such as the Humana chain, are becoming an increasingly important form. (Although the commercialization of American medicine has been commented on by many critics, including Starr, it is important to realize that it is only among *chains* of for-profit hospitals that the for-profit sector seems to be making inroads into the non-profit market.)[8] The main advantage enjoyed by the chains seems to be that, because of economies of scale, there are a number of goods that they are able to supply to their hospitals far more cheaply than can non-profit hospitals. Initially the advent of the National Health Service in Britain limited the size of the private sector, and hence the intrusion of for-profit enterprise. However, in the 1970s and 1980s private health care expanded considerably and by 1981 more than 6 per cent of the population was covered by some form of private health insurance. Here too we find evidence of an American phenomenon, the use of charitable status by organizations catering to only a relatively small proportion of the population. This has been commented on by Gladstone, who cites the Nuffield Nursing Home Trust which was founded in 1957 by the British United Provident Association (BUPA):

> 'to promote and encourage the provision of modern hospitals for the acute surgical and medical treatment of private patients'. This charitable trust, which now runs thirty-two hospitals funded almost entirely by payments from the BUPA insurance schemes, has as its beneficiaries those prepared to pay BUPA's subscriptions, which although not huge, must be beyond the means of most people on low incomes . . .[9]

But in comparison with the US, the stricter interpretation of charity laws in Britain has greatly limited the use of charitable status by organizations providing private medical treatment.

In summary: one of the important reasons for competition between charities and for-profit enterprise has been a failure to reform laws on charities in the light of changing needs in society and of the potential for market operations in the provision of certain services.

B The liberalization of non-profit corporation laws

One of the main differences between the US and England in relation to charities has been that, while in the latter charity law has been distinct from laws relating to other organizations and has been the main influence on the organizational development of charities, this is not so in the US. There the organizational and operating constraints imposed on charities emanate more from laws on non-profit corporations than from charity law specifically. These laws extend to organizations other than those which would be charitable under English law and the liberalization of these laws in recent years has contributed to the extension of the areas in which competition between charities and for-profit enterprises can develop. To understand this, it is first necessary to explain how non-profit corporate bodies, which were not charities, developed as a legal form.

Until the mid-nineteenth century there were two main legal forms that a charity, other than one which was simply a voluntary association, could take in England. It could be a trust or a corporation. The former was more common, and the latter was restricted to a relatively small number of old, but large, charities. Included among them were universities and the British Museum, and there were a number of devices, such as Royal Charter, by which a corporation could be established. But this status was a privilege and, unlike the trust form, it could only be conferred on an organization, rather than being an entitlement through certain legal requirements being met. In 1862, however, the legal concept of the company limited by guarantee was introduced by the Companies Act. To qualify for this status a company had to prohibit the distribution of profits among members. Unlike a company limited by shares, limited liability was provided not by the issuing of shares, but by financial guarantees posted by the members. Obviously, the provision of limited liability yielded advantages over organizational forms with unlimited liability, and it was a device which could be used by charities and other kinds of organization for which profit distribution was inappropriate. Essentially these latter are 'mutual benefit' or 'self-help' groups – such as sporting or social clubs, trade and professional associations and committees to manage the common structure of groups of owner-occupied flats.

In relation to our present concerns there are two significant features of the company limited by guarantee. First, while important in determining the legal position of some charities, the laws on such companies have not served to undermine the importance of the distinction between charities and other organizations. Whereas, for many purposes, non-profit corporation laws in the US have led to the non-profit organization becoming a more important concept in American law, as well as a more familiar concept with the American public, the company limited by guarantee has not achieved this status in England. Second, in England the Inland Revenue seems to have been vigilant in preventing the use of this organizational form by companies seeking to find means other than profit distribution (such as higher salaries to employee-directors) for distributing trading surpluses. Consequently, there has not been an explosive growth in companies limited by guarantee on the fringes of the commercial sector.

American charity law has its origins in English sixteenth- and seventeenth-century laws, and even today there is a great similarity between charity law in the two countries. As Gladstone notes, 'American and Australian precedents are still admissible in English courts and vice versa'.[10] However, by the mid nineteenth century most American states had adopted laws relating specifically to non-profit corporations – laws quite distinct from those relating either to business corporations or to co-operatives. NPOs became the principal organizational form of bodies entitled to charitable status, as well as of some other kinds of association, and, for charities, non-profit corporation law became even more significant than charity laws. Popularization of the terms 'non-profit corporation' and 'non-profit organization' did not occur until much later – in the mid twentieth century. The close relationship between charity law and laws on non-profit corporations in the US may be contrasted with the position in England. From its inception, the company limited by guarantee was a legal form which did not specify the particular purposes which companies must have to qualify for this status. In America, by contrast, 'at one time most non-profit laws limited the purposes for which a non-profit corporation could be formed',[11] and with some exceptions these paralleled the purposes which were charitable in law. More recently, since the second world war, there has been a pronounced change 'toward an approach that would permit use of the non-profit form by any group that sees its activities as compatible with that structure'.[12]

Despite this one respect in which the US seems to have moved towards the legal position in England, neither federal nor state income tax authorities, nor any other agencies, have been concerned with probing into organizations to determine if they are, in effect, businesses.[13] On the contrary, the liberalization of non-profit corporation law has been designed to make the corporation an alternative form of business organization employable by any kind of business. Even in those states which still restrict the purposes for which non-profits can be formed, there has been liberalization relating to the purposes organizations can pursue, although this does not usually extend to permitting manufacturing firms to be non-profits. It is within the service sector, then, that the increased use of the non-profit form of corporation is mainly to be found, including, according to White, in the hotel industry; she cites the Best West International chain as an instance of this.[14] Generally what seems to be happening is not the emergence of non-profit firms in areas that were previously well outside the sphere of non-profit operations, but an expansion into the 'boundary' areas between the for-profit sector and the non-profit domain. It is in activities involving personal care – health, welfare, education, and child care – that the expansion has been most noticeable. It is, perhaps, significant that the field which has created the greatest controversy about the exploitation of the non-profit form by firms that are overtly commercial enterprises is the nursing-home industry.[15]

Nevertheless, if liberalization of non-profit laws has enabled alternative business structures to be developed, the question must be raised as to why non-profit business should exist at all. Why would holders of capital want to tie it up in an enterprise when they are prohibited from earning interest on their investment? We shall consider the answer to this more fully later in the chapter, but for the moment we can mention briefly the two most important reasons. On the one hand, liberalization of non-profit laws in the US made possible the formation of organizational complexes containing both for-profits and non-profits. In such complexes there can be substantial commercial advantages to financing certain kinds of projects on a non-profit basis. On the other hand, wealthy charitable institutions themselves may well have the capital to finance new ventures. And it is to the more general economic role of these sorts of charities that we must now turn.

C The economic power of wealthy charities

Wealth itself does not make charities major economic actors or competitors with for-profit enterprises. It is the concentration of that wealth in particular sectors of the economy that can lead to economic power, and for the most part the trustees of such institutions do not relish the controversy that such power can generate. There are several circumstances that can lead to the acquisition of power. Before outlining them, however, it must be pointed out that in this section we are excluding consideration of charities which have extended into commercial activity relating in some way to their charitable purposes; these cases are discussed in section F.

One circumstance in which wealth leads to economic activism in a charity is the possession of an original endowment concentrated in a particular form, even though it is a 'passive' form of wealth such as land or share portfolios; sometimes there are restrictions on trustees' alienating the particular form of the endowment, sometimes it would be costly for the charity to do so, at least in the short term, and sometimes the trustees simply do not wish to deal with the problems associated with transforming the asset structure. Colleges and universities often received their first endowments in a 'concentrated' form. Many of the older Oxford and Cambridge colleges were wealthy landowners who leased their land to others. While they did not usually exert their monopoly power in local economies to their full advantage, in an era when the commercial development of land can transform the value of particular sites, colleges can become major actors in the planning process. (Universities can also be controversial landlords because they use their landholdings to maximize their income, as any commercial enterprise does, rather than in the pursuit of social objectives. Columbia University in New York found itself in this position because of its ownership of a considerable amount of land in Harlem.) Endowments for newer colleges have tended to be in the form of shares – Nuffield College, Oxford, received a large holding of shares in the Nuffield (Morris) car company, and while in this case, the shareholding was subsequently diversified, clearly there could be major problems for such institutions if they became key actors in rival takeover bids.

Whenever possible, the Charity Commission in England has sought in recent years to keep charities as 'passive' holders of economic resources. Except where a trust has granted the trustees the widest possible powers, charities must seek the permission of the Commission to engage in any financial activity that might be speculative. In the early 1970s the Commission did approve two major transactions in London, where the charities concerned wanted to develop land themselves rather than to sell it for development; the former approach was expected to generate far more profit than the latter. However, problems subsequently emerged when property prices collapsed, and since then the Commission has been even more cautious about the active (and hence speculative) creation of wealth by charities. In the US, wealthy charitable organizations have greater opportunities to engage in property development, because they are not constrained by the need to justify speculative enterprises to an independent agency. For example, the Educational Testing Service, which generated most of its capital from the sale of its services, planned in 1987 to build 447,000 square feet of offices which would mainly be rented to other companies until the twenty-first century.[16]

Another source of economic power comes when wealth is linked to restrictions on the activities in which the charity can engage, and when there are legal penalties imposed on charities for not carrying out these activities. This is a comparatively rare problem, but there is one extreme, and well-known, case of a charity competing with other charities, for-profit firms and individuals and having a considerable impact on the market. This is the Getty Trust which purchases works of art for the Getty Museum and which is so large that it has already had a considerable impact on the art market:

> The Getty trust, with total assets of around $3 billion is . . . helping to push prices up. The trust supports the museum, and assuming the assets grow at a compounded rate of 8 percent annually, by the year 2000 the museum will be required under Internal Revenue Service trust regulations to spend $430,000 *every day*.[17]

Charities too may be bequeathed enterprises which they decide to continue to operate themselves, in competition with for-profit businesses. As Ellman notes, 'The University of Texas sells oil, and the New York University Law School at one time owned a successful, profit-making noodle factory'.[18] But there are disincentives for wealthy charities in both England and the US to become active participants in the economy. Since 1950 there has been an unrelated-business income tax in the US, so that organizations that are otherwise tax-exempt do pay tax on income from earnings that is held to be unrelated to the purposes for which they can claim tax exemption from the Internal Revenue Service. That New York University would receive the profits from their noodles, and that financially strong universities might be held to benefit the public, is irrelevant; noodle-making is not linked directly to the supposed purposes of a university, and that income became taxable after 1950. In England, too, the Charity Commissioners have tried to restrict this kind of unrelated income. They made their position clear in their 1980 annual report:

> In some cases the trading or other commercial activities may form so small a part of the institution's activities as to be insignificant. In our view trading of this nature would be permissible but the profits would not enjoy exemption from income tax unless the trading was in the course of carrying out (i) a primary purpose of the charity, or (ii) the work is mainly carried out by the beneficiaries of the charity.[19]

Nevertheless, while concentrated wealth has been a factor contributing to the growth of competition between charities and for-profit firms, it is probably not among the most important factors. Far more important, for example, is the factor to which we now turn, the professionalization of fund-raising.

D Maintaining charity income through professionalized fund-raising

The problem of 'organizing' charity has been an issue in England and the US for nearly 150 years. What has changed is what it is that needs to be organized. In the Victorian period the key problem was thought to be the distribution of charity; in the twentieth century attention has switched from the distribution of funds to their supply. Increasingly business techniques have been applied to fund-raising. In the US this has given rise to devices such as federated fund-raising through payroll deductions, and to efforts to increase donations from business corporations. Fund-raising in Britain has been much less well developed than in the US, but one of the manifestations of the new entrepreneurial approach there has been the employment of professionals to raise funds on behalf of a charity; concern about certain aspects of this, including some professionals' demands to keep an excessive proportion of the funds raised, was expressed by the Charity Commission in its report for

1986.[20] (Payroll deduction schemes were also introduced in Britain after 1986.) But for our purposes, in examining competition with for-profit businesses, the most interesting change has been the growth of trading activities as a way of raising funds, a development which itself leads eventually to the employment of relevant 'professionals'.

In part the growth of marketing operations by bodies like Oxfam, which are heavily involved in raising money through donations, reflects the availability of new techniques for increasing income. But a major incentive to adopt such techniques has been the relative weakness of fund-raising efforts in the mid twentieth century. Data on contributions to charities is scarce, and data on long-term trends in charitable donations is almost non-existent, especially for England. However, from what is available two conclusions can be drawn which suggest great pressure on charities in recent decades. There is considerable evidence that charitable donations were declining in the 1960s and 1970s in both Britain and the US, and it was this perceived crisis which led to the setting up of the Filer Commission to investigate the situation of charities in the US in 1973.[21] Moreover, in the broader perspective, charities have not done very well because the percentage of personal income given as charitable donations in the US has not increased very much since the 1930s, even though personal income has grown rapidly since then and the number of charities has also increased greatly.[22] The situation in England is probably very similar, and has been made worse by the ban on charities advertising on television, though with the Independent Broadcasting Authority's acceptance of commercials for the Give as You Earn scheme in 1987, it seemed that this policy was in the process of changing.[23] Trading is an answer, then, to the failure to maintain the traditional sources of funds for charities.

As we saw earlier, although there are sources of income (including membership dues) which can be closely akin to trading, the law in both England and the US has circumscribed the expansion of trading *per se*. Nevertheless, within the limits permitted, many trading ventures have flourished in recent years. A distinction must be drawn, of course, between genuinely commercial activities and what are, in effect, solicitations for donations. The Christmas or Easter seals distributed by post are a means of 'tugging at consciences', rather than sales, because the charities have no means of preventing their use by people who do not pay for them. But, Oxfam shops, the National Trust gift catalogue, and the Christmas cards now sold by many charities are commercial ventures: only those who pay for them can acquire the goods. However, many modern fund-raising ventures embrace both commercial transactions and appeals for donations. The Live Aid rock concert in 1985 was an instance of this; money for famine relief came from two sources – from individuals and television companies who paid to attend the concerts in London and Philadelphia and to broadcast them, and from donors to whom appeals were made for gifts.[24] Sometimes the two forms of fund-raising are combined even more intimately – the prices paid for goods in a charity auction may be higher than those that would be paid in a commercial auction because the bidders are prepared to make a donation in the form of a higher bid than they would otherwise make.

The Live Aid example also exposes another issue. With a charity concert, film showing, dinner, or auction, it is often difficult to specify with whom there is actually competition in the for-profit sector. Is it reasonable to assume that the rock fan who went to the Live Aid concert at Wembley would have thereby foregone attending a commercial concert? Or is the diner at a charity dinner necessarily a customer lost to a restauranteur? Obviously, with many instances of trading involving charities the issue is much clearer: to the extent that his/her purchase is not a 'disguised donation', the customer in an Oxfam shop is presumably a potentially 'lost' customer at another second-hand shop. But the point that the impact on the for-profit sector can be an indirect one is important, because, as we will see in chapter 7, efforts at regulating commercial intrusions by charities have tended to focus on direct, *unfair*, competition.

Nevertheless, despite the pressures on charities to find new ways of raising money, even by the second half of the 1980s trading remained very much the 'Cinderella' of the fund-raising activities of those British charities which still depended heavily on donations. Even so, there has been evidence of change here. The Save the Children Fund, for example, has started opening shops which no longer follow the traditional charity shop model of primarily selling donated goods or goods made by the beneficiaries, and it has engaged in this through a commercial subsidiary company. Profits from such companies can then be covenanted to the charity, and income tax thereby reclaimed.

E Reductions in state funding

In the US, but not in Britain, the growth in the provision of state welfare services in the 1960s was largely brought about by the federal government funding other agencies (state and local governments, some for-profit businesses, and most especially charities) to provide the actual services. The dependence of charities on government money is shown in table 3.2: 44 per cent of the total income of non-religious charities in 1980 came in the form of sales to government or government grants. When, in the 1980s, the Reagan administration started to cut back on social welfare programmes, charities were faced with a shortfall in income.

Although efforts were made to increase donations, especially from business corporations, these efforts did not even come close to matching the government's reduction in funding. In order to try to maintain their income, many charities had to increase the charges they made of their clients, where this was possible, and to try to expand their revenue-producing activities. Together with the decline in donations, mentioned in the last section, federal government policy increasingly pushed charities into market operations. As we see in section F, the possibility for increased trading already existed, so that the effect of the cutbacks in the 1980s was to further encourage developments that were evident earlier.

In Britain, of course, the creation of the welfare state had involved far more direct provision of services by governmental agencies than in the US. (For example, the fees and grants paid by local authorities to charitable bodies in the early 1980s constituted no more than about one and 1.5 per cent of total local authority expenditures.)[25] Indeed, it was in the 1980s, in the attempt to reduce governmental expenditure on social services, that increasing use came to be made of charities as intermediaries. Nevertheless, there were some policy areas, of which support for universities was the most important, where charitable organizations had already become heavily dependent on state funding. Faced by reductions in funding after 1981, universities had to expand their commercial ventures greatly, a development which was actively encouraged by the Conservative government. There, as in the US, the expansion of activities in an earlier period had made organizations vulnerable to the withdrawal of funding – funding which could not possibly be compensated for by increasing the traditional financial base of such organizations, donations and income from endowments. Consequently, they had to turn to the market to survive, and in many cases this brought them into direct competition with for-profit firms.

F The expansion of the existing activities of charities into businesses

While the problems of declining donations and reduced state support have provided a greater incentive for charities to expand their trading, many opportunities for this already existed, and some had been well established by the 1960s. New industries developing at the peripheries of charities' activities were being exploited to supplement other income; often for-profit competition was dispersed and small scale, so that charity-based industries could emerge without too much controversy. Links with the principal purposes of the charities further insulated them from charges of unfair competition. An obvious example of this was the growth of foreign language programmes and summer school courses for foreign students at British universities, which saw the universities competing with commercial operators. Since this could be seen as a legitimate extension of their main activity, universities were able to obtain this income free of corporation tax.

Among the most successful of university enterprises have been their presses, many of which provide a good example of the transformation from non-profit-generating activities to businesses. Traditionally, university presses were publishers of scholarly works for which there was little public demand and which required subsidization to be produced at all. Changes in the publishing industry made it possible for presses to make a profit on a book which commanded relatively few sales. Furthermore, university presses themselves have moved into publishing books which attract a wider readership than do academic treatises, and this has brought them into direct competition with commercial publishers.[26] When they are managed efficiently, university presses may not only be among the largest publishers but can also show a high level of profitability. In Britain, Cambridge University Press is frequently said to be an outstanding example of this.

Although higher education provides many of the best examples of charities assisting in the development of new industries which has brought them into competition with the for-profit sector, it is not the only source of this competition. Museums, for instance, have taken advantage of the increased demand in the last few decades for reproduced prints of paintings, 'coffee table' books, and the like, and many now sell products which they help to design or manufacture. (In conjunction with an American company, the Victoria and Albert Museum is even producing a range of co-ordinated chintzes and wallpapers.) But of all charities, universities, together in the US with non-profit organizations in the health sector, have perhaps been the best placed to enter into commerce relating to their charitable activities. They have had the resources, in terms of both capital and labour skills, to respond to the demand for new products and services. Thus in Britain in the 1980s they have set up enterprises like science parks, sometimes in conjunction with local government or private enterprise, and have sought to become major actors in the 'high technology' fields. Ironically, one of the greatest successes of universities in creating a major industry in which it both co-operates and competes with for-profit enterprise is not in these fields, but in the spectator sports' industries in the US.

Inter-university sporting competitions have never been a feature of higher education in contintental Europe, and while they have a long tradition in Britain, only a few events (such as the Boat Race and the Varsity rugby match) have ever captured public imagination. In the US, however, interest in such sporting contests has a long history, and two features of American colleges were primarily responsible for this. In many places colleges and universities were a source of local and state pride, so that the attentive public who could become interested in these contests was much greater than the body of alumni and present students. More importantly, sporting events not only gave students a sense of identity with an educational institution, but also were used as a way of keeping alumni in contact with their alma mater. These contacts have been far more important in the US than in other countries in generating funds for a college. The transformation of this peculiar feature of American academia into a major industry was made possible by increased leisure time in the mid-twentieth century and by innovations in mass communications.

Popular interest in sporting contests enabled two sports (American football and basketball), which had been the major sports at most colleges, to establish massive support at the *professional* level in the years after the second world war. Unlike, for example, baseball and ice hockey, the professional leagues in these sports owed their success very much to the popularity of inter-collegiate competitions. Television enabled the colleges, organized through a monopoly, the National Collegiate Athletic Association (NCAA), to add greatly to the income they obtained from spectators 'at the turnstiles'. Particularly in the case of American football, the colleges were able to maintain the 'quality of their product' by an agreement that the professional league clubs would not sign players of college age and that the league would play its games on Sundays, leaving Saturdays to the colleges. Under this arrangement both college and professional football and basketball became major industries in the last four decades. College crowds were at least as large as those for professional games, games were widely televised, and, in the case of many colleges, success in these sports seemed to be linked to the willingness of alumni to contribute to their alma mater. In colluding with the major professional leagues – in effect dividing up the market between them – the colleges helped to undermine the viability of semi-professional leagues and to drive out competitors (such as the World Football League of the 1970s) to the existing major leagues. The other leagues found that they were squeezed between the college monopoly, on the one hand, and the professional league monopolies on the other.

The collective power of the colleges within the sports industry enabled them to protect their share of a rapidly expanding market, especially in regard to television revenues. By the 1980s, however, a serious split emerged within the college ranks. The better footballing colleges broke away to negotiate their own agreements with television companies, taking advantage of the demand of smaller television stations and cable television companies to broadcast college games. At the same time, though, there were competitive forces posing threats to the colleges. Although they had generally been able to prevent the National Football League from recruiting players before their four years of college eligibility had elapsed, a few college basketball players were now leaving early, claiming 'hardship', to sign for teams in the National Basketball Association. While this loss constituted no more than a small proportion of the best college players, it did expose the problems colleges might face if there was more competition from professional (and semi-professional) leagues in signing eighteen to twenty-two year olds. Of course, colleges would still retain some important advantages in recruitment, even if there was more competition. Some, though not all, do actually provide their athletes with an education while at college. This is an important benefit, given the uncertainties, even for the most gifted athletes, of making a successful career in professional sport. Moreover, outstanding college athletes attract the attention of potential employers outside the sports industry, while those who go directly into professional sport, but who fail to 'make the grade', have few such contacts on which to fall back. Thus, the possible threat of a more competitive sports industry would be unlikely to destroy the market the colleges have built up, though it might reduce the income generated by college games.

But how important has commercial sport been to American colleges and universities? For the Ivy League universities and some of the elite liberal arts' colleges, the industry has remained relatively insignificant. However, for many other colleges and universities with high academic standards, the large income emanating from sport-related events has helped to subsidize athletic activities within the institution, and in some cases other activities as well. For colleges with lesser records of scholarship, sporting events have helped to focus national attention on them and have been a device for attracting both students and funds. It is primarily, though not exclusively, with these sorts of colleges that well-publicized scandals have emerged in recent years, as they have sought to maintain successful teams. The scandals have been of three main types. The first has concerned the breaking of NCAA rules of recruitment with monetary and other incentives being offered to outstanding high-school athletes. Persistent problems of this kind over the years at Southern Methodist University, one of the best schools at American football, culminated in the football programme being closed down in 1986 because its governing body believed that the integrity of the university had been badly tarnished. Another problem has been the failure of colleges to insist that their athletes actually study while at college. In some well-known cases athletes have remained at college for two or three years, and have left having attained only the level of literacy of the average ten or eleven year old. Then there are scandals relating to pressure being put on academic staff to give passing grades to athlete-scholars. The outstanding example of this was the denial of tenure to a faculty member at the University of Georgia in the mid 1980s for her refusal to co-operate when athletes failed her courses; she was successful in suing the University, and in settlement was not only reinstated but received large damages from the University. The financial rewards for successful sports' programmes, therefore, have not only encouraged the growth of these programmes in both private and public universities, but have also provided an incentive for competing 'outside the rules'.

This particular instance of charities extending their activities into new industries suggests some of the constraints charities usually face in competing with for-profit concerns. To a large degree colleges have been able to sustain their share of the sports market because of the monopoly position of the professional sports leagues – monopolies which have been sustained by favourable court decisions and legislative inaction in Congress. Few expanding industries have been able to hold on to their monopolies in quite the way that the sports leagues have, so that the penetration of the market achieved by the colleges remains rather unusual among charitable bodies.

G Charitable input in areas of marginal economic activity

We saw in section A that some of the purposes recognized by English law in the sixteenth century as charitable were areas of activity where a market could work, at best, only very imperfectly. In an underdeveloped economy services such as health care, education, adequate housing and many others can be afforded by only a small minority of the population. But in societies at all levels of economic development there are goods or services, the provision of which is widely regarded as valuable, but where the market system distributes to only a few of the potential customers. When mutual-benefit organizations do not emerge to fill this 'gap', the state or individuals and organizations may provide funds to enable the good or service to be supplied by an organization, and (when a charge is made) at a price below that which would generate a normal rate of profit in the market. (In some cases, such as hospital treatment, the purpose has always been legally charitable and consequently the organizations concerned have been charities; in other cases they have not been charitable and rather different organizational structures have had to be used.)

There are four rather different reasons why the market may fail to distribute what is believed to be an optimal supply of services such as health care, education, adequate housing and so on, and why subsidies have to be used.

(i) The level of income of most customers is so low in relation to the price of the product as to make it irrational (and even impossible) for purchases to be made;

(ii) Even if the product can be afforded by most potential customers, the patterns of their demand for goods is such that they choose to purchase less of it than either other individuals or the state believes to be desirable. Private philanthropy or state grants could be the basis of subsidy to facilitate greater consumption by lowering the price. Stated in this way, the argument might seem to be essentially paternalistic in character: 'People don't know what is good for them.' But it need not be; the purpose of encouraging greater consumption of the product might not be for the good of the consumers, but, say, to create a greater domestic market as the basis for an export drive.

(iii) The consumers may be insufficient in number, for example, because of their geographical dispersal, to provide a normal rate of return for the supplier. A village shop requires a minimum number of customers to make it viable; the decline of agricultural employment, combined with the migration to rural areas of commuters who can do their shopping in towns, has resulted in many villages being no longer able to sustain a shop. Traditional village residents find that they can no longer purchase the goods they require.

(iv) Because of hostility to a service being supplied by for-profit firms, proprietorial firms can supply only a relatively small proportion of those who want the service. Fears about 'contract failure', of the kind discussed in chapter 1, may keep some customers out of the market, and these fears may well be understood by entrepreneurs in the for-profit sector. For example, Nelson and Krashinsky, citing Ruderman, say of day-care facilities for children, 'even many businessmen believe that this is an unsatisfactory way of providing the service'.[27]

One solution to the problem of the inability of the market to supply a good on a scale that is regarded as desirable is direct provision by the state, or state subsidies of commercial enterprises. But private organizations, such as business corporations and charitable trusts, have also sought to remove these 'gaps' in the supply of goods. Businesses sometimes cross-subsidize services, a practice best illustrated perhaps by many American law firms which use profits from private clients to finance 'public-interest' cases. Alternatively a firm might provide capital for the setting up of a separate organization which then provides services on a non-profit basis. The techniques may be combined, of course: a non-profit-distributing organization may have its initial capital supplied by for-profit firms, but then generate income for its subsidized activities from the fees of full-price clients. Thus, a director of the Centre for Employment Initiatives (CEI), a non-profit consultancy firm which advises public authorities and firms on job creation techniques, described their approach as follows: 'We are essentially a Robin Hood organization ... We earn consultancy fees from richer clients which we recycle to the poorer ones in a number of ways.'[28] CEI competes against firms in the for-profit sector, the director of one of which claimed: 'We are probably more expensive than they are. If price is the main factor we won't get [the contract], but if the creation of new jobs is the overwhelming factor, then we will.' What this case illustrates is that, with 'marginal' industries, competition between the kinds of organization may well not be 'head on'. For-profit firms might either be left to work on their own in the profitable sectors of the market, or may have advantages which reduce the losses they can expect to make to non-profits engaged in cross-subsidization.

In the US the interaction of commercial organizations and charities (as well as governments) in areas of 'marginal' economic activity is both more extensive and more complex. One of the more interesting of these developments is the Local Initiative Support Corporation (LISC), which was founded in 1979 and has 501(c)(3) status with the IRS and which receives financial support from both business corporations and charitable foundations. Its 'Support is directed to organizations in the community which are expected to develop their organisations and expand their activities. This may involve groups taking on greater commercial and business responsibilities'.[29]

Jacobs reports that in Chicago LISC backed housing projects which provided accommodation for low-income families. Here is an example of co-ordination between commercial and charitable organizations in a market which has failed to provide the services required. Obviously, we are not claiming that this kind of provision is necessarily a substitute for direct state intervention, rather it illustrates how charities and for-profit enterprises may both co-operate and compete in certain kinds of market.

The expansion of non-profits into marginal areas of the American economy has not been matched in Britain. In 1985 CEI was one of only about 80 such non-profit organizations (or community businesses, as they are often called) in Britain. One of the reasons for this is the strictness of English charity law in preventing organizations which are primarily commercial, or which involve self-help, from having the tax, and other, advantages associated with charity. A demonstrable benefit to the community is insufficient to secure charitable status when there are elements of self-help; just as village shops are not charitable, even when a village cannot support a commercial shop, so Provenhall Holdings, a group of community shops in Glasgow, cannot acquire this status. A second reason is that the growth of 'third-party government' in the US – the hiving off of service provision to non-governmental agencies – helped many non-profit organizations to become established in the 1960s; some of these were involved in 'marginal' sectors of the economy. In Britain it was not until the 1980s that there were moves to reduce some aspects of direct state provision and correspondingly increase state funding of charities.[30] A third reason is that, because of differences in both the structure of the banking systems and the tax systems, it is more difficult for community businesses in Britain to secure gifts and loans from commercial firms. The absence, in particular, of 'soft loans' in Britain presents a significant contrast to the US, where both the private sector and government have made extensive use of this device.

2 Charities and Co-operation with For-profit Firms

So far the focus of the discussion has been competition between for-profit firms and charities, and we have identified seven reasons why competition not only exists, but has grown in recent years. But, at the same time, there are incentives for individual firms to engage in *co-operative* commercial ventures with charities, partly (though only partly) because of the pressure of competition from them. Indeed, it is possible to identify four main reasons for the emergence of co-operation.

A 'If you can't beat 'em . . .'

In some cases the advantages charities have had in the market, advantages which look as if they will persist, encourage firms to come to an arrangement with individual charities that might enable them to compete more effectively. An obvious example here is the market in Christmas cards, where commercial firms started to lose some of their share of the market to charities.[31] One solution to this, which was actually adopted, was for firms to make donations from their sales to particular charities, and to state that they were doing this on the back of their cards. This made it easier for the undiscerning purchaser to confuse cards produced by charities, which benefited from all profits, from those where only a small proportion of profits benefited a charity. Clearly charities which did not have their own cards had an incentive to be involved in these latter schemes, although their success would reduce the total amount of money going to charities. However, some of the largest charities were also prepared to become involved in such schemes even when sales of their own cards were high. In their case the potential loss of revenue was less important than the publicity the charities received from having cards bearing their names on sale in stationery stores. They calculated that the possible growth in donations this might stimulate would more than offset any reduction in the sales of their own cards. Less esoteric examples involve organizations like universities in fields such as analytic testing, or the development of new technologies, where firms may find that the expertise available to them through co-operation makes profit-splitting, co-operative ventures, worthwhile.

B *Favourable publicity for for-profit firms*

A second reason for co-operation, which we discuss further in chapter 4, is that being associated with charities provides favourable publicity for firms – they can develop an image of 'social responsibility', sometimes at relatively little cost to themselves. In the 1980s, especially in the US, efforts by firms to link their advertising strategies to support for charities increased enormously. Not surprisingly, a number of these efforts received adverse publicity because of the relatively small contributions made by the firms to charities. One of the better-known examples in England was an annual 'charity' golf tournament, which was named after the entertainer Bob Hope. In the event, the commercial firm which ran it made no contribution to charity, because, after the full expenses (and fees) for the participants (including Bob Hope) had been met, the tournament was operating at a loss.

Having an ostensibly charitable purpose can also help commercial ventures that might otherwise attract unfavourable publicity or protests. One example of this in Britain has been the International Air Tattoo at Fairford. The organizers claimed that the purpose of the event was to raise money for the RAF Benevolent Fund and in both 1985 and 1986 £85,000 was contributed to that charity. However, critics have argued that the main purpose of the event was to provide a forum in which arms sales could be made to Third World countries, and some of the arms companies attending the Tattoo admitted that their reason for attending was to sell their products.[32]

The quest for favourable publicity in the market can be manifested in far more subtle forms of co-operation with charities than this. Consider the case of the Chicago-based retail store Hammacher-Schlemmer, whose distinctive features are that it sells only the 'best' of any household product, that these products are 'useful', and that they include many unusual or specialized items. In part, the company has been able to establish a reputation for meeting these objectives because the testing of any possible product is actually carried out by its own (non-profit) institute – indicating to the customer a level of impartiality that overtly 'in-house' testing might not.

C New forms of fund-raising for charities

Just as the need to raise more funds has pushed charities into commercial ventures that have created competition with for-profit firms, so the need for funds has forced them to co-operate with these firms. But not all of these schemes originate in the for-profit sector, or work primarily to their advantage. One of the most interesting of such schemes in the 1980s is the linking of major credit cards in the US to charities and political 'cause' groups. A charity can obtain cards (such as VISA) for its members, the cards bearing the distinctive logo of the organization, and typically: 'banks that issue the cards pay them $1 or so for every new member who signs up for a card, plus about one-half of 1 per cent of the value of each sales transaction, or a fixed sum'.[33]

The advantage of this kind of scheme for the charities is that, once members or supporters have been issued with a card, they receive money from transactions when it is used, so that it becomes cost-free fund-raising. The supporters can direct money to their 'favourite causes' without it costing them anything.[34] And the banks claim that they benefit because they increase the number of people holding their credit cards – people 'who tend to be bigger spenders and better credit risks'.[35]

D Exploiting the advantages of tax-exempt status

The liberalization of non-profit laws in the US has made it easier for charitable organizations to be exploited by commercial firms for advantages in relation to tax exemption.[36] The area in which this is most pronounced, and in which financial complexes embracing both commercial and charitable organizations are most apparent, is the hospital industry. The emergence of this trend has been outlined by Gray.[37]

Gray argues that a variety of new forms of *hybrid* organization are developing in this industry. Superficially, one instance he cites, the Roanoke Memorial Hospital in Virginia, does not seem that unusual. Here the four bodies at the apex of the organization are of the non-profit kind; charities owning for-profit, trading, subsidiaries are not unusual, even in England. But the Roanoke case is interesting because of the sorts of enterprises into which it has diversified. These include a collection agency, a warehouse, a conference centre, a motel, and the Roanoke Athletic Club.[38] This indicates that the point made in section 1(C), that there are disadvantages to wealthy charities operating businesses, does not apply to all non-profits. More complicated, however, is another of Gray's examples – the Voluntary Hospitals of America (VHA). Here the complex intertwining of for-profit and non-profit concerns is such that, while the legal status of each individual organization is necessarily either for-profit or non-profit, it becomes much more difficult to classify the entire complex as being one or the other. Perhaps the most important development is that within such complexes, not only may non-profit organizations own for-profits, but for-profits may also have non-profit subsidiaries. It becomes clear that in some circumstances the usual disadvantage for a for-profit firm in providing capital for a non-profit – that there is no income derived from such an investment – is insufficient to prevent its formation. Apart from profit, there may be many other economic advantages to a for-profit firm, in 'farming out' some of its activities to a non-profit subsidiary.

3 Effects on the State

Finally in this chapter we must consider the impact that economic competition (and co-operation) between charities and for-profit firms has on the state. This is important because, if as we have indicated, interaction between for-profits and non-profits is increasing, the effects on the state are also likely to increase. Since many of these developments may be expected to affect the state adversely, it seems likely that the problem of regulating the boundary between for-profits and non-profits will become more crucial. For our purposes, there are five main consequences for the state which are worth outlining.

A Demands for regulating 'unfair' competition

This is an issue we consider more fully in chapter 7, because arguments about 'unfair' competition (or 'competitive advantage', as it is sometimes called) have been at the heart of efforts to regulate non-profits in the US in the 1980s. At this point, though, it is useful to identify two of the main dimensions of the debate about 'unfairness'. One important issue is whether unfairness relates simply to the tax advantages enjoyed by charities or whether, irrespective of taxation, it is unfair for entrepreneurs to face competition from institutions that originally owe their legal status to pursuit of non-commercial purposes. If the debate is about the former, then it is largely about the principles of taxing income. If it is about the latter, then more wide-ranging problems about the appropriate legal structure for, and constraints to be placed on, organizations that do not seek economic benefits for themselves become evident. The other issue is whether the origins of competition are significant in determining whether tax exemption constitutes 'unfairness'. Some instances of competition arise from 'marginal' areas of economic activity, in which for-profit concerns can scarcely survive, being transformed into full markets. From the perspective of charities, there is no unfairness to the newer, for-profit, concerns, because they entered the market knowing that non-profits already operated there. On this view, it is only in fields into which non-profits expanded at the same time, or after, for-profit businesses that competition between the kinds of organizations can ever be unfair.

On the narrower interpretation of these disputes, the problem for the state is more likely to be confined to the smaller, though still complex, issue of devising regulations for taxing charities' trading activities in a way that provides no special advantages. On the broader interpretation, the problems inherent in using sixteenth century charity law as the basis for distinguishing between kinds of organization, for tax and other purposes, in the late twentieth century have to be confronted.

B Loss of tax revenues

On balance, services supplied by charities produce a loss of tax revenue for the state compared with full provision by for-profit suppliers. This is because the former are exempt from income tax and are usually exempt from some other taxes, such as local property taxes, as well. In general, then, the larger a non-profit enterprise becomes, the more the tax bases of various units of government are undermined. Of course, non-profit enterprise is not the only, or even the major, source of tax loss for the state; in a study of bodies that do not pay real estate taxes in the US, Balk points out that other levels of government severely erode the tax base of local governments, as, of course, do charities that are not involved in commercial activities.[39] Moreover, when considering tax losses, the state must balance them against two potential economic benefits that tax-free (or tax-reduced) status for non-profit enterprise could yield.

(i) Non-profit activity in 'marginal' areas of the economy might stimulate further economic activity that itself produces tax revenues for the state. For example, the provision of non-profit-making shops might help to revive other forms of economic activity in inner-city areas, by providing an incentive to businesses that might otherwise close down or move.

(ii) Because of their favourable tax status, non-profits may be more likely than for-profit business to subsidize services that might otherwise have to be supplied directly by the state. For example, against the claims of Herzlinger and Krasker, it has been widely argued that investor-owned hospitals in the US provide less care for the poor than non-profit hospitals.[40]

The principal loss of revenue from economic entrepreneurship by charities is from corporate income tax, but the situation is a complex one and has not always been free of controversy. In England charities have remained exempt from income taxes ever since this form of revenue generation was first introduced on a temporary basis in 1799. When he was Chancellor of the Exchequer in 1863, W. E. Gladstone proposed the abolition of this privilege. He argued that the exemption 'represented an undiscriminating public subsidy for a large group of organizations which were not subject to any form of public scrutiny', but the measure did not obtain a majority in Parliament.[41] (However, until the *Pemsel* decision resolved the matter in 1891, the Inland Revenue had a policy for some time of granting tax exemption only to those charities engaged in the relief of poverty.) Since then the privilege has been extended to new, but related, taxes, such as capital gains tax. Generally these exemptions have not provoked much public debate, although controversies about one type of entrepreneurial charity (the public schools) has drawn some attention to the issue, because in this case it is unclear that there are any benefits to people other than those who can afford to educate their children at expensive schools. With most other charities, claims that there are some benefits to a wider public have usually been more evident. The exemption from taxes linked to income and capital does not extend to other kinds of non-profit-distributing organizations, of course: non-charitable companies limited by guarantee, for example, are liable to tax on any profits they happen to make in the course of business or any capital gains on assets. Nevertheless, corporation tax can be avoided (through it being reclaimed) in the case of commercial enterprises which covenant their profits to a charity. Thus companies set up by charities to engage in trading activities can provide their 'parent' organization with income which is free from tax. The relatively small scale of these operations has prevented them so far from becoming controversial.

The tax situation in the US is rather different. 'In the early days of the federal income tax ... all nonprofit organizations were lumped together and exempted from tax as though fungible members of an undifferentiated mass.'[42] Disputes in the 1940s about the abuses of tax privileges led in 1950 to the first of several reforms. Since then the practice has been to identify different categories of non-profit organizations to which different rules apply. While the most privileged status, 501(c)(3), is more inclusive than the category of 'charity' in England, all non-profit tax categories are subject to restrictions, including the taxing of 'unrelated income' and, in some cases, of 'passive' investments as well.[43] In America too there has been considerable debate as to whether it is inconsistent to tax the income of non-profit bodies – an issue which involves analyzing the concept of income.[44]

A further source of tax loss for the state is charities' exemption from other kinds of taxes. In England most charities are exempt from 50 per cent of local property taxes (the rates), and local authorities have discretionary powers to waive some (or all) of this reduced liability. However, churches are wholly exempt from rates, while universities and other institutions of higher education are debarred from receiving the mandatory relief.[45] With regard to sales taxes, the position of charities in England was made worse by the introduction of Value Added Tax (VAT) in 1972, in that the number of exemptions available was fewer than under the previous purchase tax system. But, because they are not themselves supposedly engaged in commercial activities, English charities do not have to pay VAT on their own 'production'. Yet those charities with a turnover of more than £5,000 must register for VAT, and charities cannot reclaim VAT on goods supplied to them as final consumers. In the US, exemptions from state sales taxes and from local real estate taxes vary from state to state and from city to city. For the most part, the greater indulgence to charities found at the federal level is replicated at these lower levels. Moreover, decentralized political systems are more exposed to the power of economic interest groups at the local level than are centralized systems. Wealthy charities can exert such power, and can use it to reduce their own tax liabilities. An outstanding recent example of this was the threat by the Reverend Jerry Falwell to move his church and its associated institutions from Lynchburg, Virginia, a move that would have had a serious impact on the local economy, if the city did not remove the property taxes on his enterprises. In effect the Lynchburg city council was forced to choose between losing 2,000 jobs and a $32 million annual payroll or forgoing $400,000 a year in property taxes.[46]

Obviously, one of the issues raised by the Falwell case, and other similar incidents, is whether explicit commercial practice should be compatible with charitable status. But even in Britain religious organizations of the Falwell kind would be protected from de-registration with the Charity Commission if they could demonstrate that they actually performed their charitable purposes. Indeed, religious charities enjoy the greatest protection from charges of either commercial or political activity because virtually anything they do can be seen as helping to advance their religious purpose. The unwillingness of liberal democracies to be seen as suppressing religion makes it very difficult for state agencies to intervene to suppress the exploitation of charitable status.

C Reduction in state outlays

We have argued that a large area of commercial activity by charities may have a serious impact on a state's tax base. Obviously, there are advantanges too for the state in having successful entrepreneurship by charities. Just as greater fund-raising by charities may enable the state to reduce its own expenditures in a particular field, as it has with medical research in Britain, so also may greater revenues from commerce permit such reductions.[47] In the case of British universities, government policy in the early 1980s was directed towards increasing the share of non-governmental funds, especially through sales of services and skills, by announcing cuts in government grants in advance. Faced by a large reduction in grants from the University Grants Committee (UGC), universities vied with each other in recruiting (full-fee paying) foreign students, in setting up science parks, in establishing contracts with industrial companies and so on. (In fact, this approach was also extended to the government sector of higher education; the 1985 Further Education Act empowered state-sector institutions – polytechnics and local authority colleges – to sell on a commercial basis the by-products of their research.)

However, encouraging (or coercing) charities to turn to commercial activities as a way of reducing grants from the state is a strategy that can be extended to relatively few areas of policy. Even with universities, the American experience indicates that, whatever the vitality of non-governmental fund-raising, the state has to remain the principal source of funds for basic research, which in the sciences is the most expensive activity of all. It is a classic case of a public good. While philanthropic foundations may provide some funding, commercial interests are unlikely to provide substantial support because it yields no specific benefits to them. Consequently, in the years after 1945 there was a huge increase in the federal government's share of the funding of universities (both private and public), even though in other ways American universities became even more commercial in character. Furthermore, it is important to realize that one of the reasons why British universities were able to enter into overt commercial transactions is that they are one of the relatively few kinds of charities that are not subject to review by the Charity Commission. Government policy in this area does not require legislation to amend the laws relating to charities. Finally, of course, there are many fields in which charities operate but in which there is little possibility of government funds being substituted for commercial sales.

D The regulation of monopoly

Just as the state may have to intervene in the for-profit sector to dissolve, or regulate, monopoly or excessive market power on the part of one supplier, so too commercial activity by charities might prompt state intervention. It should not be forgotten that amongst the oldest aspects of the legal regulation of charity in England is medieval legislation relating to mortmain which was designed to prevent too much land falling into the hands of corporations that could exist in perpetuity. Today there are relatively few areas where the market power of charities, at least on a national level, is sufficiently great that anti-monopoly provisions are even possible. Nevertheless, there are two areas in the US, which we have already mentioned, where excessive market power has developed. The first is the power of colleges, working through the NCAA, in controlling part of the spectator sports industries. Here, however, public and congressional opinion has supported the continuation of the monopolies of which these are a part. The other is the Getty Trust, whose income is so great that it has already helped to increase prices in the world art market. It is not inconceivable, though, that in regard to some areas of technological innovation in the future, particular universities, say, might establish monopolies in conjunction with their for-profit collaborators. The problem of monopoly power is one, therefore, that might easily become more important than it has been in the recent past.

E Effects on social welfare

Competition between for-profit and charitable organizations has an impact on social welfare. Changes in the extent and balance of that competition can create demands for state intervention, because some social groups are adversely affected by this change. Nor is it for-profit organizations that are always responsible for the social problems which arise. To take one example at the local level. Columbia University has faced problems in recruiting teaching staff in recent decades because of the high cost of housing in Manhattan.[48] Its policy has been to buy up apartment buildings in the immediate vicinty of its campus from private landlords, and to lease them to faculty members at rents below the market rate. Non-profit organizations are exempt from the city's rent control and security of tenancy laws, although 'sitting tenants' do not lose their rights when a building is taken over by the university. In an area with an acute shortage of low-rental housing, the Columbia policy has had the result of further squeezing the housing opportunities of lower-income earners, including its non-faculty employees who are not entitled to Columbia apartments. Specific incidents, such as the eviction of a resident in 1987, intensified the controversy, and local community groups have charged the university with attempting to gentrify the area and with maintaining large numbers of unoccupied apartments.[49]

More usually, of course, it is charitable organizations whose policies are more likely to be compatible with those of disadvantaged groups and wider publics. Indeed, one objection to the entry of firms into areas of previously marginal economic activity, where non-profits had been dominant, is that less attention will be given to social aspects of the supply of the good. For example, critics of the growth of for-profit chains of hospitals in the US have argued that the displacement of non-profits will result in a reduction in care available to the indigent. It is claimed that these chains commonly engage in practices such as locating hospitals in areas where emergency cases involving the poor are unlikely, not equipping hospitals with emergency equipment, and even 'dumping' indigent patients on other hospitals in the vicinity. A related problem is that the chains are more likely than non-profits to take over public hospitals, and then to reduce their more general medical facilities. This practice has been increasing, and both Georgia and North Carolina have enacted legislation setting minimum levels of care for the indigent that such hospitals must provide.[50] Nor is it just the interests of the poor that are affected by for-profit takeovers; the leasing of the city hospital in Louisville to the Humana chain in 1983 led to the closing down of the hospital's burns unit. In this case, though, opposition by city firefighters led to a reversal of the policy.

4 Concluding Remarks

We have suggested in this chapter that there are a number of very different reasons for the existence of competition between charities and commercial firms, and also for co-operation between them. Both competition and co-operation are becoming more extensive, and this affects the state in a variety of ways. But the main point to note is that any major changes in the relationship between charities and for-profit firms are likely to increase demands for state intervention to regulate adverse consequences of these changes. The state itself has a direct stake in these relationships – for example, in connection with its own tax base. Yet, at the same time, the growing interpenetration of the commercial and charitable 'sectors' creates more complex relationships which make state regulation far more difficult than in the past.

4

Financial Autonomy and the 'Independent Sector'

Both at the level of political polemic and that of academic debate one of the most long-standing arguments about IOs is that a large sub-group of them constitute a separate 'sector' of society. Largely, but not exclusively, these IOs are charities. This 'sector' is viewed by its proponents as being distinct from both the for-profit sector and the state sector, and, as we have seen, it has been variously described as the 'independent sector', the 'third sector', the 'voluntary sector' and in many other ways as well.[1] Each of these terms delineates the 'sector' in a slightly different way, and certainly 'voluntary sector' can be a restrictive term.[2] But the arguments about the role of these sectors in a liberal democracy are very similar. The main feature of the 'sector' is an ability to respond to, and ameliorate, *needs* in society – needs which can be defined objectively. It differs from the market in that the latter can respond only to the *wants* people have, and, whether because of lack of resources, information or whatever, the wants satisfied in the market may well not be the same as needs. The 'sector' is separate from the state which is seen as ill equipped to respond to needs.

Many political writers who would describe themselves as pluralists are advocates of the 'third sector', but a pluralist is not committed by his/her support for autonomous non-state institutions to the view that the notion of a 'third sector' is a coherent one. A radical pluralist, for example, could take the view that provision for social needs should be made mainly (or even exclusively) by the state, while still maintaining that certain kinds of autonomous institutions in the economy are essential to democracy. Indeed the argument that there is a 'third sector' that can respond to need is unconvincing, and in this chapter we consider arguments about the autonomy of this supposed 'sector' in relation to the financial base of the organizations' operations. What we are concerned with in discussing 'autonomy' is the ability of organizations to set their priorities, and commit their resources, on the basis of evident need, rather than in response to other factors. At the level of the 'sector' as a whole, evidence of autonomy would be provided by the total supply of services matching the overall pattern of need, and by the absence of forces diverting these IOs' resources to other purposes. At the level of individual organization, indications of autonomy would be provided by the concentration of particular activities on objectives connected with the amelioration of need.

As we saw in chapter 3, the proportion of income organizations in the supposed 'independent sector' actually receive from donations, rents and investments is rather low. This suggests some caution in evaluating the claim that all the organizations in the 'sector' have the necessary autonomy to respond to need in the way indicated by their supporters. Establishing an overall picture of the degree of autonomy possessed by these institutions is very difficult, because the impact of market forces and the state is likely to vary between policy areas. In this chapter I want to argue against the plausibility of the 'independent sector' model. The main thrust of the argument presented here is that many of the 'independent' sources of income of IOs create obstacles to their response to need.

But what are needs? The problem of specifying social needs has long posed difficulties for political theorists.[3] A useful approach to the subject, which has been discussed by Weale, is to relate needs to the conditions required for people to devise and implement their own projects. Those who cannot do so adequately may be identified as being 'in need' or falling below the minimum standard of subsistence necessary for them to carry out their own projects. And, as Weale notes:

> subsistence is as much a social notion as a physical notion. What this means is that minimum needs are not simply satisfied by providing the physical necessities of life, for example adequate food, clothing and shelter, but require also for their satisfaction a level of provision for persons that is suitable for social agents, interacting with others in a specific society.[4]

The fact that a person can afford to buy some of the goods s/he requires to meet a minimum standard of subsistence, of course, does not somehow convert needs into mere wants. Indeed some needs, like food, can be supplied to most people in advanced industrial societies through the market; with other needs, like housing, the market system seems to work far less effectively both directly and indirectly. On the one hand, a free market in housing may still not generate housing for low-income earners, while on the other hand, unemployment may result in large numbers of people being unable to pay for accommodation. Nevertheless, we must recognize that meeting needs can be achieved through the market in many cases, so that needs are in no sense the special province of either charities or government.

The argument outlined here is that, if charities are to meet social needs they are likely to be most effective in doing so under conditions in which many of the parameters have been established by the state, and where the state itself can further respond to 'gaps' in need-provision left by charities. In other words, the argument is a restatement of the social democratic consensus about charities that dominated the first thirty years after the second world war. It constitutes an explicit rejection of the view that an 'independent sector' could partially take over from the state in meeting needs. First, though, we must distinguish between several different strands of opinion among the advocates of this separate 'sector'.

1 The 'Independent Sector' and Its Financial Base

The traditional argument about the 'sector' is one most associated with the nineteenth-century Charity Organization Societies (COSs). On this view the state's attempts to respond to needs would be defective in two ways. It would fail to distinguish between 'deserving' and 'undeserving' cases, and would thereby waste a large proportion of state revenues because the 'undeserving' would receive money or services, which would further discourage them from acquiring the motivation to become 'unneedy' members of society. Just as they opposed private doles by the rich to the poor, so the COSs opposed state aid as an encouragement to the 'undeserving' to do nothing about their plight. State provision would also break important social links between those with needs and those helping to ameliorate needs – links that were deemed important in eliminating claims about 'needs' that were in fact the product of failings in the individuals themselves.

A second, modern, version of this argument largely omits claims about the value of social contact between the needy and those aiding them. Instead, like the point about aid to the undeserving poor, it rests on neo-classical economic assumptions. The state is a bad distributor of goods because it is not subject to the constraints of the market. Consequently, there will tend to be an over-provision of services to ameliorate need. Organizations that are not open to political pressures are better adapted to supply them.

A third interpretation of an 'independent sector' is less hostile to the state playing at least some role in providing for needs in society. Its proponents do not seek to remove the state entirely from this role, and in some versions a welfare state of the scale established in post-war Britain is compatible with an 'independent sector'. But it is argued that even a democratic state is inefficient at responding to needs in society and that a clearly defined 'third sector' is required to ensure that needs are met. Douglas, for example, argues that:

> Weisbrod is surely right in assuming some majoritarian or populist constraint – whatever its precise form – on government that makes it inevitable that government will leave numbers of citizens unsatisfied and thus leave room for such citizens to supplement the activities of government voluntarily through nonprofit organizations.[5]

But what is it about these non-state organizations that enables them to respond to needs? Although the various adherents of the 'independent sector' hypothesis weight them differently, two main reasons are given. Both suggest the 'sector' operates in a distinctive way compared with the market and the state. The first reason is finance. It is argued that the institutions in the 'sector' are dependent neither on market transactions nor on funds raised through taxation, but on income that makes it genuinely independent from market forces or 'populist' political forces. This independent income consists mainly of donations to the organizations or of the interest generated from earlier gifts. The other factor contributing to institutional autonomy is the availability of a voluntary labour force. In part, volunteers raise funds for their organizations, but, it is claimed, volunteers perform a number of other tasks which would otherwise have to be done by paid employees. The point about volunteers is not just that they enable services to be provided free (or at a price well below the market price) to those in need, but that the presence of volunteers helps to ensure that organizations continue to be orientated to ameliorating need and do not pursue other objectives.

In the 1980s arguments about the role of a 'third sector' in society became popular in political debate in Britain and the US; in very general terms, incoming conservative administrations (in 1979 and 1981) raised the issue of the 'private sector' taking more responsibility for social welfare. How this was to be accomplished was never made very clear, as no schemes were propounded for having for-profit firms supply more welfare services (as they do, for example, in Japan), and there was little evidence that 'third sector' organizations would be able to finance a greater share of social welfare provision themselves.[6] In the event two rather different trends became apparent in the two countries. In the US cutbacks in the provision of services by the federal government did not come close to being matched by increased funding by agencies in the 'third sector'. In Britain there were also cutbacks in relation to demand for services, but there was some growth in the amount of state funds channelled to non-state agencies as a substitute for state provision (see section 6). Yet if contemporary experience does not suggest that an autonomous 'third sector' can partly take over from the state, it is worth considering whether the model of such a sector outlined by some writers provides an adequate explanation of how these organizations actually operate in a capitalist democracy. In this chapter we are concerned with the issue of their financial autonomy, while in chapter 5 we examine the role of volunteers.

Our starting point is the data on the sources of income of charities in England and the US (tables 3.1 and 3.2). Certainly at first glance it would appear that these do not provide much support for the argument that a 'third sector' would have the financial autonomy necessary to respond to the needs of a society. In England Posnett's estimate is that only 17 per cent of the income of non-religious charities is in the form of donations, rent or investment income (9 per cent donations, and 8 per cent rent and investment income).[7] (And this may well be an overestimate since Posnett's data indicates that government grants to charities were £0.56 billion in 1980, while the National Audit Office's estimate in 1987 was that funds from central government and grants from local government were three times this amount, at £1.7 billion.)[8] Again, in the US, Rudney's data indicates that only 29 per cent of such charities' income is from these sources (22 per cent donations and 7 per cent investment income).[9] In the US the crucial period in which charities became dependent on the federal government for finance was the 1960s. A decline in donations, a rise in costs, and the availability of government funds meant that charities had 'offers they could not refuse'. As Kramer notes:

> While there is a long history of governmental subsidies, grants, and payments to voluntary agencies, particularly in the field of child welfare prior to the War on Poverty, public funds had largely been restricted to governmental agencies . . . The 'takeoff' period for governmental funding of voluntary agency programmes . . . was launched by the 1967 Amendments to the Social Security Acts which provided for matching federal grants which could triple the value of contributed funds . . . The next stage of development occurred in 1974 . . . Title XX of the Social Security Act in 1974 broadened the boundaries of eligibility for the personal social services and made it possible for state and local governments to purchase more tangible services for a larger number of middle-class clients who have traditionally been served by voluntary agencies.[10]

The popular image, which its proponents do much to foster, of the 'independent sector' (that it has a distinctively non-market and non-state income) seems to be somewhat misleading. Nevertheless, even if a large proportion of income is from fees, sales, and state grants, there are four reasons which might be initially advanced for exercising some caution in immediately dismissing the whole notion of an 'independent sector' which has sufficient financial autonomy to respond to need.

(i) Many charities, of course, derive a much greater proportion of their income from donations, rent, and investments than does the 'typical' charity. Indeed, charities range from those which are heavily reliant on 'independent' income to those which have virtually none: towards one end of the spectrum are Oxfam, War on Want, and so on, and towards the other non-profit hospitals and private secondary schools. If there is an 'independent sector', which corresponds to the model we have outlined, then it is likely to be considerably smaller than even 'the charity sector'. Unfortunately, propagandists for the 'sector', such as Nielsen, Pifer and even Douglas, usually seek to take the broad view that organizations which are heavily dependent on market-type operations or on state funds are included.[11] This tends to obscure the peculiar contribution of organizations that do have 'independent' funds.

Nevertheless, donations still form a 'relatively' small component of the income of charities in some areas which are regarded popularly as

Table 4.1 Sources of support for US non-profit human service agencies (excluding hospitals and universities) in 1981, as percentage of total income

	% of total
Governments	41
Fees and service charges	28
Donations	20
Endowments	5
Other	6
Total	100

Data taken from: Lester M. Salamon, 'Government and the voluntary sector in an era of retrenchment: the American experience', paper presented at *The International Conference of Philanthropy*, Venice, 1985, table 4

being central to the 'charity sector'. Table 4.1 shows Salamon's data for the sources of support for (non-profit) human service agencies in the US excluding two of the most entrepreneurial and state-dependent institutions, hospitals and universities. Only one quarter of the income of these agencies – agencies which constitute a large sector of 501(c)(3) organizations – typically comes from donations or endowments. What his data also shows, in table 4.2, is that among none of the categories of these agencies do donations form more than 30 per cent of total

Table 4.2 Sources of income for US non-profit human service agencies, 1981 – by category and as a percentage of the total

	Donations	Fees and government grants	Other
Mental health	7	90	4
Institutional/residential health	11	83	5
Health	13	82	5
Employment/income assistance	13	65	23
Housing/community development	16	81	3
Legal service/advocacy	23	72	5
Social services	25	70	5
Education/research	25	59	16
Multi-service	25	67	6
Arts/culture/recreation	30	42	27

Data taken from: Lester M. Salamon, 'Partners in public service: the scope and theory of government-nonprofit relations', in Powell, (ed.), *The Nonprofit Sector*, table 6.5

income. While bodies like famine relief agencies, medical research charities, and (of course) churches do receive a large proportion of their income in gifts, they do not typify the 'charity sector'.[12]

(ii) Even organizations that derive a relatively small proportion of their income from 'independent' sources may have considerable freedom to control how they define need, and how they respond to it. Whether this is the case, or not, will depend on the constraints imposed by their fee income and state grant income. For example, a charity which receives 20 per cent of its income from donations might be able to devote much of this to projects which it deems most appropriate and which do not depend on other forms of funding. Much of the claim that charities are able to innovate in providing services depends on the ability to dispose of funds in this way. But another organization which obtains one fifth of its income from donations might have far less autonomy. Most of this income may have to be devoted to covering its fixed costs, so that the services it provides may reflect either what it can sell (to individuals or the state) or the projects the state deems to have priority and for which it is prepared to award grants. Alternatively, a charity may find itself trapped by earlier commitments into continuing to subsidize particular kinds of services, to which it would give lower priority if it could allocate afresh its funding of various projects. In other words, just how independent 'independent' sources of income makes a charity will vary greatly from case to case. There is no reason for assuming *a priori* that donations, rent or investment income necessarily gives an organization freedom that it lacks if it is wholly dependent on fees and grants.

(iii) By no means all fee income indicates that a charity is responding to wants rather than to needs. To take an obvious and common case, a charity might be unable to supply a service at all, or could supply it only to a very few people, if it imposed no charge. Thus it may subsidize the cost of providing the service, thereby lowering the cost to those who need it to a level that they can afford. Of course, subsidization by a charity itself is not evidence that a need is being ameliorated: an educational charity which uses its foundation funds to lower the fees charged to middle class-parents is not meeting a social need, because of the availability of qualitatively-similar state education.

The significance of charities is not just that they ameliorate need, but that they pay for goods (or services) to meet *needs that people cannot pay for themselves*. Sometimes this involves subsidization and sometimes the free provision of the good. Whether charging people for a good is evidence that a charity is not responding to need depends then on (a) whether that good forms part of the 'minimum standard of subsistence', and (b) whether all those who need that good can afford to pay the price now being charged for it without reducing their ability to acquire other goods which form part of that minimum standard. Making a small charge for a bed in a hostel, for example, is no indication of a failure to respond to need. Naturally, we cannot make generalizations about the whole range of services provided by charities. But one general point can be made. To the extent that a charity which provides for those who cannot afford to pay fully for a need has to impose charges, it is likely to switch from providing for the most needy to the less needy and to those who can afford to pay a market price. One of the arguments that has frequently been made about American social welfare agencies in the 1980s is that, faced by cutbacks in federal government funding, they tended to increase their charges, thereby shifting the relative weight of their work from clients who could not afford to pay to those who could.

(iv) Not all grants from the state compromise the operational autonomy of an organization. Especially where grants contribute to a relatively small proportion of operating costs, where payments are for particular services delivered, where the programmes funded do not create permanently dependent clients and where the state provides the organization with the maximum freedom of manoeuvre in the way it manages the programmes, the impact on organizational autonomy is likely to be small.[13] Nevertheless, there are numerous ways in which grants can compromise that autonomy, of which the following are, perhaps, some of the most important.

The most obvious constraint is that grants may have 'strings attached' which prevents the recipient from engaging in certain activities to which they would otherwise wish to devote the funds. There are many areas of policy where such restrictions appply. For example, Smith reports his interviews with officials of American voluntary agencies operating in developing countries: 'Twenty of the twenty-four indicated that their organizational freedom was impaired as a consequence of government support. The US State Department had forbidden them from using public subsidies in countries it politically blacklisted in Latin America.'[14] The acquisition of state funds might also lead to an organization taking on programmes that are tangential to its main purposes, and if they are sufficiently large this might alter the whole character of the organization. The fear that the organization may be unable to extricate itself from its relationship with the state is one that may underlie the reluctance of many voluntary organizations to accept too much government funding.

Again, even when the funds are for projects closely associated with one of the primary aims of an organization, excessive reliance on state grants may change the 'weight' it gives to its different objectives. This argument has been much used by critics of the high levels of federal government funding to universities in the US since 1945; they argue that, because this funding is almost entirely for research, there has been an adverse impact both on the kind of research undertaken at universities, and on the teaching in these institutions, especially undergraduate teaching.[15]

Furthermore, close financial ties to the state in one sphere of its activities may make it more difficult for an organization to campaign against governmental policy which is contrary to some of its other interests. This was one of the issues raised in the dispute within the National Trust in 1982 about its apparent lack of opposition to Ministry of Defence plans to build a 'military bunker' on Trust property at Bradenham. Some critics argued that the Trust had not been as active as it should have been in rallying opposition to the proposal because of its need to preserve a good working relationship with the state from which it acquired property that was provided by owners in lieu of death duties.

Then, even though its autonomy is not actually compromised, an IO may still be seen in this light by important groups of its clients. State funds may make it difficult, therefore, for it to carry out its activities in the way it would want to because of the likely response of its clients. Some voluntary development agencies operating in Central America have refused US government aid because they do not wish to be identified by those with whom they deal as agents of US policies.[16]

Even when none of the first five problems are likely to arise, an organization may still fear the disruption that would be caused to its operations if it relied too heavily on state funds and these funds were to be reduced subsequently, or withdrawn altogether. Many small community arts' groups flourished in the 1970s, but disbanded, or reformed on a much smaller scale in the 1980s, when grants from the Arts Council and local authorities declined. They had been unable to diversify their fund-raising sufficiently and could not survive in the form they had taken.

Finally, state funding may provide both a justification and an excuse for the establishment of state control later. The justification lies in the requirement that the disbursement of state funds be subject to proper systems of accountability; the excuse can emanate from policy failures, when the state can use its funding role to impose new policies on supposedly independent organizations. The Royal National Lifeboat Institution has long opposed receiving any funds from the British government because of the fear that control might be exercised subsequently. This would be most possible in areas like the lifeboat service where the service is provided directly by the state in many other countries. Nor are such fears far-fetched. As we shall see in chapter 6, the growth of state funding to British universities led ultimately to a transformation in the state/university relationship – from one in which the state protected university autonomy to one in which it used its power over the purse-strings to control many aspects of university policy.

Having considered, in general terms, some of the constraints both the market and the state may place on the autonomy of organizations seeking to respond to need, we must turn to consider the supposedly 'independent' source of IO income – donations.

2 Factors Influencing Donations to Intermediate Organizations

People contribute to mutual-benefit organizations either when an organization can provide a selective incentive or when factors other than the self-interest of the individual (such as an identification with the relevant community) are strong. We are not concerned here with these sorts of organizations, but with those providing benefits for other people. Many of these organizations are charities, but not all are. Some are debarred from this status because they embrace elements of self-help, some because the public benefits they provide are not recognized as charitable in law, and some because they are characterized as political.

Under British law Amnesty International, for example, is prevented from being a charity for this last reason. Why do people contribute to such organizations? Occasionally, as will be seen in the case of Henry Ford, there are circumstances in which donations are in the immediate self-interest of the donor. Self-interest can also be responsible for decisions to join bodies like the National Trust where membership provides free entry to Trust properties. However, economic self-interest cannot explain donations to the Trust, nor with the exception of a few cases like Ford can it explain most other donations. But, as we shall see, self-interest can be an influence in determining *how much* people will donate.

In the popular imagination altruism is the principal motive for philanthropy, but in many instances other factors are responsible for donations. These include inertia (the failure to stop a bank's standing order for a charity in which the donor has long since lost interest); convenience (it is sometimes easier to give donations than to argue with the person soliciting funds); social conformity (a desire not to be in the minority that is not wearing a charity flag); peer group pressure (social ostracism because of a failure to support a particular cause); social esteem (at some charitable functions in the US the donor often has to announce how much s/he is prepared to pledge, a device which helps to increase contributions); informal reciprocity ('you contribute to my fund-raising drive, and I'll contribute to yours later'); habit ('I've always given to this cause'); superstition ('if I don't give to the Cancer Fund I'm sure I'll be the one to get it'); and the feeling that contributing makes one part of a larger community (it was alleged, for example, that among many television viewers the Live Aid concerts produced a feeling of being part of such a community). In the market it is quite reasonable to assume that a willingness to maximize one's benefits (or, at least, not to minimize them) is usually the most important influence on behaviour; it is much less obvious with philanthropy that altruism is quite such a dominating influence. This creates obvious problems for any attempt to explain how and why contributions to charity vary over time and between societies. Constructing an explanation is made even more difficult by the absence of reliable data on donations for the years before the 1970s, and the virtual absence of any data for the pre-war years. What follows, then, is an attempt to examine some of the most general factors that we might expect to influence the willingness of people to respond to the evidence of need.

A The kind of altruism involved

Clearly the value placed on altruism in a given society (or community) influences donations to alleviate need.[17] However, altruism may take two forms, and the form it actually takes is likely to influence the level of donations. On the one hand, there is what Margolis calls 'goods altruism', where the satisfaction of the potential donor increases in relation to the goods others possess.[18] This kind of altruist is equally satisfied if s/he provides goods for other people or if some other agent does so. On the other hand, a 'participation altruist' is made happier by his/her *own contribution* to the happiness of others. In practice, of course, altruists are likely to combine the two forms to some degree, but the particular 'mix' may affect the overall donation. To the extent that a person is more motivated by 'goods altruism', s/he is likely to be concerned about the contributions made by others, and in many circumstances the mobilization of others may well yield greater donations. But the person who is more motivated by 'participation altruism' will contribute to a cause irrespective of the likelihood of eventual success in providing goods for others. The 'goods altruist', wants results and his/her own donations depend on evidence of a connection between contribution and outcome. Consequently, when they believe they live in a society of egoists, 'goods altruists' are likely to give less than would a corresponding number of 'participation altruists'. But, in a society where a large number of people could be persuaded to behave at least somewhat altruistically, 'goods altruists' are more likely to realize this potential among their fellows than 'participation altruists' are, because they value the contributions of others and will seek to organize them. The mobilization of others by pure 'participation altruists' comes about solely by the former following the example of the latter, and not by their being organized by them.

B Donations and affluence

One seemingly obvious hypothesis is that increased affluence leads to greater philanthropy, because people can afford to 'indulge' more in altruism. Clearly, if this hypothesis were correct, the richer an economy the greater proportion of personal income individuals would donate to other-regarding organizations in the society. The fragmentary evidence that is available suggests, at best, only a weak corelation between economic development and philanthropy in advanced economies. There is no relevant data for Britain. Jencks's data for the US, which he emphasizes must be treated with considerable caution, suggests that total contributions to philanthropy were slightly less than 1.5 per cent of personal income in the 1930s and increased to around 2 per cent of personal income in the 1950s.[19] But after that there was no upward movement whatsoever. Other commentators have even suggested that there was a fall in donations; some data shows that donations by individuals in the US declined by 15 per cent between 1960 and 1976,[20] and other data indicates that, as a proportion of real income they declined by 7.5 per cent between 1970 and 1981. Indeed, it was widely believed in the 1970s that despite post-war affluence, American philanthropy was facing a crisis.

We can examine the problem another way by considering the propensity of people to give to charities. Here it is better to begin by considering the available British data, because although less complete than the American data, it has one major advantage. In the US the ability of tax payers (until recently only those who 'itemized' their tax deductions) to deduct philanthropic donations from their income tax liabilities provided an increasing incentive for people to make donations as their income rose. In Britain, where the tax incentive was much smaller, the evidence of two Family Expenditure Surveys in 1980 and 1984 suggested a rather weak relationship between personal income and donations.[21] The 1980 survey showed that those earning more than £100 per week did contribute more than two and a half times as much as those earning less than £90 per week; but people earning more than £200 gave hardly any more than those earning between £100 and £200. The 1984 survey indicated a slightly more pronounced 'generosity' among the more affluent group, but even so, at 68p per week, they were still contributing a maximum of 0.34 per cent of their income.

There is one aspect of the propensity to donate in the US which seems to contrast with Britain. In Britain, for those individuals earning between £2,601 and £10,400 in 1984 donations as a proportion of income were remarkably similar (table 4.3). However, in the US many studies have found that there is a pronounced 'U'-shaped curve when the propensity to give is plotted against income. The poor typically give a greater proportion of their income to charity than do middle-income groups, and it is only around the $50,000 income level that the propensity to give starts to increase again.[22] Table 4.4, which relates only to those who itemize their tax returns, illustrates this tendency. It suggests one possible problem with the model of an 'independent sector' responding to need. Excluding the very rich, the greatest donors to charity in the US (in relation to their income) are the very groups that might be expected to be the main beneficiaries of policies designed to provide for social needs.

Table 4.3 Donations to charities by individuals in Britain in 1984, by income group

Annual income (£)	Percentage of own income donated by median donor in group	Total amount given to charities annually by mean donor (£)
0–2,600	not available	7
2,601–3,120	0.3	9
3,121–3,640	0.3	9
3,641–4,160	0.4	14
4,161–4,680	0.3	14
4,681–5,200	0.4	18
5,201–6,500	0.3	17
6,501–7,800	0.3	20
7,801–9,100	0.2	17
9,101–10,400	0.3	30
10,401 and above	not available	35

Calculated from data cited in *Charity Statistics 1985–86*, p. 138

Table 4.4 Donations to US charities by taxpayers who itemize their taxes, 1981

Adjusted gross income ($)	Deductions from donations as percentage of adjusted gross income	Mean charitable donations ($)
under 5,000	6.1	
5,000–9,999	6.3	181
10,000–14,999	4.5	490
15,000–19,999	3.4	574
20,000–24,999	2.7	613
25,000–29,999	2.3	643
30,000–49,999	2.3	885
50,000–99,999	2.7	1,709
100,000–499,999	4.1	6,560
500,000 and above	8.9	90,880

Data taken from: Christopher Jencks, 'Who gives to what?', in Powell, (ed.), *The Nonprofit Sector*, p. 323

C Religious observance

We might expect that the greater amount of religious observance in a society, the greater the propensity to donate to charities. Of all groups to which individuals belong, religions provide the greatest pressure to be philanthropic. There are two quite distinct ways in which this occurs. Churches and other religious organizations openly solicit funds for their own operations, and donations are easily their largest source of income. But their focus more generally on charity may be expected to increase contributions to non-religious charities as well. The first point is well illustrated by comparing Britain and the US. Depending on the measure of observance used, participation in a church or similar religious body is about four times higher in the US, where about 40 per cent of the population are regular attenders, than in Britain.[23] (Indeed, America is, by far, the most religious large industrial state in the western world.)[24] In Britain, including the income of church charities with that of other charities does increase the share of income derived from donations, rents and investments, from 17 to 24 per cent of total income. However, in the US the inclusion of religious charities increases this element of income even more – from 29 to 40 per cent of the total.

The role of religion in America is also shown, perhaps, by the 'U'-shaped curve. A large proportion of the donations by the poor goes to churches, whereas among those with high incomes, hospitals, universities and arts organizations are increasingly favoured. Jencks's conjecture is that these donations to churches, along with other donations by the poor, reflect an attitude of 'paying your dues', while among the rich the dominant ethos is that of 'giving away your surplus'.[25] But, in a comparative perspective, we have to explain why 'due paying' should be so prevalent among the *American* poor, and here the penetration of the churches into poor communities would seem to offer a possible explanation. The failure of the churches, especially the Anglican church, to penetrate most working-class communities in Victorian Britain established a tradition that was suspicious of charities and their 'Lady Bountiful' mentors. Whatever dues the British working class believed they had to pay, these were much less likely to be 'debts' to a church or a charity.

The more general hypothesis that religious observance encourages donations to non-religious charities is almost impossible to substantiate. Certainly donations are much higher in the US than in other western states, but how much should this be attributed to the tax structure, to general cultural norms which equate charity as being part of the 'American way', or to the impact of churches over the years? The data on which comparisons between countries are made is notoriously unreliable, and estimates of the difference vary. Obler cites data from 1973 indicating that Americans donate about seven times more to charity *per capita* than the British.[26] Bakal cites data for 1978 showing an even greater gap between the two countries: the average contribution in the US then was $180 per year, about nine times greater than in Britain.[27] A more recent survey conducted by the Charities Aid Foundation, in 1985, suggests that this data may have exaggerated the difference between the two countries and that the average American gives only about four and a half times as much as his/her British counterpart.[28]

D A tradition of volunteerism

One of the most widely accepted ideas among Americans is that the US has a peculiarly strong tradition of giving help to others, and this tradition of volunteering is often invoked as an explanation of why individuals today continue to give far more to charities than their fellows in other advanced economies. Now, obviously, if there were a tradition of giving to charities, we might expect, *ceteris paribus*, that this would continue in some form. But this observation merely prompts two further points – is the tradition of volunteering so especially American, and what exactly is the relationship between voluntarily helping others and donating money to charities?

In response to the first point, there are two related aspects of the American historical experience to which attention is usually drawn when discussing volunteering. On the seventeenth- and eighteenth-century rural 'frontiers', and again in the nineteenth-century multi-ethnic cities, mutual help became a central feature of social life; the absence of alternative mechanisms of aid forced communities (whether geographically or ethnically defined) into co-operation as an insurance against disaster. Furthermore, as Tocqueville noted in the 1830s, Americans tended to join associations of various kinds – something which reflected not just the frontier tradition of 'mutually insuring against disaster', but also the quasi-democratic culture which had emerged in a state without a feudal tradition. This having been said, a commentator looking at Britain and the US in the late nineteenth century might have been struck by the parallel developments in the two societies in relation to volunteering. As we shall see in chapter 5, in both countries voluntary work by the middle classes in working-class communities emerged and the Charity Organization Society was a British institution that was successfully transplanted to the US. As we noted in chapter 2, working-class institutions promoting mutual aid were arguably stronger in Britain than in the US. In the twentieth century the great American achievement has been to institutionalize voluntary help to others – the tradition of associating has, arguably, resulted in relatively more voluntary organizations than in Britain and in more participation directed through them.[29] But at the same time the market has tended to erode the voluntary spirit more in the US than in the Britain. This was an argument made by Titmuss in relation to the donation of blood; as Obler, discussing Titmuss's view, notes:

> The commercialization of blood in the United States promotes self-interest, stifles selflessness, and generally, adversely affects people's disposition to give. The British are more inclined to give blood because it cannot be sold as a commodity; there is no private market to dissuade them from giving. The private market, then, moulds people's values; it erodes altruism.[30]

If we were to try to measure the amount of voluntary aid given in Britain and the US we might well find that assistance to others that was *not* channelled through formal voluntary associations was greater in the former. As Obler's own study demonstrates, the 'volunteer spirit' survived the advent of the welfare state in Britain, though voluntarism tends to 'prosper especially in those phases of public life in which the state takes no more than a negligible interest'.[31] If there is a peculiarly American tradition of voluntary help, it probably relates more to the forums through which help is channelled than to the overall level of aid provided.

Now this last point helps to answer the second question raised above, as to the relationship between voluntarily assisting others and the donation of money to charities. The much greater institutionalization of assistance to others in the US has facilitated much greater fund-raising through donations. Along with a distrust of 'charity' which the (largely) non-religious British working-class tradition helped to bring about earlier this century, Britain has generally lacked (in relation to the US) the organizational structures to transform volunteerism into monetary gifts.

E Disasters and less immediate needs

Obviously, people can respond to need by donating money to aid those 'in need' only when they become aware of the problem. Given that there are so many needs to which funds could be devoted, even the most determined altruist would face a formidable task in deciding where to direct his/her funds. One of the most common responses is to direct funds to particular causes, in the hope that others will make different decisions and that, overall, every need, or rather every need forming part of the 'minimum subsistence' in a society, will have been responded to. But how do people decide which causes to support? Of course, much of the time habit, self-esteem and so on are involved so that the issue of a *choice* does not arise, but there are occasions when it does, and how people choose affects the amelioration of need. Often they donate to those causes in which their own families have been amongst those in need – as when a family member has suffered from a particular disease for which there is not a cure. Even when there is no personal connection of this kind, choices depend on the potential donor actually knowing about a need and regarding it as worthy of immediate attention. At one extreme are well-publicized disasters where the donating public can empathize with the victims; Aberfan (where a coal tip slid down upon a mining village killing 14 people in 1966), the Penlee lifeboat, the Bradford City fire (which killed 55 people at a fire in 1985), and the Ethiopian famine were all of this type. Occasional tragedies like this give fund-raisers few problems in commanding the attention of donors, once the disaster is actually known about. At the other extreme are cases where both the number of victims and the effects on their lives may be just as great, but where the victims are not part of a collective 'incident' which can command much attention; popular prejudice that the need is not that serious, or even the fault of the victims themselves, further increases the problems of fund-raisers. Mental illness is such a cause, and its charities have always been able to raise much less money than, say, cancer charities.

Television appears to have affected the pattern of contributions in the post-war years by giving publicity to causes that might not 'touch' most people directly. It is at least arguable that famine relief charities and those engaged in medical research would not have become such large recipients of individual gifts in the absence of vivid images of sufferers which television can present more completely than other media. Conversely, causes which impinge more on the everyday lives of people, such as charities for sick animals, can rely more on street collections to generate adequate funds without publicity on television. The main point to which we are drawing attention here, though, and it is one to which we return shortly, is the potential gap between actual need and the perception of need by donors.[32] Unlike the consumer who may be presumed to know his/her own interests best, the donor is usually most unlikely to be in the best position to determine the relative importance of different needs, even when his/her contribution involves a *decision*.

F Institutional structures

We would expect that how people respond to need when they become aware of it would be influenced greatly by the institutional structures relating to need which they face when considering a donation. In this regard three aspects of the institutional framework are worth special consideration: the organization of the need-ameliorating agencies, the part played by the state in meeting needs, and the incentive provided by the tax system to make donations. We discuss briefly these aspects in turn.

We have noted already the much greater organizational framework relating to voluntary work in the US, and the likely impact this has on overall fund-raising there. But this very framework can also impede certain kinds of responses to need. This is most clearly evident in the different response to the Live Aid concerts (held in London and Philadelphia) which Bob Geldof encountered in the US:

> We discovered that, unlike in Britain where everyone was working for nothing, in the States almost everyone expected to be paid. Only the bands and the promoters and Mitchell's crowd, Worldwide Sports and Entertainments, were working without payment; all the technical people, the PA and light companies, and everybody who was a member of a union had to be paid . . . We cursed, but we realized that we just had to live with it. Philadelphia cost $3.5 million. Wembley cost $250,000.[33]

The problem faced by Geldof was not, of course, antagonism to voluntary activity in the US; rather Geldof's plan did not fit into the philanthropic organizational structure helpers in the US were used to facing, and they responded by treating it as a commercial proposition. In Britain the much weaker penetration of society by organized charities meant that there was much greater scope for persuading people to provide their services free of charge. Businesses and employees in Britain were in some doubt as to who should be doing something about the Ethiopian tragedy, and were prepared to assume some responsibility themselves through the Geldof project. Persuasion is more difficult to implement when decision-makers have clearer views about whose responsibility a particular problem is, and how their own activity relates to that.

In some circumstances, then, a highly developed philanthropic institutional structure can actually hinder the response to need; this can occur when the existing institutions are incapable of responding sufficiently themselves, and new ways of soliciting funds have to be tried. A less comprehensive system of charity may be advantageous in stimulating private responses to emergencies.

The effect of *public* institutions on the willingness of people to contribute to philanthropic causes has long been controversial. Since the nineteenth century opponents of state welfare provision have argued that it would depress the 'charitable spirit' and lead both donors and recipients to expect that the state would always intervene. The result would be the rapid decline, and eventual obliteration, of philanthropy and self-reliance. While this argument is most usually associated with *laissez faire* economists and social theorists, it has also been a major strand in anarchist thought which has stressed the state's impact on co-operation between people.[34]

For several reasons empirical evidence relevant to the alleged crowding out of charity by state activity is difficult to interpret.[35] Many studies seek only to relate levels of state provision of services to direct financial donations to charities, so that the more general issue of whether state provision crowds out all forms of altruistic behaviour is usually not addressed. Not surprisingly, there is evidence that 'crowding out' may occur in regard to some kinds of services but not others. Moreover, since there are a very large number of variables which are likely to affect levels of individual giving, and which are difficult to build into any analysis relating state provision of services to overall donations, most of the studies are unconvincing in demonstrating a direct causal relationship.

The most radical challenge to the view of the state as the enemy of charity has come, of course, from Titmuss.[36] From his study of blood-donation, Titmuss concluded that services like the National Health Service actually provide the best environment in which the ethic of giving could thrive.

Few empirical studies have attempted to consider together the many different aspects of the relation of donations to state provision. One of the few that has, Obler's analysis of private giving in an English village, indicates a more complex situation than that envisaged by most protagonists in the debate. Obler concludes that monetary donations for the disadvantaged are depressed, especially direct gifts from donors to known recipients, by state provision and that Titmuss's example of blood is probably a highly unusual example of a state framework assisting altruism. But he also concludes that donations even in areas where the state is involved have survived, and the main thrust of his argument is that 'a society need not sacrifice private benevolence when it takes on the commitment to assure its citizens the right to economic and social security'.[37]

The impact of provisions in tax codes for allowance to be made for charitable donations has been the subject of considerable study by economists. Tax structures affect donations in various ways. Most noticeably they affect higher-income earners, and it is widely agreed that gifts from these individuals are highly sensitive to alterations in tax rates and in the conditions under which gifts can be made. The ability of donors to balance donations against their income tax liability, as in the United States, encourages giving, such that any alteration in these arrangements is likely to have a major impact on charities. This became especially controversial in the mid 1980s when federal income tax reform was being debated in Congress; several of the proposals would have eliminated the charitable tax deduction altogether, while others would have modified it. On some estimates the removal of the deduction might have reduced charitable donations in the US by one third. But high-income earners do not just give money, they often donate property – company shares as well as real estate. Changes in laws on capital gains, for example, most surely influence contributions, as do laws relating to capital transfers and death duties. One example of this in Britain is the incentive provided to owners of works of art to donate them in partial lieu of death duty, as a way of preserving the 'national heritage'. As Schuster notes, 'These provisions are . . . designed to preserve and provide access to the best examples of the nation's artistic and cultural heritage while providing tax advantages for the owner and, at the same time, limiting the actual cost to the Exchequer.'[38]

What is evident from this brief survey of the factors influencing charitable donations by individuals is that overall the link between giving and the ability of charities to respond to need seems to be, at best, indirect. In the next section a more radical thesis is outlined. There we suggest that the income provided by donations yields the very opposite of the kind of income required by responsiveness to social needs – it is similar to income generated by the market, in that it reflects individuals' wants and tastes.

3 Do Donations Provide Sufficiently 'Independent' Income for Charities?

At the heart of the arguments to be outlined in this section is a point that was made in section 2(E) above – that donors are very often in a poor position to understand the pattern of social needs in a society, so that to the extent it is dependent on donations, a 'charity sector' would be ill-placed to meet needs. This problem was partly understood by the Charity Organization Societies, who wanted to eliminate doles from the rich to the poor and to have 'scientific charity', centred on their own organizations, where decisions about the best use of donations could be made by experts. But the problem is more deep-rooted than even the COSs realized. Some arguments we consider are at the macro-level (of the 'sector' as a whole), but first mention must be made of the ways in which the tastes of, and information possessed by, the donors, as well as the activities of those raising funds, may affect the pursuit of its need-related objectives by an individual charity.

One constraint facing individual charities, which obviously varies from one to another, is that donors may place restrictions on how their gifts are to be used. Through ignorance of the relative importance of the needs which the organization is trying to ameliorate, or because of their own tastes, donors may specifically direct funds to 'marginal' projects. In many instances a charity can get round this by 'shuffling' other funds around, but in the case of large gifts a charity's activities may be determined as much by the whims of the donor as by the professional administrators' perceptions of relative need. Donor control can be increased by tax incentives to donate. Until the British Finance Act of 1980 there was a marked difference between Britain and the US in this regard, with the latter facilitating much greater donor influence by providing a tax deduction for donors. In Britain donations have not been tax-deductible for the donor, but in the case of covenants charities have been able to reclaim the income tax paid (until 1980 only at the standard rate) by the donor on the income s/he subsequently gave to them. As far as a charity is concerned, until 1980 deeds of covenant yielded two elements of income. The money coming directly from the donor could have restrictions on use placed on it. However, there was also the money coming directly from the Inland Revenue, the refunded tax paid by the donor, on which, of course, there were no donor-sponsored restrictions. However, in making it possible for charities to reclaim tax which had been paid at rates above the standard rate, the 1980 Act essentially removed one of the key differences between a tax deduction scheme and a covenanting scheme. This point has been summarized well by Schuster:

> The reforms of the deed of covenant in the Finance Act of 1980 have moved the deed of covenant closer to the charitable contribution deduction in two respects: for taxpayers with the same marginal tax rates, the financial incentives for charitable giving are now identical in both systems, and with higher rate relief donors have been given the opportunity to restrict the expenditure of a portion of the taxes foregone via the deed of covenant.[39]

Restrictions placed on the use of donations can have truly perverse effects on the amelioration of need. In the US one of the best-known instances of this was the Buck Foundation. Established in 1975 on the death of the donor, the Foundation's capital was worth over $435 million by the mid 1980s. However, the bequest provided for the needy in Marin County, California – one of the wealthiest counties in the country, where there was hardly anyone in need. None of the Foundation's income could be used to provide for the numerous poor people in nearby San Francisco or Oakland.

As well as this direct way in which donors can limit the autonomy of charities in responding to need there are indirect ways in which donations can have this effect. This occurs when, in return for a donation, a charity provides an individual benefit for the donor. The charity may then end up by gearing its fund-raising to satisfying the wants of the donors, and in some circumstances this could lead to the charity focusing more on meeting the demands of donors than in satisfying needs. In this case the *modus operandi* of the body might change. Usually, of course, the problems of 'responding to the market' arise more in relation to membership fees than to gifts. (For example, the fact that membership of the National Trust permits members to enter Trust properties free of charge might create a clientele among the membership that has wants for services from the Trust that are partially incompatible with its main objectives. It has been alleged by its critics that the Trust gives too much weight to maintaining stately homes in the south of England, which are much visited by members, and too little to acquiring open countryside, especially in the north of England, which is accessible free of charge to all.) But there are cases where specific benefits have been tied to gifts. In 1985 the Inland Revenue objected to a practice of the Royal Society for the Protection of Birds of granting free admission to its sites to people who covenanted money to it. The Revenue's objection was that such an arrangement amounted to turning a donation into a transaction. In this context the important point is that transaction-type donations may make possible some displacement in a charity's goals so that it is less responsive to the needs it is supposedly meeting.

Goal-displacement within a charity can occur in other ways as well. Fund-raising may come to dominate the activity of volunteers, so that social service agencies, for example, become less orientated towards the services they originally provided, and research bodies focus more attention on aspects of research that will best help attract funds. Most British medical research charities, for example, have supported the dual system of funding that has emerged, in which the Medical Research Council funds basic research and the charities fund research directly related to a disease. The image that they are trying to find a 'cure' for a disease is essential to their fund-raising, so that even in cases (such as AIDS) where extensive basic research is almost certainly a prerequisite for eradicating the disease, charities want to be seen to be sponsoring 'disease-solving' research. Goal-displacement is a problem common to all organizations that encounter difficulties in obtaining the money they require.[40] Bulpitt, for example, has argued that local Conservative party organizations in Britain do not have time to devote to discussing issues of public policy, because nearly all their activities are organized around raising funds for the next election campaigns.[41] In the case of charities, the greatest problems are likely to arise when changed circumstances mean that the organization should be considering a redefinition of the needs to which it responds. But sometimes the desire to raise funds actually leads to a perversion of a charity's goals. This was a problem with Boy's Town – a juvenile community organization in the US sufficently well known for a movie to be made about it in 1938 (with Spencer Tracy as its star). Later it was discovered that Boy's Town was so concerned with raising money that it admitted only those boys for whom there was a very high chance of 'reform'.[42]

The failure of a charity to replace its objectives, because they are central to its fund-raising efforts, can equally undermine responses to needs. Public identification with the provision of a particular service may be so central to its fund-raising that a charity may fail to recognize that a need might be better provided by some other means. With one exception, charities in Britain are permitted to have the same purposes as other charities, so that substantial overlap does occur.[43] In the area of visual handicap there is not only duplication, but an unwillingness to have the state involved in the provision of services. As Kramer has argued, 'Affiliates of national organizations in both England and Israel resisted the policy of referring clients to government health services for aids, appliances, and other services.'[44]

However, it is at the macro-level that the main doubts arise about the role of donations in providing for sufficient autonomy for charities to enable them to identify and respond to need. Donations, though not income from earlier donations in the form of interest and rents, constitute a highly imperfect market mechanism subject to what Fred Hirsch called 'tyranny by small decision making'.[45] There is a tendency for individuals to give to those charities which, at a particular moment, happen to capture public imagination or sentiment, and this has given rise to several problems. In the case of appeals to aid the victims of disasters where the number of victims is relatively small, public sympathy can lead to the appeal raising too much money because each individual is giving without reference to what others will give. One of the best documented instances of this was the Aberfan tragedy, to which a shocked public contributed *so* generously that the appeal fund subsequently faced controversy as to what it should actually do with the money. The problem is compounded by English charity law which circumscribes how much can be given to the victims of disasters or their relatives. (For this reason, there was considerable debate after the Penlee lifeboat disaster as to the legal form that a fund for the families of the dead men should take. It became clear that if a charity were formed there might well be problems in distributing the vast amount of money that was being sent in. The fund established subsequently for the victims of the fire at the Bradford City football ground took the form of a discretionary trust rather than a charity, and this now appears to be the preferred model in such cases.) But the problem that each individual donor is contributing without knowledge of how others will contribute has more general application than this. Even in a world of informed altruists, co-ordinating donations to a large number of charities, so that the services provided were an appropriate response to relative needs, would be extremely difficult.

Nevertheless, as we have already noted, factors apart from altruism influence donations to charity, and the vast majority of donors are ignorant about the relative merits of particular causes. Donors are at a disadvantage in that they do not experience directly what they 'buy', compared with the market for private goods, and the result is that the distribution of donations is often unrelated to need. (It is not *always* unrelated to need, as the experience of the Band Aid Trust, which became the charity with the largest income in the UK in 1985–6, demonstrated.) Thus we find that charities for the blind have always found it much easier to raise money than those for the deaf, although the resources required for special training and education by those who have the latter disability are no less. Moreover, legacies tend to reflect the popularity of causes a generation or two earlier – St Dunstan's continued to benefit from legacies, although the group of first-world-war victims for whose benefit it was set up was diminishing to relatively small numbers even by the 1960s.[46] Finally, it need hardly be added, there is the particular eccentricity of the British in contributing excessively to charities for animals rather than people: the RSPCA, for example, was one of the twenty largest recipients of voluntary income in each of the years between 1982 and 1985.[47]

So far our discussion of donations has focused on individuals; but what of companies? Are they more able through their charitable donations to reduce the problems we have just outlined? It is important to address these questions, because in the 1980s the Reagan administration, and to a much lesser extent the Thatcher administration, argued that companies should fill the gap left by state reductions in welfare provision. In fact, for all the emphasis placed on developing this aspect of philanthropy, total financial donations made by companies are fairly small in relation to those of individuals.[48] In Britain the largest two hundred company donors in 1980, and they accounted for the greater part of corporate contributions, provided a mere 0.5 per cent of all donations that year. Even in the the US, where there is a much stronger tradition of corporate donations, they still provide only 5.5 per cent of all donations annually, and philanthropy is concentrated very heavily in the largest corporations. Nevertheless, there does seem to have been an increase in corporate donations since the 1940s, as a proportion of companies' pre-tax income.[49] But this growth has been unsteady: donations more than doubled between 1940 and 1960, but then declined and did not reach the 1960 level again until 1980.

An indication of the relatively small sums involved in Britain can be seen by noting a problem facing researchers examining trends in corporate donations. In a commentary in 1986 on trends in charity finances, it was argued that a single, one-off, large donation made by Marks and Spencer in 1983–4 seriously distorted an analysis of trends in corporate giving since 1983. It was suggested that it was more appropriate to exclude this donation from the analysis. The donation which produced such distortion was for 'only' £3.4 million![50] A major advantage charities have had in the US in obtaining funds from companies is that donations can be taken as a deduction against a company's business expenses. This development, though, has had a somewhat complicated history. The 1917 federal income tax law followed the principle laid down in an English court decision of 1883 in allowing as business expenses only items that provided direct benefit to a company, and this excluded charitable gifts. However, in the 1920s donations to Community Chests (which we will discuss in section 4) were treated differently and permitted as benefiting a company directly. This was reversed by a court decision in 1934, although lobbying in Congress the following year resulted in legislation which eliminated this obstacle. Donations to other kinds of charities remained non-deductible, and it was not until 1953, in the decision of *Smith v. Barlow* that the legal basis for wide-ranging donations to charity was firmly secured.

Like individuals, companies face a myriad of organizations to which they can contribute, and like individuals most prefer to give so that their own contribution can be seen as 'making a difference', rather than dividing it between many charities in a 'balanced' response to social need. While some companies, especially in the US, employ administrators to co-ordinate their grants and donations programmes, so that some of the excesses of ignorance and prejudice manifested in individual giving are less common, there are still huge biases introduced into the overall pattern of giving. Educational organizations alone receive more than 40 per cent of total corporate gifts. Usually companies do not wish to be associated with unpopular social causes, however pressing the needs in that area are. Moreover, they are more likely to stay clear of areas which are politically controversial, or where liberal and left-wing political activists are involved with the charities. This tendency for corporations to support certain kinds of charitable activity, and not to respond evenly to the overall pattern of need in society, has been reinforced by a new development, especially pronounced in the US, of linking charitable donations to a firm's advertising.

Companies have always understood the benefits derived from being seen to contribute to charity. As the *New York Times* commented in 1985: 'Companies have long given money to a wide variety of causes to establish themselves as responsible citizens. But it is only in the last few years that they have found that they can tie a do-gooder image to their sales efforts.'[51] That year several major corporations, including American Express and General Foods, embarked on huge advertising campaigns to promote their products in conjunction with publicity for (and donations to) charities. In some instances, as with American Express, special charities were created, while in others contributions were made to existing organizations. As with all corporate gifts, image has been important. Organizations to promote community development are acceptable, as are virtually any agencies helping children, but the less popular causes have been notable by their absence.

4 Co-operative Fund-raising: a Solution to the Problems of the 'Market'?

One answer to the problem of the tyranny of small decisions in relation to charities, and to biases in patterns of donations, is to invoke the state. But if this is ruled out, as it is by those who see need-provision as the preserve of a 'third sector', what of the possibility of co-ordination of fund-raising by charities themselves? This brings us to the subject of federated fund-raising, which grew rapidly in the US (and Canada) earlier in the twentieth century, but failed to do so in England.

Co-operation among charitable groups first emerged in a few American cities at the end of the nineteenth century, in an effort to remove what was seen as the destructive competitiveness between different charities in their annual fund-raising drives. One fund-raising campaign replaced the many, and the money was then distributed between the co-operating bodies. The movement became nationwide during the first world war, with towns and cities developing 'Community Chests'; there were fund-raising drives once a year with local charities participating in the drives and in the distribution of funds. The war was a catalyst for this; new needs were emerging from the conflict in Europe, and the decentralized systems of raising money were inadequate to deal with the greater impulse to donate generated by the war. If for no other reason, consolidation of fund-raising was necessary to prevent fraud and waste in the charity arena. In the years after the second world war the

Community Chests were transformed into United Funds – organizations which today describe themselves as being part of the United Way.

The two main developments in these later years were the inclusion of several national charities, such as the American Red Cross, within the system of federated fund-raising, and the use of payroll deduction schemes in participating companies. By 1978 the income raised by the United Way each year was $1.2 billion. Moreover, it has a high visibility; for example, the National Football League pays for United Way advertisements during most televised games. Yet the apparent success of the United Way must be put in a broader context. In 1980 donations to it formed only about 5 per cent of all donations to non-religious philanthropic bodies in the US. In addition, as Kramer has pointed out, during the 1960s and 1970s the member agencies received a decreasing proportion of their income from its federated fund-raising. With 'third-party government' expanding in the US, federated funds constituted no more than about 20 per cent of the income of United Way agencies in the late 1970s.[52] The incentive to accept federal government money had been so great that in 1967 the United Way had had to change its traditional policy of discouraging member agencies from accepting governmental funds to one in which it worked in partnership with the state.

Unlike the original COSs which had been transplanted successfully to the US in the late nineteenth century, federated fund-raising did not prove equally popular on both sides of the Atlantic. It was first introduced in Liverpool in 1873 but did not catch on in Britain; an English clergyman introduced it in Denver in 1887, and it became more extensive at the end of the decade and in the early part of the twentieth century. However, the organization which became the model for others was one formed in Cleveland, Ohio in 1913, following six years of planning, by a group of businessmen involved in the local Chamber of Commerce.[53] (One minor consequence of its failure in Britain has been that several generations of British players of the board game 'Monopoly' have been puzzled by the term 'Community Chest' which plays some part in it.) Co-operation between British charities in fund-raising has occurred, but it is much more related to specific situtations in which competition would be, and would be seen to be, undesirable. For example, the UK Disasters Emergency Committee consists of the leading relief agencies which come together after a disaster has been identified. They take it in turns to be the 'public front' for particular disasters, and they pool all money donated for that cause and distribute it equally between themselves.

It is not entirely clear why permanent federated fund-raising did not become established in Britain. One possible explanation is that its rapid development in the US coincided with a weakening of ties in Britain between businessmen and charity, and it was business leadership that was crucial in the establishment of Community Chests. After the first world war British business was faced by long periods of economic depression and business leaders were less disposed to take a lead in the 'organization' of charity than their nineteenth century predecessors had been. By the time prosperity returned in the years after 1945, a welfare state was hastily being constructed and the break between business communities and charities became yet more complete. Furthermore, as Heidenheimer argues, this same period was one in which the English churches withdrew from welfare activity; citing points made by Norman, he suggests that:

> During the inter-war period, the 'acceptance of collectivist principles' had become 'very general' in the Church of England leadership, which had come to 'look to the state to initiate the required social reforms'. Thus in 1930 their convocation had urged the government to 'introduce as soon as possible legislation which will facilitate the abolition of the slums'.[54]

The orientation of the Church of England away from private solutions to welfare issues left businessmen without one of the principal allies they would have had in organizing co-operative efforts at fund-raising.

However, if co-operation through federated fund-raising in the US has resolved some of the problems of competition between charities, it has not been a solution to the problem of how, in the absence of the state, to make charities respond to an overall pattern of need. One problem has been that the unanimity among charitable organizations necessary for this sort of scheme to work has not been achieved, and the United Way has sometimes sought to impose itself as a monopoly adopting a ruthless attitude towards other charities. It has excluded charities it has not liked and has tried to coerce other charities into joining its federated funding. The large national medical research charities have usually been at the centre of these disputes, for often they have not been convinced that they would gain from participation in the United Way. But, at times, the United Way has also competed fiercely with other payroll deduction schemes. In one case an organization in southern California, the Associated In-Group Donors, sued the United Way after its income declined from $18 million in 1976 to $8.5 million in 1977.[55]

A further objection to the United Way has been that its links to business have been so close that it has tended to support safe, respectable charitable organizations catering primarily, though not exclusively, for white America. In the past this has led to lawsuits, boycotts and other action against the United Way by activists in black and other communities. To some extent it has attempted to change its image in recent years, at least by involving organizations that directly benefit ethnic minorities.

But it remains a body that must be partly responsive to the business community which has done so much to make possible its fund-raising, and this undermines its claims to always be able to respond to social need. Nevertheless, it is a measure of how important federal government funds have become, even to the United Way, that, along with many other charities, it was a vocal opponent of the social welfare cutbacks of the Reagan administration. While its close links to the business community suggest parallels with the nineteenth century COSs, there is a crucial difference between the two. Like the COSs, the United Way values voluntarism, but it cannot afford to support this to the exclusion of federal government programmes and grants.

Today, while the position of the United Way in the American charity universe is relatively secure, it is not really an expanding form of philanthropy. Its security lies in the fact that those companies which support it do not want to incur the administrative costs they would face if they let in other payroll deduction schemes. The public utility firm Consolidated Edison of New York rejected a request from employees that deductions to the Black United Fund be permitted on the ground that the company would then have to open its doors to any scheme.[56] Yet at the same time the United Way is being threatened in two ways. The share of corporate donations to philanthropy going to federated schemes has declined dramatically, as corporations increasingly deal directly with the charities themselves. Furthermore, individual donors seem to want more say in determining where their donations go, and there has been an increase in United Way schemes which allow employee participation in determining the destination of donations.[57] Implemented on a small scale this does not pose a problem for the United Way but, taken together with challenges from black and other groups, it suggests a process of fragmentation that could produce division within the United Way when some of the traditional charities find their United Way funding to be in relative decline. As Polivy has observed in relation to the participatory scheme introduced by the United Way in San Francisco in 1978:

> While the Donor Option Plan may have worked to silence some critics, it may have aroused others, particularly those member agencies that believe that their allocations may be reduced in the long run because of diversion of funds from the general campaign to designations. Critics of the Donor Option Plan claim that it is antithetical to the concept of the United Way 'where a committee of local knowledgeable individuals determines where the money should be spent.'[58]

Payroll deduction schemes today have been made relatively easy by computerization, and as the schemes now being introduced in Britain demonstrate, they can be run without an intermediary of the traditional

United Way kind. (Under the provisions of the 1986 Finance Act employers make arrangements with approved agency charities, such as the Charities Aid Foundation, which then distributes the donations to the charities nominated by the donor.) Co-operative fund-raising, then, would not seem to provide a solution to the 'market-type' problems donations pose for charities in systematically responding to need.

5 Philanthropic Foundations

There is, of course, one set of philanthropic organizations which would seem ideally placed to respond to an overall pattern of social needs – both because they have large resources and because they are staffed by professionals who can determine priorities among competing needs. These are foundations, or grant-making trusts. The foundation is an American innovation which took hold in the first thirty years of the twentieth century and which has been copied elsewhere. The principal characteristics of the modern foundation are that it derives most of its income from endowments, it makes grants to agencies for projects or administers projects directly, it is controlled by a self-perpetuating board of trustees, and it is run by a professional staff which operates independently from the original benefactor. In other words, foundation funds are not tied directly to the preferences of donors and, because those who determine foundation policy are not the agents of benefactors, more objective responses to competing needs are possible. Yet it must be acknowledged that not all foundations are of this type. Especially between the late 1930s and 1969, many foundations were set up in the US to further the interests of particular companies (by providing benefits to employees, to further the company's image with the public, or for tax-reduction purposes), and which were actually controlled by those who ran the company.

The origins of the foundation are too complex to discuss adequately here, and in the US, at least, there are several types of foundation with important differences between them. However, there are a number of factors which must be understood in explaining the emergence of the first foundations. The social tensions prompted by industrialization intensified in the 1890s, producing problems which existing non-Marxist theories of state and economy seemed unable to explain adequately or help resolve. There was a belief among some sections of the American socio-economic elite that there was a crisis in American society and that adequate knowledge as to how to resolve it was not available. With the exception of the universities, the traditional IOs in America seemed ill-suited to help in this resolution: they were too localized and too much focused on merely easing the manifestations of social tensions. (The research-orientated university, on the other hand, seemed a useful tool in the search for explanations for major social problems and, like the foundation, was to expand greatly in the twentieth century.) Again, the federal government could not be instrumental in crisis-resolution in the way that national governments in Europe could. The structure of institutions set up by the Founding Fathers, the continuing influence of the Jeffersonian-Jacksonian traditions of power devolution, and the settlement which was reached at the end of Reconstruction in 1876 all worked against the use of national political institutions. Indeed, it was not until the Great Depression that a political leader could even contemplate a central role for the federal government, and then it was used mainly to alter power imbalances in American society and economy.[59]

Trusts for specific purposes had existed in nineteenth century America, and indeed have a long history in English law, but the crucial innovation of the twentieth century was that trusts were to be created for which specific purposes were not designated, so that neither the donors nor later trustees were restricted with respect to the needs with which the foundation could concern itself.[60] However, to use their funds most effectively, many foundations did choose to direct attention to a relatively small range of needs – for example, by concentrating on the eradication of a disease. Whatever control a philanthropist might hope to exercise over his/her creation, the normal pattern was for foundations very quickly to come under the direction of a professional staff. By the 1920s foundations had rapidly reached a position of being prominent, wealthy and largely independent bodies operating in the general area of social policy.

Grant-making trusts were also created in Britain, but not only have most of them been much smaller than their American counterparts, they also came into existence in very different socio-political conditions. If the British state was not that successful in resolving the 'social question', at least it was attempting to grapple with some of the issues. Hence if the language of 'partnership' is best used to describe the relationship between the state and voluntary social service organizations after 1945, the role of foundations before then is best seen as complementary to the state role, and not as in the US, an alternative to state action. In fact, in the twentieth century grant-making trusts – such as Wellcome, Cadbury and Nuffield – were in a sense merely an addition to a pre-existing structure. Since the middle ages, livery companies, for example, had used their wealth for grant-giving purposes, but the innovation of the new foundations was that they followed the American initiative in using their resources for research into 'social issues'. As in the US, medical research was prominent among the causes funded by them.

The role of foundations in British society has been altogether a smaller one than that of their American counterparts. But in relation to other sources of funds for philanthropic organizations in their own country, British foundations are relatively more important today than are foundations in America. Excluding the state-supported Arts Council, grants from grant-making trusts in 1982 amounted to £239 million, or about 3.5 per cent of the estimated income of non-religious charities in 1981.[61] In 1981 American foundations made grants totalling $2.4 billion, which was 2.5 per cent of the income of non-religious charities that year.[62] In relation to donations, the contribution of British foundations was also greater – forming about 38 per cent of donations to non-religious charities, while American foundations' grants constituted only 11 per cent of donations to non-religious bodies. This is scarcely surprising when we remember the relatively small scale of individual giving in Britain: British foundations are 'big fish in a small pool'. When compared with American foundations, though, they appear to be 'minnows', even if for the purpose of comparison we assume $2 is the equivalent of £1. Ten American foundations in 1981 made grants larger than those made by the biggest British foundation, the Wellcome Trust; forty-three American foundations made grants larger than the fifth largest British trust, the Leverhulme Trust; and between them the largest 200 grant-making trusts in Britain made grants that were only one and a half times as great as those made by the largest US Foundation, the Ford Foundation.

Because of their independence, both with respect to funds and the ability to decide which needs should be attended to, foundations are often thought to lie at the very heart of 'the third sector'. Both directly and indirectly they influence social conditions, yet they are neither part of the government nor in any way beholden to the market or popular tastes about suitable objects for charitable intervention. Despite their apparent potential for responding to social needs, foundations have been controversial institutions at times, and many of the controversies have related to the issue of their independence. For the most part these disputes have centred on American foundations, because of the far more central part foundations were supposed to play there in resolving 'the social question'.

At the outset foundations encountered opposition from those who saw them as yet another device for institutionalizing the power of the wealthy. Epitomizing this opposition was the fight in Congress from 1910 onwards to prevent Rockefeller from having his foundation granted a federal corporate charter. In 1913 he abandoned this attempt at legitimization for his venture, and the foundation was incorporated under New York law. Nor in their early years did most of the foundations help to overcome these fears: John D. Rockefeller Jr, for example, became the first President of the Rockefeller Foundation, and it was not until the 1920s that many of the early foundations established independence from their founders. Nevertheless, most of the original founders were largely philanthropic in their intentions and this, combined with the success of many of their projects in the first world war and the 1920s, helped to legitimize the organizations they had established.

By no means all the later foundations involved such an obvious degree of disinterest at their founding. Corporate foundations were an example of organizations of another type – devices enabling companies to retain close control over their donations and to direct philanthropic endeavours to areas that might best benefit the company. Another line of criticism, though one which did not raise doubts about the autonomy of the institutions being established, was that foundations were often established to reduce taxes. The most spectacular case of this concerned Henry Ford, an outspoken opponent of philanthropy, who discovered that the foundation could not only be a device for reducing taxes but also a means by which family control of his company could be retained. The result was the wealthiest foundation in America. The case has been described well by Bakal:

> By setting up the foundation and bequeathing 90 per cent of their Ford Motor Company stock to it, the noncharitable Henry Ford and his son, Edsel, enabled their heirs to avoid an inheritance tax bill that would have come to $321 million. If the stock had passed directly from Henry and Edsel to their heirs, most of it would have had to be sold to pay that hefty tax. In parting with their holdings, the heirs would also have lost control of the company, but to forestall this possibility, all the stock given to the foundation was nonvoting. The 10 percent retained by the family had total voting power, maintaining the family's domination of the company. Moreover, the voting stock passed to the family tax-free, saving another $42 million, because the wills of Henry and Edsel provided that the taxes on this bequest be paid by the foundation.[63]

The belief that foundations were a device to broaden the power of the wealthy also affected the kinds of projects which some foundations sponsored in the 1930s. They wanted to be seen to be successful. Consequently, they tended to focus on projects where demonstrable achievements within a few years were a realistic hope. For example, in the area of public health, foundations made a major contribution to disease control and eradication. Buck and Rosenkrantz describe the resulting situation in 1937 as follows: 'In marked contrast to the situation ten years earlier, with the exception of tuberculosis and pneumonia, contagious diseases no longer ranked among the ten leading causes of death.'[64] And in answer to their question of whether 'the foundations made medicine look good, or conversely, was it medicine that legitimated the foundations' role as instruments of the public interest?', they conclude the former is correct.[65] One problem in the early years, then, was that the need to acquire legitimacy among the American public arguably made some foundations less autonomous in identifying priorities among different needs in American society. By the 1960s the position was very different. While some foundations' activities abroad in furthering US interests made them the subject of criticism from those on the left, their independent policies in the domestic arena brought attacks from the populist right. The involvement of foundations in civil-rights-related areas inevitably drew them into conflict with southern-based populism which had always been antagonistic to centralized economic power. In 1969 these political forces in Congress inserted provisions into the Tax Reform Act placing a number of new restrictions on the behaviour of foundations.

The 1969 Act was a wide-ranging measure which was partly directed at the wealthy, and largely 'independent', foundations and partly aimed at the corporate and family foundation, the growth of which had been spectacular since the late 1930s. Foundations were now subject to a tax on their investment income and were prohibited from political activity which might in any way be partisan. (Among the political activities which had gained considerable publicity the previous year were Ford Foundation grants given to aides of the late Bobby Kennedy.) But foundations were also required to be other-regarding. They had to distribute all their net income annually, or a fixed percentage of their total assets if this were a greater amount, and there were a number of provisions to prevent donors benefiting from the assets of a foundation once it had been established. The result was a dramatic decline in their numbers, as foundations set up out of self-interest tended to cease operations.

This decline constitutes one of the grounds for the argument that foundations are in a state of crisis. Another element of this argument is that much of the work sponsored by foundations has little to do with providing 'minimum subsistence' either at home or abroad. A senior foundation official has even argued that 'Not one tenth, probably not one twentieth, of their grants have any measurable impact upon the major social problems confronting the nation at the present time'.[66] Nor is this altogether surprising, since 'colleges and universities have long been the major instruments and beneficiaries of foundation giving',[67] so that foundation control over the relevance of the projects they fund to social problems is rather weak. Even though foundation funding of educational institutions has been in relative decline in recent decades, foundations still have a strong tendency to fund projects that benefit

Table 4.5 Purposes funded by US foundations in 1981, as a percentage of total grants made

	%
Welfare	26.2
Health	22.5
Education	21.1
Cultural	15.3
Sciences	6.9
Social sciences	6.0
Religion	2.0
Total	100.0

Data taken from: Paul N. Ylvisaker, 'Foundations and nonprofit organizations', in Powell, (ed.), *The Nonprofit Sector*, table 20.5

middle-class clienteles as much as those 'in need'. Certainly, as table 4.5 indicates, while 'welfare' may obtain more foundation money than any other single policy area, purposes which are more likely to benefit people who enjoy a standard of living well above minimum subsistence, including culture and education, are heavily funded. Finally, the one significant area of growth among foundations has been among community foundations – bodies which draw their income from present-day donors rather than from the investment income of one original donor. For those who see the foundation as the prime example of 'third sector' bodies' ability to respond autonomously to needs, the community foundation has two disadvantages. It is explicitly local or regional in character, and thus it cannot focus *directly* on issues that are national in scope. Moreover, because these foundations allow donors to specify the purposes for which their gifts may be used, we return to the problem of co-ordinating individual wishes so that an overall pattern of needs may be met. Indeed, in some respects, community foundations are more like local United Ways than they are like the traditional philanthropic foundation.

6 State and Charity Interdependence

The main argument in this chapter has been that the 'independent income' of charitable organizations does not provide a 'sector' of organizations that is able to meet a complex pattern of needs in a society. Of its nature, the overall response of charities is haphazard, because of the decentralization of the philanthropic system. To accept this point is not to deny that charities have an extremely important role to play in identifying and ameliorating needs. But the 'social democratic' assumption that has been widely accepted in Britain since the advent of the welfare state, that it is the state which largely defines the boundaries of need, still holds. To argue in this way is not to say that charities are merely 'gap fillers' in the provision of welfare. Indeed, if they were responsible for 'gap filling', it is not clear that they would be very effective at doing so. Sosin's important recent study of private welfare agencies in the US substantiates this point. His findings contradict the claim that private agencies will fill gaps left by public agencies. He argues:

> There is no statistically significant relation between public welfare expenditures and the extensiveness of the private network, and thus no proof that private agencies are more *common* when public expenditures are low. In addition, there is a *more* extensive private network when there is a more extensive public network, and this flatly contradicts the gap filling hypothesis.[68]

As social democrats have long recognized, it is in the interaction between state and charities, and not in a truly 'independent sector', that the best hope for 'plugging gaps' lies. To the extent that they operate in separate spheres, there is less supervision of gaps in the provision of needs when they arise.

Until the 1970s the points raised above would have been regarded as commonplace. The increasing favour with which the notion of 'rolling back' the welfare state has been viewed in the 1980s has resulted in a partial rejection of a welfare partnership between state and charities, where the former was to be the dominant partner. The alternatives to this are unattractive precisely because they ignore the nature of donative charities discussed in this chapter. The virtual elimination of the state from welfare provision ignores not only the fact that most modern charities are heavily dependent on non-gift income, but that a reliance on donative income inevitably leads to huge gaps in providing for 'minimum subsistence' within a state. A more modest withdrawal of the state would lead to the problem identified by Sosin, that charitable agencies do not go to the areas of least state provision. Rather it is the ability of state and private agencies to cross-check each other that provides the best hope for removing such gaps.

The same objection applies to the policy that has been applied in Britain in the 1980s – of replacing some direct state provision with grants to charities to supply the service. One of the most significant developments in Britain in the 1980s has been the vast growth in central government grants to voluntary organizations, although grants from local authorities may now be starting to decline. In the five years between 1979–80 and 1984–5 the former increased from £93 million annually to over £224 million.[69] Even in real terms this represents an increase of 57.8 per cent, close to 10 per cent per annum. In most cases grants have been straightforwardly for the provision of services. But, as in the US, some grants have also been given to support organizations that have some of the characteristics of pressure groups – albeit ones that are less overtly political than some of the recipients of grants in America. An example of this was a grant (of £5,000) made by the Department of Health and Social Security in 1987 to the group Parents Against Injustice (PAIN). PAIN's goals were to discover cases of wrongful diagnoses of child abuse and to reunite families. Although they were due to receive charitable status, the group had been controversial, because its activities had been seen by critics as perpetuating the belief that child abuse was uncommon in Britain.[70]

In general, charities in Britain have been affected in two rather different ways by Conservative government policy. On the one hand, in areas where government departments believed charities could do more from their own resources, there have been noticeable cutbacks in funding. One of the best known disputes this occasioned was that in 1986 between the government and medical research charities.[71] Their argument was that the charities' own success in fund-raising was working against them, because they were now having to finance aspects of research to which state funds had been devoted earlier.[72] They claimed that the gap in funding brought about by government cutbacks was not one they could easily fill. The state had generally provided long-term support for research, such as in the purchasing of capital equipment, and the charities' dependence on the uncertainties of fund-raising made them ill-suited for this.

On the other hand, charities are an excellent instrument for making government cheaper. Wage rates are usually lower than in the state sector, in some instances voluntary labour can replace paid labour, and there is also the possibility that in the longer term the state can squeeze some organizations into providing more from their own resources when the cost of service provision increases. Moreover, the use of 'third party agencies' might reduce the direct impact of 'voice' from clients when services decline in quantity or quality. In the growth of grants to voluntary agencies in Britain since 1979 we see 'third-party government' emerging, just as it did on a far larger scale in the US in the 1960s. But there is a crucial difference between the two cases. In the US it was the attempt to expand federally funded welfare provision that brought this about, whereas in Britain it is the attempt to restrain state spending on welfare (in relation to demand) which is the motivating force.

What is actually happening in Britain, therefore, is very different from the model of an autonomous 'third sector'. Charities are becoming more dependent on the state financially (both directly for funds and indirectly in areas where they are under pressure to fill gaps left by the state's withdrawal).[73] As we have suggested, that the state does not leave to charities the task of identifying the overall pattern of needs is clearly desirable if needs are to be met. But the more significant problem is that the erosion of a two-tier system in which state and charities were both active in the same fields, and could check gaps left by each other, makes it more likely that some needs will simply not be satisfied. Part of what has made this possible, though, has been an exaggeration of how effective non-state welfare provision alone can be, an exaggeration which, it must be added, has generally not been made by the charities providing the services. Indeed, the main rhetoric about the existence and significance of a distinctive 'third sector' has often come from defenders of institutions like universities and non-profit hospitals, which are frequently the least dependent on that supposed source of 'independent' income, donations.

5

The Growth and Transformation of Volunteering

One of the most important ideas to emerge during the rise of liberal democracy has been that of the volunteer. Although liberal democracy has its roots in commercial society, and reached its full development in industrial society, the market mechanism has not always been seen as the most appropriate way in which needed labour should be supplied. It has been widely believed that in some areas of social life tasks should be performed, where possible, by volunteers. The essence of volunteerism is that those labouring are not paid for their work and they are free to withdraw from the activity without thereby seriously harming their own interests. (Volunteerism can be based on 'unconditional' altruism or on reciprocity, but the volunteer is always free to quit.) This modern view of the volunteer as an unpaid actor, in contrast with a 'professional', differs markedly from the older, military, distinction between a volunteer and a conscript. A volunteer in this sense is someone who agrees to serve voluntarily (in an army) and has to be paid at a rate to make it worth his/her while, and a volunteer army is often referred to, therefore, as a professional army; a conscript is *required* to serve, and usually is paid little more than a subsistence rate.

Volunteerism can exist only when there is a sufficient economic surplus that individuals can choose to donate their labour, and it is to be distinguished, therefore, from mutual co-operation in peasant societies where the individual cannot survive long without conforming to customary co-operative practices. Among democrats there has been considerable conflict as to exactly which activities should be the domain of volunteers, as well as disagreements about the possibility of establishing areas of activity in which volunteerism is strong. In this chapter we discuss five themes: the growth of volunteerism; the use made of volunteers in the mid- and late twentieth century; the reasons why volunteers are used in those activities where their numbers are significant; the consequences for the state of their deployment; and possible changes in volunteerism in the future.

1 The Growth of Volunteerism

In this section we identify three main strands of volunteerism – emanating respectively from mutual benefit activities, from the politicization of the urban working class and from the charitable impulses of the middle classes. At the outset, however, it must be recognized that these strands are themselves interrelated and that the rise of the volunteer in industrial society was an extremely complex process which we can only touch on briefly here. Neverthess, it can be admitted immediately that volunteerism had a very limited role to play, both at mass and elite levels of society, in the early stages of the commercial revolution. Of course, at the mass level there were many tasks in agricultural communities for which peasants and small farmers had always had to pool their labour, but the basis of this was convention. These conventions, recognized as obligations by the parties themselves, had their origins in the uncertainties of communal life in feudal society. In towns the organization of the economy around guilds meant that the shared interests of those engaged in a particular trade were provided for through formal structures which required the members of a guild to provide whatever resources were necessary. But, as in rural communities, co-operation for mutual benefit lacked one of the main elements of volunteerism – the ability of the participant to withdraw from an arrangement without seriously undermining his/her own interests.

Moreover, charity in feudal society, and then in commercial society, had far more to do with the giving of money or land than with personal, voluntary, service on the part of the donor. Neither of the two western traditions of charity, the Greco-Roman and the Judaeo-Christian, which became fused in the charitable practices of medieval Europe, gave prominence to personal service.[1] The wealthy in the Greek city state were expected to take on the burdens of public office, but the philanthropist in that society was one who contributed money to civic causes rather than one who devoted his/her own labour to something. Indeed, requiring those who were not generous with their wealth to take on burdensome public offices was one way of encouraging philanthropy.[2] The Judaeo-Christian tradition differed in its concern for the poor and disadvantaged, but here too it was material resources that were required from the donor. In medieval Europe people who took the strictures of the church to heart would give their wealth to one of its institutions for some charitable purpose, and devote their time to prayer or other religious activities. While the parable of the Good Samaritan, and other passages in the Bible, provided scope for religious movements which emphasized direct personal service by the wealthy to the poor, for obvious reasons this was not a dominant theme in medieval life. It was far easier for the person concerned about the fate of his/her soul to dispense with part of his/her wealth than to abase himself or herself.

The need for volunteer labour first becomes apparent when conventions regarding collaboration between neighbours in rural communities, and the power of the guilds in the cities, declined. Rational self-interest required certain kinds of co-operation between economic actors who were often unable to provide for all contingencies themselves. It is not surprising, therefore, that it is in some of the American colonies of the seventeenth and eighteenth centuries that we find some of the first examples of volunteerism – of freely assumed co-operation between individuals. The willingness to form associations in America, which so struck Tocqueville in the 1830s and which remains the popular image of the 'American way' of conducting social activity to this day, stems in part from the need for co-operation on the frontier. The market could not provide for every need, and in the absence of long-standing conventions determining how collective goods would be provided, the ethos that people should contribute their time and labour to community affairs became established. If self-interest provided an initial stimulus to the cult of the volunteer in the US, it spread to other-regarding activities among 'concerned citizens', a development promoted further by the War of Independence.

The independent economic actor (especially the smaller farmer and trader) provided the basis for much collective action utilizing the labour of contributors. But, of course, the growth of market societies provided problems of how to generate collective goods for other groups. The poorest groups simply lacked the resources with which to combine their labour, but in the skilled working class we find movements like the Friendly Societies enabling members to provide some insurance against the future. Similar developments can be found among successive generations of non-British immigrants to the US, where co-operation by members of a particular ethnic group to teach the English language, for example, was practised widely. There are several points worth emphasizing about the stimulus for volunteerism which emanated from the 'collective action problem' in the advanced stages of commercial society and in the transformation to industrial society. Many of the earliest mutual benefit initiatives in commercial societies, such as the Friendly Societies, were formed around informal assistance as well as financial benefits for members. Eighteenth-century Friendly Societies are an important link between the convention-governed, non-voluntaristic co-operation of feudal society and the volunteerism of the twentieth century, where there is usually no cost whatsoever to a member leaving an organization. In small communities 'exit' was not entirely cost-free. But the primary motive for joining Friendly Societies was economic – they provided some insurance against the future. Though lacking appropriate legal structures, many small-scale co-operative efforts did survive and thrive. With the availability of new legal forms, many kinds of association became institutionalized but have continued to rely to a high degree on volunteer labour. Thus organizations as disparate as chambers of commerce in small towns and gardening clubs still depend heavily on members performing certain tasks; they cannot afford to pay and membership would decline drastically if there was a large increase in membership subscriptions to cover wages. Nevertheless, for the most part, increased affluence means that economic self-interest alone cannot explain the mobilization of volunteers to provide mutual benefits today. As in the eighteenth century, volunteer-based organizations are likely to be centres of social activity as well as suppliers of specific collective goods, or to be bodies where the distinction between self-interest and broader social goals is somewhat blurred, or to be providers of non-economic goods to the participants. We return to this point shortly.

The need to organize to produce certain collective goods in the advanced stages of commercial society also facilitated the growth of forms of political organization, in direct and indirect ways. Friendly Societies provided a front for trade unionism and for more political activities, and as Thompson has noted:

> In the simple cellular structure of the friendly society, with its workaday ethos of mutual aid, we can see many features which were reproduced in more sophisticated and complex forms in trade unions, co-operatives, Hampden Clubs, Political Unions and Chartist Lodges.[3]

In America the need to translate co-operation for mutual benefit into political activity was espoused by those who saw it as the basis for a check on elite dominance in the new political system. In Ackerman's words, the authors of the Federalist Papers placed: 'a high value on public-regarding forms of political activity, in which people sacrifice their private interests to pursue the common good in transient and informal political association'.[4] The independent-minded volunteer, who became politically active only when circumstances demanded and was the model citizen sought by the Founding Fathers, has continued to serve as an important myth in the popularization of American democracy.

When volunteers joined forces with political elites, as they did in the Jacksonian era, the result was a major transformation in the *practice* of

American democracy. The willingness to join organizations had not produced permanent, volunteer-based parties at the beginning of the Republic. A party system based on local elites, and operating through the Congress, arose in the mid 1790s but in the early nineteenth century this collapsed into a loose one-party system. Jacksonianism spread the cult of democracy and encouraged the participation of all male citizens. But introducing volunteerism at the mass level into political parties did not produce the democratic ideal of an informed, participatory, citizenry whose members enjoyed economic independence. Instead, volunteerism was grafted onto existing party organizations that were controlled by elites, and whose corrupt practices were already worrying British conservatives in the 1820s.[5] The rapid growth of patronage politics from the 1830s onwards culminated in the urban party machines of the mid nineteenth century.[6] The influence volunteers had in the Jacksonian movement waned, so that in the nineteenth century the US moved from having political control exercised directly by socio-economic elites to them having influence through, and in conjunction with, party bosses.

Although, as Tocqueville saw, the US was a nation of 'joiners', the ethos which encouraged banding together to produce collective goods did not at the same time produce extensive volunteerism as a supplement to philanthropy. It is only much later in the nineteenth century that we find the growth of volunteerism as an important element in dealing with the problem of poverty. Nor is this surprising. While as Owen has said of England in the early nineteenth century, 'The times called not for impulsive charity but for care and discrimination, for greater personal interest on the part of donors, who only in this way could separate the deserving from the impostors and the idle', in neither Britain nor the US did this require volunteer work with the poor from the philanthropist.[7] This was to come later with the scientific charity of the Charity Organization Societies. In the earlier part of the century the wealthy were expected to be more discriminating than their predecessors two generations before, but it was essentially their money that was demanded of them by their philanthropically inclined peers. Of course, when the idea of the philanthropist having direct and continuing contact with recipients did develop towards the end of the century, the American tradition of forming associations helped to strengthen this movement more than in Britain. But it took further changes in attitude to bring this about.

The second major thrust to the mobilization of volunteers came from the politicization of the urban working class. The social upheavals of industrialization had produced, of course, a class that was largely lacking in political resources, but which nevertheless enjoyed some of the civic freedoms denied the poorest economic groups in peasant societies.

Limited rights of assembly, their numbers, and the close proximity in which they lived gave the urban working class some resources with which to mobilize in pursuit of their common interests. Obviously, there were serious problems to be overcome in creating working-class political movements. Bourgeois civic freedoms were often interpreted by the courts in ways hostile to trade unions or working-class political groups. The impoverishment of sectors of the working class, and their total dependence on wage labour, meant that they were operating in conditions where the 'Olson problem' – the absence of an incentive for an individual to contribute to the provision of a collective good – was most apparent. Nevertheless, movements such as Chartism in the 1840s were able to mobilize large numbers of people, and they relied heavily on the participants devoting time to attend meetings and demonstrations, and in proselytizing among their fellows. This was, indeed, voluntary, mass politics.

Nevertheless, there were two linked difficulties facing these sorts of movements in the use of their potential numbers as a political force. The first was that of sustaining volunteer enthusiasm after the movement had suffered setbacks. This is a central problem for all movements based on volunteers. The classic solution to it has been to provide a permanent framework for participation, with dimensions other than the political, so leaders can retain close contact with participants during 'fallow' periods for the movement. One device for maintaining a commitment of joint action is ideology, but developing this among a large group itself requires organizations so that the central beliefs can be disseminated. More fundamentally, then, political mobilizing demands that certain facilities (possibly social and recreational, or possibly services for the mutual benefit of members, such as insurance schemes) be supplied as an incentive for activism. In fact, when they could, socialist parties did attempt to provide such facilities, and these became an important element in attracting members in the late nineteenth and early twentieth centuries. Among the best-known examples of this in Europe were the stamp collectors' clubs operating under the auspices of the parties in Austria and Germany. But for much of the nineteenth century a lack of resources made it difficult to keep participants in political movements, and there was a strong tendency, therefore, for movements like Chartism simply to break down. Moreover, many of the mutual-benefit organizations growing up among the skilled working class (craft unions, Friendly Societies and so on) did not always support overtly political movements – either because they were regarded as undermining their own interests or because they threatened their more covert political activities. Of the earlier part of the nineteenth century Thompson has noted:

despite the weight of legislation, there was a hazy area in which some kind of

> trade union activity was still, in practice, accepted as permissible . . . trade clubs – such as those in the London crafts – which emphasized their function as benefit societies, and which kept quiet as to their national correspondence and negotiating functions, might go for years unmolested, until some conflict or strike offended employers or the authorities.[8]

Channelling and maintaining political volunteerism was difficult, then, until most of the working-class mutuals could be persuaded to participate in broader political movements – which in Britain was not until towards the end of the century.

A second problem facing these movements was primarily confined to the US, though states like Canada exhibited it as well, and this was that the mass parties which had mobilized before industrialization were strong rivals to working-class parties. In the US mass parties had developed in the 1830s – a wide franchise generating competition for the people's vote. In the cities, of course, the growth of large party machines, based on patronage and on an 'exchange relationship' between bosses and 'members' meant that strong electoral organizations existed during industrialization, and voting loyalties among the working class were already established. The machines did not want or need political volunteers, and parties to rival the Democrats and, after the 1850s, the Republicans did not survive in the long term.

What we find in nineteenth-century Britain is working class political volunteerism that was harnessed only gradually by permanent organizations. Nevertheless, by the first half of the twentieth century trade unions and their allies in constituency Labour parties had established an institutional framework enabling them to make use of voluntary labour in elections and in other political activities. But neither the British Labour party, nor the bourgeois parties which copied its mass membership organizational style, provided quite the scale of social and recreational facilities found in some continental socialist (and religious) parties, so that their 'tapping' of the potential volunteer workforce was not as great. Moreover, while all socialist parties, as well as many other parties after the extension of the franchise to the working class, had an incentive to recruit volunteers, volunteers were also a possible threat to parties, so that many were disinclined to utilize this resource fully. Essentially parties wanted members who were sufficiently motivated to give their time to political activity, but who were also sufficiently involved in the social side of the party that they would be less tempted to 'rock the boat' on matters of principle. The price of making working-class volunteerism more effective over the longer term was to restrict the impact it might make in the short term.

The third main strand of volunteerism emanated from the idea of scientific charity which became popular in both Britain and the US in the last three decades of the nineteenth century. The COSs, through which the idea was propagated, accepted in a rigorous form the distinction between the deserving and the undeserving poor. This distinction had been a cornerstone of the Poor Law Amendment Act of 1834 but that Act, in abolishing 'outdoor' relief for the poor, had done little to make provision for the 'deserving'. The COSs were an attempt to fill this gap. On the one hand, they provided certain kinds of relief for those thought to be deserving, while on the other they hoped to organize charity within the geographical areas each COS covered, so as to try to eliminate any private doles to the undeserving. The latter would then be forced back into the workhouse, in which conditions were sufficiently bad that they would soon be rid of their alleged idleness. The belief that charities should attempt to distinguish between categories of the poor in this way was not new: it had been attempted in Glasgow by the Reverend Thomas Chalmers between 1819 and 1823, but it was not copied elsewhere at the time.[9] It was not until 1869 in Britain, and 1877 in the US, that the first COSs were formed to organize charity on this principle.[10] (The formation of these bodies so late in the century is significant, at least in respect of the development of social welfare policy, because the COSs were trying to organize 'scientific charity' at the very time that ideas about the role of the individual in industrial society, on which they were based, were starting to be questioned more thoroughly.) For our purpose the importance of the COSs is that separation of different categories of claimant for relief necessitated detailed information about individual cases. Charities before this had not sought such information because it could be obtained only by a labour-intensive programme of interviewing and visiting claimants. The work was carried out by volunteers attached to a COS, and the use of volunteers was not just for reasons of economy. 'Friendly visiting' was to yield a form of social control of the masses by providing them with moral guidance:

> the visitor saw in her client less an equal or potential equal than an object of character reformation whose unfortunate and lowly condition resulted from ignorance or deviations from middle-class values and patterns of life-organization: temperance, industriousness, family cohesiveness, frugality, foresight, moral restraint.[11]

The COSs did not rely entirely on volunteers. In addition each district office would have an agent, who was paid, and in some cases one or two other paid employees.[12] As well as providing some continuity in administrative matters, the agent played a key role in liaising with Poor Law relieving officers, and with other private charities, to ensure that the 'less eligibility' principle embodied in the 1834 Act was put into practice. But volunteerism was seen as essential if scientific charity was to work. Indeed, when in the first thirty years of the twentieth century professional social workers started to be employed by COSs, many in the COS movement expressed opposition because the transformation from volunteerism to social work seemed contrary to its aims.

If it was the COSs which provided the initial forum for this new form of volunteering, there were several developments subsequently that were to change its character. The notion that the middle class should participate in activities that would bring it into contact with other classes spread. But if the volunteer ethos gave rise to bodies, like the Boy Scouts, which also aimed directly at social control, there were other organizations, such as Toynbee Hall in England and the settlement houses in the US, that were founded on a more progressive social philosophy. Again, while the COS pioneered charitable volunteerism, it was also largely responsible for the emergence of case work and the profession of the social worker; while the volunteer was still needed, it was very much as a back-up to the professional, who was the person now 'diagnosing' individual problems and strategies for overcoming them. Furthermore, once the welfare state was established in Britain, and the quasi-welfare state in the US twenty years later, volunteers were not discarded as a hang-over from an earlier era. On the contrary, there were many areas where the state wanted to encourage volunteering, so that services which were essential but which would strain state budgets would still be provided. It has been estimated, for example, that volunteers in charities in the UK form the equivalent of a full-time workforce of about 400,000 people.[13]

But why did this kind of volunteering emerge in the late nineteenth century and thrive subsequently? A full explanation is far too complex to present here, but some of the main elements can be mentioned briefly. The urban middle class who were the backbone of volunteering had increased greatly since the 1830s and 1840s; certainly by the end of the century in the US there was a relatively large group of college-educated women, for whom most careers were not open, and for whom virtually all were closed after marriage; mid-nineteenth-century improvements in sewage and water supplies, together with the growth of regular police forces, had made 'visiting' the urban poor considerably less dangerous than it had been in the first three or four decades of the century; and far more was actually known by the 1870s about the conditions in which the poor lived, so that more complex ideas about how they might be both controlled and reformed were now possible. In the twentieth century there was a continuing expansion in the available numbers of the group that was most important for volunteerism – middle-class women, especially married women – until after the second world war. Although extensive use was made of women in the workforce in the two world wars, the first war did far more to legitimize volunteer work than employment among the female middle class. The war was a catalyst in legitimizing women's participation in voluntary organizations – not just as visitors, but as fund-raisers, and in providing ancillary services, especially in nursing and the care of the wounded.

2 Volunteerism in the Mid- and Late Twentieth Century

As we have already noted, many of the early mutual-benefit organizations which utilized the voluntary efforts of members were already giving way in the nineteenth century to much larger bodies with an interest only in the financial contributions of members. In most cases effective control by the membership was lost with expansion. But, if the increasing affluence and organization of the skilled working class led to the demise of the original mutuals, there were two important ways in which this kind of volunteerism was to survive in the twentieth century. Affluence provided opportunities for leisure that had not existed before. Churches and political parties used their resources to provide facilities for social and recreational activities, but even they were unable to satisfy much of the demand. Associations of relatively small groups of people were thus formed; and even today they are the principal ways in which amateur footballers, railway modellers, and many others pursue their leisure interests.

The other way in which volunteerism in mutual benefit bodies has expanded is through the development of associations to help individuals deal with personal problems through interaction with people who have similar problems. In these cases the volunteer is aiming to help himself or herself through his/her interaction and participation with others. As we saw in chapter 2, Alcoholics Anonymous is perhaps the best (and probably the best-known) example of this kind of organization. The ethic that 'people can only help themselves', and can best do so in conjunction with fellow 'sufferers' is a central tenet of such organizations. The strictly 'mutual' principle underlying these bodies is revealed in several ways. They reject the notion that people can simply be 'treated', so that the commercial provision of a service to aid them could enjoy only limited success. Cures 'cannot be bought' because the person would not have acquired the appropriate motivation to deal with his/her problem in the longer term. Any lapses or failures, for instance, could then always be blamed on something else. They also reject the idea of help from outside agencies. The constitution of Alcoholics Anonymous, for example, prohibits the acceptance of donations and bequests. Having received a large bequest in 1985 it found that under the law it could not actually refuse a gift, although it insisted that it did not want gifts 'of such magnitude as would, if accepted in the whole, endanger the principle of self-help upon which Alcoholics Anonymous operates'.[14] It had to get a Private Act of Parliament passed, The Alcoholics Anonymous Dispositions Act 1986, which allowed it to decline gifts. These strict self-help groups also refrain from acting as cause groups in the political arena, leaving it to other bodies.[15]

The idea that mutual self-help is different from, and superior in quality to, the provision of services through charity and, most especially, the market, is found in other groups too. Indeed, it can be a source of tension between members in clubs and other associations when the scale of operations increases to the point that certain services can now be provided on a commercial basis, rather than by members volunteering their efforts. These tensions parallel those in the COSs over the introduction of professional social workers – something about the nature of the activity is lost if commercial relationships replace non-commercial ones. Volunteering in mutual groups, then, has survived partly because in many instances the scale of activities is too small to sustain a market, and partly because there are activities where the market is held to be incompatible with values central to them.

When we turn to politicization as a source of volunteer labour, we find that social change in the twentieth century has contributed to an increase in this kind of volunteerism. However, it was not the politicization of the working class that was its main component. Indeed, generally political parties became less competitive in recruiting members through the social and recreational facilities they could offer to the working class as new forms of mass entertainment and leisure activities became available. Rather, it was in the expanding middle class, who increasingly had time to devote to other-regarding activities, that volunteer politics were to become far more important, and in the longer term parties in Britain and the US found it more difficult to channel this form of participation. To understand these developments, however, it is important to realize that in the US the Progressive era had earlier witnessed an upsurge of middle-class involvement in socio-political affairs. The impulses for this were complex. The religious convictions of Protestants, which gave rise to the visiting of the poor also produced participation in moral reform organizations like the Anti-Saloon League. On the other hand, the more progressive views which produced middle-class activism in Hull House and other settlement houses could go hand-in-hand with involvement in promoting women's suffrage. Moreover, the very venality of American party politics in the nineteenth century provoked middle class indignation, resulting in laws to control the organization and procedures of parties and the hiving off of certain governmental functions – to the professions and to new areas of expertise that were claiming professional status. Some of these political movements (for women's suffrage and temperance) were also found in Britain, but in general British socio-political structures, including political parties, tended to contain and restrict middle-class activism in this period.

Why, then, did this upsurge of middle-class political activism not become a permanent feature of, at the very least, US politics? Once again the explanation is too complex for us to do more than briefly outline an answer. One consideration, as Hirschman has contended, is that there seems to be a cycle involving the pursuit of private ends and public affairs.[16] Concern with public aspects of people's lives seems to decline after a period of intense political activity.[17] Then, too, success with some of their objectives simply takes the steam out of political movements, and it becomes more difficult to sustain activism: the adoption of party primary laws and other institutional reforms had this effect on progressivism. Moreover, once an issue forms part of the agenda of politicians in the electoral arena, there is a disincentive for activism even before the objectives have been realized. This is because the forums in which the issue is discussed and eventually resolved are now ones where the mass mobilizing of activists is unlikely to be very effective. Mass activism is most effective as a resource against identifiable opponents, and least effective after a consensus has been established that *something* has got to be done about a problem. Finally, external events can make previously central issues marginal ones, or can lead to their being decided without a real fight. Two world wars, and the largest-ever economic depression that occurred between them, radically changed domestic policy agendas in Britain and the US. Consequently, it was not until the very late 1940s that elements of a new mobilization of middle-class political volunteers began to appear in both countries. By then the continuing increase, and diversity, in the middle class was to dramatically alter the potential for this form of political activism.

As I have argued elsewhere, one of the main causes of this new political mobilization was the absence of many alternative, and acceptable, ways for the middle class to socialize with each other.[18] In many respects the late 1940s and the 1950s were highpoints for participation in British and American political parties. This was to change very rapidly, partly because social mores were to change and partly because increasing employment among women, especially married women, meant that there were fewer people available for the really time-consuming aspects of political participation. At the same time, though, the limitations of parties as the main forums for participation were becoming more obvious. Often parties were embarrassed by the issues their members or activists took up and sought to disown them or to express some opposition to the cause, while at the same time that cause may well have had support from outside the party. Consequently, the single-issue group, which had long been an important element in both political systems, came to even greater prominence. In Britain the formation of the Campaign for Nuclear Disarmament (CND) in 1958 marked the beginning of a new era of middle-class volunteering. In the US it was the Vietnam war, together with the rapid disintegration of Democratic party organizations, that was significant in the new mobilization of 'cause' groups. The explosive growth of what Walker calls 'citizen groups' is well documented; his survey revealed that 60 per cent of the groups had been formed since 1960, a finding compatible with other studies of interest groups.[19]

If the vast increase in numbers of well-educated members of the middle class and the great increase in their leisure time made possible much larger voluntary political movements, it was sustained also by other changes in society. A significant development was that a large segment of this class (in education, in some of the professions and in some of the neo-professions providing welfare services) was now dependent on the state, directly and indirectly, for its livelihood. Efforts at reducing state domestic expenditures from the 1970s onwards helped to politicize individuals and to draw them into contact with political activism. A few years earlier the political confrontations of the 1960s had produced a sub-culture that gave prominence to the idea of self-determination. This was most advanced in Germany, where it was to become manifested not just in newer forms of political organizations (like the Greens), but also in self-help groups providing kindergartens and youth-care centres.[20] This ethos found many adherents too in Britain and the United States. Moreover, in Britain, the importance of 'relevant experience' for those wishing to undertake professional training in fields like psychology and social work meant that many future 'professionals' undertook voluntary work in the social services as a way of establishing their credentials for training. One consequence of this was that it frequently brought individuals into contact with 'grass-roots' socio-political groups in which they would participate. Thus there has been some merging of political volunteerism with more traditional philanthropic volunteerism. This has affected religious, as well as other, charities. A survey of religious organizations by the Council on Foundations, published in 1985, found a noticeable growth in support for projects advocating social change, human rights and advocacy issues.[21] But the scale of such developments in relation to traditional philanthropic volunteering must not be exaggerated. As Gerard has noted, in discussing a Gallup poll of charity activists in Britain: 'Contrary to expectations ... political activism ... has minority appeal – even among new style groups – and is largely restricted to community-work and overseas aid fields.'[22] Overall, though, the merging of political and philanthropic volunteering has probably had some effect in reducing the impact of the 'private ends–public affairs' cycle on political volunteerism.

In relation to the philanthropic component of volunteering, we must begin by noting again that the growth of the welfare state has been accompanied by state encouragement of individuals to volunteer. In Britain there has been a notable change in this regard since the early 1960s. Older children, like the fictitious Adrian Mole, are now encouraged by their schools to undertake certain kinds of voluntary work, whereas in the 1950s such service was not regarded by most boys' grammar schools in Britain as a substitute for service in the school's military cadet corps.[23] But, as Gerard has pointed out, despite such encouragement the young are generally under-mobilized in voluntary work. Those between eighteen and twenty-five form only 10 per cent of volunteers.[24] This low level of volunteering persists despite the fact, which we noted earlier, that in Britain there is an incentive for some young people to volunteer, because of the linking of acceptance on certain professional training courses to relevant voluntary experience.

These sorts of developments must be weighed against a decline in the availability of people who traditionally formed the heart of the volunteer movement. Most especially, the increase in the number of married women in employment is undercutting the base of philanthropic volunteerism. This has been most obvious in those areas where volunteerism was strongest – the American suburbs. One area where the problem of declining volunteerism has been observed is the New York suburbs, where the proportion of women in employment outside the home increased from 39 to 47 per cent of the total in just ten years after 1975. In the more affluent suburbs escalating property prices have also meant that 'civil servants and employees of local businesses who once made up the bulk of the members of volunteer fire companies can no longer afford to live in the communities where they work.'[25] In addition, the rise of single parent families has put pressure on the voluntary services, because of the decline in time available to women with children. Of course, there are categories of people who might potentially replace some of the lost volunteers – such as the retired – but the increasing tendency, at least in the US, for them to live in special retirement communities reduces this source of volunteer labour. Finally, of course, secularization is slowly reducing the vast amount of volunteering that has traditionally formed around religious organizations.

If in the long term there are forces gradually reducing the supply of volunteers to some philanthropic bodies, it is only in certain kinds of communities that the threat to voluntary services has been realized so far. There is still a lot of voluntary activity going on, and overall the amount of time devoted to volunteering has increased. In part, this is because the number of organizations in which people can participate seems to be increasing greatly. A rather crude indication of this is suggested by data presented in table 5.1. showing the growth in the number of registered charities in England, and in the number of 501(c)(3) organizations in the US, between 1968 and 1985. Although some of the newly registered organizations may have existed before 1968, and some of those registered may no longer be operative, and not all of them would actually provide for volunteerism, the huge increase in their numbers indicates that opportunities for volunteering have probably grown considerably. Moreover, there is survey evidence of the scope of volunteering in the two countries. Verba and Nie's study in the early 1970s revealed that 40 per cent of American adults reported that they were active members in one or more organizations.[26] Even though these organizations included non-philanthropic bodies, this figure is still very high. Weitzman's data suggests that in 1980 just over half of American adults donated time to working for non-profit organizations. Their work has been estimated as the equivalent of 4.9 million employees, or about 4.5 per cent of the US workforce.[27] This represents a three-fold increase since 1964.

Table 5.1 Number of charitable organizations in the US and England and Wales, 1968–1985

	Organizations classified as 501(c) (3) by Internal Revenue Service	Organizations registered with the Charity Commission
1968	137,487	71,000
1978	293,947	129,212
1985	366,071	154,135

Data taken from: *Reports of the Charity Commissioners for England and Wales, 1970, 1978 and 1985*, and General Accounting Office, *Tax Policy: Competition Between Taxable Businesses and Tax-Exempt Organizations*

In Britain where the tradition of formally joining an organization is less strong than in the US, we have already seen that on one estimate the contribution of volunteers amounts to the equivalent of 400,000 full-time workers, about 1.5 per cent of the total workforce – a lower contribution than in the US. The Wolfenden Committee Report of 1978 indicated that about one sixth of British adults were in 'voluntary organizations', which would suggest that about three times as many Americans were volunteers and would confirm the widely-held belief that volunteering is a distinctly American phenomenon.[28] Yet a survey published in 1987 suggested a very different situation. It indicated that a much greater proportion of British adults were involved in helping charities than Wolfenden found were active in 'voluntary organizations'. The later data showed that 51 per cent of respondents gave some time to charity work, and that the average time given up to this work was actually greater than in the US![29] As in the US, the typical volunteer is a middle-aged woman from the middle-class: over half the volunteers are from the top half of the social scale and from non-manual occupations, and about 60 per cent are women.[30] Women volunteers in Britain, though, are even more important than this suggests, because the average woman volunteer devotes 60 per cent more time to volunteering than the average man.[31] However, the bias towards middle–class participation in Britain is not as pronounced as is widely believed. And, while the composition of the middle class is changing, and some elements of it now have less time for volunteering, we must remember that overall this class continues to grow. Any crisis in philanthropic volunteering affects only certain traditional kinds of volunteering and is basically long term.

3 Why Is Voluntary Labour Undertaken at all in an Advanced Capitalist Society?

If volunteerism is so extensive in organizations like recreational clubs, 'cause' groups, and philanthropic associations, it can be asked why it should exist at all in market societies, and certainly in the most advanced economies. After all, if markets worked as they are supposed to, all goods and services for which there was demand would be supplied by entrepreneurs who would employ paid labour. In our discussion in this and earlier chapters we have already indicated several aspects of the answer to this question, and here we recapitulate, and expand, on these points as well introducing further arguments.

Firstly, one of the main reasons volunteerism survives is that markets cannot always supply the goods people want. With smaller organizations there may be insufficient demand in the relevant locale for an entrepreneur to find it worthwhile setting up in business. It is only by expending some of their own labour that those who want a local gardening club, or whatever, will be able to have it. Moreover, in the case of goods and services which are on the margins of profitability, there is an advantage to self-help, in that once established it is less likely to put the organization under continual threat of closure. This is one of the reasons mutual sporting clubs survive, even though with some capital-intensive sports there is now a strong market to which commercial companies are responding. The other main problem with markets is that for most people the labour market works in a highly imperfect way. The bank official who spends a couple of weekends every spring helping to repair his/her cricket club's pavilion would, in a perfect economy, work extra hours for his/her employers and use this additional income to pay a lower wage rate to someone to do his/her share of the repairs. But, like most salaried employees s/he cannot undertake paid overtime, and there may well be an additional problem in a small club of finding someone willing to undertake relatively small items of repair and maintenance. This point about inflexibility in labour markets applies even more to married women with children of school age. Often the relatively small number of hours they would be free to take on paid labour makes them of little value to employers, even though they may have valuable skills, and it is not surprising that they have formed the backbone of the philanthropic voluntary labour force.[32]

Secondly, given these imperfections in real-world economies, volunteering can be used as a device in rationing scarce goods. We have already noted the use made of 'relevant experience' in allocating places in Britain to trainees in some professions connected to the social services. Its value lies in the fact that only those most suitable for such training are likely to undertake voluntary work or do well at it. More generally, in an era of high unemployment, voluntary work experience may make potential employees attractive to employers because references for them can draw attention to their commitment to hard work, trustworthiness and so on. To the extent that volunteering experience is valued as indicative of certain attributes on the part of those who undertake it, it imposes a cost on those who do not. The greater the need for rationing, the greater such costs to non-participants may become.

Thirdly, the ideology of middle-class volunteerism which emerged in the late nineteenth century continues to be widely accepted. At first glance this might seem odd, since that kind of volunteerism was based on patronizing attitudes towards the working class that were widely resented. There are several reasons why it survived and now commands wide support.

The most obnoxious aspects of volunteering, of the 'friendly' visits by the middle class to the less fortunate in order to provide for their moral welfare, were reduced gradually as volunteers were replaced by professional social workers in the most sensitive areas of encounter between classes. The tasks to which volunteers were mainly confined in social welfare agencies in the twentieth century were ones where conflict arising from their motives was less likely to occur.

Also, when the state assumed the main responsibility for the provision of welfare services, it had a strong incentive to support the ethos of volunteering; this was especially so in the US where voluntary agencies were the primary suppliers of federally funded programmes. But in Britain too volunteering was vital for the state. The cost of replacing volunteers and the organizations they worked in would have been enormous, and in many cases services could not have been provided. The state legitimized the middle-class ethic of volunteering by transforming it into an ethic of service for the community – an essentially classless ethic.

Then too it became apparent that service by individuals could be useful to far more radical social projects than would have been acceptable to the nineteenth-century pioneers of volunteering. In the 1960s a number of charities working with the poor and homeless were started, which made use of volunteers but which were committed to changing the causes of poverty, a commitment which drew them further into *overt* political activity at the mass level than had been usual with earlier charities.[33] (The COS and many of the leading nineteenth-century philanthropists were highly active in elite politics, but at the mass level their objective was depoliticization, which in itself, of course, was a form of political action.) Many of the volunteers on these projects were involved with, or subsequently drawn into, overt political activity. In some ways typifying this new style of charity in the 1980s is Youthaid, which fights against youth unemployment; it has published pamphlets publicizing state benefits to which the young are entitled, but which the British government itself had refused to publicize. The new acceptability to the left in Britain of many new style charities was also demonstrated by the much greater use made by Labour-controlled councils of donations to some of these charities.

Fourthly, although changes in class structure as well as growing affluence had helped to undermine the commitment to local mutual benefit activity, which the nineteenth century working-class organizations had fostered, it did not disappear completely. Part of the effort in mobilizing people in areas of poor housing, for example, has been directed to building up attitudes of community pride and solidarity so as to sustain the kind of local volunteering necessary for these projects to succeed. It is not class and community solidarity which has eroded but rather low-level working-class institutions outside the workplace through which solidarity could be expressed on a regular basis.

Fifthly, just as in real-world economies there are imperfections which result in entrepreneurs not coming forward to supply certain goods, so too in the political arena entrepreneurs may not emerge to organize campaigns for particular collective goods:

In fact Salisbury (1969) and Frolich, Oppenheimer, and Young (1971) have argued that the formation of advocacy organizations is . . . problematic because it requires entrepreneurs who perceive opportunities to advance their own careers and perhaps the patronage of privileged actors.[34]

Indeed, failure in the political market is likely to be that much greater because the individual goals an entrepreneur might hope to advance (such as his/her political career) are that much more difficult to estimate than even profitability in a market. Given the 'Olson problem', it might seem that political movements could never get started. Yet, most certainly, they do. Volunteers contribute their time to campaigns sometimes because there are selective incentives to do so (such as peer group pressure) but also for reasons other than self-interest. Notions of a duty not to free ride are often as important as any sense of companionship participants may derive from their activity. It is at least arguable that the very difficulties political entrepreneurs face actually help to sustain a sense of obligation as a factor in the mobilization of political activists; if people suspected that the 'market' might work they would be far less inclined to volunteer. This is a variation on the Titmuss argument about altruism: in some circumstances the market can drive out other-regarding behaviour.[35] There is another way too in which political entrepreneurism, were it more predictable, might have an adverse effect on volunteering. Elite-based organizations would find it that much more difficult to invoke peer group pressure against non-contributors than do organizations and movements that arise from volunteering within a community: their moral force is much less. In other words, it is the failure of political entrepreneurism which may partly contribute to the survival of political volunteerism.

Finally, certain kinds of activities are sometimes considered to be done less well if a market relationship is involved, or to be 'tainted' by people being paid to provide them. We have seen already that, in cases like alcoholism, it has been argued that it is primarily by assisting each other that people can overcome their problems. But the argument that the market can be an unsuitable mechanism for providing goods and services is much broader than this. Some anarchists and socialists have rejected the market as a basis for providing any goods and, of course, there have been numerous experiments at organizing relatively small communities using uncoerced self-help. Individuals provide their labour (and other resources) to assist others and receive their help in return. But even those who have embraced the market as the best means of distributing most goods have rejected it in the case of others. As we will see in chapter 6, aspects of religious observance, basic research and artistic creation and performance have all been identified as activities that lie (at least partly) beyond the scope of either the market or the state. But in the twentieth century we also find a widespread rejection of market values in relation to the operation of a democratic polity itself. The voluntary political activist has been widely, though not universally, regarded as making a more valuable contribution to the polity than the person who is paid to undertake political work.[36] Late nineteenth- and twentieth-century political reformers have bitterly opposed the practices of machine politicians in paying (through jobs and in other ways) those who mobilize voters for them, while these same reformers have usually been highly supportive of the market system. Their opposition has not usually been based on straightforward self-interest – an inability to practice patronage politics themselves. Rather it derives from a belief in the separability of the political and the economic, with the former being seen as an arena in which rational argument and discussion should prevail. On this view, political volunteers are a significant element in the polity because, in mobilizing support for their causes, they require others, including elected politicians, to engage in public discussion about issues. Those who are employed to perform electoral tasks are likely to have little interest in initiating public debate, and thereby political conflict is more likely to be about differing loyalties to parties and about the personalities of political leaders, rather than about issues.

Of course, opposition to a paid workforce as the means of providing a service was at the centre of the dispute about the introduction of professional social workers. Those who resisted the introduction of professionals in the COSs, claimed that both sides of the charitable relationship would suffer. The poor would be denied the particular kind of moral leadership that a volunteer could bring, while the latter would be denied the uplifting experience of meeting those who had to overcome adversity. Although today such attitudes would be rejected as naive, they are significant in that even those who were among the greatest supporters of the market system did not want that system to embrace all areas of social life. Not all social interaction involved 'products'. The attempt to extend ideas of economic exchange to social relationships emanates much more from some strands of late twentieth-century, 'New Right' economic thought, especially in the US, than directly from nineteenth century views. In this 'New Right' perspective any activity that is not guided by liberal economic principles will produce inefficiencies, and society would be better served by its elimination. The social order sought by the COSs would now be maintained solely by the acceptance of the order of the market place. This view is not opposed to philanthropy, after all people may do what they like with their money, but it is opposed to inefficient allocations of resources, such as the diversion of funds by corporations to philanthropy and to volunteerism as a way of supplying goods. Thus within modern conservative thought we find an important division, between supporters of a 'third sector', and its peculiar attributes like volunteerism, which has its origins in late-nineteenth-century views of *social* institutions, and an 'economic' conservatism which is founded entirely on the institution of the market. With the important exception of adherents of this latter view, the main dispute about the value of volunteering in market societies has not been about whether it is desirable at all, but about those areas of social life in which voluntary labour is supposedly superior.

4 The Consequences for the State of Volunteerism

If voluntary labour emerges in any capitalist state, what are the consequences for the state? Or, more precisely, what difference is it likely to make to the state whether a relatively smaller, or larger, amount of activity is being undertaken by volunteers? From our preceding discussion it is clear that one consequence of a weak tradition of volunteering in the social services, or a decline in volunteering, would be to require the state to provide more or to force it to let some needs go unmet. Volunteers do partially 'fill gaps' in state provision, even if, as Sosin has shown, voluntary agencies do not tend to operate in those places where the 'gaps' are greatest.[37] But the contribution of volunteers is not just the millions of hours of unpaid labour they supply in the social services. Volunteers are also instrumental in raising funds for organizations – funds which are unlikely to be raised in any other way, the absence of which would also necessitate either greater state expenditure or the non-provision of services. But should volunteers be too successful in this, there may be an incentive for the state to reduce its own expenditures and to let the voluntary agencies assume a greater share. In view of the point we made earlier about the general pressure on fund-raising in the mid- to late twentieth century, it would seem that this is not a common problem faced by the agencies. But there is one area where it has occurred – medical research in Britain. Fund-raising by these charities is heavily dependent on volunteers, many of them relatives of people affected by the particular disease in question; in 1979 the state (through the Medical Research Council) spent about twice as much on research as the members of the Association of Medical Research Charities, but by 1984 the former's share of their combined expenditures was only about 56 per cent.[38] A steady growth in the charities' income of about 9 per cent a year in this period was then countered by a 'levelling off' in state funding after 1981.

A second aspect of the effect of volunteering on the state concerns the consequences of citizen participation in social and political affairs. One long-standing argument about participation is that the experience of it tends to decrease the likelihood that a person will place his/her own individual interests ahead of the group in which s/he participates. Interaction with others modifies the perspective of the participant. Obviously, the impact of this on the state depends on the forums in which volunteering occurs. On the one hand, it might be argued that volunteering may increase the stability of a political system because involvement, say, with others in a social welfare agency will encourage a view of society in which shared interests are emphasized. Concern for the poor would then manifest itself in reformist views – policy changes within the context of the survival of the political system. On the other hand, the group with which participants come to identify may not so much be the whole community as one component of it; the collective action that this gives rise to will more likely be in support of a class or section of the society, and this is more compatible with radical socio-political demands, including the transformation of the regime. One of the reasons why involvement in some charities is now supported by left-wing activists is that they are no longer seen as promoting reformist views among participants and those with whom they come into contact. Charities which promote left-wing values can maintain the political commitment of their volunteers and can help to radicalize those whom they are helping.

In the case of explicitly political volunteering, volunteerism is likely to have a significant impact on the nature of politics within the liberal democratic state. The precise form that this takes in particular states is more difficult to specify. Political volunteers are primarily concerned with issues and causes, though some may be mobilized by other factors, such as the comradeship involved in campaigning. One of the interesting features of political parties, even supposedly ideological parties like socialist parties, is that most recognized very early on that ideology would be insufficient for recruiting a mass membership. Their social and recreational facilties were important incentives for many who became members, and one effect was that internal clashes over issues and policies were not as destructive as they might have been in parties of ideologues; members tended to limit the intensity that such conflicts would be allowed to reach. For party leaderships this was important in that it made compromises in government easier to effect. However, the declining attractiveness of their recreational facilities has meant that many parties are now attracting more participants who are solely interested in ideology and public policy issues than they used to. And, of course, these new, largely middle-class, political volunteers are far more attracted to single-issue cause groups, in preference to parties, than were political activists at the beginning of the twentieth century. This has two effects on the style of political conflict within the state. One is that it becomes more difficult for elected politicians to keep disputes out of the public domain and to deal with them through a process of elite compromise. Even though there is little evidence that issue activists are extremists in their views, or are attracted to high-risk electoral strategies, as some early studies supposed them to be, the very openness of a conflict can make it less easy for a compromise to be reached. Volunteerism makes political management more complex. In addition, volunteers are often involved in controversies where an agreed solution is less easy anyway. Moral arguments about abortion, say, are less amenable to compromise than conflicts on economic issues, and the same is true of unilateral nuclear disarmament. The absence of acceptable intermediate positions which opposing sides can agree to does make volunteer politics today more dificult to manage. Nevertheless, this argument must not be overstated. As Tesh has argued in the case of single-issue politics in the US, the system of government itself forces these groups to compromise.[39] To have any impact at all, they must focus on short-term objectives – such as the maximum duration of a pregnancy in which abortion is permissible, or on the removal of particular kinds of nuclear weapons.

It is important to distinguish the arguments presented here from two misleading arguments about the nature of volunteer politics. We are arguing that volunteerism creates problems for political management partly because volunteers may have few ties to their organization other than a commitment to its cause, and partly because many of the issues around which volunteers mobilize today are ones where the 'middle ground' is largely missing. But volunteer politics have been criticized by others for the alleged extremist positions on issues many volunteers assume, and for a lack of concern to moderate their positions if elections are to be won. In brief, volunteers are supposed to be both extremists and risk-takers. These charges against volunteerism have quite a long history; for example, they formed a major theme of Wilson's study of Democratic political clubs in the US in the 1950s.[40] But are volunteers extremists? Certainly survey evidence suggests that participants in politics have views that are slightly different from others; as Nie et al. found in relation to party activists in the US: 'The data on the Republican activists indicate that they have a conservative bent like the ordinary Republicans, only more so.'[41] But it is important to bear in mind two points about this relation of activists to others. On many issues levels of information and the ability to conceptualize the issue may be rather lower among the wider public, so that it is scarcely surprising if, overall, activists have more firmly held views or want more extensive changes in public policy. Moreover, it is the belief that such changes are necessary which prompts individuals to become active in a cause in the first place, so that it would be surprising if they were representative of a broader public. So the real question is whether volunteers are not just different, but *radically* different in their views from other people. Of course, there are some organizations, like the Paedeophilia Information Exchange, which have commanded virtually no support at all, but these are tiny groups. The causes in which the vast majority of political volunteers are to be found are generally ones for which some measure of much wider support exists. Organizations that have little chance of mobilizing support from others do not usually try to do so. But bodies like CND and the anti-abortion lobbies can, and do, point to considerable opinion poll data indicating majority support for at least some of their objectives and policies. And while their overall position may not command majority support, they still represent significant currents of minority support. If they did not, their opponents would not have to work so hard in mobilizing against them.

What then of the charge of risk-taking? Sometimes this is what critics actually mean when they accuse volunteer politicians of being extremists: they are not bound by the usual constraints facing other actors in the political process. There are several points to consider in answering this. The first is that earlier studies, in the 1950s and 1960s, which suggested that volunteers in American political parties were quite prepared to let their party go down to defeat with 'purist' candidates, are being re-evaluated.[42] It now appears that instances of volunteers seemingly imposing unelectable candidates on their parties are related to whether the groups doing this had systematically been excluded from influence in the party and to simple misjudgements about who was electable. (If 'extremist' George McGovern was unelectable in 1972, then experience was to show that 'mainstream' Walter Mondale was equally unelectable twelve years later.) As Rapoport and his colleagues have shown, a strong commitment to particular issues and policy stances can go hand-in-hand with party loyalty and a commitment to the party winning.[43]

However, where critics of political volunteerism are on stronger ground is in arguing that political volunteers are less likely to be involved regularly in parties now, and are more likely to channel their participation through 'cause' groups, so that the constraints imposed by a party no longer apply. Certainly, there is something to this argument: issue groups follow election returns in a much less direct way than parties. But, for three reasons, this argument does not really substantiate the claim that there are no constraints on the demands issue groups can make in the political system. The first is that public opinion is important to them because if, quite demonstrably, they lack even significant minority support, governments will have no incentive to meet any of their demands. In addition, there is the argument advanced by Tesh that many supposedly single-issue groups – and she cites organizations in the clean air and nuclear weapons fields in the US – are actually multiple-issue groups.[44] Even when they begin as single-issue bodies, there is often pressure from some volunteers to take stances on, or campaign on, issues which fall outside their original brief. For example, CND in Britain opposed the Vietnam war in the 1960s and in the 1980s linked its opposition to nuclear weapons to an anti-nuclear fuel policy. A broader agenda does force groups to take account of how their other aims will be affected by a high-risk strategy in relation to one of them. Furthermore, a failed high-risk strategy might cripple a cause permanently. For example, one high-risk strategy open to CND might be to conduct a mass invasion of an American nuclear base in Britain, in the expectation that in the confusion some US servicemen might kill or seriously injure some CND members, thus provoking public reaction against the bases. But depending on just what happened, an invasion might well provoke sympathy for the American guards and completely erode CND's credibility. This is why peaceful resistance was such a successful strategy for Gandhi in India and for the civil rights movement in the US in the 1960s: it was difficult for protestors to be shown up in a bad light. It is a relatively low-risk strategy, but one consequence of that is that if the authorities can find a way of removing demonstrators without using violence any publicity value is greatly decreased. (Of all the sit-in campaigns in segregated facilities in the American south in the 1960s, the one in Albany almost failed for this very reason and came close to stopping the momentum which the civil rights movement was then gathering.) But, at least a failed low-risk strategy is unlikely to blight the long-term prospects for a cause in the way failed high-risk strategies can.

5 Changes in Volunteerism in the Liberal Democratic State

In this chapter we have indicated several ways in which volunteerism is continuing to change. The traditional middle-class female base of philanthropic volunteerism is being slowly eroded by changing employment patterns and family structure; radical politicians have discovered that philanthropic volunteering through the appropriate organizations can be compatible with, and possibly contribute to, more general political mobilizing of the working class; and political volunteering has become increasingly important, both inside political parties and, most especially, through issue groups. In concluding this chapter, we must now consider the question of whether certain kinds of volunteering are likely to be replaced by organizations that do not rely on volunteer labour. We begin by looking at the special case of political parties, then look at social movement organizations and more generally at interest groups, and conclude by considering the possible relevance of these arguments to other kinds of voluntary bodies.

The argument has been stated most clearly in the case of parties. In 1951, in the first (French) edition of *Political Parties*, Duverger argued that mass membership parties, pioneered by socialists, were the most advanced form of party organization.[45] By collecting dues from members they had devised a way of acquiring the finance necessary for running a large organization; at the same time members would be available to perform political tasks as part of their commitment to its collective goals. Sixteen years later Epstein argued against Duverger that the mass membership party was not the model that other parties would have to copy to remain competitive.[46] Rather, he claimed, new techniques, originating in the US, of campaigning through television, combined with the raising of funds from major economic interests, would make a large membership unnecessary for a party. The distinctive role of the member, in making direct contact with voters, would be rendered partly, though not wholly, redundant. Indirect campaigning would replace direct campaigning.

Since the 1960s further developments in opinion polling and the use of computers and word processors to distribute and target direct mail, both for propaganda and fund-raising purposes, have been seen by some as confirming Epstein's view that an army of volunteers could be dispensed with in electoral campaigning in the US. Certainly there have been campaigns where candidates have overcome the apparent disadvantage of having few volunteers by concentrating on media campaigning; one instance was Edward Koch in his successful bid for the mayor's office in New York in 1977.[47] However, it has also become clear that the comparative advantage of the new forms of campaigning cannot always be realized, and that there are serious costs to a party if it is organized without a large mass membership base.[48] Even Epstein was to argue in a new edition of his book that the American party model might not predominate outside the US in quite the way his earlier arguments may have suggested.[49] Nevertheless, there is little doubt that in many circumstances the availability of new methods of fund-raising (from business and direct-mail solicitations) does allow parties to modify the Duverger principle of expanding their membership bases as much as possible. There are now partial substitutes for members.

Paralleling this development in parties there have been rather similar developments among social movements in the US. Traditionally, organizations formed around social movements, such as those active in support of civil rights in the US in the 1950s and early 1960s, gained their resources from a large volunteer base. Even when there was no *formal* membership or membership dues, it was the members who were responsible for raising the necessary money. In the 1960s, though, relatively new kinds of organizations, to which McCarthy and Zald gave the name 'professional social movement organizations' started to appear and to operate alongside the 'classical' social movement organizations (SMOs). One of the main features of the former is that they 'direct resource appeals primarily towards conscience adherents and utilize few constitutents for organizational labour'.[50] That is, those who are to be the ultimate beneficiaries of successful collective action are not mobilized, and to the extent that labour is required, it is paid for on a commercial basis. Campaigning is conducted through the mass media, and through such devices as bringing law suits, rather than through marches, demonstrations and so on.

Obviously, this raises two questions – where do the resources for the new kind of organization come from, and why has it been in the years since the mid 1960s that this form has come into much greater prominence? The resources come from two kinds of 'conscience adherents' – individuals who sympathize with the cause (and donate money) and, most significantly in the early years of forming an organization, wealthy institutions, such as foundations, churches and governmental agencies. In the case of individuals, support from traditional donor groups, such as Jews in the civil rights movement, was supplemented greatly by the growth of sectors of the middle class with political interests that went far beyond narrowly-defined economic ones. The rise of so-called 'postmaterialist values' has produced a greater propensity for political activity,[51] and this has resulted not just in greater participation in politics by the post-materialist middle class, but also a much greater willingness to donate funds to organizations with goals they support. With elite institutions there has been disagreement as to their reasons for funding professional SMOs. Haines has argued that their funding of civil rights organizations stemmed from a desire to support more moderate bodies, and thereby remove the threat posed by radical civil rights groups.[52] Jenkins and Eckert agree that elite institutional funding was primarily 'reactive' in the case of civil rights, and arose from a perceived threat to national elites; however, they argue that the consequences were rather more complex than others have claimed:

Patronage may well have diverted leaders from indigenous organizing. It may also have exacerbated organizational rivalries and created the appearance of symbolic gains that weakened mass support for further organizing. Quite clearly, it ensured that the organizational vehicles for movement activity were increasingly professionalized. In short, patronage channelled the movement into professionalized forms. But it did not divert the movement from its concern with the 'black power' agenda or drastically reduce the role of protests.[53]

At the same time as new forms of organizations associated with social movements were emerging, so too were new kinds of interest groups. Some of the environmental and 'public interest' lobbies that developed in the 1960s and 1970s were organized on explicitly mass membership lines; Common Cause is an outstanding example of this. But at the same time, smaller groups, drawing their funds from foundations, government programmes or similar sources were also finding it easier to survive. Foundations, in particular, were a central source of initial funding for these groups, referred to by Walker as citizen groups:

Government agencies and foundations both made contributions to the founding of a few groups in the profit sector, but their efforts are clearly concentrated in the mixed, nonprofit, and citizen sectors. After 1945 the government supplanted foundations as a source of start up money for groups in the nonprofit sector, while foundations shifted more of their attention toward the citizen groups.[54]

Their reasons for becoming involved in funding political activity were also summarized well by Walker:

Several of the country's largest foundations only began serious operations in the 1950s and were in search for a meaningful role in American life. Foundation officials believed that the long-run stability of the representative policymaking system would be assured only if legitimate organizational channels could be provided for the frustration and anger being expressed in protests and outbreaks of political violence during this period.[55]

In other words, as with organizations built around social movements, elite patronage stemmed from a belief that perceived imbalances in the political system had to be corrected through the injection of financial support to groups that otherwise might not form.

But how do these developments relate to those in Britain? Although some aspects of the new campaign technology have been embraced by political parties, tight controls on candidate expenditure and a tradition of strong membership organizations have prevented the emergence of wholly elite-based parties. Moreover, with respect to SMOs and interest groups the British experience has also been very different. The very strict distinction between political and non-political activities has prevented British foundations from following the American lead in funding organizations that are explicitly political. Also Britain did not expand its welfare services by making grants available for which private agencies could compete, as the US did in the 1960s. The state funding around which 'professional' interest groups could develop was much less, and it was not until the 1980s, with the Thatcher government's commitment to reducing direct government provision of services that these contracting relationships started to develop. New groups formed around the issues of poverty, third world development, and environmental protection, for example, have started in the last two or three decades, but these agencies are far more likely to resemble 'classical' organizations in being membership, and participation, orientated: 'New-style agencies tend to adopt a progressive view of society and a participative organisation structure.'[56] And those charitable trusts that did make contributions to organizations engaged in community work, and other projects designed to benefit the poor, were not doing so from fear that the political process was under pressure. Indeed, trusts were often sympathetic to the idea of funding projects that could demonstrate activist support and more sceptical of supporting 'professional' organizations for whom participation was of relatively little importance. Where, in the longer term, new ways of raising funds will have the greatest impact on volunteerism in both Britain and America relates to volunteer-dominated philanthropies that are primarily concerned with raising money. Medical research charities are a good example of the current use of volunteers to co-ordinate local fund-raising events. Computerized mailing lists and other devices will not remove the need for volunteers, but they are likely to reduce the number of mundane tasks for which traditionally volunteer labour has been required.

Finally, we must return to the issue we raised at the beginning of the last chapter, and which prompted our examination of volunteerism. We suggested that proponents of the notion of a distinct 'third sector' in the capitialist democracies, which can respond to objectively defined needs in society, see the autonomy of such a sector lying in two of its features: its financial independence from the both the market and the state and the role played in the constituent organizations by volunteer labour. In the last chapter we suggested that the arguments about the financial autonomy of many of these organizations have been overstated. But what about the contribution of volunteerism? Many of the larger organizations that are claimed to be part of this 'sector', universities and hospitals for example, either rely on volunteers relatively little or use them to perform largely menial tasks. If volunteerism is to provide a distinctive character to a supposed 'third sector', it is because volunteers have an impact on the nature of the activities engaged in by an organization. This is not to say that volunteers must be involved in the national decision making of an organization for volunteerism to make a difference – this would be too strict a test. But clearly, at the local level, in how they perform their tasks, volunteers must have some measure of control. And all that we can do here is admit that there is enormous variation between organizations in this regard. Even in political parties, which are often regarded as among the most elite-dominated membership organizations, the extent of member control does vary greatly.

Consequently, if there is an argument about a distinctive 'third sector' responding to social needs, it must surely be considerably smaller than 'third sector' proponents have usually been prepared to acknowledge. Not only would it exclude, as the proponents would admit, some of the explicitly political volunteer bodies, but many others as well. Organizations responding to social needs in which volunteers play a major role are much fewer in number than legal charities or, even, voluntary social service agencies. Thus, while the idea of a state sector or of a commercial sector requires us to overlook complex sets of relationships involving organizations in both sectors, the notion of a *sector* still remains a clear one; it is far from evident that the 'third sector' is not merely an almagamation of disparate organizations, although at the 'core' there may well be organizations that are distinctive in the way 'third sector' proponents suggest. But this 'core' is far smaller than most discussions about the 'third sector' usually indicate.

6

Dangerous Areas of State Involvement?

This chapter is about three kinds of organization which share one important feature – a feature which is widely regarded as crucial in explaining the need for at least some IOs in the liberal democratic state. They are all seen as providing benefits for society that would be critically compromised were their provision to be in the hands of government. At the same time these benefits are not likely to be provided for fully in the market system, as there is the possibility that the benefit would also be undermined were it the object of economic exchange. These organizations are churches (and similar religious bodies), institutions conducting 'pure' academic research, and those creating, exhibiting or performing artistic works. There are several points we must make immediately in connection with the claim that the goods generated by these organizations are such as to make both market and governmental supply either impossible or undesirable.

It was certainly not the case in the centuries before the rise of liberal democracy that there was widespread acceptance that these activities should be engaged in by autonomous or semi-autonomous institutions. In the case of religion, as we have seen, the Roman church claimed to be *the* state, but if the Reformation entailed a changed relationship between church and state, it did not lead directly to church autonomy within the Protestant states or to a belief in the value of a plurality of religions:

> To most minds of the seventeenth and eighteenth centuries an established church reflected the proper relationship between the post-Reformation church and government.... even the French Huguenots who would have gained freedom from persecution thereby, tended to agree that diversity in religion was unseemly in a nation. The United States Bill of Rights (1791) seems to have been the

first constitutional recognition that pluralism in religion might be positively justifiable in its own right.[1]

An established church would help to prevent the erosion of state power, for as Pye has argued of the process of political development in Europe:

the typical legitimacy crisis in Europe involved a clash of church-state relations. Secular state authority had to compete against religious, parochial, and other forms of institutionalized authority in which the erosion of authority that is related to industrialization and social modernization had not as yet disrupted the more traditional bonds of society.[2]

Until the state had established supremacy against potential rival sources of power, religious pluralism and independence for the church could not be granted. Consequently, the view that there should be autonomous religious institutions within a sovereign state is one that started to become widely propagated only in the early stages of the emergence of liberal democracy.

The view that researchers and artists should similarly enjoy protection from interference by the state came even later. Of course, not all the benefits provided by religious, research and artistic institutions potentially involve the problems of compromising values when supplied by the state or the market, and, indeed, this is the source of one of the main difficulties in establishing appropriate sets of relations with the state. Moreover, although the shared feature of these kinds of institution provides an important reason for considering them together, there are significant differences between them, and this has a considerable impact on their varying relations with both market and state.

The argument, advanced by liberals, for the propagation of religious knowledge and experience to be conducted by non-state agencies is that understanding and appreciating either deities or moral codes is sufficiently complex that it is a matter about which even reasonable people are likely to disagree. For the state to train and organize religious leaders, much as it might civil servants, would be to make it more likely that false orthodoxies or practices would be perpetuated. Competition among ideas is necessary for two reasons. With religion it is difficult to distinguish between valuable and worthless changes in understanding and practices; and attempts at stifling conflict are likely to intensify opposition by heretical groups. The modern idea that pluralism in religious beliefs was preferable to conformity, even if it led to the propagation of false doctrines, is one that spread slowly as the liberal creed of devolving other kinds of decisions to individuals spread. But the possibility that competition between religions could intensify divisions within a society has meant that even liberals have often been wary of fully extending *laissez-faire* principles to this area.

Similarly, the argument for having 'pure' research conducted by independent bodies also has to do with the problem of specifying in advance how progress is most likely to be made.[3] The state, it is argued, may stifle unorthodox research because it does not conform to conventional assumptions, and as a result potential advances in knowledge may be lost. Now this argument does not assume a Popperian view of the scientific community, in which there is open competition between alternative views. Its proponent could accept Kuhn's view that the scientific community tends to exclude the unorthodox, but s/he *might* argue that having governmental agencies directly controlling academic research further exacerbates conservatizing tendencies.[4] But why can the market not provide for pure research? Two factors are relevant here: the high, and increasing, cost of pure research in the twentieth century, and the unknowability of its results mean that no commercial enterprises would bother to finance it, at least on grounds of self-interest. Such enterprises will only be interested in funding research when there is likely to be some tangible benefit to them at its conclusion. Consequently, there is a gap which other institutions have to fill. This argument about the market is rather different in the case of religion. With pure research there is a public good that would not be supplied if for-profit enterprises were the only actors involved; with religion the argument is that treating the relationship between priests (or whatever) and followers as if it were mainly a commercial transaction is likely to destroy part of what is valuable about religious experience. Of course, some religious leaders, including evangelical television preachers in the US, have followers who are quite happy to know that their religious leaders are making large sums of money, but for the most part congregations are suspicious of income-maximizing behaviour.

With the arts the difficulties posed by market and state provision are slightly different again. In the market there may be not enough demand for some artistic forms, or, as with opera, the cost of providing the goods may be high in relation to demand, so that too little of the good would be provided in relation to what is perceived by some to be an appropriate amount. Clearly, this notion of what is an appropriate level of supply involves non-market considerations – views about what an emotionally and intellectually healthy community requires to function properly. The market might be an adequate mechanism for producing some of these goods, but not all of them. In the case of the arts, unlike that of pure research, therefore, the market may be capable of providing much, though not all, of what is needed. As with research, though, direct state intervention could lead to the stifling of certain kinds of initiatives – initiatives that might prove important in the future development of some art forms – because political decision-makers may seek to impose their own tastes or views on artists and those who manage artistic enterprises.[5]

Given the sensitivity of possible state intervention in at least some of the activities of these three kinds of organizations, several aspects of their relations with the state are worth examining. In this chapter we focus on the following: state financial aid to these organizations, how the state has dealt with potential conflict between the 'sensitive' activities of the organizations and other activities in which the state has a legitimate interest, and the ways in which these organizations can be regulated to prevent financial and other abuses.

1 Financial Aid from the State

A Churches

In relation to state funding, churches and other religious bodies have been treated very differently to research or artistic institutions. Among those who have rejected the establishment of a single religion, the consensual view has been that the churches, and their members, should be responsible entirely for funding their activities.

The Bill of Rights in the American Constitution explicitly prohibits the establishment of religion; even if the First Amendment was to be treated far more narrowly than it actually has been by most courts, it would be difficult to reconcile it with government financing of sacramental activities. As we have noted, the Bill of Rights is the first example of a constitutional commitment by a state to what might be called 'voluntaristic pluralism' – the idea that people should have the opportunity to *decide* which religion to practise. The US was not to be like the 'mother country', in that a person would be able to choose his/her religion, and, of course, it was an idea which meshed well with the values of economic choice being propagated in this advanced commercial society. With the mass immigration of Catholics (and, later, Orthodox Christians and Jews from eastern Europe) in the nineteenth century, this idea of 'voluntaristic pluralism' gradually became interlinked with a rather separate notion associated with 'cultural pluralism'. This was the idea that different ethnic groups, many of which were distinctive partly because of their religious beliefs, were entitled to equality of respect. It was the ethnic group, as much as the individual, which became the focus of religious freedom.

Developments in Britain were rather different. While most of the legislation which discriminated against non-Anglicans was repealed by the end of the nineteenth century, the idea that it was desirable for individuals to be able to choose their religion from a wide range of religions never became popular. Instead, changes in attitudes to religious pluralism were brought about, in the later twentieth century, by immigration to Britain in the 1950s and 1960s from the Indian sub-continent. It was the recognition that Britain was now a culturally pluralistic society that helped the emergence of the view that, for many purposes, other religions had to be treated as the equal of Anglicanism. Thus, there has been a growing acceptance in twentieth-century Britain that the maintenance of an established religion is compatible with religious pluralism in society. At the same time, there has been a recognition that there should not be direct state financial support for any churches, even Anglican ones. To a large extent, such a position was made possible by the complex history of the Church of England itself, which at its founding can be seen as embracing elements of both 'nationalization' and 'privatization'.

Henry VIII's break with Rome led to political control of the English church switching from the Pope to the English monarch. Appointments to senior positions in the church were placed in the hands of the Crown, thereby giving the monarch, and subsequently prime ministers, a considerable source of patronage. Nevertheless, this 'nationalization' of the church was restricted in two ways. First, power to appoint to many lower livings in the Anglican church came once again to rest not with the Crown, but with private individuals, so that the English church never had the characteristics of a pure state agency. As Youings notes:

> In the diocese of Canterbury the amount of lay patronage more than doubled between 1533 and 1553, from 16 per cent to 38 per cent, a surprisingly high proportion in an area so dominated by the primate, but the situation was not dissimilar in other dioceses. Advowsons were, and still are, a form of real, that is freehold, property, and along with tithes, could be bought, sold and also leased.[6]

Second, the Crown takeover did not necessitate state financial aid to sustain the church; to the contrary, the accumulated wealth of the church had been a potential source of conflict with the civil state since the middle ages, and the opportunity to confiscate the wealth of the monasteries was itself a strong incentive for the Reformation in England. At the parish level, churches were maintained by tithes, but in many cases after the Reformation 'the ownership of tithes had passed into the hands of laymen and had developed a nearly unfathomable complexity.'[7] Titheing remained controversial, but its maintenance represented an *indirect* form of state aid. It was only later with dwindling congregations, and the consequent need to close churches, that the question of direct state aid might have arisen. But, with the acceptance of the idea that

England was a multi-denominational society, the possibility of direct financing by the state to subsidize sacramental activity within one denomination never arose.

But if direct state financial aid has not been extended to religions, there are several important indirect ways, in addition to the preservation of tithes, in which it has. The most long standing of these have been those derived from religions being entitled to charitable status. Implicitly the Statute of Charitable Uses recognized the 'advancement of religion' as a charitable purpose and there have been few political challenges to this. Before explaining the exact financial benefits which stem from charitable status, it is first necessary to explain how religion has been conceived in law. In this respect it is also important to distinguish between England and the US. Since the nineteenth century, English law has given a liberal interpretation to the nature of religion in two respects – 'both as to the range of faiths which may be "advanced" and as to the methods which may be adopted in endeavouring to advance them'.[8] But English law has restricted what is to count as advancing religion in other respects. For example, it must involve some form of worship of a deity, so that bodies merely advancing ethical principles are not charitable. Again, law in England does not allow all activities pursued by a body that is recognizably a religion to count as charitable. In some cases the purposes of the organization have been held by the courts not to benefit the public and are therefore not charitable. Thus, a trust to establish a convent for nuns who would remain entirely cloistered from the rest of the world has been denied charitable status.[9]

Even though American trust law has remained remarkably similar to English law, the situtation in the US is very different. There are two reasons for this. The prohibition in the Constitution of the establishment of religion has actually been interpreted by governmental agencies, and indeed by the courts, to limit any investigations they might carry out to determine whether an organization is religious and how that organization operates. American courts have also held that nontheistic organizations are entitled to tax exemption, if this is available to theistic groups.[10] Nor has the Internal Revenue Service, federal income tax legislation, nor any US Treasury regulation, ever defined the terms 'religious' or 'religion'.[11] Moreover, since it is laws on non-profit organizations, rather than laws relating to charitable trusts, which are the ones most affecting religious groups, there has been a tendency towards a much more liberal interpretation of what can be registered as a religious group. For example, Oleck notes that:

> in early 1970, atheist Madelyn Murray O'Hair, well known for her opposition to all religion, said in Austin, Texas, that she and her husband, Richard, had

organized the Poor Richard's . . . Church for tax evasion purposes. She said, 'From here on we're going to take every exemption.'[12]

Oleck goes on to observe that there have also been advertisements in newspapers explaining how people can 'turn themselves' into churches. Like federal legislation, state legislation has been unconcerned with religion: non-profit laws have rarely addressed the question of what is to constitute a religion, and this has permitted religion to become a broad category in non-profit legislation.

As charities, religious organizations receive two main kinds of financial benefit from the state in both Britain and the US. The most important is that they are wholly exempt from income tax – in the US every state exempts churches from state income taxes in addition to their being free of federal income tax. In fact, their treatment in America has often been better than other charities, in that income from so-called 'unrelated business' activities has also been tax-exempt. This was not challenged at all until 1969, when a case in New York held that revenue from property leased by a religious organization to a day camp was taxable income.[13] Of course, this ruling applies only to that state, and in most states all church income, from whatever sources, is tax-free. This explains why Ms O'Hair was so keen to organize her life as a church. The Tax Reform Act of 1986 confirmed the generally favourable status granted to churches. One provision of this Act repealed the exemption 501(c)(3) non-profits had enjoyed in regard to commercial-type insurance they had provided, but:

there are exceptions to taxation. One is the exemption for property and casualty insurance provided by a church plan for a church or for an association of churches. Similarly exempt is the provision of retirement and welfare benefits under church aegis for its employees or their beneficiaries.[14]

However, there has been some tightening of the special provisions of which churches can take advantage under federal income tax. Under legislation in 1950 concerning the unrelated business income of non-profits, churches were exceptional in being excluded explicitly from the requirement to pay taxes on such income. This was changed by the Tax Reform Act of 1969, though the legislation did not come into effect until 1976. The congressional Joint Committee on Internal Revenue Taxation pointed out that such legislation was necessary because some churches were operating publishing houses, hotels, factories, radio and TV stations, bakeries, restaurants and other enterprises.[15] Nevertheless, the 'kid glove' approach to churches remains in that, unlike other non-profits, churches may not be audited except by a direct order from a Regional Commissioner in the Internal Revenue Service.[16] In England churches enjoy the same income tax exemptions as other charities, and are subject to similar liabilities in relation to profits from trading; as we will see in chapter 7, all British charities are prohibited from trading if this constitutes more than a small part of their activities.

The other tax benefit enjoyed by churches in both countries is freedom from property taxes. In England, indeed, churches are specially advantaged by this in comparison with other charities, in that they are wholly exempt; for other charities a distinction is drawn between the mandatory relief on the rates to which all charities are entitled and the discretionary relief which is decided upon by individual local authorities.[17] Generally, in the US only those non-profits deemed to be charitable receive property tax exemption, and there is no special treatment for churches. This idea that churches are not treated exceptionally was important in the Supreme Court's decision in the *Walz* case in 1972 when it held property tax exemptions to churches were constitutional. The Court noted that:

> New York . . . has not singled out one particular church or religious group or even churches as such; rather, it has granted exemption to all houses of religious worship within a broad category of property owned by nonprofit, quasi-public corporations which include hospitals, libraries, playgrounds, scientific, professional, historical, and patriotic groups.[18]

Unlike their English counterparts, American churches are also usually exempt from sales taxes, unless they are engaged in business. This is a privilege churches share with other American charities, whereas successive British governments have withstood pressure from charities for them to be exempt from Value Added Tax.

For the most part, then, churches have enjoyed tax concessions broadly similar to other organizations which would be charitable in law, although in the US the enforcement of tax laws in relation to churches has probably given them an advantageous position. The other source of indirect state aid to churches is more difficult to assess, however. This is the money they receive from governmental agencies to provide services, such as schools, day-care centres, foster homes and so on which they have tended to provide as part of their pastoral work. In some instances, the money received is in the form of grants designed to provide state subsidies for services the churches have been providing anyway, while in other instances governments pay fees which amount to the full cost for the service. Especially in the US, where churches have been important 'third party' agencies in the expansion of welfare provision, contractual arrangements between local governments and churches constitute a major element of state-church relations. In New York City, for example, only about 10 per cent of foster children are housed in city-operated homes.

The remainder are provided for under contracts, totalling about $300 million a year in the mid 1980s, between the City and 57 private agencies, most of them with religious affiliations.

Although contracting of this kind has occasioned disputes about the policies religious agencies may pursue in relation to individuals whom they are being paid to care for, in the US it has been in connection with grants that controversy about the separation of state and church has been greatest. Aid to church schools has been a major political issue for some years, and court decisions in this area have attracted criticism about the confusion generated by attempts to separate church and state.[19] For the most part, American courts have sought to distinguish between secular and sectarian purposes, and they have allowed state funding for the former but not the latter. However, defining secular purposes is difficult. The Supreme Court has permitted aid for bussing children to schools and for the costs of administering state-prepared tests, but not the lending of equipment to religious schools. But, of course, any kind of aid, whether it be for state-required purposes or not, necessarily helps a church by paying for items which it would otherwise have to buy itself, if it were to continue to run a school. In England, where the history of church-state relations means that the modern state is less concerned with maintaining a strict separation of the two, direct aid is made available to schools – and not merely to Anglican schools. The theory behind this is that schooling for their pupils would have to be provided anyway, and providing grants is a cheaper solution than the state having to replace those church schools which would close because of a lack of funds. In the US this rationale, of the state obtaining a 'good deal' through making use of church facilities, is more widely accepted in relation to payments made for non-educational services such as day care. In part this is because the relationship between church and state is supposed to be a strictly financial one, and away from areas like education, where the issue of religious indoctrination is problematic, it is possible to view churches as similar to any other kind of organization with which the state might enter into a contract.

But are churches actually advantaged by the contractual relationships into which they enter? One view is that churches, like other charities, tend to be the victims of the state in that they cannot charge the full economic price for the services they supply, and that, especially in periods of cutbacks in government spending, they are under pressure from governments to absorb more of the costs of a service. The state knows that a sense of duty, as well as possible public hostility, forces churches to continue to provide services even when they would rather not. Another view, however, is that, of all charities, churches are among the best able to protect themselves from attempts to have them bear the costs of service provision. For example, when in 1987 the Catholic diocese of New York was considering terminating its contracts with New York City for the provision of foster homes for children, the church itself admitted that this would reduce its income by $100 million, but this was a loss it was prepared to sustain.[20] Moreover, the cost to a church of providing these services is often secondary to the benefits it gains, in terms of building social networks, from being a major supplier of services. It increases its penetration of communities – providing a church with access to potential converts and to active members, creating further activities with which to involve members of congregations and generally favourable publicity to the church. In short, service provision helps churches to counteract the pressures towards secularization by placing them more at the centre of a whole network of social relations in a community. In this sense, any state financial aid helps to preserve religious institutions. This is consistent with the widely-held view in the US that the intention of the Founding Fathers was merely to prevent the establishment of a *single* religion, and not to prevent the state from facilitating religious organizations, as a whole, from entrenching themselves in American society.

B Colleges and universities

Academic research and the arts are more like each other than either resembles a religious organization in relation to financial assistance from the state. But there are important differences both between these two policy areas and also between the US and Britain. Universities present the more complex case. Colleges and universities are part of a rather small category of English charities – ones which receive their status by Royal Charter. Before the Reformation the relations between the two old English universities and the state were, in Berdahl's words, 'many and various',[21] but they did not, of course, include financial aid. Nor after the Reformation was this an issue – rather the sources of conflict between the two centred on such matters as loyalty to the Crown and later the self-indulgence of the universities, which in the nineteenth century was to lead to state-imposed reforms. The older colleges of Oxford and Cambridge had large endowments, and it was only with the establishment of new colleges in the nineteenth century that the question of financial aid arose. A special grant was made when the University of London received its charter in 1836. Further requests for grants for newly-founded colleges were denied until 1882, but a system of annual grants, varying from £500 to £1,800, was started in 1889. This system expanded, and in 1919 a University Grants Committee (UGC) consisting of academics was established to administer the grant for universities provided by the Treasury.[22]

By this means of direct financing distributed through an independent body, the British state became the major source of income for British universities, and this dependence on the state continued to grow. Parliamentary grants accounted for 33.6 per cent of university income in 1920–1, but by 1955–6 they constituted 72.7 per cent of income and this trend continued through the years of expansion in higher education in the 1960s. Correspondingly, income from fees, endowments and donations declined from 1920–1, when they formed 46.9 per cent of total income, to 1955–6 when they amounted to no more than 15.5 per cent of the total.[23] Now, and this is a point discussed further in the next section, in funding universities the British government was financing a much wider range of activities than pure research, but it was the complex interaction of these activities which formed the basis for the conduct of that research. Two other sources of state funding in the years after the second world war further bolstered the state's role. Research Councils, attached to government departments, became key funding agencies for research, and new councils, such as the Social Science Research Council, were created to extend state sponsorship to areas where it had previously not been involved. (Under a system of 'dual funding', the UGC provided items such as buildings, basic equipment and teaching staff, while grants from the research councils for specific research projects paid for other research costs, including staff.) Again, a system of mandatory local government grants for university students meant that much of the fee income earned by universities also originated with central government – because of the relatively high proportion of local government income emanating in grants from central government.

Despite the immense financial involvement of the British state in all universities, a set of procedures was established by which governmental and parliamentary pressure on the universities was minimized. The members of the UGC itself were academics, and neither political nor policy considerations seem to have been invoked in appointments to it. Grants were made to cover a five year period, and the quinquennium system removed universities from the public eye. The Treasury, to which the UGC was formally responsible did not attempt to influence how money should be spent by the universities, and successive governments greatly restricted information to Parliament which might have enabled it to oversee this area of public expenditure. By these devices political pressure on the UGC was minimized. Indeed, in the 1950s the autonomy which the UGC and the universities had established led to disagreement between the Treasury and the Public Accounts Committee of the House of Commons, as to whether the former was providing the latter with sufficient information for it to be able to perform its accountability function.[24]

This stable system of state finance and university autonomy broke down from the early 1960s onwards, and by the 1980s it had been replaced by much more direct state intervention in the universities. There were a number of interrelated factors bringing this about. The whole question of national policy in relation to higher education had been debated since the second world war, but it was not until the early 1960s that a policy for rapid expansion of higher education was implemented. A much larger university sector increased greatly the state's financial stake in the universities. Because universities now formed part of a more wide-ranging higher education policy, responsibility for funding them was transferred from the Treasury to the Department of Education and Science, where there was no tradition of guarding jealously the autonomy of the universities. Moreover, in the later 1960s the Labour government expanded the provision of tertiary education by making more funds available to the local government run polytechnics, institutions which were much cheaper to fund, at least as far as undergraduate education was concerned, than universities. Some polytechnic departments, though not all, became active in pure research, so that it was no longer the case that all such research was being conducted in supposedly autonomous organizations. This was to weaken the case for university autonomy when, in response to the problems facing the British economy, governments sought to reduce their expenditures in the 1970s.

The first break with the mid-twentieth-century way of handling state-university relations was the effective abandonment of the quinquennium system in the early 1970s. Successive governments slowly undermined UGC authority. However, the Conservative government elected in 1979 was to adopt an approach that was to make the UGC unviable in the long term, and was to lead to its replacement. In the short term, though, the UGC took on a broader role in relation to the universities – a role which had been envisaged for it as early as 1946.[25] The Conservative government thereby converted the UGC into little more than an agency for implementing the policies of the Department of Education and Science, and in the 1980s it sought to effect greater control over the kinds of subjects to which emphasis in research and teaching would be given. In the mid 1980s the UGC even began evaluating the merits of different university departments, with a view to persuading universities to give relatively greater funding to the supposedly better departments, and curtailing funds to what were described as 'below-average' departments. In some cases even the closing of departments was recommended. The reduction in funding to some universities was so great that plans for dismissing tenured members of staff had to be initiated. Moreover, one policy that was being discussed seriously in 1987 involved the teaching of courses being conducted on market principles, with institutions submitting bids to teach particular courses: the lowest tender getting the contract.

In Britain, then, state funding of academic research was largely absent until the end of the nineteenth century, and then expanded enormously in the twentieth century. Expansion was first undertaken in conjunction with a policy of autonomy for the universities, but this was later undermined and more direct forms of control, based on the financial dependence of the universities, was initiated. In America too concern has been expressed that the traditional independence enjoyed by 'private' colleges and universities since the early nineteenth century has been undermined in some ways, but the main problems there have been rather different than those in Britain. To understand this we need to understand the somewhat different history of American higher education. As in England, the first colleges in colonial America were private institutions, although some like Harvard College were initially joint ventures between private philanthropy and a state government. However, two conflicting approaches to private corporations in the US emerged at the end of the eighteenth century. In much of the north, especially New England, private institutions were valued while, in the south, the Jeffersonian tradition was suspicious of private centres of power. When attempts at public control of private colleges were thrown out by the courts, and the *Dartmouth College* case of 1819 is usually cited as a turning point in providing private institutions with freedom from state intervention, the only alternatives to autonomous private colleges were public ones. This indeed was the response both of those opposed to centres of private power and also of regions where there were not major philanthropists willing to found new private colleges. Nevertheless, in the nineteenth century it was the private colleges which became the dominant element among institutions of higher education in the US – with respect to size and reputation for excellence. In the twentieth century two developments were to modify this position. First, the growing emphasis on research, and on the research university in which it would be conducted, led the most prestigious private institutions to curtail their expansion of student enrollments. They concentrated much more on research than on undergraduate education, thereby creating a vacuum which would be filled by other institutions. In 1915 five private universities (Chicago, Columbia, Cornell, Harvard and Pennsylvania) accounted for over 9 per cent of all college student enrollments; by 1939 they enrolled just over 3 per cent of all students.[26] Second, the growing cost of research in the sciences prevented expansion of higher education in the private sector commensurate with the demand for it, and this produced pressure for governmental action from important groups in state electorates. Especially after the second world war, virtually all state governments greatly expanded access to public universities. While the long-established, elite, private universities retained their reputations for excellence, they were now a much smaller component of the higher education sector.

One argument, then, about American universities has been that the private sector has shrunk too much in relation to the public sector, and that this has been the main factor undermining the goals and policies pursued within higher education. This is not a convincing argument for three reasons.

It is far from clear that the forms of control found in state universities do actually undermine academic independence in ways different from that found in American private universities. It is true that during the McCarthy era publicly supported institutions in the US were vulnerable to investigations by state legislatures into 'un-American' activities. And critics can point to controversies like that over loyalty oaths at the University of California in the late 1940s as examples of gross interference with academic freedoms. But the overall record of private universities in the hiring and tenuring of left-wing academics probably differs little from that in the public sector, and even those institutions that now display pride in their record against McCarthyism were often far less scrupulous than they claim to be. For example:

> Recent evidence suggests that even Harvard, which has long congratulated itself for stubbornly resisting McCarthy's onslaught, secretly pressured ex-Communist faculty members to inform on former party associates when asked to do so by the FBI or other government investigators. Moreover, Harvard's much acclaimed defence of academic immunity did not extend to nontenured faculty, administrators, or graduate students.[27]

Again, whatever protection for academic independence could be provided by private universities would surely be provided by their continuing presence, rather than by their maintaining a particular share of student enrollments.

Furthermore, it can be argued that the influence of for-profit firms on private universities can be at least as pernicious as that of the state on public universities in undermining the indepedence of institutions. One much-publicized recent example was the decision by the University of Rochester to rescind the registration of an employee of the Fuji photographic film company in a course that would have involved him sharing classes with employees of the Kodak company.[28] Kodak, which is based in Rochester, has long been the main corporate supporter of the university and was worried that the Fuji employee would gain access to sensitive information.

A more serious debate has been about the growing influence of federal government funding on all universities. As with governmental financial support in Britain, the federal government supports universities in a number of indirect ways now, including for example the provision of loans to students to enable them to finance their studies. But the most important area has been in providing funds for research, especially pure research. As the costs of research have increased, universities have become more dependent on securing these funds. Indeed, they are required not merely for keeping research teams in employment, but as an important source for cross-subsidizing other aspects of university work. Unlike the British Research Councils which do not permit universities to add on to any research grant proposal a proportion of the total cost as a charge for administering the grants, a generous surcharge, far in excess of the actual administrative costs, is permitted by the federal government. These 'overhead' fees are then attached to the university's general funds. Thus, a failure to replace expiring large grants with new ones not only affects the prestige of a university department and the livelihood of its supporting staff, but may have serious consequences for other departments as well; this increases the pressure on all academic staff to be successful in 'grantsmanship'. The first arguments about the possible adverse effects of grant-dependence were raised in the 1970s, but since then there has been a spectacular growth in grants for research and development to universities and colleges. The growth has been greatest for pure research which increased from $1.2 billion in 1974 to $4 billion in 1985, while total grants rose $2.2 million to $6.3 million in that period.[29]

Three main criticisms have been made of this dependence, at least as it bears on the issue of preserving academic independence so that conditions necessary for optimally advancing knowledge can be sustained. The first is that it orientates universities towards a particular way of organizing their activities, and tends to lead to the downgrading of activities such as teaching which are still important in an indirect way for the 'research culture' of an institution. Second, because funding comes from so many sources in the federal government, rather than being centralized in organizations like the British Research Councils, there is a tendency for a market-type mechanism to come into effect. Researchers gear their research proposals very much to what they know the grant-giving agencies are interested in, so that the very decentralization of the grant-giving process tends to discourage unusual or high-risk research. Under a more centralized system, an overview of the entire field for possible funding would partially restrict this orientation towards 'grantsmanship'. Third, it has been disputed whether much of the funding which is classified as pure research really warrants this description, and it has been argued that the federal government's agencies are still far more interested in research that will be of direct use to them.

But there is a fourth criticism of the high level of state funding of research which is applicable to Britain as well as to the US. It is that, if the state commits itself to funding research, and then subsequently reduces its commitments, it forces universities and their researchers to look to whatever commercial applications of research there may be. This was described by the President of Harvard as making 'our campuses highly dependent on forces beyond their control',[30] and he argued that faculty members would tend to stray from their academic goals as they attempted to market their skills in 'extra-mural ventures' that provide them with a 'mounting source of excitement, variety, status and income'. The main difference between Britain and the US in this regard in the 1980s was that in Britain there was a deliberate government policy to encourage such ventures, while in the US it was an unintended consequence of the developing pattern of federal government contracting for research.

We can now summarize the principal differences between the two countries in regard to state funding of academic research. In Britain there were no state universities, but the universities, all of which had the legal status of charities, became heavily dependent on direct government funding.[31] Directly they became dependent on grants from the Research Councils, and indirectly they depended on grants from the UGC, which was initially distributed, though, in a way designed to maximize university autonomy. In the US a parallel structure of universities developed – private universities relying on income from fees, donations and endowments, and public universities supported by income from fees and funds from state and, in the case of New York, city government. In Britain the heavy dependence on the state facilitated extensive intervention in the universities in the 1980s, when they were encouraged by the government to become far more active in commercial projects relating to their research programmes. In the US the financial dependence of private universities in the twentieth century was indirect, as were the pressures to commercialism, but here too high levels of state funding for research, and the unavailability of alternative sources for pure research, partly undermined the 'pursuit of knowledge'.

C The arts

With regard to the arts, Britain and America are alike in that state funding emerged relatively late, but when it did emerge a form of funding developed in both countries which was very similar to the period of UGC autonomy in British higher education.[32] Both countries differed from many states in continental Europe where there was a strong tradition of state patronage, and in some cases control, of the arts. In Britain and the US there was a wide spread belief, until well into the twentieth century, that a lack of private 'consumers' for artistic endeavour, was of no more concern to the state than was inadequate demand for any other kind of good. Along with churches, universities and other bodies, arts' organizations which were charities did not pay corporate income tax, and might have their property tax liabilities reduced, but there was no permanent direct aid in Britain until the 1940s and until the 1960s in the US. Nor is this slow development difficult to explain. The services an artist or an arts' organization could supply were not needed by governments, nor did they seem important in the way that academic research did, from the late nineteenth century onwards, to the long-term success of an economy or the military. Although there were long-established examples of state commitment to the arts, such as the British Museum or the National Gallery, in Britain there was:

> a public attitude of detachment: while all other European states founded, encouraged and subsidized theatres and opera houses, national and municipal, Britain left such matters to chance on the supposition that entertainment, even in its highest aspects, was a matter of business and thus the business of the individual.[33]

Similarly, in the US cultural 'goods' were partly provided for by the market. Although his fame today rests on his 'low-brow' entertainment, P. T. Barnum also catered to the 'high-brow' market such as it was.[34] As DiMaggio has argued:

> High culture, as we now define it, did not exist in the United States until after the Civil War, nor did many nonprofit organizations offering exhibitions or performances to the general public. Serious art and popular works intermingled promiscuously in public performance.[35]

In parts of the US, though, of which Boston is an example, socio-economic elites started to compensate for their declining power in city politics by founding systems of non-profit organizations which enabled them to maintain some control over the community even while they were losing their command of its political institutions.[36] Prominent among these non-profits were arts' organizations.

The second world war was the turning point for the funding of the arts in Britain. The Council for the Encouragement of Music and the Arts (CEMA) was formed in 1939 to support cultural activities and for this it was able to obtain government funds. Its success in providing concerts, plays, exhibitions and so on during the war led to the establishment of the Arts Council in 1945. Unlike the UGC, whose autonomy during its first forty to fifty years depended on good will and the acceptance of tradition by state bureaucracy, the Arts Council was given formal quasi-independent status through being created by Royal Charter. It was a conduit for providing money to the arts, and significantly it sought to supplement organizations' other sources of funding rather than having bodies which were wholly dependent on it. The scale of funding provided by the Arts Council in relation to other grant-making trusts can be gauged by noting that its income of £102 million in 1985 was equal to the combined income of the next 22 largest trusts. Since these include both the Wellcome Trust and the Nuffield Foundation, it can be seen just how extensive government patronage of the arts became, as well as, indirectly, how relatively small English foundations are. The major change in the operation of the Council has been, as Ridley argues, that after 1965 it moved from merely responding to requests for funds to the more active role of encouraging certain kinds of developments in the arts. As he says, though, 'it is no planning unit, drawing up a cultural blueprint of its own.'[37]

In the US the federal government's first foray into funding for the arts was in the New Deal with the WPA arts' projects but, as with several other of the more innovative aspects of the New Deal, this initiative had been abandoned by the early 1940s. It was not until 1965, with the establishment of the National Endowment for the Arts and Humanities, that a permanent source of funding was introduced.[38] But, as Zukin has noted:

> The terms that justified the strong state of the 1960s differed fundamentally from the terms that introduced the New Deal in the 1930s. Unlike the WPA, arts policy of the 1960s did not view art as an instrument of economic recovery. Instead, the new state patronage of the arts gave the Welfare State the role of improving the quality of life.[39]

It was no coincidence that a state arts policy developed at the very time that federal government commitments in the field of social welfare were expanding rapidly; it was widely believed that the government had the resources to do more than it had done, and in comparison with the west European states America was doing little to promote an area important to international prestige. Thus, a belief that there was money available for the arts and that they were a significant element in America's claim to moral leadership of the western world combined to bring about a radical change in policy. Between 1965 and 1980 the annual budget of the National Endowment rose from $2.5 million to $150 million. However, even before the Reagan cutbacks of the 1980s, this budget was little more than the annual budget of the Arts Council which in 1982 amounted to more than £81 million.

Even if we allow for the growing contribution by state and local governments, especially to the performing arts, the US remained very much at one end of a continuum of direct state aid to the arts. Data in this area is extremely incomplete, and sometimes misleading, but some idea of the role of governmental funding can be gleaned from data gathered by Montias.[40] In the 1970s American non-profit organizations in the performing arts continued to acquire more than half their income from 'earned sources' – from payments for performances – while in continental Europe only between 20 and 30 per cent of income usually came from this source. State subsidies there formed a much larger share of income. Britain, and indeed most of the ex-British dominions, tended to fall between these two extremes, with earned income accounting for closer to 40 per cent of total income. As in many other areas, the American practice has been to rely more heavily on the incentive to donate provided by the income tax deduction to both individuals and corporations. Since there is a strong relationship among higher-income groups between income and the incentive to donate to 501(c)(3)s, and 'high art' has traditionally been patronized by the wealthy, it is not surprising that non-profit arts' organizations have been among the greatest beneficiaries of the US federal income tax deduction. Corporations, too, have given disproportionately more to 'culture and art' organizations – in 1984 they received about 11.4 per cent of total corporate gifts.[41] For corporations such donations are relatively 'safe' targets of largesse, unlikely to offend any sector of the general public.

In both Britain and the US the market intrudes in rather different ways among arts' organizations from its role in the area of academic research. Among the former, the main problem is that the market may not sustain certain kinds of art forms or may not sustain them to the extent that is thought to be necessary for maintaining and nurturing cultural development. But the structure of an industry can also be responsible for a failure to supply art forms for which there is a demand; this is most clearly demonstrated by examining the case of public television in the US. Television progammes, especially drama, can be expensive to produce, and in the commercial sector in the US the more expensive programmes are made by independent producers for one of the three networks which in turn supply them to their affiliated stations. Individual stations themselves produce some programmes (such as local news broadcasts), but they do not make programmes for sale to stations elsewhere. Over the years the networks have displayed one form of behaviour associated with oligopoly – they have competed with each other for a share of the market, and in doing so have tended to produce programmes which will always attract a mass audience, rather than ones catering to minority interests. One result has been a dearth of serious drama productions and classical music concerts on commercial stations. One response to this from the early 1960s onwards was the growth of so-called 'public' television stations which were intended to fill this gap in the market. These stations solicited donations from individual and corporate donors, and in the 1960s and 1970s public television also received large grants from the federal government. However, they were among the organizations most affected by the cutbacks in funding initiated by the Reagan administration.

With academic research, however, the limitation of the market is that usually there is no one with sufficient incentive to fund pure research. In the absence of the state, or independently funded bodies which can cross-subsidize this research, it simply will not be carried out. This difference from the arts, in which it is the *level* of supply which is problematic, is reflected in the organization of the two sets of activities. In the arts there are several areas where the market has worked reasonably well; in the US a large market has so far sustained a thriving movie industry which provides popular entertainment as well as serious films. In Britain the commercial film industry collapsed during the 1960s and 1970s, and the issue of how this art form can be sustained became a more serious one. Where the market does prove insufficient, there is more likely to be a commercial sector and a subsidized sector operating alongside each other, or, where the market is especially unable to provide what is required, only subsidized organizations tend to exist. With the theatre the former is the case, while with orchestras, ballet and opera, wholly commercial enterprises have found it more difficult to survive. With academic research we find organizations (universities) performing a number of tasks – pure research, the education of undergraduates, applying research in conjunction with commercial enterprises and so on. There are some areas where universities are in competition with commercial enterprises, but this does not extend to the activity where state interference is regarded as most problematic – namely, in setting the agenda for, and overseeing, pure research.

2 State Intervention: the Problem of 'Sensitive' Activities

The argument that there are some activities which should not be subject to state intervention, because the activities themselves will be harmed, has become well established with the rise of the liberal democratic state. But a continuing source of dispute has been how to 'protect' these areas while still permitting the state to intervene in aspects of the organizations' activities where the state has a legitimate interest. (There has been further dispute about the precise respects in which the state does have a legitimate interest.) The areas where conflicts are likely to arise are rather different, of course, in the three cases, and we examine each in turn.

With religion the danger of state intervention is that it may help to undermine one set of religious beliefs, because it acts in a partisan way in support of groups holding some other set of beliefs. It was precisely this problem which was contentious in the New England colonies and which led to the US Constitution formally embracing freedom of religious practice. The liberal argument is that because we cannot know which, if any, set of religious beliefs is 'correct', it is socially unjust to discriminate against any one religious group, and in the long term the repression of one set of beliefs might prove to have been unwarranted on utilitarian grounds. However, not all religious beliefs are compatible with the maintenance and operation of a liberal state, and there are two main types of belief of which this is true. There are those which deny the legitimacy of the state and whose adherents seek to overthrow it, or which dispute the legitimacy of a particular law and refuse to recognize it. Then there are also beliefs which have been acquired by followers as a result of means which made them unfree at the time they acquired them.

The former problem is less significant. Virtually all modern religions which deny the legitimacy of the state, or refuse to acknowledge it, do not advocate its abolition by force. Instead, like the Amish, they find some way of accommodating themselves to the state, and in turn the state will often devise ways of legitimizing the failure of the members of these religions to be able to accept certain laws or practices of that state. But in some circumstances this is not possible without undermining the enforcement of a law more generally in the society. For example, had exemptions been made to Sikhs not to have to wear motorcycle helmets when this became compulsory in Britain, it is quite possible it would have encouraged greater disobedience of that law. In general, though, it is not the character of particular beliefs but the means used in getting followers to acquire them that prompts the greater disputes about the legitimacy of state intervention.

The problem of religious sects is not, of course, new. Heretical religious movements developed regularly during the middle ages and were suppressed regularly. In nineteenth-century America, sects, often unpopular with state government officials, emerged periodically and quite often in the same places, as in upstate New York's 'Burnt-Over' District (This area around the Finger Lakes was so called because of the intensity of religious revivals there.) As with the Mormons, direct suppression of sects was not necessary, because ultimately they could usually be persuaded to move on to other states and eventually to the frontier where there was only the federal government to deal with. In the twentieth century the problem of sects has become more acute. The Jonestown experiment (Jim Jones's People's Temple cult) notwithstanding, this is partly because there are few frontiers to which sects might migrate, but it is also because there is now greater recognition that in many circumstances a person may be unfree when joining a religious community. The problem with many sects is that they indoctrinate and manipulate a member into accepting ideas, beliefs, practices and ways of life which the person would probably not accept were it not for the means deployed to recruit him/her. The idea that people should not be exposed to such practices, irrespective of whether they now accept the sect's creed, has become an important value within the liberal democratic state. Conflicts have arisen, therefore, on issues such as the deprogramming of young adults lured into groups like the Moonies, and about a balance to be maintained between the right to practice a religion and the state's obligations to maintain freedom of choice for individuals by preventing indoctrination and manipulation. Not surprisingly, we find a rather different approach in the US from that prevalent in Britain, and this reflects different attitudes towards state intervention in general.

In Britain the duty of the state to intervene has been less controversial, and there is greater public acceptance that the state should intervene to stop some of the practices with which the Moonies, Scientologists and others were associated. Although forcible deprogramming has been ordered by some courts in the US it has been controversial.[42] The American Civil Liberties Union, for example, has been critical of such interventions, and state governments have been reluctant to intervene in the activities of sects. The freedom of religion clause in the Constitution, in effect, has given considerable licence to groups describing themselves as 'religions' to do much as they please in relation to their followers. The prospect that a sect might be banned from operating in a state, as it could be in Britain, is virtually non-existent. However, even in Britain laws on charity have worked to the advantage of religions. Even when courts have found sects to have been dangerous, they have been able to retain their charitable status. The Charity Commissioners have taken the view that they have no power to deregister charities affiliated to such sects, unless the charities themselves have contravened charity law.

However, if sects have a relatively privileged position in relation to the American state, the argument from the autonomy of the individual does still have some standing there, and in some respects possibly more so than in Britain. A good illustration of this is provided by a recent case in New York City. Catholic agencies there were responsible for placing nearly a quarter of all the children in the care of city government in foster homes, a service it provided under contract with the city itself. The city's policy had been to place Catholic children with Catholic agencies, Jewish children with Jewish agencies and so on. A case brought by the American Civil Liberties Union challenged this arrangement on the grounds that it discriminated against black, and mainly Protestant, children. In 1986 a court ruled against this practice, and also required foster-care agencies not to impose their own religious beliefs on children or require them to attend religious services. A further requirement of the court, that children in foster homes have access to contraception and abortion services led the archdiocese of New York to threaten not to renew its foster home contracts with the city. The significance of this case is that it illustrates the greater weight given to the child's freedom to make up his/her own mind than to the convenience for the city of particular existing arrangements for providing social services.[43] British local authorities are less concerned with the particular social values which welfare bodies connected with mainstream religions might introduce to those in their care.

With academic research conflict arises from the close connection between the 'sensitive' area of state involvement, the advancement of knowledge, and other aspects of higher education for which state intervention is not in itself controversial. It is widely accepted that there should be state policy relating to, among other things, the number of graduating students there are in particular disciplines. Shortages of graduates in some areas may have a major impact – for example, on the performance of key industries, or on the ability of the state to provide teachers in primary and secondary schools. Market forces may not work well in the labour market for a number of reasons – there are likely to be long time-lags in the working of higher-wage incentives in occupations where there are labour shortages, and cycles of over-supply and under-supply may be generated. In Britain, the second world war was a major catalyst in prompting discussions about the need for positive state leadership in developing an overall policy for higher education. As Berdahl notes, 'Between 1944 and 1947 [the] theme of producing qualified experts for a society in a state of rapid change increasingly came to be the central focus for discussions about university education.'[44]

However, it was not until the early 1960s, with the publication of the Robbins Report that the scale of state 'investment in the production of experts' increased greatly. The vast expansion of places in higher education meant that this was no longer a relatively small backwater of government policy. In the US, where market forces helped to increase the demand for college education greatly in the years after the war, America's assumption of leadership of the western world was to create periodic crises about the numbers of certain experts being produced in the US. In particular, the achievement by the Soviet Union in 1957 in putting a satellite in space before the Americans, produced a radical reassessment of the need for greater numbers of scientists. As we have noted already, though, the federal government sought to achieve its goals through more indirect means of funding universities than was the case in Britain, where universities were now heavily dependent on direct financial aid channelled through the UGC. In addition to its 'indirectness', another feature of the American financing of research has been its strong links to military needs. One consequence of the Reagan administration's Strategic Defense Initiative (SDI) was that in the 1986 fiscal year the Pentagon became the largest source of new funds for pure research.[45]

The problem with state planning of higher education, as it affects the advancement of knowledge, is three-fold. First, because historically pure research has been conducted primarily in institutions where students are also educated, rather than in entirely separate organizations, any policy for higher education will have some impact on how knowledge is advanced. Second, there is an overlap between those who conduct pure research and the sort of research which governments are interested in sponsoring for their own purposes. Most especially, though this is not the only aspect of governmental policy which intrudes on universities, advances in military technology in the twentieth century have drawn researchers into the sphere of government. Large programmes, such as the Strategic Defense Initiative, inevitably affect what research gets conducted overall. Third, interaction with the state and its programmes of research also affects the orientation towards pure research among scholars: attitudes towards what is valuable in research may change. In claiming this, it is not being suggested that there ever was a golden age in the 'groves of academes' when open competition between fiercely independent scholars maximized advances in our understanding of the world; rather, it is merely being suggested that the state's proper concerns with educating a population with certain kinds of skills, with providing adequate government services and with defending itself from external threats intrudes upon the conduct of pure research.

With the arts the potential threat from state intervention is different again. In this case it relates more to aspects of access to the arts. If a benign state might want to protect artistic expression, then it might also wish to ensure that, for the most part, state funds help to increase public access to the arts. These two objectives can, and do, conflict. The ethos behind the emergence of state funding of the arts in both Britain and the US was indeed that more people should be able to enjoy artistic works and performances than was possible with supply through market mechanisms. If 'art for the people' is the goal of state intervention, then how many people have themselves taken up painting or a musical instrument, or attended concerts, may be one test of the success of the policy. But this is to introduce market-like criteria in evaluating programmes, and may lead to less emphasis being given to experimental and currently unpopular art forms which may nevertheless prove to be of great importance subsequently for the development of culture in that society. Consequently, as in the funding of pure research, peer group review has become an important element in evaluating projects in the arts which seek state financial support. Artists themselves have been to left to decide whether projects display talent or not.

However, peer review arguably poses less difficulty in the case of research, because the question of what the relevant academic community *is* is more clearly defined; it has been defined by the institutions, mainly universities, in which most of those who conduct pure research are employed. While there are serious inter-disciplinary disputes, and even intense controversy within disciplines, there are still well-defined structures from which peer review can begin, and in which disputing claims can be mediated. Whatever its limitations, the idea of shared values and a shared purpose is supported by a number of practices; for example, in appointments at British universities, and in tenuring at American universities, academics from other disciplines usually play a part in the process. The situation is very different with the arts. There are no institutions which have brought together, say, folk dancers, painters and opera singers. Not surprisingly, then, the use of experts to judge experts has tended to favour elite, establishment, art forms at the expense of more popular forms. In Britain in the 1970s this was to lead to a major controversy, as to whether the Arts Council was allocating too much money to the opera, ballet, symphony orchestras and large theatre groups, at the expense of community arts' projects. In response several local authorities controlled by the Labour party started to change the traditional pattern of local authority support for the arts in favour of projects operating at the community level. The problem with the arts is that there is no agreement as to what the arts are, and how important different art forms might be in relation to each other. The scholar of French history and the physicist are more likely to be able to agree on what constitutes important research, than the folk dancer and the portrait painter on what the advancement of culture in a society would entail. This means that any schemes for funding the arts are, from some points of view, going to be open to the objection that they will discourage certain art forms and developments – whether it be popular art, 'high' art or whatever.

If we accept, then, that safeguards like peer review cannot limit the adverse impact of government funding, in the way that they might be able to with pure research, there is little that can be done to prevent state intervention 'distorting' the process of artistic development. But what follows from this? One point which must not be overlooked is that private patronage can have similarly 'distorting' effects to state aid. Moreover, while controversy cannot be excluded from the determination of priorities in spending on the arts, the *form* of state funding seems to be important. Some mechanisms help to reduce the pressures on artistic development which come from public criticism of specific controversial projects which have received state subsidies. The real advantage of funding through an agency like the Arts Council is that its 'indirect' approach helps to soften the impact of the criticism that public funds should not be used for projects of a particular type – because they are not 'art'.

3 State Regulation: some Preliminary Remarks

Because the dangers of the state becoming too closely enmeshed in regulating these kinds of organizations have been recognized, state regulation in the twentieth century has often been rather loose – even in comparison with other types of charitable organization. Nevertheless, in making this claim it is important to recognize several points. First, in general, regulation of all charities has been rather lax simply because of the absence of the structures necessary for effective enforcement and because it has not been an area of high public controversy. Second, early- and mid-twentieth century sensitivities about the need for academic autonomy were not matched in the nineteenth century or before – for example, in Britain there were major state-initiated reforms of Oxford and Cambridge in the mid nineteenth century, amidst considerable opposition from within the universities themselves. Furthermore, developments in the 1980s suggest that the consensus that 'academic freedom' is necessary in defining research priorities has partly dissolved in Britain, and much greater supervision by the state is now accepted by some elements of the British political elite. Third, the 'hands off' approach to religious organizations is peculiarly American – and has its roots in the very origins of some of the ex-colonies. Fourth, in relation to the arts, the recognition that state control of the purse should not be used to control 'artistic content' has often gone hand-in-hand with the enforcement of laws (relating to public morals and blasphemy, for example) which have certainly involved state regulation of art.

What this suggests is that, with the exceptional case of religion in the US, the commitment to independence for these activities is far from open-ended. The willingness to allow for a high degreee of autonomy in the early stages of public funding does not guarantee that far more control will not emerge later on. The continuing dispute about access to the arts in Britain suggests that political disputes about the use of public funds may become just as important there as they have been in relation to universities. In the case of religion, of course, direct state funding is not at issue, but here too there are signs that tighter state control may emerge, even in the US. Religious organizations have lost their privileged status in relation to the taxing of unrelated income, and the more open involvement of preachers in politics during the last decade may partially weaken public support for the additional privileges churches have enjoyed over other charities in America. This tendency may be reinforced by the growing exclusivity of fundamentalist churches in relation to children's education, for example, which increasingly creates conflict with secular politics. Conflict too has arisen over the explicit use by some churches of their economic power to obtain concessions from governments. One of the most notorious incidents is the example cited earlier of the pressure exerted on the city of Lynchburg by Jerry Falwell where his enterprises are major employers. The more religious groups become politically controversial the more, albeit within the constraints imposed by the US Constitution, they may find the peculiar privileges they have enjoyed being squeezed. In 1987, for example, the Sub-Committee on Oversight (of the House Ways and Means Committee) scheduled hearings into the political activities of churches. While no legislation was expected to emanate from these particular hearings, they provided an indication of shifting attitudes to the abuse of charitable status. Having made these observations, we must now turn to the more general issue of the regulation of IOs.

7

The Regulation of Intermediate Organizations

In a number of places in this book the issue of state regulation of IOs has been raised briefly. In this chapter we focus in more detail on the ways in which the state in both England and the US has sought to regulate the activities of these organizations. Regulation has become more important and controversial in the late twentieth century as many IOs are now very different in character from the kinds of IOs evident, say, fifty years ago. As we have seen in earlier chapters, there has been a considerable interpenetration of charities and the market, while at the same time many of the older mutuals have become simply a part of the commercial sector. Moreover, and for a variety of reasons, the politicization of IOs has tended to increase, while, and this has been one of the the causes of politicization, the state has increasingly used IOs as agents of its policies. This blurring of the boundaries between market, state and IOs has helped to focus public attention on the inadequacy of many of the mechanisms for regulating the affairs of IOs.

Indeed, one of the most interesting aspects of regulation in this area is that, while it has a very long history, it is not currently extensive. Even in the case of English charities, where at first sight the Charity Commission would seem to be a kind of regulatory agency, the extent of its regulation is actually rather limited. For one thing the Commission does not like to describe itself as a *government* agency, let alone a regulatory one. In part its reluctance to identify with government, despite the fact that it most clearly is a department of government, may stem from its responsibility for religious organizations, and a disinclination to have this responsibility identified with government interference or control over matters of faith. But it also arises from the Commission's definition of its activities, in which the provision of assistance to charities is seen as a more important part of its work than the task of investigating activities by charities that may be contrary to the public interest, or even illegal. As a 1987 report by the National Audit Office (NAO), which was critical of the Commission, pointed out:

> Providing information and advice to all charities, and assisting them in all possible ways both at establishment and subsequently, is regarded by the Commission as one of their essential functions imposed by statute. A significant proportion of their staff resources has been, and is, devoted to this aspect of their responsibilities.[1]

Nor is the example of the limited extent of regulation of charities in England an exceptional one among IOs.

To understand how the state in the two countries does regulate different kinds of IOs, it is useful to distinguish between seven purposes the liberal democratic state might have when introducing and re-evaluating mechanisms for regulation. Some aspects of intervention reflect the state's protection of its own interests, others involve protecting groups or individuals affected by the activities of IOs, while others provide protection for IOs themselves.

(i) The state may wish to ensure that certain services which could be provided by particular kinds of IOs are supplied, or will continue to be supplied. These organizations serve as instruments of public policy, and any failure by them to supply the services could have serious consequences for the functioning of the state, or could force the state to intervene and to provide the services itself. Thus, regulation of this kind is designed to remove impediments to organizations operating in a way most compatible with the interests of the state.

(ii) The state may seek to protect those who provide money or other resources to IOs, especially when there are barriers to the contributors (or members) themselves making certain that they obtain what they intended to get from the organizations. There are various problems the contributors might face: there may not be an adequate legal framework for them to operate in; as with legacies, their contribution might become effective only on their death; the goods or services they want supplied might be for consumption by other persons; or the sheer size of the contributing group might make it difficult for any one of them to supervise the organization's activities. And this is not an exhaustive list of the barriers to contributor and member control.

(iii) The state may want to protect those for whom services are provided – to make certain, for example, that certain minimum standards of delivery are maintained. Once again, there may be unusual conditions preventing the recipients doing this themselves – as with a charitable gift; because the recipient is not the same person as the donor, s/he has no claim on the service actually being provided at all.

(iv) The state may seek to protect those working in IOs – whether, employees, members or volunteer helpers. Here, state intervention is designed to ensure that an IO's functions do not harm those engaged in performing the relevant tasks.

(v) Where the state itself is paying for services to be supplied by an IO, it has an interest in introducing mechanisms to ensure that it obtains value for money and that supply is as efficient as it could be.

(vi) When IOs enjoy certain advantages in providing goods or services in comparison with for-profit organizations, the state may wish to prevent the former from engaging in unfair competition with the latter. Most especially, when the former are not liable to pay income tax or tax on their profits or capital gains, the state may find that there are some areas of trade in which the tax advantage is exploited and where the legitimate trading interests of bodies liable for tax are adversely affected.

(vii) Again when there are certain privileges attached to particular legal forms of IO, the state may seek to prevent organizations which take these forms from using these privileges to gain access to the political system. Here there are a number of grounds that could be invoked to justify regulation, including the question of fairness in relation to other kinds of organizations and the desirablity of preventing the privileged bodies from gaining too much influence over the state itself.

Some of these purposes of regulation give rise to issues that are quite special to IOs, while others reveal problems that are very similar to those of other types of organization. In this chapter we focus attention on the former, and omit altogether consideration of three purposes. We do not discuss the protection of beneficiaries of services, because there are clear links here with other measures to protect 'consumers' of services, especially personal services. Again, for the most part, there is nothing especially distinctive about state regulation designed to protect those working in IOs, and neither do we examine how states obtain value-for-money in their contracting with IOs. The problems of a state which is heavily dependent on commercial sector suppliers closely parallel those areas where the state is dealing with IO suppliers.

1 Maintaining the Supply of Services

State intervention and regulation to ensure that non-state agencies do supply the goods and services which they are capable of providing has a long tradition. It was precisely because the late Tudor state was worried by the prospect of there being insufficient organized philanthropy that existing laws on regulating charitable uses were codified in 1601 and a system of regulation through commissioners introduced. Earlier, the only way of preventing mismanagement and fraud in charitable uses was through Chancery, and this did not produce the kind of deterrent necessary to ensure charitable gifts were used efficiently and for the purposes for which they were intended. After 1601 the Lord Chancellor could appoint the bishop of a diocese and others to act as commissioners to investigate abuses. As Chesterman says:

> These commissioners were empowered to use such methods of investigation as they thought fit. In practice, they would call on overseers of the poor, who were the justices of the peace, to advertize any forthcoming commission in order that local residents might bring forward allegations of misuse of charity property, and to empanel a jury of twelve men.[2]

The powers of the commissioners to issue decrees were broad, and this system of supervision of charities was used widely in the first half of the seventeenth century. After this, it came to be employed much less frequently, partly because of the growing use of another device, the relator action, which is brought by the Attorney General at the behest of a private individual. But this latter procedure: 'fell on evil days in the eighteenth century by virtue of a general decay on the procedural side of Chancery. In the eighteenth and early nineteenth centuries, all Chancery proceedings became slow and expensive to an extraordinary degree.'[3]

This reliance on action through the courts in the eighteenth century, even though it had become cumbersome, rather than through commissioners, was to be important in distinguishing the British approach to the regulation of IOs in the nineteenth century from the American approach. The British were again to emphasize *administrative* supervision – in relation to both charities and now to mutuals. In 1840 the Royal Commission chaired by Lord Brougham, which had taken twenty-one years to conduct its extensive investigation into charitable trusts, eventually published its report which demonstrated that many of them were now of little value and that mismanagement of trusts was widespread. Although this report was completed at a time when *laissez faire* views are considered to have dominant among the British political elite, the resulting legislation in 1853, 1855 and 1860 set up a permanent Charity Commission responsible for supervising the administration of charitable trusts.[4] If a dual system of, primarily, indoor relief (workhouses) provided by the state and outdoor relief supplied by private philanthropy, was to work effectively to ameliorate the social problems caused by industrialization, then there had to be means of ensuring that philanthropy was not squandered through mismanagement. It was seen that this could be achieved only by extending the principle embodied in the 1601 legislation of regulation involving administrators, and not just through the Court of Chancery.

At the time of Independence, the former British colonies in North America did not face a problem with long-established, mismanaged charities nor could they see in contemporary Britain a model for administrative supervision of charities. The early-seventeenth-century approach to charity regulation had largely been forgotten. Consequently, there were two rather distinct approaches to charitable institutions to be found in the US. Strong support for (unregulated) philanthropic corporations was emerging in some states, while in the states where Jeffersonianism became dominant there was suspicion of centres of private power, and a demand for state institutions rather than private institutions. But neither of these approaches called for state regulation of either charities or of other kinds of non-profit-distributing organizations. Indeed, since the mid-nineteenth-century triumph of the private corporation (of both the for-profit and non-profit kind) the American approach to IOs as instruments of public policy has been to emphasize the 'carrot' rather than the 'stick'. Tax concessions and other privileges have made for large-scale, indirect governmental support, at all levels of government, for many organizations. At the same time policing of these organizations has been left at the federal level to the Internal Revenue Service, which has not had the resources, nor indeed has it been set up in the most appropriate way, to act as a regulatory agency. At the state level, neither the Secretaries of State nor state Attorneys General have had the sorts of facilities necessary to investigate whether IOs are indeed performing in ways compatible with the purposes of the state.

In Britain too the experience since the mid-nineteenth century has been one of relatively limited intervention by the Charity Commission, even after its role was redefined by legislation in 1960. (The main thrust of the 1960 legislation was to extend the Commission's purview to non-trust charities and to require all charities to register with the Commission and to submit accounts to it.) From the mid-nineteenth-century until comparatively recently, it was widely believed that the vast majority of charities were not mismanaged. Scandals could always be dismissed as isolated incidents. The NAO report on the Charity Commission in 1987 indicated that the Commission's lack of information, and of resources necessary to effect any supervision of charities, could mean that there was considerably more mismanagement than that of which the Commission was aware. The reports' sample survey of charities indicated that perhaps less than 40 per cent of charities had actually submitted any accounts to the Commission within the previous five years, despite the requirement that they submit accounts annually.[5] However, one issue has not yet been placed on the political agenda. This is the question of whether the category of organizations defined as charitable in the 1601 Statute, which still forms the basis of charity law today, constitutes the most appropriate classification of organizations to which certain privileges should be granted. In the case of other kinds of IOs in Britain, we find similarly little centralized state direction and rather narrowly defined regulation, despite the fact that, once again, a quasi-regulatory agency, the Registry of Friendly Societies, was established in the mid- nineteenth-century. The limited use to which the Chief Registrar of Friendly Societies, a civil servant appointed by the Treasury, was put is best illustrated in the case of the Building Societies. Extending home ownership in Britain has been an important objective of domestic policy of virtually every government since 1945, and Building Societies have been a central instrument in this policy. But relations between the societies and the Chief Registrar have not been the main channel through which housing policy has been worked out, although the Registry of Friendly Societies has remained responsible for ensuring that individual societies operate prudently so as to protect the interests of investors. While the Registry was represented on the Joint Advisory Committee on mortgage finance, which was set up in 1973 following instability in the housing market in the previous two years, it was not a major actor on the state's side. It was the Department of the Environment which was at the centre of the Committee's work in liaising with the Building Societies Association.

Thus, although IOs have remained important for the state in supplying services, which have been of both direct and indirect benefit to the state, their regulation to ensure efficient supply has remained weak. It has taken major crises, as in early-nineteenth-century Britain with the scandals over the abuses of charitable trusts, to prompt reform.

2 The Protection of Members and Donors

The Registry of Friendly Societies provides a good example of state intervention for the second purpose we identified earlier – to protect the interests of those who have placed money with an organization, or who have made donations to an organization. The main problem with Friendly Societies in the early nineteenth century, one which they shared with banks and similar organizations in the commercial sector, was that it was difficult for potential members to know how safe their deposits with a society would be. Nevertheless, as Gosden notes, 'The view that the state should go no further than help Societies through requiring returns, collecting and publishing such data as was collected became widely accepted.'[6] The key area of state intervention was in certifying a society's rules, and an Act of 1834 transferred this responsibility to the barrister who was appointed to certify the rules of savings banks. In 1846 this post was given the title 'Registrar of Friendly Societies', but while the incumbent's powers did expand somewhat as a number of other kinds of mutual-benefit organizations (Building Societies and co-operatives, most notably) came within his purview, his office was lacking in power even in comparison with the Charity Commission. This was true even after the Friendly Societies Act of 1875: 'The powers of the Chief Registrar ... were wider than those of his predecessor but they remained very strictly confined.'[7]

Because of their potential influence in capitalist economies, trade unions have long been the subject of state regulation, and often this regulation has been more extensive than that of other mutuals. For the most part, regulation has been directed at their activities in relation to employers, rather than at intra-union affairs, although like other organizations their financial arrangements have been subjected to control. In the US, where many states have enacted legislation banning union shops (closed shops) and where, at the federal level, there is statutory provision (under the Taft-Hartley Act) for 'cooling off' periods in industrial disputes and for strike ballots, there is little *special* legislation relating to unions' internal affairs. Some unions, therefore, like the Teamsters, and at various times the United Mine Workers, have been dominated by elites who have been able to insulate themselves from effective challenges by members.[8] In Britain too, until the 1980s, regulation of unions was aimed primarily at their external relations. However, operating on the assumption that the members were less 'militant' than local and national leaders, and would thereby exercise a 'moderating' influence on policy, the Conservative government considered measures for controlling unions' internal affairs. Measures so far enacted include secret postal ballots before strikes and the requirement that voting members of national decision-making bodies be *elected* to their positions. By 1987 it was widely expected in the union movement that further legislation requiring elections to be held at least every five years would also be introduced. An interesting aspect of such legislation is that, since the government's justification for such intervention has been in terms of members' control, it might provide the basis for future governments with very different ideologies to extend internal democracy to other kinds of IO.

In the case of charities we find, as with most mutuals, limitations on state intervention to protect the individual contributor. The Charities Act of 1960 has permitted the Charity Commission to investigate complaints of fraud or mismanagement in fund-raising. Yet, in 1969, only one member of the staff was engaged in investigatory activities, and even in 1987 only thirteen of its 330 established posts involved investigations, including enquiries from the press. The Commission lacks the staff to do anything other than respond to actual complaints, rather than, for example, having a system of random 'spot checks' to encourage compliance with the law.[9] Furthermore, the 1960 law gives the Commissioners relatively limited powers. This has meant that, even when abuses are being investigated, those perpetrating them may continue to do so during the course of the investigation.[10] Chesterman's explanation of this is that the 1960 legislation paralleled the nineteenth century Acts in focusing primarily on charitable trusts, and not on fund-raising charities.[11] Again, it was not until the 1986 Finance Act that the Inland Revenue was permitted to pass on information to the Commission about charities they suspected were being used for fraudulent purposes. Consequently, while at least in theory the British state can deal with many kinds of abuses in charities, it is not well equipped to protect the potential donor from fraudulent or incompetent fund-raisers. The position is broadly similar in the US. At the federal level, the IRS may be able to catch up with some incidents of fraud, especially when they have been 'tipped off' in advance, but it is a body whose main function is tax-raising and not the supervision of an 'industry'. Similarly, at the state and local levels, offices such as those of the Attorney General, lack the resources to do more than investigate the most obvious of scandals.

However, in contrast to Britain, several states have ordinances regulating the proportion of funds that charities may devote to fund-raising. Charities, excluding religious charities, must have financial returns to show they comply. (Fears about charities in Britain incurring excessive administrative costs were expressed in the NAO Report in 1987.)[12] This device does not, however, provide the donor with quite the protection s/he deserves. It is not clear that excessive bureaucracy or the commitment of too great a proportion of resources to fund-raising is as serious a problem among charities as fraud or maladministration. Moreover, this disadvantages some donors and volunteers – those 'goods altruists' who wish to set up an organization and to draw also on the altruism of others. This is because ordinances limiting administrative expenses work to the disadvantage of certain kinds of charitable cause. Charities promoting unpopular or 'new' causes may well find it much more difficult to raise funds and may have to devote a far greater proportion of their income to sustaining fund-raising. Thus, if, as in some US cities, there is simply a 'blanket' limit on the proportion of funds that may be ploughed back into fund-raising, and if this is set too low, it will prevent certain kinds of charities from operating effectively; if the ceiling is set sufficiently high to avoid this problem, it is likely to permit highly 'bloated' bureaucracies among non-volunteer-based charities.

The inadequacy of the state in protecting the donor has led to private attempts in North America at 'certifying' charities – both by 'umbrella' organizations of charities themselves and by Better Business Bureaus (These bureaus are set up by local businesses and seek to encourage fair trading practices.) There are three main difficulties with this form of regulation. First, while it does lead to the identification of certain kinds of 'cowboy' charities, it cannot hope to control many forms of incompetent administration, because of the huge costs this would entail in gathering information. Second, there have been instances, in Canada for example, where the ways in which the certifying body has presented its information have drawn criticism from reputable charities as being misleading.[13] Third, the lack of publicity that is often given to these lists of 'acceptable' charities means that the vast majority of potential donors remain unaware of which organizations do not meet the minimum standards.

In Britain too there has been some private regulation among charities, in this case via the national associations of groups operating within a particular policy area. This corporatist kind of control has been described by Wilson and Butler in the following way:

> Self-regulation through the national associations, with the state taking a back-stage role, is particularly evident in voluntary organizations that are either unique in the services they provide or largely independent of any substantial state funding (RNLI and Oxfam are examples). Furthermore, whether or not a voluntary organization is deemed charitable by the state does not preclude representation on any of the national associations.[14]

However, this kind of self-regulation is not designed so much to protect members and donors, as to provide for intermediation between groups and the state in policy areas of concern to the state.

Once again, we find that, with certain partial exceptions like trade unions, IOs have been subject to remarkably little regulation in order to protect their members and donors. At best, private regulation can only be incomplete, and yet in many kinds of IOs there is a serious problem for members and donors in establishing whether their contributions are being used efficiently and towards the objectives they would wish to see pursued.

3 The Regulation of Unfair Competition

If the problem of protecting donors and members has been largely unpublicized until recently, the issue of unfair competition has been far more controversial, so we must give considerable attention to it. Where special tax privileges are available to certain kinds of IOs, the state faces two potential problems. If these organizations are either exempt from any taxes, or pay them at a lower rate than commercial firms, there is a loss of tax revenue to the state if the activities from which the organizations generate income are ones that could be provided by for-profit businesses. The state has an interest in IOs not becoming overly large suppliers in market economies. Again, where IOs exploit their tax privileges, they may distort market conditions and, for example, weaken businesses that would be important in foreign markets. Naturally, pressure from for-profit businesses themselves, because of what they perceive as unfair competition, is likely to be a major catalyst for government intervention. In this section we consider the contrasting experiences of Britain and the US in relation to the issue of unfair competition, and begin by considering mutuals.

The history of the policy of the state in Britain and in the US towards the economic activities of mutual-benefit organizations can, very crudely, be divided into three stages. In the first period these organizations' activities were regarded with considerable suspicion, because they were seen as linked to, and sometimes 'fronts' for, trade unions and other associations that were believed to be anti-state in character. In Britain, especially, hostility in the late eighteenth and early nineteenth centuries to the mobilization of the working class coloured attitudes to mutual-help organizations, even among those who saw in bodies like Friendly Societies a potential source of social stability. Yet, as Gosden notes:

> Even while fears of the possible political consequences of friendly societies remained serious, members of the influential classes were active in putting forward schemes designed to improve the security of the insurance offered by the societies and to use the societies to relieve the expense and burden of the maintenance of the poor through the existing parish relief system.[15]

During the first three quarters of the nineteenth century the value of working-class mutual-benefit organizations to the state became increasingly evident. For one thing, the experience of trade unionism among skilled workers indicated that by no means all forms of unionism fostered political or social revolutions. Furthermore, it was becoming clear that co-operative economic activities – in insurance, retailing and house building – would actually encourage the sorts of beliefs and values the 'influential classes' wanted to see propagated amongst the working class, as well as helping to reduce possible dependence on the state.

The second stage of government policy towards mutuals, from the late nineteenth century until the mid-twentieth century, was marked by the removal of many earlier constraints on them, and in some respects special privileges being granted. Mutuals were responsible for creating markets which for-profits concerns could not, and for helping to provide many members of the working class (and, in the US, small farmers as well) with at least some stake in the maintenance of capitalism. In the US:

> the Congress sought to aid organizations operating for the benefit of lower income individuals and wage earners. The exemption from federal income tax of marketing and purchasing cooperatives, small property (fire) insurance companies, mutual irrigation companies, and the components of the Farm Credit Administration, benefits farmers.[16]

These privileges were introduced when corporate taxation itself was introduced, and it was clear that a desire to encourage thrift among the poor, or the potentially poor, was important in the granting of tax privileges to a whole range of institutions, some of which were made tax-exempt by administrative action. In the US Savings and Loan Associations were made exempt from income tax, and while in Britain Building Societies have been subject to corporation tax, we have already noted (in chapter 2) an advantage they enjoyed from 1894 to 1985 in the calculation of the income tax they paid for their depositors.

In many ways, then, the years around the turn of the twentieth century represent the high point for mutuals. They had grown large and created major areas of economic activity primarily, though not exclusively, among the working class, and they were widely accepted by successive governments as having a central role to play in social organization, and in return some of them enjoyed tax advantages not available to for-profit businesses. Indeed, at the end of the nineteenth century the Chief Registrar of Friendly Societies could write:

> it remains as one of the great glories of the Victorian era that . . . welfare has been established in a very large degree by the labours and the sacrifices of working men themselves, and by the wise and judicious legislation which has permitted and encouraged their endeavour in the direction of self-help.[17]

However, over the next fifty years the Friendly Societies were, in a sense, brought down – partly by their own limitations, and partly by their very success. The real problem of mutuals as welfare agencies was the limited range of services they could supply. They could run insurance schemes to assist the temporarily sick and to provide for the most basic of medical care, but they could not, as they were constituted, provide extensive systems of old-age pensions or complete health-care programmes. As demands for more extensive welfare programmes increased, there was always the danger that direct state provision would undermine some mutuals. This happened in Britain when state pensions were first introduced in 1911. Friendly Societies were embraced by the state, but only as very junior partners in the relationship, and their marginalization was completed with the introduction of the welfare state after 1945. Now it was by no means inevitable that greater state involvement should have marginalized them – when federal welfare provisions were greatly expanded in the US in the 1960s, it was through these sorts of agencies (especially Blue Cross/Blue Shield in the case of health insurance) that services for the many were actually provided. But in Britain the Friendly Societies' suspicion of state pensions was a key element in insuring that they would play little part in welfare provision this century.

When they were successful in excluding the state from their areas of activity, mutuals faced a rather different problem: the emergence of competition from for-profit rivals. In the nineteenth century the Friendly Societies had already drawn competition from commercial insurance companies, and, later, in the US, alternative forms of health provision to that available under the Blue Cross/Blue Shield type of scheme were to develop. We have seen too that Building Societies were to draw competition from banks in making loans for house purchases. Together with the fact that, especially after the Great Depression of the 1930s, it was less obvious that mutuals were necessary to provide a kind of 'social glue' to prevent social revolution, there was less incentive for the state to provide tax benefits for this kind of IO. Thus the third stage of state policy to the mutuals has been characterized by the gradual reduction in their special treatment for tax purposes. This has been most noticeable in the US. Mutual savings banks and Savings and Loan Associations lost their tax-exempt status in 1951 'when the Congress found that these institutions had grown so large that they no longer needed tax exemption to carry out their function of helping wage earners.'[18] Farming co-operatives had their exemptions removed in 1962, and the 1986 Tax Act removed much of the exemption for medical insurance organizations like Blue Cross/Blue Shield. In Britain the declining importance of mutuals in providing 'social glue' is shown not so much by a reduction in any special privileges, but by the Conservative government's encouragement to the Building Societies, since 1979, to develop other kinds of financial business and by the decision to convert the Trustee Savings Bank into a commercial company. The peculiar place of the large old 'working-class' mutuals has now all but disappeared, and policy towards them reflects more their ability to help in pursuing the government's particular policy objectives.

In general, then, the question of 'unfair competition' between mutuals and for-profit enterprises, which might have arisen from the economic viability of areas of activity in which only mutuals could operate earlier, has been resolved. This has been achieved by removing many of the tax advantages enjoyed by the mutuals, and by their full integration into the commercial sector. But what of competition between for-profit enterprises and other kinds of IOs, especially charities? Here the British and American experiences differ more radically, although as we shall see there are problems common to both countries.

In the US the issue of unfair competition first arose in the 1940s, and after congressional hearings changes in tax law were initiated in the 1950 Revenue Act. The most controversial cases involved universities buying property from commercial firms after arranging to lease it back to them at highly favourable rents. The deals suited both the universities and the firms involved. The latter could take advantage of the former's tax-exempt status so that, while the universities got a market rate of return on their capital outlays, the firms were able to lower their costs in comparison with their rivals. Such deals had been made possible by court decisions in 1924 and 1938 which gave tax exemption on *all* income to any organization which had tax-exempt status.[19] The 1950 Act changed this and drew a distinction between 'related' and 'unrelated' business income for a tax-exempt organization. The latter was now taxable, and unrelated business was defined as 'any trade or business the conduct of which is not substantially related . . .to the exercise or performance by such organization of its charitable, educational, or other purpose or function constituting the basis for its exemption.[20] Consequently, to take the example of a museum, a tax-exempt institution could generate at least three possible categories of income: (a) income from non-business sources, such as from membership dues, (b) non-taxable business income, such as from sales of books related to items in a collection and (c) taxable income from, say, a shoe shop it had been given in a legacy.

Now, aside from the obvious problem that there will always be 'borderline' difficulties with this sort of distinction, there were four main limitations to this attempted solution to the unfair competition issue. Firstly, the Act did not address the more fundamental problem of whether all the kinds of organizations that traditionally had been tax-exempt warranted this status. The basis for granting 501(c)(3) status was broadly the same as that for granting charitable status in England, and, of course, ultimately this derived from the Statute of 1601. There were some kinds of organizations, such as fee-paying private schools, for which the issue of tax exemption was at least controversial, since the benefits went to those who could afford to educate their children privately. In other words, irrespective of whether there was competition from for-profit concerns, there were some organizations which continued to be tax-exempt but which had little claim on grounds of public benefit to such favourable treatment.

Secondly, and of more concern to us here, the solution contained in the 1950 Act continued to allow non-profits to compete with for-profits, without taxation, providing their purpose was one which had been tax-exempt. But, of course, just as social changes during the nineteenth century had made profitable commercial insurance business among the working class, so there were activities that had earlier been impossible to organize on a large-scale commercial basis, but which had become or were becoming *industries* even in 1950. Hospitals, and health care more generally, were one example. If commercial provision was now possible, the justification for continued tax exemption for 'non-profit' suppliers became problematic. In the 1980s this issue was to become highly contentious in the case of hospitals, with at least one study purporting to show that non-profit hospitals were both less efficient than for-profit hospitals and also less inclined to provide for social needs such as care for the indigent, though other studies indicate the opposite. [21] Even if non-profit hospitals do actually provide greater social benefits than their for-profit rivals, there remains the question of *how much* better we would expect them to perform in order to warrant any tax privileges. The point is, therefore, that the 1950 Act did not provide means for dealing with industries emerging from marginal areas of the economy.

Thirdly, the way in which the 1950 Act was interpreted was also backward-looking, in that some business activities were allowed to qualify as 'related businesses' because they were long established, even though their connection to the purposes of their organizations was no more direct than other income sources which were designated as unrelated. To take one example, the income universities acquire from spectactors paying to attend games played by their sports teams (and more importantly today the income from the television rights to those games) is deemed related income. This is on the ground that universities teach physical education, and university teams competing in different sports are an aspect of that education. But it is not all clear that having a university basketball team to watch contributes in any way to the education of a student. Even if it did there is no reason for not taxing income from all non-student spectators and from television contracts. Yet American universities are taxed on any income they earn from renting student accommodation, or other rooms, to conferences which are not sponsored by their own departments. (Interestingly, in Britain such income is not taxable and has constituted an important element of universities' income for some years.)[22] In both cases the income could help to subsidize important educational activities, as could sales from a noodle factory, but unlike income from tuition fees the connection with the purpose of the institution is indirect rather than direct.[23]

The fourth problem with the 1950 reform was that it provided no means for dealing with the later expansion of existing non-profits into new, and profitable, activities related to their primary purposes. Changes in technology made it possible for certain kinds of non-profits, especially universities and organizations in the health-care field, to start up new fee-paying services which were extensions of their 'charitable' purposes, but which could also be provided by for-profit enterprises. The growth of high technology sectors of the economy made the border between related and unrelated business a problematic one – something which, obviously, could not have been foreseen in 1950.

However, as an expedient measure for dealing with the aspects of unfair competition which had become prominent in the 1940s, the 1950 Act was successful. Organized lobbies campaigning against the tax privileges of non-profits had ceased, and the areas of contention between the two kinds of organization had been much reduced. This was to change in the 1970s, and by the mid 1980s lobbying efforts for reform were intensifying again; the Small Business Administration (SBA) published reports on the issue, and, rather surprisingly, it was ranked as the third most important issue facing small business by participants at the White House Conferences on Small Business in 1986.[24] At the same time the Sub-Committee on Oversight (of the House Ways and Means Committee) was developing an interest in the activities of tax-exempt organizations, following hearings it held on foundations in 1983. (These 1983 hearings were the first major congressional review on the taxation of foundations since the reforms of 1969.) This led, in 1987, to five days of hearings on unfair competition, and to proposals for amendments to the unrelated business income tax provisions affecting non-profit organizations. There were two main causes of this renewal of the debate. In the thirty years after 1950 there had been significant changes in economic markets: high technology industries brought non-profit and for-profit institutions into competition with each other, and some areas of activity in which economic markets could not operate effectively earlier had now displayed levels of demand which could draw in for-profit firms. Moreover, there were stronger incentives for many kinds of non-profit to expand their commercial activities. Cutbacks in federal government programmes, especially with the advent of the Reagan administration, had reduced income derived from government in the form of fees and grants. In order to offset this decline, many organizations sought to boost their commercial activities and this tended to draw them into competition with for-profit concerns.

The industries identified in 1984 by an SBA report as ones in which small businesses were experiencing pressure from non-profits included: audio-visual services, analytic testing, consultancy in fields such as engineering, travel operators, research services, computer services and the manufacture and retailing of hearing aids.[25] The complexity of the issues involved, and the difficulty of reforming the present system of regulation based on the related–unrelated business distinction, is best shown by examples from some of the areas of conflict.

In the first place, there were some cases of non-profits simply expanding their range of activities into areas that might well have made them liable for tax even under present law. One example was the Monterey Bay aquarium which was a non-profit corporation established in 1984.[26] It was highly successful in drawing additional tourists to Monterey (more than two million people visited the aquarium in 1985) but at the same time tended to take visitors *away* from the town's famous Cannery Row. The dispute with local traders was inflamed when the aquarium's bookshop started retailing best-selling books, in addition to books on topics related to its exhibits, and by its plans to open fast-food stalls inside and outside its building. In 1986 the traders succeeded in getting the local council to pass an ordinance which, among other provisions, compelled the bookshop to comprise at least 90 per cent of its stock from scientific and educational books. It is possible, though by no means certain, that the kinds of commercial activities into which the aquarium had expanded might have been taxable under the 1950 law, and clearly IRS regulations could be modified rather easily to take account of the 'best-seller' problem, although restrictions on the sale of food would seem a more complex issue.

However, it is important to reaffirm a point (made in chapter 3) that not all entries into the market by American non-profits are intended to generate income. Social service agencies which charge their clients may do so because their endowments, government grants, and so on still do not enable them to provide their services free of charge. But this economic activity may still have an impact on for-profit firms. Consider a case reported by the SBA in 1984. The University of Michigan (a state university, though a private university might well have concluded the same sort of deal) negotiated with Apple Computers for the bulk purchase of $2 million worth of computers which were to be resold to faculty members and students. The discount offered by Apple enabled the university to resell them at just over half their normal retail price, and the decline in sales at local computer stores was predicted to lead to some local stores going out of business. The SBA cites this as an instance of unfair competition, but unlike the aquarium case, it is not at all obvious that it should be conceived as such. The university's purpose was, presumably, to increase the use of computers by its members, and it used its purchasing power to do so. This is little different from the activities of a consumers' co-operative which similarly exploits discounts from suppliers to reduce the price to members. Here, however, the university itself initiated the purchase to further an education-related objective. The purchase may well have reduced federal tax revenues, and this highlights the points that tax exemption on other forms of income for non-profits is revenue reducing, and that all tax laws granting privileges to non-profits require justification on grounds of equity. But tax revenues may be reduced when there is no adverse effects on for-profit firms, or when adverse consequences for them are unintended. In the Michigan computer case the question of *unfair competition* does not seem to arise because the university was not intending to raise revenue or otherwise financially advantage itself through its bulk purchase.

What this suggests is that there are at least three aspects of the activities of non-profit-distributing bodies, which are sometimes conflated under the general heading of 'unfair competition'. There is unfair competition in a strict sense which involves an NPO attempting to generate income for itself from sales in an area of activity where for-profit firms can operate, and where its tax status provides the NPO with an advantage in its pricing policy. Then there is the point that not taxing income to non-profits is revenue-reducing for the state – whether that income be in the form of gifts, interest on investments or sales of goods or services. This raises questions of fairness – in relation to the distribution of tax burdens – but not ones of *fairness in economic competition*. Then again an organization may have to charge for some of the goods and services it provides, and because these products can be supplied on a commercial basis, some for-profit firms are thereby disadvantaged; here the purpose of the sales is not to produce income for the organization but to maximize the distribution of the good. In relation to this third element it should be noted that not all adverse affects on for-profit firms provide a justification for regulation. Consider the computer case again. Providing goods directly relevant to education at the lowest possible price is linked directly to the principal purpose of the university; it cannot afford to give computers to the university community, just as it cannot provide tuition free of charge, but on academic grounds it wants to encourage the widespread use of computers for research and study. However, if the university's intention in bulk buying some goods were to be to drive certain businesses into bankruptcy, or it was using discounted, non-academic goods as a supplement to the salaries of its employees, there might well be a case for state intervention to protect affected businesses. The *raison d'être* for this, though, would not be unfair competition, for the university is not attempting to make this an income-earning enterprise, but the misuse of power.

Indeed, a number of the examples which are sometimes referred to in the US as 'unfair competition' are really cases of institutional power being used in inappropriate ways. A university which tried to drive some local firms out of business, or which sold discounted washing machines to its employees, would be using its power for ends that, at best, were only indirectly connected to its main purposes. Strict controls on unfair competition might remove some of these abuses, but there will be many that it cannot. This is because they are really unconnected with the issue of *competition*. The trouble is, that short of some more general regulatory agency supervising the activities of non-profit institutions, it is difficult to see how the use of institutional power could be controlled.

A different problem has been revealed in the case of many YMCAs in America.[27] With physical fitness becoming increasingly fashionable among the middle class, the demand for well-equipped gymnasiums and squash courts has greatly expanded. The YMCAs, which have traditionally given considerable emphasis to sporting activities in their programmes for disadvantaged youths and young men potentially 'at risk', were in an ideal position to extend their facilities in many cities to make available competitively-priced sports facilities for the middle class. In this relatively new industry, they came into direct competition with recently-formed for-profit enterprises. The question of whether there is significant head-on competition is not disputed, as it is, for example, in the aquarium case. Rather, the YMCAs' defence of their position rests on two claims. They argue that they have always been concerned with people's fitness, so that it was natural for them to enter the market for sports facilities; it is the for-profit concerns that are really the 'late comers', and because of this the contention that there is an issue of fairness at stake is specious. These businesses knew when they started that there would be YMCAs operating in this 'industry'. The second claim is that as the YMCAs need to recruit individuals to help as volunteers in their youth programmes, having middle-class members in their more exclusive facilities enables them to recruit volunteers, and hence carry out their 'charitable' purpose.

From the viewpoint of governmental regulation these two claims raise very different considerations. One is how to deal with activities for which there used to be little market demand, but for which there is now a great deal. Since the services will be provided anyway, and since the state is losing tax revenue from having non-profits continue to operate in this field, there is little justification for permitting this source of income to remain tax-exempt. However, prior involvement in the activity presumably does constitute some kind of claim for the removal of tax exemption being phased in gradually rather than implemented immediately. (In fact, the YMCA case is not quite so clear-cut an instance of marginal economic activity becoming profitable as were, say, hospitals earlier in the twentieth century. While the YMCA can claim to have been involved for a long time in helping people to keep physically fit, their earlier efforts were directed primarily at the socially disadvantaged, and not at the sorts of people over whose custom there is now intense competition.) Nevertheless, in terms of both tax loss and fairness to would-be businesses, there is a strong case over the longer term for removing tax privileges when an activity becomes widely marketable. As we saw earlier, this is precisely the sort of approach that was adopted with mutuals.

The second claim is not, of course, that the YMCAs would suffer financial harm from having this relatively new source of income made taxable, but that they would be less able to recruit volunteers for their other activities if they lost members because taxation forced them to raise their prices. Clearly, if the removal of tax-exempt status were to have a serious effect on volunteerism, arguments about the need to maintain particular volunteer-based activities would have to be weighed by the state against arguments about tax loss and fairness. In some circumstances it is possible that the commercial and volunteer components of an activity might be so intertwined, and the need to preserve volunteerism so great, that what would, in effect, be a state subsidy might well be warranted. In the case of the YMCAs, though, it is hard to believe that the erosion of volunteers would be so great that there would be a case for maintaining tax exemption solely on these grounds.

Different again are many of the examples of competition in fields like analytic testing, consultancy, research services and computer services. Here organizations, mainly universities and health-care non-profits, are exploiting commercially techniques or products which have been developed in the course of either basic research or for use within an organization itself. These cases usually differ from the YMCA case in two respects. The organizations cannot claim that there is some long-established activity, which for-profit concerns are now attempting to 'muscle in' on. These are new industries, and while in many cases the tax-exempt organizations may have made them possible through their research programmes, there is no claim on the basis of prior involvement in pre-market conditions. Again, there is no suggestion that any non-financial losses would be suffered (volunteers who might not be recruited, for example) by the non-profits if this income was taxable. There is in these cases a connection between the organizations' main purposes and their commercial ventures, and they illustrate well both the problem of 'policing' the related/unrelated business boundary when new industries are involved, and the more general issue of whether unfair competition is really only a small part of the problem of commercial activities by non-profits.

Many of the profit-making consultancy and research activities in which universities and non-profits in the health-care sector now engage are at least as closely connected with their organizations' primary purposes as are, say, income-earning sports teams to colleges and universities. The organizations have been able to stake a claim to 'related income' in these areas because, in part, it is activity in pursuit of their own primary purposes which has made the industries possible. In many instances the commercial competitors are former employees or collaborators with the non-profits, but in effect the non-profit and for-profit concerns are entering the market at the same time. It can be argued that the presence of competition is a good litmus test in deciding whether previously 'related' income should now become taxable. This is because it shows that the techniques involved have gone beyond the early stages of development, when, arguably, tax exemption is needed to encourage further research and development. But the absence of competition does not demonstrate that a fully-fledged industry has yet to emerge, for the IOs may have been able to stifle competition through collusion with groups in the for-profit sector. Perhaps the best-known example of this is not in the high technology sector, but sport, in which American colleges' collusion with professional leagues has helped to stifle semi-professional and professional leagues that might otherwise have competed with colleges for the services of young athletes, especially in basketball and American football. In other words just as the exercise of power by non-profits in the commercial arena is at least as important an issue as unfair competition itself, so actual competition between for-profits and non-profits is not the only kind of evidence that non-profits are exercising unwarranted commercial power. Consequently, regulating non-profits on the basis of competition is likely to be of only limited utility in reducing unwarranted tax privileges or reducing non-profits' commercial power.

Another aspect of the problem of competition involving American non-profits is that of the growth, especially in the health-care field, of complexes of organizations, some components of which are for-profit enterprises and others non-profits. These were discussed in chapter 3. Groups of organizations which make use of these arrangements can generate untaxed capital for themselves, through skilfully channelling certain kinds of activities to non-profit components, and entire organizational complexes can thereby acquire advantages over their competitors. Once again, it is in connection with high technology that these complexes are most apparent, and their appearance prompts questions about the basis of the distinction between for-profit organizations and tax-exempt IOs. Here too, it is not just the issue of unfair competition which is at stake, but equally the ability of corporations to reduce their tax burden. Indeed, it is in relation to these complexes that the American approach to non-profit status, in liberalizing non-profit corporation laws at the state level and in the taxation of non-profits at the federal level, most starkly contrasts with one feature of the British approach. This latter approach has sought to segregate 'charitable' organizations as a special category and to prevent the merging of commerce and charity. It is useful, therefore, at this point to turn to the British approach to 'unfair competition'.

It is correct to say that there has not been any substantial controversy about unfair competition by tax-privileged organizations in Britain. As in America, there has been growing concern with the ease with which charitable organizations can be used to further the self-interest of those who establish them.[28] Charities do provide a way in which commercial enterprises, often family companies, can 'launder' their money, and there have been well-publicized scandals such as the use made of the Vincent Foundation by the Marcos family.[29] It was with the inability of the Charity Commission to deal with this sort of commercial exploitation of charities that the NAO Report in 1987 was concerned. But the 'unfair competition' issue has been largely absent. Apart from occasional, localized, complaints about charity shops, most of the complaints received by the Charity Commission have concerned community associations operating out of village halls. Some of these associations have become social clubs engaged in the regular sale of alcohol to members, and thereby they have entered into direct competition with local pubs. The Commission has responded to this minor arena of competition by recommending that the sale of alcohol on a regular basis should be 'done through the medium of a separate non-charitable club'.[30]

In part, as we have noted, this lack of controversy about 'unfair competition' in Britain is due to the centrality of the distinction between charities and non-charities in English law, and it has meant that there has been a less 'porous' boundary between tax-exempt organizations and others. In theory at least, 'seepage' by commercial organizations into the former category is more difficult than in the US. The incentive to become a charity is also reduced by the view of the Charity Commission, cited in chapter 3, that its partners in regulation, the Inland Revenue, would tax trading income that was not derived from carrying out a primary function of a charity or if the work was not performed by the charity's beneficiaries. In practice, this has provided a greater barrier to enterprise by charities than the 'unrelated income' provision in the US. There is also the fact that several categories of charities, including universities, do not come under the jurisdiction of the Charity Commission, and it is these organizations that have been among those most closely involved in competing with for-profit enterprises. (Although the Department of Education and Science have sought the opinion of the Commission in relation to the potential legal problems raised by the former's encouragement of greater trading by universities, the Commission has no power to investigate these organizations.) Denied a formal agency with which to lodge any complaints, these firms have not joined forces with enterprises facing competition from those charities which are the responsibility of the Commission. In other words, any lobby that might form in England finds mobilization more problematic than does its American counterparts.

In addition, when a charity has been engaged in trading, the concern of the Commission has not been directly with the issue of whether it has been in competition with for-profit firms, let alone whether it has competed unfairly, but with the extent of this trading in the context of the organization's overall activities. The Commission's aim is that a charity's income should not become 'unbalanced'. If trading is a relatively minor part of the overall activities of an organization it is permitted. This policy restricts the level of trading but does not deal specifically with competition when it arises. Furthermore, the way that trading is defined by the Commission and the Inland Revenue leads to the exclusion of certain kinds of income as being derived from trading, and hence possibly subject to taxation. Fees charged for services that are part of a charity's primary (charitable) purposes do not constitute trading – even if commercial firms are also supplying similar services on a for-profit basis. Consider again the example introduced in chapter 3 – the income the National Trust derives from entrance fees to its properties and from membership dues. Neither income source constitutes *trading* for the purposes of taxation, yet the private owner of a stately home would be liable for tax on entrance fees and on any season ticket schemes s/he devised. The 'competitive advantage' enjoyed by the Trust, and by many other charities with for-profit competitors, is bolstered, then, by the narrow definition of 'trading'.

What makes this narrow definition so important in explaining the failure of 'unfair competition' to emerge as an issue in Britain is the greater centralization of the state. In both Britain and the US commercial firms engaged in competition with charities are relatively small and come from a wide range of industries. Resolving the 'collective action' problem is especially difficult for them. One of the reasons why a lobby against 'unfair competition' developed in the US was that the SBA took a part in publicizing the issue for the concerned firms. The role that departments of an administration (at both federal and state levels) play in acting as agents for the interests they deal with, and sometimes regulate, is far more developed in the US than in Britain. In the decentralized US state not only is access to the administration easier, but there is a greater incentive for branches of the administration to develop and cultivate client groups.[31] The only unusual feature of the lobby the SBA helped to cultivate was that it was a part of the for-profit economy which found itself in a relatively disadvantageous position in mobilizing against its opponents; more commonly, it is for-profit enterprises which enjoy the advantages.

4 The Political Activities of Intermediate Organizations

The final area of state regulation concerns the political activities of IOs. At issue is the right of those organizations which enjoy certain kinds of privileges from the state, especially tax privileges, to engage in overtly political acts. The granting of these privileges (such as the right to reclaim tax on covenants, or the right of donors to take their donations as tax deductions) to *political* groups may be objected to on three grounds. First, there is the argument that the greater the number of tax privileges granted, the more inequitable the tax burden is likely to be; exemptions, therefore, should be granted only in cases where essential services would not be provided at all, and with political groups, it is far from clear that tax concessions are required to bring about mobilization. Second, it might be argued that it is far from clear what benefits to a society as a whole emanate from tax exemptions and other privileges being granted to 'cause' groups. Third, the ability of the state to act as an arbiter between competing groups in society might actually be reduced by high levels of politicization among groups, especially those providing services funded by the state. On this view, maldistributions of resources are likely to develop, as the best organized groups are more able to sustain state support for programmes in which they are involved.

On the other hand, those who support the extension of tax privileges to political IOs contend that its opponents overlook several serious problems. In practice, the distinction between the political and the non-political is virtually impossible to implement fairly. Moreover, distinguishing between IOs in this manner is politically biased, since the groups which are most overtly political are those which want to change certain social arrangements, and, therefore, are usually the more liberal or left-wing groups. But, in any case, in a democratic society helping to remove costs of mobilization (through tax advantages) from those with few resources is actually to advance democracy, because it grants access to the political system to those who are relatively powerless – such as the disabled. Undoubtedly, those who support the extension of tax privileges to groups which are politically active are correct in claiming that the present system is grossly unfair. However, it can be argued that the most appropriate way of removing this unfairness would be to eliminate tax privileges from many of the categories of groups that already have them, rather than extending the privileges.

At the risk of oversimplification, it is possible to distinguish three main stages in both England and the US in the state's approach to this issue. First, there was the period up to the early years of the century when the issue was not addressed directly, and when a number of organizations that were advancing indubitably political goals were permitted to have charitable status. In Britain these included organizations like the Lord's Day Observance Society – bodies which would probably not be granted charitable status today, if they had to apply for it anew, because of their lobbying activities. Even more important, perhaps, were the Charity Organization Societies which sought to affect both mass behaviour and the content of some Acts of Parliament.[32] In the US some courts held political objectives to be charitable and some even found bequests to political parties to be charitable; for example, there was a case in New York in 1914, where a particular political objective was held to be charitable, and 'where a disposition to defray the expenses of a political organization was sustained as charitable on the theory that the donor intended to use a political party only as the agent for advancing a political objective.'[33]

The succeeding period was characterized by the attempt to create a well-defined category of tax-privileged organizations which were not political. In England this began with the decision by Lord Parker in the *Bowman* case of 1917 when, in relation to political objects, he said the judiciary had 'always refused to recognize such objects as charitable'.[34] In the US the IRS's establishment of what later became known as the 501(c)(3) category of tax-exempt organizations, ones that could receive tax-deductible donations, similarly established the principle that political activity was not 'charitable'. In the second period there was a general consensus that 'charities' were a special kind of IO that were both non-political and non-market orientated. The third stage (beginning in the mid 1960s), however, has been marked by growing challenges to both the fairness and the enforceability of this prohibition on political activity, and in turn this has contributed to questioning of whether there really is a 'charitable' or 'independent' sector in society that is clearly different from both market-orientated organizations and political organizations.

How are we to explain this move, in both countries, first towards restrictions on the political activities of charities, and subsequently towards a more liberal interpretation of this distinction? In fact, slightly different explanations have to be given for the two countries. In England it was perhaps inevitable that, once 'unpopular causes' started to seek charitable status, a court case might result in judicial opinion resolving an area of legal uncertainty in favour of the easiest solution – prohibiting the pursuit of political objectives. Nor, once this had happened, was there likely to be much immediate pressure to have the decision reversed – those groups that were concerned about the issue did not have the power to get it on to the political agenda. It was the easiest solution, because for a court to have allowed some political objectives as charitable would almost certainly have necessitated further parliamentary action to define the boundaries of permissible political activity. Instead, since the *Bowman* decision, it has been held that a trust promoting political objectives cannot be charitable, as the courts have no means of determining whether the proposed change in the law advocated by an organization would be of public benefit.

There were three differences in the context in which political activity by charities was dealt with in the US. There were no federal laws relating to charities; some states and some courts had, even by the early twentieth century, given relatively liberal interpretations as to which objects were charitable; and for many purposes the laws on non-profit organizations, rather than those on charitable trusts, were the ones affecting most 'other-regarding' organizations. However, the IRS too opted for the administratively easiest solution of following the general thrust of the 1601 Statute when deciding which kinds of organizations were to be granted tax exemption and permitted to receive tax-deductible donations, and they rejected the case for those with political objectives. The major court ruling which confirmed their approach was *Slee* v. *Commissioner* (1930). In this case the court agreed with the Commissioner of Internal Revenue that an organization devoted to repealing legislation was not charitable, and that contributions to it were not tax deductible.[35]

The instability of this solution to the issue of political activity, which had been arrived at in both Britain and the US, was brought about by both socio-political changes in the two societies and also by the ways in which governments conducted their affairs in the mid-twentieth-century. We consider these two factors in turn.

As many studies have revealed, the rise of new elements of the middle class in the twentieth century has generated new kinds of issues in political debate. 'Other-regarding' politics among the middle class has taken many forms, including most recently, of course, the emergence of groups and parties organized around ecology and 'green' issues. But there are two features which all of these movements have tended to have in common compared with other styles of middle class politics. They have not been concerned with promoting the *overt* economic self-interest of the participants, and have often portrayed themselves as being 'public regarding' in character. And they have also tended to reject traditional ways of political organizing through hierarchical political parties in favour of smaller or more loosely coordinated structures. Both of these features are relevant for our discussion.

On the one hand, the kinds of issues which these groups have promoted have often been objects which have traditionally been charitable – the alleviation of homelessness and the preservation of the environment, for example. Of particular importance, because of their size, have been charities providing aid to third world countries. They are largely a post-colonial phenomenon, although Save the Children dates back to 1919 and Oxfam was founded originally to relieve problems associated with war-time refugees in Europe. They have never shirked from proclaiming that they are concerned with the causes of poverty in the third world, and in an interview published just before a lobby of Parliament in 1985 the point was made that: 'As Oxfam's [director] Frank Judd says: "If we see a government whose citizens we're helping use scarce resources to buy arms beyond its means, we have to be prepared to tell them, 'We're dealing with the consequences of your policies.'"'[36]

The problems posed by these agencies, though, are not so much that they try to change a government's policies – proceeding through official channels has always been recognized as compatible with charitable status – but with two aspects of how they seek change. One aspect is that the borderline between education of the public (which is charitable) and propaganda (which is not) is extremely indistinct, and many development agencies have publicity programmes that exhibit these difficulties very well. The second aspect is that the operational style of some of these agencies – in seeking to mobilize large numbers of people in support of their cause, and getting them to do more than just raise money – is incompatible with the older model of charity-state relations which saw elite contacts through 'normal channels' as the proper mode for lobbying by charities. Faced by these problems, and with limited staff resources, the Charity Commission has, in effect, acquiesced in campaigning activities that it might have rejected thirty or forty years ago, while at the same time it has sought to eliminate the most overt political actions by charities.

On the other hand, organizing in bodies other than parties, and having non-political, as well as directly political activities in these organizations, has appealed to many participants and has sometimes made possible the formation of organizations that are charitable or are affiliated to new charities. Perhaps the best example of this kind of organization in the field of third world aid is War on Want, which was founded by members of the Labour party and which has a democratic, membership-based structure. Of all the third world aid organizations, it has been the one most associated with highly political grass-roots activists, and with investigations into political involvement by the Charity Commissioners. In brief, then, a new political agenda, and new styles of socio-political organizing, have made it much more difficult to maintain a consistent distinction between a non-political charitable 'sector' and a 'political' sector.

In Britain the pressures on the existing distinction between charity and politics have been evident in the situation facing the Charity Commission in dealing with complaints that a particular charity has been engaged in political activities – activities that fall outside the area of those permitted as ancillary to a charitable purpose. For the most part, the Commission seems to have preferred to issue warnings, to discuss how infringements might be avoided, to deregistration. Similarly, Chesterman has said of the Inland Revenue: 'there are no publicized cases in which they have withdrawn tax relief from a registered charity on the ground of political activity.'[37] When the Commission has had to intervene one solution open to a charity has been to start up a new, non-charitable, subsidiary to carry out the overt political activities, and to be more careful in confining its own activities to those that can be argued to be educational or whatever. Moreover, since the Commission permits officials of charities to express political views in a personal capacity, further flexibility is possible.[38] At the price of some inconsistency, such devices have let the Commission 'off the hook'. This 'fudging and mudging' in Britain of the issue of political activity by charities was not possible in the US, because there the problem of this sort of activity reached a crisis point in the later 1960s.

There were two sources of this crisis. One was the use of funds by foundations for quasi-political purposes:

> Most of the salvos were launched by particular persons and groups with particular vexations (Taft Republicans angered by the support given Eisenhower by liberal Republicans closely associated with the Ford and other foundations; Congressman Patman unforgiving of Huntington Hartford's A&P for driving his father out of the grocery business and ever-suspicious of the eastern financial establishment).[39]

The congressional inheritors of Jeffersonian hostility to private power, and especially Wright Patman, scored a major victory in 1969. After 1969 the activities of foundations were constrained in a number of ways. But at the same time it was clear that other kinds of 501(c)(3) organizations were actually disadvantaged by the then laws on lobbying. The earlier laws provided that 501(c)(3)s could retain their status if they did not engage in 'substantial' amounts of lobbying. However, organizations found that their status was threatened by their use of funds to oppose the policies of, especially, organized business interests. In particular, the long-established environmental group, the Sierra Club, got into trouble with the IRS. The Club's argument was that they had to undertake public campaigns to counteract the lobbying and advertising of their opponents, which the latter could claim as a tax-deductible expense. The growing political power of environmental groups, and the fact that the politics of that period were conducive to raising issues of fairness in the political process, led to a change in the law in 1976.

Rules proposed under new legislation, the Tax Reform Act, enabled 501(c)(3) organizations either to be subject to the older guidelines about lobbying or to register under a new section, 501(h). Those registering under the latter would be subject to strict guidelines as to the amount they could spend on lobbying, but in general they would be allowed to devote rather more to this than the IRS had allowed in the past. The IRS was to promulgate new regulations within ten years on this basis. In fact, the first draft of these regulations was far more constricting than the 1976 law and, according to Independent Sector, it actually made the situation more difficult for 501(c)(3)s than the pre-1976 regulations. The reason for this difference between the clear intent of the 1976 Act and the regulations presented by the IRS in 1986 seems to have its origins in specific difficulties the IRS had experienced in dealing with some tax-exempt organizations in that decade. There was no evidence that the IRS was actually trying to undo the reforms enacted by Congress.

At the same time the state itself was making it more likely that charities would become active in politics. Here, once again, the lead was taken in the US when the Great Society (and other) programmes of the 1960s used 501(c)(3)s extensively in the delivery of services. This meant that many organizations had an immediate stake in protecting particular programmes. (As we have noted, it was only later that similar, but smaller, efforts were made in Britain to extend the involvement of charities in the provision of state funded welfare services.) Sometimes state encouragement to the formation of advocacy groups was unintended; as Jenkins has argued:

> The National Organization for Women (NOW) . . . was initially organized by political activists attending the White House-sponsored National Conference on the Status of Women in 1966. Although the Johnson administration had not intended to create an independent advocacy group for women, its sponsorship inadvertently organized an entrepreneurial cadre with heightened awareness of women's issues.[40]

However, in some policy areas the state actually wanted to create groups that would be politically active, in order to carry out its own policies. Walker's data indicates that in the US more than 10 per cent of 'citizen groups' founded between 1945 and 1980 received government grants at their founding.[41] In policy areas where these groups could be useful in informally monitoring developments, grants would be given to help in their establishment. For example, 'the federal government . . . has become an important source of seed money in the formation of large, multiple-issue environmental' citizens interest groups.[42]

Again, cutbacks in federal government funding in the late 1970s and 1980s, and greater competition for the available funds, were to lead to far greater lobbying activity, and grass-roots mobilizing, by those bodies that had now become heavily dependent on government funding. This was, of course, especially evident in the social welfare field, but one of the most controversial instances has been the use of lobbyists by individual universities to secure research funds for themselves:

> Increasingly, lobbyists are using their contacts in the capital to bypass the established peer review' system through which most Federal funds are distributed to colleges . . . Such reviews do not occur when lobbyists go after specially 'earmarked' funds by attaching a specific spending allocation on an appropriations bill for a particular agency, whether from the Education Department or the Bureau of Mines.[43]

The net result of these different developments was that, by the second half of the 1980s, the state in Britain was facing problems in regulating the political activities of charities, while in the US yet more difficulties of regulation were becoming evident. The problems in Britain were various.

First, the Charity Commission, lacking the resources to 'police' most charities once they were registered, was attempting to guard against possible political activities by would-be charities by scrupulously checking the proposed objectives of any organizations that appeared to infringe present law. In practice, one consequence of this policy was to deter a number of apolitical bodies from obtaining charitable status, because they became tired of the correspondence they had to enter into with the Commission.[44]

Second, both among many organizations that have long been registered charities, and among those that have been able to 'slip by' the Commission, some kinds of (especially) local political mobilizing exists alongside the more traditionally charitable activities of these groups. These organizations, however, tend to be concentrated in particular policy areas – notably overseas aid and community work. In relation to *all* charities, they are not that large a sub-group, and, indeed, Gerard has argued that among the rest there had been 'a worrying degree of complacency'.[45] But, as we have seen, the number of charities has been growing so rapidly that, even though the Gallup survey revealed that 90 per cent of charities do not have explicit political objectives, there are still a lot of organizations which do have them.[46]

Third, because the Commission lacks the staff and resources to conduct even 'spot checks' on organizations, the cases of political activity that are exposed usually result from complaints by MPs and other individuals well-placed to obtain publicity for their viewpoints: it is a system which regulates, therefore, largely on the basis of complaints by opponents of particular groups.

Fourth, even those organizations which have fallen foul of the Commission are usually able to reorganize their affairs so that, by splitting their activities between a charitable and a non-charitable body, they can overcome the prohibition on political activity by charities. As with War on Want, this solution is not always completely successful, though, because of the difficulties encountered in providing funds for the political organization. But the very increase in the number of quasi-political activities undertaken by organizations that have purposes which are undoubtedly charitable in law raises important questions as to whether the present system of regulation is both consistent and enforceable. Because of their growing involvement with the state, and because many charitable purposes (including the elimination of poverty) have important political aspects, a growing number of charities do not now appear to be the apolitical bodies that were identified in the *Bowman* decision.

Thus, regulation of charities today poses a dilemma for the state. If, as in Britain, it continues only to permit attempts at influencing government through 'official channels', there is the danger that the law will be seen as arbitrary and irrelevant in an era when the nature of many charities, including the best-known ones, has changed. And it is important to realize that the problem lies not so much on the fringes of charitable activity, but in core areas like poverty relief where changing the state's policies, when necessary, is now widely regarded as being intimately connected with alleviating the plight of the poor. To maintain the ban on political activity is to ignore the facts that the thrust of much charitable activity differs from that of charities sixty years ago, and that charities' relations with the state are also very different now.

However, to liberalize the law, as the US Congress did in 1976, can pose even greater dangers if it is not done carefully. In the following decade there was growing evidence of two problems. Some organizations simply took advantage of the weak position of the IRS in scrutinizing political activities and used funds in 501(c)(3) organizations for purposes that do not qualify for that status. Among the best publicized of these cases have been the deployment of funds by right-wing fundamentalist churches for political campaign purposes, and the channelling of funds to the Nicaraguan Contras in the 'Irangate' scandal.[47] The other problem has been the exploitation of 501(c)(3) status by politicians and organizations taking advantage of the 'educational' category in the IRS classification of non-profits. Perhaps the most openly political development here has been the establishment of political foundations by nationally known politicians:

> Although these organizations must be nonpartisan to qualify for tax-exempt status as public charities under the Internal Revenue Code, they can give political candidates a vehicle for assembling intellectual resources and developing policy expertise that could benefit them in their campaigns.[48]

Publicity (and scandals) about the use of 501(c)(3) status for political purposes led in 1987 to congressional hearings and then to the introduction of a Bill in the House of Representatives (HR 2942) by the Chairman and the Ranking Minority Member of the sub-committee on Oversight (of the House Ways and Means Committee). This Bill was intended to prevent overtly political organizations operating as 501(c)(3)s.

It is interesting to note that in the 1980s the Canadian authorities have encountered rather similar difficulties relating to the political involvement of charities. Faced by new kinds of charities, which clearly had political aspects to them, federal law was changed in 1985 to allow for a greater allocation of resources to political activities by charities, providing this was to further their charitable purposes and did not dominate their charitable work. As a Revenue Canada Information Letter explained:

> The political activity must ... be 'incidental', that is, it must be minor or subordinate to the charitable purposes for which the charity was established and registered. An example of an activity which is not 'incidental' is a charity spending a *major* part of its time, effort and money on political activity.[49]

Nevertheless, this reform did not resolve all the difficulties Revenue Canada faced in dealing with complaints about political activity. Most especially, it did not address the question of how to treat religious groups (such as some anti-abortion groups that were advocating civil disobedience) which claimed that their actions were necessitated by the religious principles that themselves made the organizations charitable. Such lobbies have also posed problems in relation to the ban on *partisan* activity. Of Canada's three major parties, the New Democratic party is the only one with an explicit commitment to free choice on abortion, so that *any* intervention by anti-abortion groups in electoral politics could be interpreted as having a partisan dimension.

There are, of course, two distinct issues to be faced in considering how the state should attempt to regulate the political activities of charities. The first is that in neither Britain nor the US (nor, indeed, in Canada) in modern times has there been an appropriately resourced agency to effect *wide-ranging* regulation. It has not been thought necessary, so that hope of effective regulation of any kind must depend on a radical change here, as the Charity Commission itself indicated in 1987.[50] The second issue is that it is far from obvious how to resolve the dilemma we have identified. A solution at one extreme would be to make all political purposes charitable. At the other extreme, tax privileges might be initially removed from all organizations that presently enjoy them, but then reinstated under licence (subject to regular review) to *some* organizations that were deemed to provide especially important services on behalf of the state. These latter organizations might then be prohibited from engaging in specific kinds of political activities, which might vary depending on the sorts of services they provide. In between these two extremes there are a variety of other possible solutions. The Canadian solution, of granting greater flexibility to charities (providing political activities do not predominate) and of banning all partisan activities and all activities in relation to candidates for public office, is an example of one possible approach. The difficulty is that few of the alternative approaches would seem easy to operate because of the great variation in the organizations that enjoy charitable status. This, indeed, is the nub of the problem: English charity law. Both England and the US continue to make use of a category that is so broad, and, after 380 years, so inconsistent and ill-fitted to modern social organizations, that any solution which is based on this category would seem to be impossibly complex.

In this chapter we have explored how the liberal democratic states of Britain and the US have dealt with the question of how to regulate IOs. Regulation is necessary for a number of purposes – to ensure an adequate supply of goods, to protect members and donors, and so on – but in many respects it has been conspicuous by its absence in these countries. There have been several consequences of this, but perhaps the most important is that it has contributed to the erosion of the boundaries between IOs and both the state and the market system. This erosion has important implications for pluralism and, more generally, for democratic theory, and it is to these issues that we now turn.

8
Intermediate Organizations and Democracy

In an examination of the evolution of IOs we have noted considerable changes within these organizations, as well as in their relations with the market and the state. This transformation, and the increasing complexity of the relationship between public and private institutions, whose boundaries IOs straddle, demands a re-evaluation of their role in modern democracy. The idea that IOs are a key component in democracy has been particularly important in pluralist political thought, so it is with this critique of IOs that we begin.

As we shall see in the concluding section of this chapter, the idea of pluralism in democratic theory has been ambiguous, and the term has acquired meanings and connotations that it did not originally have.[1] For the moment, though, we shall employ the term in the way that it has come to be used, albeit sometimes misleadingly, by many political scientists in the last two decades. In this sense pluralism is identified with the kinds of economic and social institutions that developed with the rise of capitalism in western Europe and North America.

In the pluralist view, IOs can constitute key institutions between the profit-distributing sector and the state. On the one hand, they can mediate the impact of intense economic competition. For example, McConnell argues that 'private associations' helped to moderate the 'savage methods of competition' of the early twentieth century.[2] They have been seen as *private* institutions in that they are believed to be legally and financially independent from the state. Some IOs are also private in the different sense that they primarily serve their members rather than a wider public, while many others are explicitly concerned with advancing the interests of others. But they are distinct from profit-distributing bodies in that they do not seek to raise income which can later be distributed to individual members or contributors. Again, with some exceptions, their involvement with the state is largely intermittent – it occurs as and when issues arise which affect them. Unlike profit-making organizations which have the resources, and often the incentive, to retain semi-permanent lobbying facilities, most IOs are usually seen by pluralists as being more peripherally involved with the state. When they need to they can become part of the pressure group universe, but, especially in Truman's version of pluralism, their *potential* for political action still makes them central elements in the state.[3] Their lack of dependence on the state for resources and the general infrequency of their political activities enable them to retain a high degree of autonomy when dealing with a government and its institutions. In Dunleavy and O'Leary's words: 'pluralists valued groups and organizational autonomy, activity and diversity.'[4]

The other main characteristic of IOs as idealized by mid-twentieth-century pluralists is the role of their members and activists. Pluralists have not been so ill-informed as to believe that most IOs are controlled on a democratic basis by their members, but they have seen participation in IOs as producing rather different kinds of constraints on how these organizations operate than the constraints imposed by the market on for-profit firms. The volunteers in a social service agency and the members of a club exercise influence over how their organizations arrange their affairs precisely because they conduct the activities themselves and they are free to withdraw from them if they wish. As Dahl and Lindblom argued in 1953:

> It is much more difficult for leaders to tyrannize over members of their organizations if these members can withdraw and join another organization with substantially equivalent benefits. In this situation the tyrannical leader will become a leader without a following. Thus there is a core of sound common sense in the liberal preference for voluntary organizations as against the corporatist preference for compulsory ones.[5]

In the market too there is freedom – employees may quit and customers can stop purchasing, but firms are typically organized hierarchically and markets can be less than fully sensitive to the preferences of the latter. The *indirectness* of the market provides for less participant influence than in an IO, where there are less rigid hierarchies and either an identity between 'supplier' and 'consumer' or close interaction between them. For pluralists the market was only one of the mechanisms in a democracy, and it did not provide the basis for all social relations:

> although they defended the merits of political individualism, pluralists were aware of the dangers of a society where self-interest was the dominant motive and traditional social ties were absent. This understanding still differentiates pluralists from the individualism of some new right thinking.[6]

What, then, are the major changes in IOs in Britain and the US which we have identified in this book? First there is considerable evidence that certain kinds of IOs have been increasing in numbers. In both countries there are now more IOs enjoying tax-privileged status – as registered charities in Britain and as 501(c)(3) organizations in the US (See table 5.1.). But, second, important elements in the spread of this kind of IO have been advocacy groups and other kinds of socio-political groups; relatively more IOs today are involved in political activity both at the level of lobbying and in mobilizing at the mass level. While many IOs continue to fit the pluralist model of being largely apolitical, it is the growth in organizations seeking to influence the state both directly and indirectly which is most noticeable. This is related to a third point – changes in patterns of volunteerism. The extent of these changes must not be exaggerated, but there seems to have been a growth in participation in political and quasi-political bodies. This extends from explicit socio-political mobilization in community organizations, through participation in organizations like Oxfam, which are frequently involved in publicity to change the policies of governments, to organizations, like medical research charities, seeking to obtain state support for research in addition to their own efforts.[7] While older styles of participation – volunteer firefighting, 'meals on wheels' helpers and so on – persist, and perhaps still constitute a major portion of volunteer effort, there is evidence of problems in recruiting these kinds of volunteers and there also appears to be a marked shift in patterns of volunteering in both Britain and the US towards more political activities.

In turn these developments in volunteering can be linked to a fourth point – the rise in state funding of certain kinds of IOs. These are usually organizations that are providers of services, and often, though not always, they have charitable status. In the US the growth of state-financed IOs was occasioned largely by the expansion of welfare services in the 1960s when the federal government lacked the structures necessary for direct state provision. But there are also several advantages for the state in using IOs as intermediaries in the provision of services, and after 1979 the Conservative government in Britain started to channel funds towards IOs – a radically different approach from one which emphasizes an *independent* 'third sector'. These advantages include lower labour costs, greater flexibility when subsequently cutting back programmes and altering policy priorities, and reducing direct client pressure on the state when programmes are eliminated or reduced. But state funding also creates relationships of dependence which can intensify efforts at lobbying by individual organizations to secure funds for themselves.

However, dependence on the state for money has also contributed to a fifth change in IOs in recent decades – the need to generate income from fee-paying activities, and this brings some IOs into competition with for-profit enterprises. When state funds are reduced, supplementing income by supplying goods and services to individuals and organizations on a fee-paying basis becomes crucial to the survival of many IOs. But other factors have also helped to bring about this considerable erosion of the lines of demarcation between IOs and the commercial sector; as we have seen, technological changes and the emergence of some activities from 'marginal' areas of an economy have also been important factors. This competition is even more extensive than it initially appears, especially in Britain, because some kinds of 'fee income' are not classified as trading, and some forms of what are, in effect, fees for services that are also supplied in the for-profit sector appear as membership subscriptions in the accounts of some IOs. The expansion of competition between tax-privileged bodies and for-profit firms has brought about demands for its regulation in the US, but in Britain there are fewer affected firms and so far they have not mounted a lobby against 'unfair competition' or abuses of power by large IOs.

Finally, the membership-based, working-class IOs established in the nineteenth century have ceased to constitute a distinctive form of socio-economic organization. Even in their primitive forms, the boundary between them and the for-profit economy was not so clearly drawn as it might appear, but in the twentieth century the successful organizations, like Building Societies, have become fully integrated into capitalist economies. They have lost most of the peculiar features of membership-orientated organizations. Of the older mutuals, some British Friendly Societies did retain this older ethos, but they were marginalized with the establishment of the welfare state. The mutual principle has survived – in clubs of various kinds, and in new forms of self-help groups – but in the twentieth century, at least, the commercialization of marginal areas of the economy was associated with the effective abandonment of mutuality as a distinctive organizational form. Preserving participation and democracy in commercial enterprises may not be impossible, but clearly considerable planning in the construction of policy-making structures is required if they are to be retained, and this has been largely absent.[8]

The picture which emerges from this is one which is rather different from the pluralist account. This is not to deny that there are a great many IOs which are largely dependent on non-market, non-state sources of income, which are only occasionally involved in politics and in which the activists play a major role in shaping how they conduct their affairs. But there are a great many IOs which do not share all these characteristics, and some do not display any of them. Even medical research charities which, in many ways, come close to the pluralist ideal of an IO have to be more permanently involved in lobbying activities because of the role of the modern state in funding research and providing care. While Douglas's remark, that the distinction between, 'governmental, business, and voluntary' sectors is artificial and academic, and that actually they form 'a seamless web of the institutional fabric of society' is correct, the problem for the pluralist is that the core of that third 'sector' seems to be rather small.[9] It is only by including a large number of 'borderline' and 'hybrid' organizations that it is possible to produce something large enough to call a 'third', 'voluntary', or 'non-profit' *sector*. Certainly the core of such a 'sector' is far smaller than the cores of the state or commercial sectors.

Yet, having made these points, care must be taken not to suggest that we have dismissed the case (even a pluralist case) for the importance of IOs in a democracy. We have not. By taking the classic pluralist models (models which have their origins in the analyses of Truman and Dahl) too seriously we may fail to appreciate the role that IOs do play in sustaining democracy. A parallel may be drawn here between this and arguments in the 1950s about party government and the role of parties in advancing democracy. Anglo-American political scientists tended to take the British version of party government as *the* model of party government, and, of course, most states could then be seen as having an underdeveloped popular input via parties into the state. But, as we now know, party influence on both society and the state can be great even when the British model of two-party competition, and single-party government, is not operative. For example, as Hine has noted of post-war Italy:

> Party government was . . . fairly rapidly established as the norm after 1945. The parties dominated political recruitment, they were essential pathways to increasing numbers of non-elected careers, they exercised wide influence over the interest group universe, and in the absence of a prestigious self-consciously evangelical bureaucratic elite, they dominated the process of policy making.[10]

In the remainder of this chapter we examine whether, in the light of our understanding of the 'real world' of IOs, the myriad of IOs found in Britain and the US are capable of performing the functions attributed to them by some democratic theorists, especially pluralists. Of the nine functions identified in chapter 1 we may dispose of two of them with a fairly short discussion because they relate only briefly to issues we have examined in chapters 2–7.

The argument about superior service delivery by IOs in comparison with the state has not been addressed at all in this book. Since in different policy areas state institutional structures differ, as does the organizational capacity of the relevant IOs, it is likely that this is an issue demanding a wide-ranging and complex investigation. The claim about the ability of non-profit-distributing bodies to provide certain guarantees to donors or members when they might face exploitation by for-profit firms was discussed briefly in chapter 1. It was suggested that it is not an especially plausible claim, but our subsequent discussion of the comparative performance of for-profit firms and IOs where they compete has been too brief for us to resolve this matter.

1 Provision of Goods and Services not Supplied by the State or the Market

Arguments about the ability of IOs to supply goods and services which the state and the market will *fail* to supply has raised, as we saw, debates about the origins of alleged failures in both state and market. But equally there are serious problems in relying on IOs to fill these 'gaps'. There is the collective action problem in relation to self-help groups – groups may fail to form because the potential members cannot see their contributions making a difference. Pluralists like Douglas are right to point to the diversity of supply that can be achieved by IOs, but to do so the groups around which IOs form must have the resources necessary for inducing people to join them. Then there are difficulties in relying on philanthropy. The issue is not that people are selfish, but that they give relatively little in relation to the resources required to meet social needs. As studies in the US have shown, donations of money are closely related to the tax concessions available to donors. Again both individual and corporate donors often give to causes which are not the 'neediest', sometimes out of ignorance, sometimes because the neediest are 'unpopular', sometimes because there is greater publicity in placing their money elsewhere and for a variety of other reasons. Moreover, even if donors were attempting to respond to social needs, IOs themselves cannot co-ordinate donations so that services are provided where they are most needed. As we have noted, research like Sosin's has shown private welfare agencies do not tend to cluster in areas where state provision is weakest. Rather they tend to be found where state activity is already strong.[11] Institutionalization too can get in the way of responses by IOs in providing goods where markets and states fail. The problem is not that welfare states dampen the willingness to give, for there is little evidence that, overall, altruism is undermined by state services, but rather that institutionalization may make it more difficult to respond to new needs when they arise. The contrast between the British and American responses to Live Aid illuminates this point. Live Aid was easier to set up in Britain, partly because the lower level of institutionalization among charities meant that corporations and organizations whose co-operation was required were more willing to accept that a new organization could properly be responding to the new needs posed by the east African famine. In the US the Live Aid project did not fit into the philanthropic framework other organizations were used to dealing with, and they were much less willing to devote time and resources free of charge to the project.

The central argument, then, about the role of IOs in supplying goods and services that market and state do not concerns the value of the state offering tax (and other) concessions to either donors or IOs to facilitate greater supply by them. Proponents of tax deductions to donors to IOs point to the variety of services that can be supplied by IOs. Opponents focus on the lack of correspondence between the services IOs actually supply and the overall patterns of need in a society. Generally pluralists support at least some assistance to IOs to provide for greater diversity of supply, while their opponents question whether the groups this will encourage to form are those most likely to provide for the greatest social needs, and hence whether more direct state supply would not be more efficient. Inevitably, though, at the level of individual programmes and incentives there are considerable variations in the relation between IO provision and social need, so that pluralists may be equally opposed to particular forms of incentive. For example, it would be quite consistent with a pluralist position to argue that the present range of institutions in the US whose donors may receive tax deductions on their gifts is too wide, and that concessions should only be available to programmes providing services for the poor.

In brief, the debate over the role of IOs in filling gaps in service provision suggests that, while they do fill some gaps, there remains considerable doubt over their efficacy in responding unaided to the areas of greatest need.

2 Provision of 'Non-market Goods'

Virtually all twentieth-century pluralist writers have argued in favour of those activities at the heart of religion, basic research and the arts being beyond direct state control; their claim is that certain central aspects of these activities would be likely to be compromised if the state were involved in their provision, or at least were a dominant influence in their provision. Indeed, even those who reject other arguments often associated with pluralist thought, such as a commitment to the market economy, could argue in favour of a role for IOs in this area. As we have seen, however, all three of these activities actually involve close interaction between IOs and the state in both Britain and the US. With basic research and the arts there has been a growing financial dependence on the state to sustain the activities while 'secular' aspects of the activities of churches (as in the provision of welfare services, such as foster-homes) have also drawn them into large-scale financial relationships with the state. Of these three areas, it is with basic research, where the state has a direct interest in the 'final product', that financial dependence has produced the greatest threat to the autonomy of IOs. To a large extent this has been because research has traditionally been conducted in multipurpose organizations, universities, in which the state too has an interest – in securing an adequately trained workforce. But the growing cost of research also produces dilemmas – the state must allocate funds efficiently between competing projects without biasing the overall direction of research. One mechanism for achieving this has been peer review, but in the US this has been breaking down, as individual universities increasingly lobby Congress to secure resources for themselves.[12] Their increasing reliance on federal government funds has helped to introduce more explicitly political considerations (such as the geographical location of particular institutions) into the allocation of research funds. In Britain much greater government direction of all facets of higher education has been undertaken in the 1980s.

The contrast with the financing of the arts is significant here. Arts' organizations are far less central to the state, so there is less pressure on intermediate structures to gradually cede their powers of allocating resources to the state itself. Political controversy is far more likely to concern the need for 'balance' in the distribution of funds, when absence of agreement may be expected even in a system of peer review, because of the heterogeneity of the activities embraced within the arts. But this represents much less of a threat to the independence of IOs than do state interests in the generation of basic research.

With the obvious exception of those cults which seek to undermine the state, having responsibility for religious practice in the hands of non-state organizations is valued by most democrats, even those who reject other aspects of pluralism. There are, however, three qualifications to this. First, even among pluralists, there is disagreement as to the rights of the state in preventing manipulation of people during the recruitment of members by religious organizations. Second, religions which are branches of international organizations, such as Roman Catholicism, might (and have) intervened in the state on the basis of policies and judgements emanating from outside the state itself; in some circumstances this could constitute a challenge to the practice of democracy in the state. Generally, the Catholic church, in western Europe and North America at least, has sought to limit conflict with states in the twentieth century, precisely because this might turn even democrats into supporters of some form of state regulation of religion. (Although there are several instances, as with the legalization of divorce in Italy, when it has not followed this course.) Third, there is disagreement as to how narrowly religious activity is to be interpreted. This has become increasingly problematic as contracting between the state and church agencies in matters of social welfare has spread. Churches maintain that their welfare efforts are an expression of their religious activity and that they should not be expected to conform to some rules the state may wish to impose on secular organizations with which it contracts. This point was made in response to the court-imposed accord in New York, requiring foster-home agencies to take children on a 'first come, first served' basis and to provide them with full access to services such as family planning:

> Monsignor Arpie said the issue for the Archdiocese was not just one of control but of religious purpose.'We must maintain our religious principles', he said, 'Religion for us is the fundamental from which we spring. If it weren't for our religiousness, we wouldn't be in this business.'[13]

Other democrats, including some pluralists, have argued that the area of religious activity protected from the state should be narrow in scope, and confined to wholly sacramental matters.

3 Facilitators of Social and Political Integration

In chapter 1 we noted the argument that 'voluntary organizations' are unlikely to be of much use in integrating highly divided communities, though in less divided ones they may facilitate integration into the wider community. But what happens when societies become more homogeneous? Individuals have less need for some of the specialized IOs, and correspondingly they play a reduced role in integrating people into society. Of course, such tendencies must be placed in context. Suburbanization and the breakdown of (white) ethnic, inner-city neighbourhoods in the US have not destroyed all ethnic organizations – churches, for example, help to keep communities together which are geographically more dispersed than they used to be. However, while some IOs (for example, self-help groups teaching new immigrants English) simply disband, others are able to survive by changing the focus of their activity. Consider Catholic schools in New York City. Originally, they supplied an alternative to the secular education provided by the city for practising Catholics who wanted their children educated in a specifically Catholic environment. Gradually, there has been a decline in the demand for this kind of education, as first and second generation

European Catholics have become more completely absorbed into American society. At the same time, though, there has been an increasing demand for private education, because of problems in the city's school system, from parents who cannot afford the fees charged in the more exclusive secular private schools. The Catholic schools have responded to the possibility of having to close down, by de-emphasizing the religious elements in their education and thereby attracting a much wider clientele than they used to. In this case institutions have been able to survive by transforming themselves from more exclusively religious organizations and by competing more generally for students in the education market; a similar transformation has also occurred in many colleges.

The argument made here, of course, is not that IOs do not provide for social integration, but that with secularization and the absorption of immigrant groups into a society, the distinctive integrative role of some IOs has been reduced. We must raise now the question of whether IOs actually make any substantial contribution toward social integration in Britain and the US? This is not an issue we have examined directly, but one or two points we have considered are relevant in attempting to answer it. While there are very large numbers of IOs in both countries, greater prosperity, secularization, new opportunities for leisure and several other factors have reduced the time people spend in organizations where attitudes and values are likely to be formed or modified. The decline of the nineteenth century working-class mutuals constitutes one aspect of these changes. The more closed world of the Friendly Society, the trade union, the social club and possibly the local church have been replaced partly by activities of a more strictly commercial and individual kind: the purchasing of television, car and home computer entails largely non-group-based activities. Thus, even if we were to accept the view that involvement in formally organized groups was central for social integration, and this point is controversial, it can be argued that IOs are now far less important in this regard than they used to be. It is true that much more time is now devoted to volunteering than it was even twenty years ago, but there are now many more groups for which individuals simply do a job and which do not embrace most aspects of their lives or those of their families.

The group-dominated world conceived by American analytic pluralism must be understood in the context in which it arose. For Bentley in 1908 social groups would appear far more central to understanding a polity than they would today, just as for Truman in 1951, in reconstructing Bentley's ideas, it was pressure groups that seemed to dominate the American policy-making universe.[14] But neither of these authors attempted to examine how individuals were actually influenced by the groups they belonged to – it was merely assumed that they would be influenced – for in their conception there were really nothing but groups in society. In Truman's version, even unrepresented and unorganized interests were potential groups – groups that politicians had to take account of for fear of mobilization against them.

But what of the argument, based on the evidence of Walker and others, that there are now many more politically active groups than there were even in Truman's time? Certainly there has been an increase in tax-privileged IOs so that, in one sense, the group-based society valued by pluralists is perhaps more evident today than, say, two generations ago. But the sorts of groups which have been growing are those from which members can 'enter' or 'exit' more or less at will. (It is a phenomenon which is, perhaps, most aptly described as a 'Book of the Month Club' style of politics.)[15] Political cause groups or fund-raising charities do not usually provide the continuity of participation and involvement which provides for integration into the society. But, for the political system, this might be thought to be a source of stability. To the extent that loyalties to unions, for example, tended to strengthen group, rather than community-wide solidarities, their decline might facilitate greater integration into the polity as a whole. However, for Britain and the US, such an argument is not especially convincing. With a few exceptions, in the twentieth century working-class organizations (like unions) in these countries have effected relatively low levels of encapsulation, so that loyalties to the state have survived alongside group loyalties. The erosion of these older loyalties in Britain and the US has relatively few benefits for the two states, while the growth of organizations exhibiting 'Book of the Month Club' characteristics does little to develop loyalties among citizens to wider publics.

4 Facilitators of Diverse Opinions

Two of the points just raised are relevant in looking at the ability of IOs to provide for diversity of opinion within a society. On the one hand, reduced contact between the individual and organized groups has restricted the potential for groups actually playing a major role in forming opinions. On the other hand, the growth in socio-political groups might seem to increase the range of opinions to which individuals will be exposed, and hence decrease conformity to accepted views. Certainly, new-style electoral politics are associated with weakened attachments to particular parties, and with far more volatile electoral behaviour.[16] But the new kinds of political, and quasi-political, IOs are as much a response to the breakdown of older political loyalties and to the emergence of new sources of opinion, as they are shapers of these opinions. Volunteer work in local community projects, in environmental protection groups and in similar groups do help to modify, solidify and even form opinions, but:

> Although effective political organization and access to resources are crucial aspects of issue formation, these factors alone are not sufficient to determine how an issue will affect public opinion. The ways in which issues are defined and the manner in which they are transmitted by the mass media are probably the major elements in the issue formation process.[17]

And it is the ways political elites respond to issues raised by IOs that are significant in the definition of an issue.

If many democrats have argued for a plurality of opinions in a democratic society, they have also often viewed the political process as involving debate over the merits of different proposals – debate which in turn leads to changes in opinion among the participants and wider publics. But if issues have become relatively more important in electoral campaigning, it has not been in the context of this model of the process. Rather, there seems to be a tendency for political elites to adopt ambiguous stances in campaigning and not to confront alternative policy positions directly.[18] Issues tend to emerge and disappear, as politicians find they need pay less attention to affected organized interests, without opinions having been changed among those most affected, or even having been fully formed among wider publics. Consequently, when competition between ideas is lacking, it is far from clear why diversity of opinion would actually be valuable within a democracy. All that IOs are contributing to is a less stable political agenda in which issues tend to be taken up by politicians when they provide useful political symbols and to be dropped when they have served their purpose. The instability of modern 'issue-orientated' politics can be seen not as a contribution to democracy but as its antithesis.

5 Mobilization of Interests and Demands in a Society

This last point bears on a further role which has been attributed to IOs by pluralists – mobilizing interests in a society, so that competing demands can be considered and aggregated. In one version of pluralism a 'neutral' state acts as an arbiter of the competing demands made on it.[19] Whatever the state actually does to respond to these demands, it can be argued that debate among political elites about them is only indirectly part of the arbitration process. Yet, irrespective of more radical criticisms that can be made of the arbiter model, it is clear that in many areas of public policy, especially social policy, the state has been one of the causes of the growth in IOs. And the state's role in facilitating the creation of IOs, and in some cases actively encouraging them to form, has increased as state funding of services has grown. Walker's data on financial aid received by American groups at their formation is illuminating in this regard. Comparing groups formed in the period 1840–1945 with those formed between 1946 and 1980, Walker found that in the earlier period 10.4 per cent of groups in the 'non-profit sector' had received government grants at their founding but that 31.4 per cent of them received such aid in the later period.[20] Among what he terms mixed-sector groups (mainly occupational groups), the proportion receiving governmental aid doubled between the two periods from 6.3 per cent to 12.5 per cent. There were also smaller increases in initial funding to groups in the for-profit sector and among citizen groups. Quite clearly, in a period in which there has been a dramatic increase in IOs, the state has made a major contribution.

Yet, if the state does not conform to the arbiter model of some versions of pluralism, there remains the issue of the IOs themselves – are they mechanisms for channelling demands from society? One of the main criticisms of pluralism by Schattschneider and others was that those groups which were most active and influential in the political process tended to be business groups, and that other kinds of groups found it more difficult to get onto the policy agenda.[21] Despite the vast increase in the number of groups, the bias in favour of business groups at the *national level* of politics has not only been maintained, but actually seems to have increased. There are three reasons for this. Many, though not all, of the new IOs were service providers that did not have to become politically active so long as funding for their programmes was maintained. Those groups that were more political, such as groups operating some of the Great Society programmes, were directed towards local political action, and lacked the resources to become involved at the federal level. Furthermore, the groups best equipped to take advantage of the further decentralization of power in the US Congress in the 1970s were business interests. They had the resources necessary for opening public relations offices in Washington, for retaining lobbyists and so on. The result was that, as Schlozman concluded in 1984:

> For all the newborn organizations representing the interests of diffuse publics, minorities, poor people, the elderly, and other disadvantaged groups, business actually is a more dominating presence in Washington now than it was two decades ago. For all organizations having representation in Washington the proportion representing the interests of business rose from 57 per cent to 72 per cent since 1960.[22]

In Britain too the increase in single-issue political groups and of other forms of political volunteering has done little to increase access to the policy agenda for interests previously unrepresented or under-represented. Although British administrations can choose which groups to give 'insider' status to, and which to exclude as 'outsiders', it is primarily trade unions, and business and professional associations that are candidates for the more privileged positions. Even charities involved in aid to the third world have to rely far more on 'going public' with their argument than in using their connections with the Overseas Development Administration. (Their lack of influence in the 1980s is indicated by the fact that, as a proportion of GNP, official development assistance fell by 50 per cent between 1979 and 1984.)[23]

6 Arenas of Participation

In chapter 5 we saw the widespread involvement of people in various kinds of IOs – in self-help groups, in charitable organizations aiding other people and in various other organizations. While there are pressures on certain kinds of volunteerism, in other respects it is probably expanding. In spite of the spread of the market to various activities for which it was not feasible previously, and in spite of the growth of state provision of welfare services, volunteering remains a strong element in social relations in both countries. The state itself has encouraged it, and the expansion of markets and the emergence of 'New Right' ideologies extolling the market have failed to destroy it. For pluralists, of course, the survival of these arenas of participation is crucial. Before examining whether they are right to place such faith in participation in IOs, it is important to see why they have valued it.

As we have seen earlier, pluralists saw the dangers of a society in which the pursuit of self-interest dominated social life. It would be destabilizing. Pluralists recognized that in liberal democracy direct political participation would be restricted, because of the very size of the polity. The electoral mechanism could play only a limited role in constraining political leaders and ensuring that they tried to aggregate demands in the society optimally. The most effective device for checking them was a citizenry that might be mobilized. As Dahl and Linblom noted:

> the problem is not so much one of insuring that every citizen is politically active on every issue as it is of insuring that all citizens have approximately equal opportunity to act, using 'opportunity' in a realistic rather than legalistic sense.[24]

But the use of these opportunities depended on there being organizations which could 'spring into action' when state policy threatened citizens' interests. In Dahl's terminology polyarchy (liberal democracy) required social pluralism, by which he meant a diversity of social organizations with a high degree of autonomy with respect to one another.[25] The strength of organization was that: 'A lone citizen speaking only for himself can often be intimidated by officials; but a spokesman for a body of citizens is less easily cowed.'[26] But IOs also checked the pursuit of self-interest because membership of multiple groups by a citizen would discourage extremism and recklessness by group leaders in the pursuit of their goals. For pluralists, then, participation in IOs was valuable primarily for two reasons. It gave organizations the strength with which to intervene, when necessary, in the political process, and it provided the basis for limiting the pursuit of self-interest within the state.

In the American pluralist view, then, the significance of participation in IOs is instrumental rather than developmental. It is not, for example, that it helps to make citizens more community-orientated, or gives them a greater sense of efficacy in the pursuit of collective goals, but that it is the means by which demands in a society can be more optimally aggregated and conflicts over the pursuit of self-interest reduced. The objections to their analysis are two-fold. As we saw in the last section, there is the problem of access to the political system, which is dominated by economic (and mainly business) interests. Then again it is far from clear that the existence of more groups actually entails a greater willingness to compromise. The increase in the number of groups, especially since the 1960s, has been accompanied by the rise of conflicts over less obviously economic issues (such as abortion and nuclear defence policies) which seem less amenable to compromises acceptable to the IOs concerned.

Nevertheless, if we abandon the traditional pluralist framework, there still seem to be facets of participation in IOs that might help to extend democracy. The pluralists were correct in seeing an all-pervasive market system as undermining democracy. Market relations help to reduce the commitment to shared values in a society and they do not provide opportunities for learning the skills of collective action, skills which are essential for participation in the political system. The centrality of this kind of training in participatory democratic theory has been summarized by Pateman:

> for maximum participation by all the people at [the national level of representative institutions] socialisation, or 'social training', for democracy must take place in other spheres in order that the necessary individual attitudes and psychological qualities can be developed. This development takes place through the process of participation itself .... Subsidiary hypotheses about participation are that it has an integrative effect and that it aids the acceptance of collective decisions.[27]

Radical democrats, though, have tended to focus on democracy within industry or at the level of the local community as the most appropriate arenas in which this 'training for democracy' might occur. Nor is there any reason to doubt that the centrality of the workplace and the neighbourhood in people's lives would make them the principal places for instituting reforms to facilitate more democratic control. But the failure of attempts to establish greater participation in these arenas in the 1970s, and the accession to power of conservative administrations in Britain (in 1979) and the US (in 1981) wholly opposed to democratic control, and committed to the extension of the market system, forces us to ask whether IOs might not, at least, play some part in citizen training.

As we have seen, volunteering in IOs is a relatively broadly-based activity in both countries, and has been encouraged (for reasons of self-interest) by the state. Sceptics about its value, though, can point to the limited scope of democracy within these organizations. For example, of the major third world aid charities, War on Want is the only one with a democratic structure based on a mass membership. In spite of the rise of new-style agencies, with a participatory ethic, most IOs are still hierarchical in character. Yet, there are two reasons for believing that their relevance to 'training' for democratic citizenship is worth considering. First, even in agencies where volunteer input to the national level of policy making is limited, considerably more scope for initiative, and for providing specifically local responses to local needs is left in the hands of volunteers. If volunteers are not to quit, they have to be given some sense that their contribution makes a difference. It is only with infrequent activities, like elections, that most volunteers will accept undertaking purely mundane tasks which leaves them no scope for displaying initiative. Because the volunteer is a volunteer, it is far more difficult to impose rigid directives on him/her. Among many kinds of IOs, the hierarchical structures possible in the for-profit sector, or in the state, are more difficult to sustain at the local level. Second, the transference of service provision to IOs provides an opportunity for participation-orientated bodies to become involved in the distribution of welfare services – something which is less possible within a state agency. In 1987, in the immediate aftermath of the third consecutive general election victory for the Conservative party, one leading social democrat John Lloyd, the editor of the *New Statesman*, argued:

> Part of the 'realignment' of the opposition parties over the next period will include, I judge, their giving a much more central role than in the past to . . . voluntary activity – and explicitly advancing this as a partially publically funded adjunct to some state activity. . . . And the augmentation of state-provided welfare by a multitude of endeavours which were personal, tangible and on an individual

human scale could allow any politician embracing this 'wave of the future' to speak from somewhere closer to the gut than they could earlier this month.[28]

But it is only an *opportunity* for greater participation that some IOs can provide, and many of the agencies which obtain grants and contracts may be far more like universities or non-profit hospitals in their structure than the volunteer-based IO. Charities, such as those engaged in helping the poor or unemployed or in promoting community development, which can provide for volunteer participation are only one kind of IO. The danger for social democrats, then, in seeking to find a way of promoting democratic values, in an era when conservative administrations are dismantling elements of direct state provision, is of believing that IOs necessarily constitute an 'Achilles heel' for conservatism. The IO universe is *not* largely populated with participatory organizations, and many of them are partly orientated to providing services on a market basis – as we have seen from their reliance on fee income. By utilizing IOs in providing services, the state is not thereby decentralizing power to volunteers. Nevertheless, the growing use of IOs probably tends to limit the spread of purely market values, and, without doubt, there are now more participatory bodies that provide some basis for citizenship training through the role they cede to members in organizing the distribution of services. The IO cannot be ignored by democrats in quite the way that it was in the first few decades of the welfare state.

7 Countervailing Power

Perhaps the most interesting arguments about the value of IOs to democracy concern their alleged 'checking' role – either in countering the power of the market or of the state. Obviously, the arguments about the two are very different, and we consider each in turn. In relation to the market, IOs have been seen as providing countervailing power in three distinct ways: through organizations established to counter for-profit firms directly, through alternative structures to for-profit suppliers and through the propagation of values that counter the pursuit of self-interest.

Of all the interests that might be adversely affected by the operations of for-profit enterprises, the best organized have been trade unions. And, traditionally, when discussing power to counter the business sector, it has been unions that have been thought to provide the major check. This check has been controversial, of course. Free market economists have tended to see unions as an impediment to the efficient working of markets, while socialists have often extolled them as the main way of defending working-class interests against the vagaries of the market. In both Britain and the US, though, trade unionism has been in decline. The problem in the US has been evident for far longer, and is largely connected with two changes in American industrial structure. Unions have failed to recruit many members in the growing white-collar sectors of the economy, while their blue-collar base has been in decline. In the twenty years after 1956, the proportion of unionized workers in white-collar jobs only rose from 13.6 per cent of the total unionized workforce to 18.4 per cent of the total, although this was a period of rapid transformation in the American economy. Consequently, while at its peak, in the first decade of the post-war years, 'union density' in America was generally over 30 per cent, by the mid 1970s only a little over a quarter of the workforce was unionized.[29] The other problem contributing to this decline was the shift of manufacturing industries, especially the newer ones, away from the heartland of union strength in the north-east and mid-west of the country to the southern and south-western states, where unionism had always been much weaker.

In Britain 'union density' has always been much higher than in the US, and in the 1970s it actually *grew* considerably so that by 1979 it was about twice as high as in the US. The success of British unions lay in their much greater penetration of white-collar sectors, especially among state employees. (The direct provision of services by the state, compared with the 'third party' approach in the US was an important element in this greater unionization.) But blue-collar employees still accounted for about two-thirds of union membership, and with the great increase in unemployment in the 1980s, especially through massive job losses in some of the traditional industries, union density in the UK declined from its peak of 54.4 per cent in 1979 to less than 44 per cent in 1985.[30] Even if in the 1990s administrations more sympathetic to trade unions were to come to power in both countries, the continuing relative decline of older manufacturing industries makes it unlikely that union memberships will reach again the levels they did in the US in the early 1950s or in Britain in the 1970s.

Unions have been able to overcome the collective action problem partially through the selective incentives (such as closed-shop agreements) they have been able to provide for potential members. This is not the case with most other interests which may be affected by the activities of for-profit enterprises. Consumer interests are often cited as the best instances of potential IOs that were largely unorganized until the later 1960s. A combination of middle-class volunteers, with the time available to take part in groups and campaigns in support of consumer interests, and highly publicized scandals such as General Motors' hounding of Ralph Nader led to the formation of various consumer action groups in the US. In the late 1960s and early 1970s they enjoyed considerable success in getting legislation supportive of consumer interests passed at federal and state levels. But, although they gained access to the political process and succeeded in placing a number of major issues on the political agenda, such groups faced the usual problem of cause groups of how to sustain their activities when the first flush of enthusiasm wore off. The same was true of environmental protection groups organized to combat the external costs, including pollution and the destruction of unique landscapes, some industries were imposing on the communities in which they operated. One result, as we saw in section 5, is that for all the new diversity among American interest groups, business lobbies have taken advantage of their resources to increase their lobbying presence in Washington. For-profit firms and business associations have become more adept themselves at countering the possible checking power of American IOs.

Since the late nineteenth century the British state has played a much greater role than its American counterpart in one aspect of the protection of the physical environment from externalities imposed by for-profit firms – land use. But in some other areas of environmental policy – especially pollution control – the absence of IOs has been far more significant. And in relation to consumer issues too, especially those affecting manufactured goods, the centralization of the British state and the problems of collective action for IOs have contributed to rather less control of business 'externalities' than in the US.

In both countries non-union IOs, when they have formed, face difficulties in being effective at all levels of government, or in relation to all industries in which the interests of other parties are adversely affected by those of for-profit enterprises. Their membership may be concentrated in particular locales, and hence be far more concerned with certain kinds of pollution, or whatever, than with others. It was often argued of environmental lobbies in the US in the mid 1970s, for example, that they were more interested in preserving the open countryside to which the middle classes had access, than with those pollution issues, such as garbage collection, which had more impact on the lives of the poor. Nevertheless, new forms of political volunteerism have contributed to an increased capacity for IOs to check some aspects of the power of for-profit firms, although it still remains rather limited.

A rather different conclusion emerges when we consider the alternatives to for-profit enterprise provided by IOs. One of the clearest trends we have identified has been the decline of the nineteenth-century working-class mutuals – either through the taking over of their functions by the state, or more especially through their transformation into fully commercial organizations. Whereas many of the original mutuals had social objectives, as well as being vehicles for advancing the individual interests of members, organizations like Building Societies and even consumer co-operatives now conduct their affairs largely, if not always exclusively, in order to maximize the size of their business. The socialist argument that markets tend to destroy the distinctive features of IOs has been vindicated. It is true that among producer organizations there have been experiments at running commercial enterprises on more participatory lines; examples include agricultural co-operatives, some retailing co-operatives like the John Lewis Partnership and workforce 'buy outs' of plants that would otherwise be sold off or shut down. However, the very fact that these organizations are usually competing with for-profits forces them to modify whatever social objectives they might have. The most successful ones rely to a large degree on a high level of attachment to the community by the co-operators. In asking whether the renowned Mondragon co-operative might be a model for others elsewhere, Bradley and Gelb indicated that there were places where it might succeed, but that: 'A dynamic analysis over the lifetime of an enterprise suggests a less favourable outlook because of the generally high mobility and relative absence of community attachment in major industrial regions.'[31]

Mutuals have survived in marginal areas of economies, where more sensitive mechanisms of control than those usually provided in markets are required, and where an activity is held to be incompatible with the market ethos. But, at least in Britain and the US, mutuals have not proved especially effective vehicles in providing for either member control or the promotion of social objectives, when faced with competition with for-profit enterprises.

Perhaps the greatest difficulty in reaching conclusions in connection with the alleged countervailing power of IOs concerns their roles in propagating values that are contrary to the pursuit of individual self-interest on which the market is based. The difficulty arises for two rather obvious reasons. There is conflicting data as to the spread of the market ethos. In the 1960s and 1970s there was considerable evidence of the growth of 'post materialist' values in western democracies, and the electoral success in the 1980s of parties like the West German Greens indicates that such values may continue to be prominent among certain social groups.[32] Nevertheless, it is clear that from the mid 1970s onwards there was also a remarkable growth in the politics of self-interest, most noticeably among those who believed they had a firm stake in the economic system. (Already in the mid 1970s the American writer Tom Wolfe had identified the 'me-generation' that was emerging in the US, long before it was seen as having an electoral impact.) The consensus established in the immediate post-war years, that the state had at least some responsibility for protecting the welfare of the disadvantaged, was now a source of division, with (at least) a significant minority now willing to let market forces take their toll. The election (and re-election) in both countries of the most market-orientated administrations since the second world war was not, however, accompanied by marked changes in opinion among the public regarding the provision of services for the disadvantaged and for communities as a whole. For example, opinion polls taken on the day of the 1984 US presidential election, when Ronald Reagan won nearly 60 per cent of the vote, showed that 80 per cent of the electorate favoured no reduction in public expenditures on the poor and 40 per cent actually favoured increases.[33] At best, then, the market ethos has probably made only a restricted advance in public appeal at the expense of other values.

The role played by IOs in either facilitating or hindering the politics of self-interest is difficult to determine, partly because the precise impact such institutions have on opinion formation is not fully understood. Yet, even allowing for this, we would expect the combined impact of IOs to be complex. On the one side, the sustenance of non-market values through the proliferation of various kinds of IOs – including charities and new kinds of self-help groups – and the maintenance of high levels of volunteering suggests that a wide variety of non-market values are likely to survive, even among those who give high priority to the market system. Indeed, in many ways, such as in the establishment of philanthropic foundations and in fostering volunteering through organizations like the United Way, American capitalism has continually created institutions that propagate values and policies that are only partly consistent with the spread of the market ethos. As Douglas has said of the big foundations – they have supported a 'sophisticated conservatism',[34] a conservatism which seeks to protect the interests of those who have done well out of capitalism, by supporting changes that make the status quo more efficient and acceptable. And, to a large degree, this involves promoting values other than the market ethos, because the full rigors of the market operating over a wide range of social activities has been seen by those who control foundations as divisive and ultimately threatening to the interests of the greatest beneficiaries from capitalism. If one of the major dangers to capitalism is the behaviour of the economic actors themselves, and if it is difficult to curtail the absolute pursuit of self-interest in economic relations themselves, then sustaining other kinds of institutions that can seek, in different ways, to moderate the impact of this behaviour becomes an obvious strategy for its supporters. From the viewpoint of 'sophisticated conservatism', though, this approach itself has its dangers, in that the institutions may come to develop interests of their own (through, for example, dependence on state funds) or they may later be controlled by those who partially identify with the interests of the disadvantaged. Such developments can then provide for a much weaker buttressing of the ideology of the market than the 'sophisticated conservative' would want. Certainly by the late 1960s American foundations had come to be seen by their opponents as one of the main props of the *liberal* eastern establishment.

On the other side, however, one of the most pronounced developments among IOs has been their commercialization. We have noted the full commercialization of the nineteenth-century mutuals and the growing reliance on fee income by other IOs, especially charities. Now, although reliance on fees does not necessarily indicate a more commercial approach to relations with clients, or increased support for a market-orientation in their activities, this tendency may become more pronounced when the maintenance of income becomes crucial for an organization. Hospital chains in America have put pressure on non-profit hospitals in what in recent decades has been openly referred to as the *hospital industry*, and this makes it more difficult for the latter to sustain all the non-market activities they used to perform. Universities too have become more aggressive merchants of their services, and in some ways this has made it more difficult for them to promote the values with which they are associated traditionally. The same is true of many other kinds of IOs. The problem is not so much that the organizations propagate an overtly pro-market ideology – often they do not and continue to insist that their aim is to provide service to their communities – but that their commercial activities are seen to compromise their claims to have a non-market orientation. 'Concealed' market orientations tend to undermine their claim to moral leadership.

IOs, of course, have been seen by some democrats as a bastion not so much against the market as against the state. Moreover, it is not just defenders of western democracy who have seen the need for bodies to be able to exercise power against the use of power by the state. For example, Julius Nyerere rejected European multi-party democracy, arguing that multi-tribal African states could not afford the cleavages which competition between parties might create. In his version of democracy, *ujamaa* villages would be recreated and socialism practised at the level of community organization. The villages would provide a safeguard against the abuse of power at the state level, and would provide a vehicle for popular participation. The crucial point about any intermediate body is that to be able to check the state it must be autonomous. Obviously, legal autonomy is insufficient if the state controls resources vital to the operation of an IO. But, equally, a checking function can still be carried out if there is dependence on both sides of the relationship. One of the features of the relations between the British state and the Roman church in the medieval period was that neither could completely dominate the other. To some extent this applies to many modern IOs – the state requires them to deliver certain services – but their disadvantage *vis-à-vis* the state would seem to lie in the fact that they represent a relatively small area of activity in relation to the state's overall responsibilities, even within a single policy sector. The growth in financial dependence on the state might seem to have paved the way for the subsuming of IOs under the state.

Indeed, there is one clear example where this has happened – the case of British universities. Rather surprisingly, however, there are many areas where financial dependence has not resulted in loss of control by IOs. In his four-country study of voluntary agencies in the welfare state, Kramer discovered that: 'In England, there were practically no complaints about governmental interference, partly because there were fewer regulations than in the United States.'[35] and that: 'evidence in the United States and Canada suggests that the impact of government funds in controlling social service organizations may be much less than is commonly believed.'[36] Kramer argued that a variety of factors, including the inability of the state to exercise control over all organizations, the diversity of the agencies' income sources, and the mutual dependence inherent in many relations, contributed to this failure to reduce autonomy. Such is the independence that IOs can create for themselves that in the US the groups most active in advocacy are the ones receiving the highest proportion of government funds.[37] The idea, then, that the state *necessarily* erodes the autonomy of IOs is clearly false.

Nevertheless, there are two other possible aspects of the growing financial dependence on the state that might seem to bear adversely on the ability of IOs to act as a countervailing force against the state. One is the 'trimming' that can result in cases of conflict through a desire on the part of IOs to retain the 'normal' relationship with a state agency. Critics accused the National Trust of this in the Bradenham controversy involving the construction of a Ministry of Defence installation on Trust property. The other aspect is the growing politicization of IOs which is caused by their need to secure funds, on the one hand, and to secure state benefits for client groups on the other. In a sense, of course, this last form of politicization constitutes a form of checking of the state but, for those democrats who have argued for an entirely separate sector of IOs, advocacy activities are incompatible with the claim that IOs check best when they are most detached from the state. One of the difficulties posed by the 'contracting state' is that it further blurs the distinction between the self-interest of IOs and the standards and values they demand of the state in its operations in a particular policy area. In brief, critics argue that the checking power of IOs as *detached* 'watchdogs' of the state is being eroded. Whether this last point should be taken very seriously is questionable. In the past IOs have often had their own interests, and, of course, many were established to advance the interests of particular classes or groups. While some of them (for example, the universities and, today in Britain, churches) have often claimed to be impartial arbiters of conflicts in society, it is far from clear that they have ever been quite as impartial as their own propaganda would suggest.[38] If they are to play a checking role, it is far more likely to result from their interests being sufficiently different from those of the state and from the major business interests in society.

But the politicization of IOs which results from the quest for funds, together with the rise of groups committed to social action does raise problems in both England and the US about the privileges granted to some kinds of organizations. As we argued earlier the tax privileges available to charities in both countries have excluded political organizations, but, increasingly, employing this as the basis for a fundamental distinction between IOs is becoming difficult to both enforce consistently and to justify. Yet politicized IOs are likely to be just as important in checking state power as apolitical IOs, and arguably they will be even more important in an era when the state still accounts for a large proportion of GNP.

8 Postscript: Pluralism and the Future of Social Democracy

We have argued in this concluding chapter that in many respects claims made by democrats, most especially pluralist democrats, about the contribution of IOs as they are presently constituted to the advancement of democracy, cannot be substantiated. It might seem, therefore, that we have reached a conclusion that would have meshed well with arguments that were commonplace in the early 1970s, to the effect that pluralist theories of democracy were badly flawed. However, today, such a conclusion is rather less comforting to social democratic critics of pluralism than it would have been then. In the intervening period it has become more obvious that control of the state does not generate all the advantages that many social democrats once thought it would. Such control has not decentralized power to citizens, nor has it brought as much social and economic equality as socialists assumed that it would. This is not to say that control of the state does not make a difference; there is considerable evidence that the policies of states do vary depending on which sorts of parties form the government.[39] Nevertheless, even the most optimistic social democrat would have to admit that controlling the state has not extended to citizens as much control over their lives as it was imagined that it would. Moreover, the 'New Right' has sought to exploit discontent with state bureaucracy and the unpopularity of certain forms of taxation in an effort to 'roll back' the great success of twentieth century social democracy – the creation of the welfare state. Ultimately such efforts may be doomed,[40] but the 'New Right' has at least shown that the state may not be quite as popular an arena on which to focus debate about the distribution of power in society as social democrats used to assume. This suggests that in looking for ways to realize its objectives, social democracy should consider institutions, other than the state, through which power could be decentralized.

When examining the possibility for fostering participation in socio-political activities and for providing checks on the exercise of power both by the state and also in the market, IOs may well have an important role to play. Even socialists, who reject the idea that most economic production and distribution should be in the hands of private entrepreneurs, might see several advantages in having certain kinds of autonomous organizations operating within the state. And this brings us to one of the great ambiguities in the study of democracy in contemporary political science – the idea of pluralism itself.

In a sense all democrats (and, indeed, socialists) are pluralists because they value the dispersion of power among many centres – to the people. Nevertheless, pluralism is most usually associated with the claim that democracy requires certain kinds of autonomous organizations in society, and not just the decentralization of power. As Dahl has argued:

> if a socialist economic order were to be democratic, it would necessarily have to contain many relatively autonomous organizations, including economic enterprises; that is, it would necessarily be organizationally pluralist. . . . if it were *not* organizationally pluralist, I do not think it could be democratic.[41]

The reason why it seems there *has* to be a connection between democracy and organizational pluralism is that, in the absence of autonomous organizations, it is far from clear how individuals could prevent the erosion of their power to the state. Even if we are sceptical of a claim of Michels, that there is an inevitable tendency to the concentration of power within political leaderships, the problem of how to prevent this tendency is a complex one for the democrat. The electoral mechanism, for example, is a relatively weak instrument in this regard.[42] However much we may regret that democracy at the level of the small community cannot be replicated at the level of the nation-state, it is difficult to avoid the conclusion that, for the latter, we must look to organizations to protect democracy.

However, organizational pluralism does *not* require that ownership of the means of production be in the hands of capitalists; it is compatible with worker-owned (and controlled) enterprises and also with community-owned enterprises. Indeed, it might be argued that it is precisely these non-capitalist organizations that could be expected both to prevent the centralizing of state power in the hands of particular interests, and also to encourage democratic practices within their own structures. Pluralism is about the dispersion of power, and a radical pluralism, which seeks to reform social and economic institutions so that they provide for some degree of membership or user control, is not a self-contradictory notion. Rather, it could be argued that it is through these structures that the best hope for the genuine extension of democratic control lies. Moreover, such an approach does have, at least, *some* connection, albeit indirectly, with one set of mainstream pluralist ideas – those of early twentieth-century English pluralism, and especially with the ideas of G. D. H. Cole.

This strand of pluralism largely died out in Britain, partly because, after the Labour victory in 1945, social democracy came to be associated with state ownership of essential industries and with state provision of welfare. Thus, to the extent that there were distinctly pluralist political ideas in post-war Britain, they tended to be influenced by American pluralism. In the US pluralist ideas had not been linked, as in Britain, to theories of social organization, but were more narrowly political in focus: pluralism was identified with the decentralization of power to groups of the kind currently existing in western democracies – groups which were mainly hierarchically-organized and non-participatory. Consequently, both its proponents and opponents alike tended to ally pluralism with democracy of the kind which developed under capitalism. In this sense, pluralism was certainly a 'small c' conservative theory of politics.

However, not all American pluralist writers had made the naive assumption that pluralism was possible only under capitalism. Indeed, some recent writers seem to ignore the complexity of much earlier pluralist theory in favour of a simplified account equating pluralism with capitalist democracy. For example, Manley, in discussing a book published by Dahl in 1982, claims that: 'he takes a step that, in the historical context of pluralist theory, can only be described as transformative: *he breaks the connection between pluralism and capitalism*.'[43]

This connection between democratic politics and existing economic arrangements was not a necessary one, as both the early-twentieth-century English pluralists and also Dahl, even in his early scholarship, had recognized.[44] There is no reason, then, why social democrats and socialists should not try to reconstruct democratic theory on pluralist lines and to develop socialist programmes within a pluralist context; that is, accepting that hierarchies in state and economy need to be kept in check, and that autonomous organizations are a means of effecting this. While this is not compatible with the Marxist-Leninist tradition of state dominance, such a theory could undoubtedly still be socialist – in the sense that economic power would be transferred away from managers and non-worker owners. Dahl himself has attempted to 'clear the ground' for a theory of economic democracy.[45] Indeed, it would be ironic if, at a time when both the Soviet Union and China are attempting to decentralize economic decision making, social democrats too did not seek to devise mechanisms for increasing popular input into hierarchical structures in state and economy.

However, in addition to economic organizations, democratic socialists would also have to provide an account of how non-profit-distributing organizations were to contribute to the decentralization of power under socialism. As we have seen, IOs do, perhaps, provide some potential for the development of participation in society and in checking the pursuit of self-interest. But, unless checks are placed on them, IOs are also organizations that can develop their own interests, and they can become indistinguishable from commercial operations or heavily dependent on the state. However, in an era when social democrats are struggling to find new ways of redistributing power and resources in society, given the limitations and relative unpopularity of state control in achieving this in the last fifty years, it would seem that a pluralist approach might be worth exploring. This will first require a more complete understanding of IOs, as they have actually developed in the western states, than we have hitherto possessed. Yet, it may be that, as we come to understand more about the 'real world' of IOs, it will be possible to utilize the potential of some kinds of IOs in the reconstruction of social democracy.

Notes

Chapter 1 Introduction

1. In using the term 'intermediate organizations', I recognize the possible confusion this may cause owing to the ways in which the term 'intermediate' has been employed by others. For example, the Wolfenden Committee Report used the term 'intermediate bodies' in a restricted sense to refer to the so-called 'co-ordinating bodies' in Britain which operate between government and voluntary organizations. See Wolfenden Committee Report, *The Future of Voluntary Organizations* (Croom Helm, London, 1978), p. 100. For my purposes, the value of calling the organizations I am looking at 'intermediate organizations' is that it does not presume that these organizations rely at all on volunteer labour or on donations, nor does it incorporate the peculiar institutional biases that would be involved in using the American term 'non-profit organizations'.
2. For example, as Cousins suggests in discussing British local government, it is possible to construct a *continuum* of organizations ranging from the purely voluntary organization, established without the assistance of local government and receiving no assistance from it, to the local authority itself. On this nine-point continuum, it is difficult to determine where the boundary between 'state' and 'private' is to be drawn. Paul F. Cousins, 'Quasi-official bodies in local government', in Anthony Barker, (ed.), *Quangos in Britain* (Macmillan, London, 1982), pp. 154–5.
3. Robert A. Nisbet, *Community and Power* (Oxford University Press, Oxford, 1962), p. 109.
4. A modern statement of this argument is provided by Michael Taylor, *Anarchy and Cooperation* (John Wiley, London and New York, 1976).
5. See especially G. D. H. Cole, *Self-government in Industry* (G. Bell and Sons, London, 1919), *Social Theory* (Methuen, London, 1920), *Guild Socialism Restated* (Leonard Parsons, London, 1920), *Chaos and Order in Industry*

(Methuen, London, 1920) and Harold Laski, *The Grammar of Politics* (Allen and Unwin, London, 1948).

6. For an analysis of the pluralist viewpoint see David Nicholls, *The Pluralist State* (Macmillan, London, 1975), esp. chs 2 and 3.
7. Ferdinand Tönnies, *Community and Society* trans. Charles P. Loomis, (ed.), (Harper and Row, New York, 1963).
8. Fred Hirsch, *Social Limits to Growth* (Routledge and Kegan Paul, London, 1977), pp. 79–82 and Richard Titmuss, *The Gift Relationship* (Pantheon, New York, 1971).
9. Examples of the use of these different terms include the following: James Douglas subtitled his book *Why Charity?* (Sage, Beverly Hills and London, 1983) – *The case for a third sector*; 'Independent Sector' is the name adopted by one of the main 'umbrella' organizations lobbying on behalf of non-profit bodies in the US; the major research handbook edited by Walter W. Powell, under the auspices of the Program on Nonprofit Organizations at Yale University, was entitled *The Nonprofit Sector* (Yale University Press, New Haven, 1987). Some indication of the problems evident in identifying the boundaries of this 'sector' may be seen in the different names used by the various authors of the research papers submitted to the Filer Commission: 'Private voluntary charitable sector' (Gabriel Rudney), 'Non-profit charitable sector' (T. Nicholaus Tideman), 'Not-for-profit sector' (Dale L. Hiestand), 'Voluntary non-profit sector' (Burton A. Weisbrod), 'Voluntary sector' (Gordon Manser, also Stephen H. Long) and 'Private voluntary sector' (Adam Yarmolinsky and Marion R. Fremont-Smith): *Research Papers of the Commission on Private Philanthropy and Public Needs* (Department of the Treasury, Washington DC, 1977).
10. Jan-Erik Lane, 'Introduction: public policy or markets? The demarcation problem', in Jan-Erik Lane, (ed.), *State and Market* (Sage, Beverly Hills and London, 1985).
11. This example is discussed by Grant, who himself cites the passage from Hood and Mackenzie quoted in the text; Wyn Grant, 'Corporatism and the public–private distinction', in Lane, (ed.), *State and Market* p. 169, and C. Hood and W. J. M. Mackenzie, 'The problem of classifying institutions', in D. C. Hague, W. J. M. Mackenzie and A. Barker, (eds), *Public Policy and Private Interests* (Macmillan, London, 1975), pp. 422–3.
12. Lane, 'Introduction: public policy or markets?' p. 46, citing L. Johansen, 'The bargaining society and the inefficiency of bargaining', *Kyklos*, 32 (1979), pp. 479–522.
13. Nicholls, *The Pluralist State*, p. 88.
14. Joseph A. Schumpeter, *Capitalism, Socialism and Democracy* (Allen and Unwin, London, 1943).
15. James Douglas, 'Political theories of nonprofit organization', in Powell, (ed.), *The Nonprofit Sector*, p. 47.
16. The best example of this sort of view is John Plamenatz, *Democracy and Illusion* (Longman, London, 1973), ch. 6.
17. The classic statement of the collective action problem in the modern era is,

of course, Mancur Olson, *The Logic of Collective Action* (Harvard University Press, Cambridge, Mass., 1965).

18. 'Contract failure' is the term devised by one of the proponents of this view, Henry B. Hansmann. See 'The role of non-profit enterprise', *Yale Law Journal*, 89 (1980), pp. 835–901. Another account of this sort is provided by David Easley and Maureen O'Hara, 'The economic role of the non-profit firm', *Bell Journal of Economics*, 14 (1983), pp. 531–8.
19. Douglas, 'Political theories of non-profit organization', pp. 48–9.
20. Judith Tendler, 'Turning private voluntary organizations into developing agencies', *AID Program Evaluation Discussion Paper No. 12* (US Agency for International Development, Washington DC, 1982), p. 108.
21. Douglas, 'Political theories of nonprofit organization', p. 47.
22. See, for example, A. Lijphart, *The Politics of Accommodation* (University of California Press, Berkeley, 1968).
23. John Stuart Mill, *On Liberty*, Everyman edn (Dent, London, 1910), p. 119.
24. The significance of the 'pillar' system in the Netherlands has been well summarized by Smith:

    > The phenomenon of the three 'pillars' of Dutch society, its *Verzuiling*, was an expression of the existence of at least three distinctive sub-cultures: Catholic, Protestant, and a general latitudinarian one – the last of which itself subdivided into liberals and socialists on a political plane. We may describe this as a vertical division of Dutch society; its effect was to cut across the horizontal divisions of the class structure, preventing the formation of 'armed camps' which one naturally associates with sectionalism.

    Gordon, Smith, *Politics in Western Europe*, 4th edn (Heinemann, London, 1983), p. 14.
25. The best known, and arguably the most important, statements of this approach are by David Truman, *The Governmental Process* (Knopf, New York, 1951) and Charles E. Lindblom and Robert A. Dahl, *Politics, Economics and Welfare* (Harper and Row, New York, 1953).
26. The idea of pressure groups 'cross-cuts' that of IOs. The former are groups which seek to influence government – that is they are defined in terms of a particular sort of relation to the state. While many IOs are pressure groups, so too are commercial firms and, often, governmental agencies themselves. On the other hand, IOs are defined in terms of their legal structure, and not their activity.
27. J. Roland Pennock and John W. Chapman, (eds), *Voluntary Associations* (Atherton Press, New York, 1969).
28. Excellent accounts of the different theories are provided in Henry Hansmann, 'Economic theories of nonprofit organization', in Powell, (ed.), *The Nonprofit Sector* and Estelle James and Susan Rose-Ackerman, 'The nonprofit enterprise in market economies', *PONPO Working Paper No. 95* (Institution for Social and Policy Studies, Yale University, New Haven, 1985). Among the more influential theories so far have been: Burton A. Weisbrod, 'Towards a theory of the voluntary non-profit sector in a three-sector economy', in Edmund S. Phelps, (ed.), *Altruism, Morality and Economic Theory* (Russell Sage, New York, 1974), Hansmann, 'The role of nonprofit enterprise', Ira Ellman, 'Another theory of nonprofit corporations', *Michigan Law Review* 80 (1982),

pp. 999–1050, Avner Ben-Ner, 'Non-profit organizations: why do they exist in market economies?', *PONPO Working Paper No. 51* (Institution for Social and Policy Studies, Yale University, New Haven, 1983) and Michael Krashinsky, 'Transaction costs and a theory of the non-profit organization', *PONPO Working Paper No. 84* (Institution for Social and Policy Studies, Yale University, New Haven, 1984).

29. In the English context, the term is not used in a generic sense to refer to a wide range of non-profit-distributing bodies, but in a much narrower sense to refer to organizations on the boundary between commercial enterprise and charity. In a letter to the author an employee of an organization discussed in an article in the *Financial Times* commented on the problems of operating on the charity–industry boundary:

> Ours is a company limited by guarantee, a form of organization which, as you will probably have gathered from the *FT* articles, has not proved to be entirely satisfactory. Particularly, this form tends to be associated with charities, with a resulting further confusion in the minds of traditional institutions such as banks over our 'not-for-profit' status. To many, a company such as ours must either be commercial (i.e. profit motivated) or else a charity.

30. Estelle James, 'The nonprofit sector in comparative perspective', in Powell, (ed.), *The Nonprofit Sector*, p. 404.
31. Douglas, *Why Charity?*.
32. Weisbrod, 'Towards a theory of the voluntary non-profit sector in a three-sector economy' and *The Voluntary Non-Profit Sector* (D. C. Heath, Lexington, Mass., 1977).
33. See Anthony Downs, 'Why the government budget in a democracy is too small', *World Politics*, 12 (1960), pp. 541–63.
34. Burton A. Weisbrod, 'Private goods, collective goods: the role of the non-profit sector', in Kenneth Clarkson and Donald Martin, *The Economics of Nonproprietary Organizations* (JAI Press, Greenwich, Conn., 1980).
35. David Easley and Maureen O'Hara, 'The economic role of the non-profit firms'.
36. Hansmann, 'The role of nonprofit enterprise', p. 845.
37. This was a point made by one of Hansmann's earliest critics', Permutt, who conducted a telephone survey in New Haven to discover public recognition of prominent local NPOs. Respondents were asked which of a list of organizations 'are most likely non-profit organizations as opposed to being for-profit'. In the case of five of the eleven NPOs a majority of respondents thought the organizations were for-profit concerns, and in some instances it was a large majority that had this misapprehension. Steven E. Permutt, 'Consumer perceptions of nonprofit enterprise: a comment on Hansmann', *Yale Law Journal*, 90 (1981), p. 1626.
38. However, there are a few notable exceptions to this – including the work of Peter Dobkin Hall; see, e.g., *The Organization of American Culture, 1700–1900* (New York University Press, New York, 1982) and 'A historical overview of the private nonprofit sector' in Powell, (ed.), *The Nonprofit Sector*.
39. Herbert A. Simon, 'Rationality as process and as product of thought', *Papers*

and Proceedings of the American Economic Association, 68 (1978), p. 4.

40. Douglas E. Haynes, 'From tribute to philanthropy: the politics of gift giving in a western Indian city', *Journal of Asian Studies*, 46 (1987), p. 340.
41. Hui-chen Wang Liu, *The Traditional Chinese Clan Rules* (J. J. Augustin, Locust Valley, NY, 1959), p. 126.
42. This diversity of organizational forms engaged in activities providing goods or services for others became greater still in the late Ming and early Qing. In addition to older forms of aid provided by, for example, lineages and the state, this period saw the rise of benevolent societies. See Joanna F. Handlin Smith, 'Benevolent societies: the reshaping of charity during the late Ming and early Ch'ing', *Journal of Asian Studies*, 46 (1987), pp. 309–37.
43. However, as the Woodfield Report states, 'The Inland Revenue are effectively the determining body for charitable status in Scotland since organizations apply to them for fiscal relief on the grounds that their activities are charitable. For fiscal purposes English charitable law is part of Scots law and therefore the Revenue follow the English interpretation of charitable status.' *Efficiency Scrutiny of the Supervision of Charities* (HMSO, London, 1987), p. 48.
44. Kenneth Ch'en, *Buddhism in China* (Princeton University Press, Princeton, 1964), p. 295.
45. John Neville Figgis, *Studies of Political Thought from Gerson to Grotius, 1414–1625*, 2nd edn (Cambridge University Press, Cambridge, 1923), p. 4.
46. Antony Black, *Guilds and Civil Society in European Political Thought from the Twelfth Century to the Present* (Methuen, London, 1984), p. 174.
47. E. P. Thompson, *The Making of the English Working Class* (Vintage Books, New York, 1966), p. 425.
48. Indeed, even early Victorian attitudes to state intervention in the affairs of private individuals and organizations are far more complex than popular accounts of the 'triumph of *laissez-faire*' usually allow for. See William C. Lubenow, *The Politics of Government Growth* (David and Charles, Newton Abbot, 1971).
49. Hall, 'A historical overview of the private nonprofit sector', p. 4.
50. Ibid., p. 5.
51. Lester M. Salamon, 'Partners in public service: the scope and theory of government-nonprofit relations', in Powell, (ed.), *The Nonprofit Sector*, p. 101.

Chapter 2 Mutuals and the Supply of Goods and Services

1. For a brief discussion of the rise of such groups in Germany, and their relation to the hierarchical, traditional charities, see Dietrich Thränhardt, 'Established charity organizations, self-help groups and new social movements in Germany', *Discussion Papers in Political and Administrative Science No. 3* (Institut für Politikwissenschaft der Westfälischen Wilhelms-Universität Münster, Münster, 1987).
2. Henry B. Hansmann, 'Mutual insurance companies and the theory of nonprofit and cooperative enterprise', *PONPO Working Paper No. 89* (Institution for

Social and Policy Studies, Yale University, New Haven, 1985), p. 2.

3. Hansmann, 'Mutual insurance companies and the theory of nonprofit and cooperative enterprise', p. 3.
4. P. H. J. H. Gosden, *Self-Help* (Batsford, London, 1973), p. 23.
5. Robert Michels, *Political Parties* (Free Press, New York, 1962), originally published in 1911.
6. For a discussion of some of these issues see Alan Ware, *Citizens, Parties and the State* (Polity Press, Cambridge, 1987), ch. 6.
7. Gosden, *Self-Help*, pp. 180–1.
8. Herman Stolpe, 'The cooperative movements', in Erik Allardt et al., *Nordic Democracy* (Det Danske Selskab, Copenhagen, 1981), p. 360.
9. For the years 1947–54, see *Monthly Digest of Statistics* (Central Statistical Office, London), *Report of the Chief Registrar of Friendly Societies* (HMSO, London) and *Statistical Abstracts of the United States* (US Department of Commerce, Washington DC) for each of these years.
10. *Royal Commission on the Taxation of Profits and Income* Cmnd 9474 (HMSO, London, 1955), p. 175.
11. Peter G. Whiteman and David C. Milne, *Whiteman and Wheatcroft on Income Tax*, 2nd edn (Sweet and Maxwell, London, 1976), p. 254.
12. Henry B. Hansmann, 'The role of nonprofit enterprise', *Yale Law Journal*, 89 (1980), p. 889.
13. Ira Ellman, 'Another theory of nonprofit corporations', *Michigan Law Review*, 80 (1982), p. 1048.
14. For an analysis of one example of this, see Keith Bradley and Alan Gelb, 'The political economy of "radical" change: an analysis of the Scottish Daily News worker co-operative', *British Journal of Political Science*, 9 (1979), pp. 1–20.
15. There are, however, a few examples of producer co-operatives which have objectives other than maximizing the income of the members. One case is the artists' co-operatives in New York, which are discussed by Zukin, but she regards them as an unstable form of institution when faced by the market: 'In the 1950s . . . the New York School had their co-op galleries on Tenth Street, and in the 1970s many of the new galleries in SoHo were co-ops. As long as the artists who use them depend solely on the art market for their livelihood, however, the artists' co-ops enjoy only a brief success. Eventually some of the artists are either picked up by professional dealers – who are glad of the 'screening process' that artists' co-ops provide – or the co-ops themselves hire professional 'directors' with the explicit idea of improving the gallery's position in the marketplace.' Sharon Zukin, 'Art in the arms of power: market relations and collective patronage in the capitalist state', *Theory and Society*, 11 (1982), p. 432.
16. Leon T. Kendall, *The Savings and Loan Business* (Prentice-Hall, Englewood Cliffs, NJ, 1962), pp. 4–5.
17. Martin Boddy, *The Building Societies* (Macmillan, London, 1980), p. 7.
18. Kendall, *The Savings and Loan Business*, p. 6.
19. Mark Boléat, *The Building Society Industry* (Allen and Unwin, London,

1981), p. 177.

20. George and Weedon Grossmith, *The Diary of a Nobody*, 5th edn (J. W. Arrowsmith, Bristol, 1910).
21. Boléat, *The Building Society Industry*, p. 8.
22. See, for example, Paul Barnes, *Building Societies: the myth of mutuality* (Pluto, London, 1984).
23. Kendall, *The Savings and Loan Business*, p. 78.
24. Boddy, *The Building Societies*, figure 3.7.
25. Boléat, *The Building Society Industry*, p. 352.
26. *Statistical Abstracts of the United States 1985*, p. 492.
27. *New Statesman*, 18 January 1985, p. 10.
28. Derek Fraser, *The Evolution of the British Welfare State*, 2nd edn (Macmillan, London, 1984), p. 108.
29. Gosden, *Self-Help*, p. 119.
30. Fraser, *The Evolution of the British Welfare State*, pp. 165–6.
31. Speech by Lord Beveridge in the House of Lords, 22 June 1949, *Hansard*, vol. 163, col. 94.
32. Registry of Friendly Societies, *Report of the Chief Registrar for 1981–1982*, p. 39.
33. Hansmann, 'Mutual insurance companies and the theory of nonprofit and cooperative enterprise', pp. 14–15.
34. Hansmann, 'Mutual insurance companies and the theory of non-profit and co-operative enterprise', pp. 12–13.
35. Boris I. Bittker and G. K. Rahdert, 'The exemption of non-profit organizations from federal income tax', *Yale Law Journal*, 85 (1976), p. 356.
36. The corruption of Teamster officials even led to the union being expelled from the American Federation of Labor-Congress of Industrial Organizations (AFL-CIO) in 1957; Graham K. Wilson, *Unions in American National Politics* (Macmillan, London, 1979), p. 4
37. Of course, the availability of a wide range of pubs or commercially-owned clubs does enable the drinker to select one where she feels 'most at home' with fellow customers. But with a for-profit concern the customer has no direct control over changes in its policy. As most of the former regulars at the 'White Horse' in Leamington Spa, Warwickshire, would argue, the pub had a very different atmosphere after it was modernized with a view to attracting a new kind of customer. And, although there are a great many other pubs in the area, none of them has quite the ambience of the 'old' 'White Horse'. Similar complaints have been voiced about pub modernizations throughout Britain during the last few years.
38. Like clubs, charities might be thought to be organizations that could facilitate or hinder the integration of groups into the wider society. Like clubs, too, many of them in the past have provided benefits specifically for members of one sex, ethnic or national group. However, because of the burdens the removal of discrimatory practices would impose on some charities, they have generally been unaffected by legislation against such discrimination. As Gerard notes, 'charities enjoy a degree of immunity from recent anti-

discrimination legislation and are able to confer benefits on individuals on the basis of their sex, nationality and ethnic origin.' David Gerard, *Charities in Britain* (Bedford Square Press/NCVO, London, 1983), p. 51.

39. Under Public Law 63 (an ordinance of New York City) a club is regarded as being not 'distinctly private' if it has more than 400 members, provides regular meals, and regularly receives payments of dues or fees for the use of space, facilities, services, meals or beverages from non-members who use the club for trade or business purposes. This ordinance prohibited clubs from discrimination on the grounds of race or sex, and it was upheld in a case involving the University Club. While this club voted subsequently to admit women, the Union League Club hoped to take the issue as far as the US Supreme Court, if necessary. *New York Times*, 6 June 1987.
40. In the case of *Rotary International v. Rotary Club of Duarte* (1987) the Court held that admission to rotary clubs was not sufficiently selective for them to be treated as wholly private clubs. *New York Times*, 5 May 1987.
41. *All England Law Reports* (Butterworth, London, 1973), vol. 1, p. 529.
42. Rose himself analyses the 'welfare mix' in terms of provision by three kinds of social institution – the household, the market and the state; Richard Rose, 'The state's contribution to the welfare mix', *Centre for the Study of Public Policy Paper No. 140* (University of Strathclyde, Glasgow, 1985), p. 4. He argues that the supply of welfare by voluntary agencies is merely a variant of market supply, because most of them are provided by paid employees and the goods and services produced are then sold (p. 46).
43. Richard G. Lipsey, *An Introduction to Positive Economics*, 2nd edn (Weidenfeld and Nicolson, London, 1963), p. 252.
44. Ibid., p. 248.

Chapter 3 Economic Competition Involving Charities

1. Gabriel Rudney, 'A quantitative profile of the nonprofit sector', *PONPO Working Paper No. 40* (Institution for Social and Policy Studies, Yale University, New Haven, 1981), table 8.
2. Posnett's data for 1985 shows that the income of registered charities constituted 4.1 per cent of GNP that year, but 10.9 per cent of this income originates with government in the form of grants. Since this data excludes charities not registered with the Charity Commission (such as universities), it may be concluded that at least 3.7 per cent of GNP can be said to originate with charities. This data relates only to charities in England and Wales, and not to charities in other parts of Britain. John Posnett, 'Trends in the income of registered charities, 1980–1985', *Charity Trends 1986–87* (Charities Aid Foundation, Tonbridge, 1987), p. 6.
3. English data for 1985, the year of the Ethiopian famine and the Live Aid concert, does show some increase in the share of charity income provided by donations – from 12.2 per cent of the total in 1980 to 15.2 per cent in 1986. Even so, donations remain a relatively small item of total charity income. See Posnett, 'Trends in the income of registered charities,

1980–1985', p. 6.

4. The first charity Christmas card was introduced in 1949 by UNICEF, but it was not until the 1960s that they started to be sold in large quantities. Today cards sold directly by charities account for about 15 per cent of the total market, while a further 10 per cent of the market is accounted for by cards sold by commercial enterprises which make a donation to the charity identified on the card.
5. Michael Chesterman, *Charities, Trusts and Social Welfare* (Weidenfeld and Nicolson, London, 1979), p. 135. Condition (i) (IV) the seemingly 'catch-all' category of other purposes which the law recognizes as charitable, is actually rather narrowly defined in practice. Generally court decisions since 1601 have tended not to stray too far from the purposes illustrated in the preamble to the 1601 Statute, or from the extensions to them which the courts have accepted as new needs have arisen. But conservatism in this regard has meant that the notion of 'public benefit' employed in charity law bears little relation to widely accepted notions of 'public benefit' in modern political discourse.
6. Edith L. Fisch, Doris Jonas Freed and Esther R. Schachter, *Charities and Charitable Foundations* (Lond, Pomona, NY, 1974), p. 229.
7. Data on private schools in England and Wales is contained in John Posnett and Jim Chase, 'Independent schools in England and Wales', *Charity Statistics 1984–85* (Charities Aid Foundation, Tonbridge, 1985), pp. 81–7.
8. Paul Starr, *The Social Transformation of American Medicine* (Basic Books, New York, 1982). For alternative views of the development of the American health industry, see Daniel M. Fox, *Health Policies, Health Politics: the British and American experience, 1911–1965* (Princeton University Press, Princeton, 1986) and Bradford H. Gray, (ed.), *The New Health Care for Profit* (National Academy Press, Washington DC, 1983). On recent changes in the structure of the hospital industry, see Bradford H. Gray, 'The new entrepreneurialism in health care – overview: origins and trends', *Bulletin of the New York Academy of Medicine*, 61 (1985), pp. 7–22.
9. Francis Gladstone, *Charity, Law and Social Justice* (Bedford Square Press/NCVO, London, 1982), p.66. While Gladstone's point about the inability of people on low incomes to pay for BUPA subscriptions is correct, his argument is a little misleading. The large growth in private medical insurance in recent years has largely been a result of companies paying to have their employees join, rather than individuals on middle and high incomes themselves paying to do so.
10. Gladstone, *Charity, Law and Social Justice*, p. 45.
11. Ira Ellman, 'Another theory of nonprofit corporations', *Michigan Law Review*, 80 (1982), p. 1004.
12. Ibid. p. 1005. On the two approaches, see 'Nonprofit corporations – definition', *Vanderbilt Law Review*, 17 (1963), pp. 336–42.
13. Although there are federal laws relating to non-profit organizations in Canada, these are different again. A sharp distinction is drawn in these laws between mutual-benefit organizations and charities, and only the latter are

entitled to register with Revenue Canada for tax-exempt status which provides tax-deductible benefits for donors. If Revenue Canada believes a profit motive lies behind an attempt to so register an organization, registration will be denied.

14. Michelle J. White, 'An introduction to the nonprofit sector', in Michelle J. White, (ed.), *Nonprofit Firms in a Three-Sector Economy* (Urban Institute, Washington DC, 1981), p. 2.
15. The classic popular exposé of the corruption of the American nursing-home industry is that by Mendelson. She argues strongly against the view that non-profit status provides much protection against unscrupulous practices in this industry; Mary Adelaide Mendelson, *Tender Loving Greed* (Knopf, New York, 1974), ch. 9. For a brief review of attempts to reform the nursing-home industry, see Catherine Hawes, 'Nursing-home reform and the politics of long-term care', *PS*, 20 (1987), pp. 232–41.
16. *New York Times*, 28 April 1987.
17. *New York*, 20 May 1987, p. 36.
18. Ira Ellman, 'Another theory of non-profit corporations', p. 1028.
19. *Report of the Charity Commissioners for England and Wales for the Year 1980* (HMSO, London, 1981), p. 7.
20. *Report of the Charity Commissioners for England and Wales for the Year 1986* (HMSO, London, 1987), pp. 14–15.
21. The Commission (its full title was the Commission on Private Philanthropy and Public Need) sponsored a number of research reports, as well as making its own reports; all these reports were published in 1975.
22. On trends in philanthropic contributions in the US, see Christopher Jencks, 'Who gives to what?', in Walter W. Powell, (ed.), *The Nonprofit Sector* (Yale University Press, New Haven, 1987), especially table 18.6.
23. *Observer*, 15 March 1987.
24. On the role of 'moral blackmail' in the acquisition of the resources required to put on the concerts, see Timothy Kenyon, 'The politics and morality of "Live Aid"', *Politics*, 5 (1985), pp. 3–8.
25. For data on this, see Eric Major and Mark Ashworth, 'Local authority support of charitable bodies', *Charity Statistics 1984–85* (Charities Aid Foundation, Tonbridge, 1985), tables 2 and 6.
26. To some extent university presses have long been involved in publishing books, such as the dictionaries produced by Oxford University Press, for a wider market. In recent years, however, a much greater range of books for non-academic readers have been published by these presses.
27. Richard Nelson and Michael Krashinsky, 'Two major issues of public policy: public subsidy and organization of supply', in Dennis R. Young and Richard R. Nelson, (eds), *Public Policy for Day Care of Young Children* (D. C. Heath, Lexington, Mass., 1973), p. 55. See also F. Ruderman, 'Child care and working mothers', (Child Welfare League of America, 1958).
28. *Financial Times*, 9 July 1985.
29. Brian D. Jacobs, 'Non-profits in the US private sector and their role in community development (with reference to the Local Initiative Support

Corporation)', paper presented at the *Annual Conference of the American Politics Group of the Political Studies Association*, Durham, 1984, pp. 8–9.

30. See ch. 4, section 5.
31. Ironically, though, one of the stimuli to the rapid growth in sales of charity Christmas cards in the mid 1960s was one of the largest manufacturers of cards which saw this development as providing an *additional* market. It was only later that it became apparent that the charity cards might become competitors to commercial cards.
32. *Guardian*, 18 July 1987.
33. *New York Times*, 7 February 1987.
34. There is an important difference between this scheme and one introduced by the Bank of Scotland in 1987. The latter linked the opening of a VISA account, and purchases made by card users, to contributions to a particular charity, the NSPCC; (see *Observer*, 1 November 1987). Under the Bank of Scotland scheme, therefore, there was no choice open to potential card users as to the cause or charity to which the money could be directed.
35. *New York Times*, 7 February 1987.
36. On the legal position of joint-capital-raising ventures involving Internal Revenue Service, see Michael H. Schill, 'The participation of charities in limited partnerships', *Yale Law Journal*, 93 (1984), pp. 1355–74.
37. Gray, 'The new entrepreneurialism in health care'.
38. This diversification is far from unusual among contemporary American hospitals. Among the other activities they have become involved in are cleaning services for schools and factories, catering services using hospital kitchens in off-hours, and computerized billing services for local doctors. *New York Times*, 25 January 1987.
39. Alfred Balk, *The Free List* (Russell Sage, New York, 1971).
40. Regina E. Herzlinger and William S. Krasker, 'Who profits from nonprofits?', *Harvard Business Review*, 65 (1987), pp. 93–106. The selective use of data by these authors was much commented on when this article was published, and the debate received considerable publicity in the American press; for example see *New York Times*, 2 April 1987. Data indicating that the behaviour of non-profit and for-profit hospitals differs is presented, among other places, in Theodore R. Marmor, Mark Schlesinger and Richard W. Smithey, 'Nonprofit organizations and health care', in Powell, (ed.), *The Nonprofit Sector*. For evidence that, in the area of mental-health care, for-profit firms provide fewer staff resources for patient care and fewer services with community-wide benefits, see Mark Schlesinger and Robert Dorwart, 'Ownership and mental-health services', *New England Journal of Medicine*, 311 (1984), pp. 959–65.
41. Gladstone, *Charity, Law and Social Justice*, p. 58.
42. Boris I. Bittker and G. K. Rahdert, 'The exemption of non-profit organizations from federal income tax', *Yale Law Journal*, 85 (1976), p. 302.
43. Ibid.
44. Ibid. and Henry B. Hansmann, 'The rationale for exempting nonprofit organizations from corporate income taxation', *Yale Law Journal*, 91 (1981),

pp. 54–100. See also the excellent discussion of the rationales for tax exemption in John G. Simon, 'The tax treatment of nonprofit organizations: a review of federal and state policies', in Powell, (ed.), *The Nonprofit Sector*, esp. pp. 73–81.

45. Chesterman, *Charities, Trusts and Social Welfare*, pp. 243–4.
46. *New York Times*, 4 September 1986.
47. *Times Higher Education Supplement*, 18 July 1986.
48. In large cities attempts by universities to increase the housing facilities available to students can pose equally serious problems for local communities. New York University, which in recent years has built six new dormitories near its campus in Greenwich Village, is like Columbia in having been accused by local residents of destroying the neighbourhood. Given the shortage of land, new buildings can only be erected if older ones – many of which were local shops or housed people not concerned with the university – are demolished. *New York Times*, 20 September 1987.
49. *New York Times*, 20 April 1987.
50. *New York Times*, 25 January 1985.

Chapter 4 Financial Autonomy and the 'Independent Sector'

1. See ch. 1, n. 9.
2. See Tom Deans and Alan Ware, 'Charity-state relations: a conceptual analysis', *Journal of Public Policy*, 6 (1986), pp. 121–35.
3. On some of the problems of specifying needs in relation to the concept of 'interests', see William E. Connolly, *The Terms of Political Discourse* (D. C. Heath, Lexington, Mass., 1974), pp. 61–2.
4. Albert Weale, *Political Theory and Social Policy* (Macmillan, London, 1983), p. 35.
5. James Douglas, *Why Charity?* (Sage, Beverly Hills and London, 1983), p. 114.
6. On the difference between Japanese and British firms as communities and as providers of welfare benefits to employees, see Ronald Dore, *British Factory – Japanese Factory* (Allen and Unwin, London, 1973), esp. ch. 8.
7. Calculated from data presented in John Posnett, 'A profile of the charity sector', *Charity Statistics 1983–84* (Charities Aid Foundation, Tonbridge, 1984), pp. 56–7.
8. National Audit Office, *Monitoring and Control of Charities in England and Wales* (HMSO, London, 1987).
9. Gabriel Rudney, 'A quantitative profile of the non-profit sector', *PONPO Working Paper No. 40* (Institution for Social and Policy Studies, Yale University, New Haven, 1981), table 3.
10. Ralph M. Kramer, 'The voluntary agency in a mixed economy: dilemmas of entrepreneurialism and vendorism', *PONPO Working Paper No. 85* (Institution for Social and Policy Studies, Yale University, 1985), pp. 2–4.
11. Waldemar A. Nielsen, *The Endangered Sector* (Columbia University Press, New York, 1979), ch. 1, Alan Pifer, *Philanthropy in an Age of Transition*

(Foundation Center, New York, 1984), p. 56 and Douglas, *Why Charity?* and 'Political theories of nonprofit organization', in Walter W. Powell, (ed.), *The Nonprofit Sector* (Yale University Press, New Haven, 1987), p. 43.

12. However, by no means all agencies involved in aid to the third world, especially in the US, depend exclusively on donations. Some American agencies receive up to 80 per cent of their income from the federal government, and more than one third of the agencies listed with the US government received at least 50 per cent of their income from it. See Peter Burnell, 'Third world charities in Britain and official funding', *Politics Working Paper No. 46* (University of Warwick, Coventry, 1987), p. 3.
13. On this issue in relation to voluntary social welfare agencies, see Ralph M. Kramer, *Voluntary Agencies in the Welfare State* (University of California Press, Berkeley, 1981), pp. 157–66.
14. Brian H. Smith, 'US and Canadian PVOs as transnational development institutions', in Robert F. Gorman, (ed.), *Private Voluntary Organizations as Agents of Development* (Westview, Boulder, Colo., 1984), p. 138.
15. For example see Nielsen, *The Endangered Sector*, p. 61.
16. Brian H. Smith, 'US and Canadian non-profit organizations (PVOs) as transnational development institutions', *PONPO Working Paper No. 70* (Institution for Social and Policy Studies, Yale University, New Haven, 1983), p. 32.
17. It is worth remembering that the argument, that altruism would be inadequate in providing for social needs in a state and that state intervention would be required, can be traced back at least as far as Hobbes. Hobbes noted 'And whereas many men, by accident unevitable, become unable to maintain themselves by their labour; they ought not to left to the Charity of private persons; but to be provided for, as farforth as the necessities of Nature require, by the Lawes of the Common-wealth. For as it is Uncharitablenesse in any man, to neglect the impotent; so it is in the Soveraign of a Common-wealth, to expose them to the hazard of such uncertain Charity' (*Leviathan*, Everyman edn.(Dent, London, 1914), pp. 184–5).
18. On the distinction between 'goods altruism' and 'participation altruism', see Howard Margolis, *Selfishness, Altruism and Rationality* (Cambridge University Press, Cambridge, 1982), ch. 7.
19. Christopher Jencks, 'Who gives to what?', in Powell, (ed.), *The Nonprofit Sector*, table 18.6.
20. Ralph M. Kramer, *Voluntary Agencies in the Welfare State*, p. 131.
21. See Mark Ashworth, 'Individual donations to charity', in *Charity Statistics 1982–83* (Charities Aid Foundation, Tonbridge, 1983), pp. 14–5 and Linda Rajan, 'Donations to charity by individuals: a comparison between 1980 and 1984', *Charity Statistics 1985–86* (Charities Aid Foundation, Tonbridge, 1986), pp. 138–41.
22. Jencks, 'Who gives to what?', p. 324.
23. For comparative data on religious commitment in several liberal democracies, see David McKay, *American Politics and Society* (Martin Robertson, Oxford, 1983), p. 23.

24. Moreover, the US differs from Britain, the Netherlands and West Germany, though it is similar to Austria in that: 'despite the tides of secularization, many offspring in these two countries profess to be more church-going than their parents.' M. Kent Jennings, Klaus R. Allerbeck and Leopold Rosenmayer, 'Generations and families: general orientations', in Samuel H. Barnes and Max Kaase, (eds), *Political Action* (Sage, Beverly Hills and London, 1979), p. 465.
25. Jencks, 'Who gives to what?', p. 324. Jencks's argument is that the sense that a church is a community of equals prompts the poor to contribute disproportionately more than they would if everyone contributed strictly in relation to their ability to do so. An alternative view might be that, in a world which is not providing them with very much else, the religious poor are especially grateful for whatever comforts their religion provides them, and hence they give relatively more than others.
26. Jeffrey Obler, 'Private giving in the welfare state', *British Journal of Political Science*, 11 (1981), p. 27.
27. Carl Bakal, *Charity USA* (Times Books, New York, 1979), p. 9.
28. Susan Saxon-Harrold, 'Patterns and attitudes to charitable giving: A household survey 1985–6', in *Charity Statistics 1985–86*, p. 131.
29. On the role of voluntary organizations in the provision of social services in Britain, see, for example, Hugh W. Mellor, *The Role of Voluntary Organizations in Social Welfare* (Croom Helm, London, 1985) and Maria Brenton, *The Voluntary Sector in British Social Services* (Longman, London, 1985).
30. Obler, 'Private giving in the welfare state', p. 20.
31. Ibid., p. 48.
32. This gap is most clearly evident in the case of AIDS. When AIDS was identified primarily as a disease affecting homosexuals, fund-raising for research was difficult. Once fund-raisers in America were able to convince potential donors of the dangers to heterosexuals, the trend was reversed and by the end of 1987 some scientists were worried that AIDS was now syphoning off funds from diseases which were taking a larger toll. *Newsweek*, 28 December 1987.
33. Bob Geldof, *Is That It?* (Penguin, Harmondsworth, 1986), p. 356.
34. Obler, 'Private giving in the welfare state', pp. 18–19.
35. For a brief and useful summary of some of these studies, see Richard Steinberg, 'Nonprofit organizations and the market', in Powell (ed.), *The Nonprofit Sector*, p. 132.
36. Richard Titmuss, *The Gift Relationship* (Pantheon, New York, 1971).
37. Ibid., p. 48.
38. J. Mark Davidson Schuster, 'Tax incentives as arts policy in western Europe', *PONPO Working Paper No. 90* (Institution for Social and Policy Studies, Yale University, New Haven, 1985), p. 21.
39. Ibid., p. 17.
40. For example, in relation to charities providing aid for the third world, Burnell has argued: 'The ways in which charities tailor their activities and

construct their images of the third world so as to attract donations from the public have been the subject of much criticism. They provide the main concern for Lissner. Roberts (p. 104) also notes how the needs of donors can come to be awarded priority over the third world clientele, thereby introducing inflexibility into the deployment of resources by agencies that are normally more flexible than government departments.' Burnell, 'Third world charities in Britain and official funding', p. 76. The research he cites is J. Lissner, *The Politics of Altruism* (Lutheran World Foundation, Geneva, 1976) and Hibbert R. Roberts, 'The domestic environment of AID-registered PVOs: characteristics and impact', in Robert F. Gorman, (ed.), *Private Voluntary Organizations as Agents of Development* (Westview, Boulder, Colo., 1984).

41. Jim Bulpitt, 'English local politics: the collapse of the *ancien régime*?', paper presented at the *Annual Conference of the Political Studies Association*, England, 1976.
42. Bakal, *Charity USA*, p. 224.
43. The exception is charities for the disabled which, under the National Assistance Act of 1948, are required to register with a local authority and which may be refused registration, if that authority believes its purposes are already fulfilled by another charity. Michael Chesterman, *Charities, Trusts and Social Welfare* (Weidenfeld and Nicolson, London, 1979), pp. 270–1.
44. Kramer, *Voluntary Agencies in the Welfare State*, p. 139.
45. Fred Hirsch, *Social Limits to Growth* (Routledge and Kegan Paul, London, 1977), p. 40.
46. On the controversy over St Dunstan's, see Benedict Nightingale, *Charities* (Allen Lane, London, 1973), pp. 256–9 and Chesterman, *Charities, Trusts and Social Welfare*, pp. 376–81.
47. *Charity Statistics 1985–86*, p. 184.
48. It might be argued that this is to ignore the contribution some firms, including Marks and Spencer, make by allowing their staff to undertake certain kinds of philanthropic work on 'company time'. But, once again, in relation to the amount of time individuals volunteer, the overall contribution is relatively small.
49. Michael Useem, 'Corporate philanthropy', in Powell, (ed.), *The Nonprofit Sector*, p. 341.
50. *Charity Statistics 1985–86*, p. 7.
51. *New York Times*, 3 September 1985.
52. The term 'third-party government' refers to the use of non-governmental agencies ('third parties') by governments to provide services which could be supplied directly by governments themselves. For an analysis of the significance of 'third-party government' in the US, see Lester M. Salamon, 'Rethinking public management: third party government and the changing forms of public action', *Public Policy*, 29 (1981), pp. 255–75.
53. William D. Norton, *The Cooperative Movement in Social Work* (Macmillan, London, 1927), pp. 68–82.
54. Arnold J. Heidenheimer, 'Secularization patterns and the westward spread

of the welfare state, 1883–1983', *Comparative Social Research*, 6 (1983), pp. 23–4. The passage he cites is from E. D. Norman, *Church and Society in England 1770–1970* (Clarendon Press, Oxford, 1976), p. 349.

55. Bakal, *Charity USA*, pp. 420–1.
56. *New York Times*, 8 March 1985.
57. Ibid.
58. Deborah Kaplan Polivy, 'A study of the admissions policies and practices of eight local United Way organizations', *PONPO Working Paper No. 49* (Institution for Social and Policy Studies, Yale University, New Haven, 1982), p. 89.
59. On the interpretation of the New Deal as an era of changing balances of power in the US, see Samuel H. Beer, 'In search of a new public philosophy', in Anthony King, (ed.), *The New American Political System* (American Enterprise Institute, Washington DC, 1978), pp. 6–13.
60. On the development of foundations in the US, see Barry D. Karl and Stanley N. Katz, 'The American private philanthropic foundation and the public sphere, 1890–1930', *Minerva*, 19 (1981), pp. 236–70.
61. Calculated from data presented in *Charity Statistics 1982–83*, pp. 45–6 and from data presented in Posnett, 'A Profile of the Charity Sector', pp. 56–7.
62. Calculated from data presented in Gabriel Rudney, 'A quantitative profile of the non-profit sector', and Brian D. Jacobs, 'Non-profits in the US private sector and their role in community development (with reference to the Local Initiative Support Corporation)', paper presented at the *Annual Conference of the American Political Group of the Political Studies Association*, Durham, 1984.
63. Bakal, *Charity USA*, p. 52.
64. Peter Buck and Barbara Gutmann Rosenkrantz, 'The social ecology of small foundations', paper presented at *Davis Center Colloquium on Medical and Welfare Policy in the United States, 1860–1980*, Princeton University, 1985, p. 2.
65. Ibid., pp. 4 and 36.
66. Bakal, *Charity USA*, p. 57.
67. Paul N. Ylvisaker, 'Foundations and nonprofit organizations', in Powell, (ed.), *The Nonprofit Sector* (Yale University Press, New Haven, 1987), p. 370.
68. Michael Sosin, *Private Benefits* (Academic Press, Orlando, Fla., 1986), p. 76.
69. *Charity Statistics 1985–86*, p. 128.
70. *Observer*, 5 July 1987.
71. *Times Higher Education Supplement*, 18 July 1986.
72. For an analysis of the privatization of medical research, see Nicholas Wells, *Crisis in Research* (Office of Health Economics, London, 1987).
73. Although expenditure on some welfare services actually increased in Britain in the 1980s, the state can be seen as withdrawing from the provision of welfare in that maintenance of the level of services established in the 1970s required an even greater increase. This is because, both absolutely and in

relation to the rest of the population, the old and the unemployed (who are heavy users of these services) are more numerous now.

Chapter 5 The Growth and Transformation of Volunteering

1. On the difference between the two traditions in this regard, see Gerald Handel, *Social Welfare in Western Society* (Random House, New York, 1982).
2. Ibid., p. 44.
3. E. P. Thompson, *The Making of the English Working Class* (Vintage Books, New York, 1966), p. 423.
4. Bruce A. Ackerman, 'Neo-federalism? The contemporary relevance of the Federalist Papers', paper presented at the *Political Thought Seminar*, Columbia University, New York, 1987, p. 14.
5. David Paul Crook, *American Democracy in English Politics 1815–1850* (Clarendon Press, Oxford, 1965), p. 134.
6. An excellent account of change in politics in New York City between the 1820s and the Civil War is provided by Amy Bridges, *A City in the Republic* (Cambridge University Press, Cambridge, 1984).
7. David Owen, *English Philanthropy 1660–1960* (Belknap Press of Harvard University, Cambridge, Mass., 1965), p. 103.
8. Thompson, *The Making of the English Working Class*, p. 505.
9. Handel, *Social Welfare in Western Society*, p. 73.
10. As in Britain the COS movement grew rapidly in the US once it was established. The first COS was formed in Buffalo in 1877, and by 1900 these organizations were to be found in 138 US cities. Walter I. Trattner, *From Poor Law to Welfare State*, 3rd edn (Free Press, New York, 1984), p. 92.
11. Roy Lubove, *The Professional Altruist* (Harvard University Press, Cambridge, Mass., 1965), p. 16.
12. Handel, *Social Welfare in Western Society*, p. 74.
13. David Gerard, *Charities in Britain* (Bedford Square Press/NCVO, London, 1983), p. 18.
14. *Times*, 29 November 1985.
15. Until the early 1980s the voluntary groups in the alcohol field tended to be engaged in competition, rather than co-operation with each other. See I. R. Baggott, 'The politics of public health: alcohol, politics and social policy', PhD thesis, University of Hull, 1987, p. 77.
16. Albert O. Hirschman, *Shifting Involvements* (Martin Robertson, Oxford, 1982).
17. There is also the argument that, in the US, swings in support for religious doctrines contribute to varying levels of political activism. This point is made by Heidenheimer: 'What we seem to see more markedly in America are pendulum swings in religious opinion which interact with cyclical trends in political preference. The greater number and articulateness of . . . sects at times can serve to help launch great populist movements, whereas equivalents in Europe only produce ripples on the socio-cultural scene . . .

More than in secularized Lutheran countries like Sweden and Germany, where class-based organizations serve to stabilize support patterns, American political and reform organizations may tend to replicate the off-and-on recruitment patterns of religious groups.' Arnold J. Heidenheimer, 'Secularization patterns and the westward spread of the welfare state, 1883–1983', *Comparative Social Research*, 6 (1983), p. 30.

18. Alan Ware, *The Breakdown of Democratic Party Organization, 1940–1980* (Clarendon Press, Oxford, 1985), pp. 76–8.
19. Jack L. Walker, 'The origins and maintenance of interest groups in America', *American Political Science Review*, 77 (1983), p. 395.
20. For a brief discussion of these organizations, see Dietrich Thränhardt, 'Established charity organizations, self-help groups and new social movements in Germany', *Discussion Papers in Political and Administrative Science No. 3* (Institut für Politikwissenschaft der Westfälischen Wilhelms-Universität Münster, Münster, 1987).
21. *New York Times*, 26 January 1985.
22. Gerard, *Charities in Britain*, p. 113.
23. The means by which volunteering is sometimes encouraged in state schools is well captured in this entry from Mole's diary: 'Monday January 19th. I have joined a group at school called the Good Samaritans. We go out into the community helping and stuff like that. We miss Maths on Monday afternoons. Today we had a talk on the sort of things we will be doing. I have been put in the old age pensioners' group. Nigel had got a dead yukky job looking after kids in a playgroup. He is as sick as a parrot.' Sue Townsend, *The Secret Diary of Adrian Mole, Aged 13 ¾* (Methuen, London, 1982), p. 20.
24. Gerard, *Charities in Britain*, p. 79.
25. *New York Times*, 10 October 1986.
26. Sidney Verba and Norman H. Nie, *Participation in America* (University of Chicago Press, Chicago, 1972), p. 41.
27. Gabriel Rudney, 'The scope and dimensions of nonprofit activity', in Walter W. Powell (ed.), *The Nonprofit Sector* (Yale University Press, New Haven, 1987), p. 60.
28. Wolfenden Committee Report, *The Future of Voluntary Organizations* (Croom Helm, London, 1978).
29. Susan Saxon-Harrold, 'Patterns and attitudes to charitable giving: a household survey 1987', *Charity Trends 1986–87* (Charities Aid Foundation, Tonbridge, 1987), table 2.
30. Gerard, *Charities in Britain*, pp. 79–80.
31. Susan Saxon-Harrold, 'Patterns and attitudes to charitable giving', table 2.
32. Nevertheless, employers in Britain have responded to the availability of a pool of labour whose members could not undertake full-time jobs, and part-employment among women has been increasing in the 1980s.
33. For an analysis of the origins of these groups, see P. Whiteley and S. Winyard, 'The origins of the "New Poverty Lobby"', *Political Studies* 32 (1984), pp. 32–54.

34. J. Craig Jenkins, 'Nonprofit organizations and policy advocacy', in Powell, (ed.), *The Nonprofit Sector*, p. 303.
35. Richard Titmuss, *The Gift Relationship* (Pantheon, New York, 1971).
36. However, a more sympathetic account of the 'professional' political activist in relation to the volunteer is contained in James Q. Wilson, *The Amateur Democrat* (University of Chicago Press, Chicago, 1962). See also Edward C. Banfield and James Q. Wilson, *City Politics* (Vintage Books, New York, 1966).
37. Michael Sosin, *Private Benefits* (Academic Press, Orlando, Fla., 1986).
38. *Times Higher Education Supplement*, 18 July 1986.
39. Sylvia Tesh, 'In support of "single-issue" politics', *Political Science Quarterly*, 99 (1984), pp. 27–44.
40. Wilson, *The Amateur Democrat*.
41. Norman H. Nie, Sidney Verba and John R. Petrocik, *The Changing American Voter* (Harvard University Press, Cambridge, Mass., 1976), p. 202.
42. Of the earlier studies of American party volunteers, those by Wilson (cited above) are perhaps the best known, but see also Aaron B. Wildavsky, 'The Goldwater phenomenon: purists, politicians and the two-party system', *Review of Politics*, 27 (1965), pp. 386–413.
43. Ronald B. Rapoport, Alan I. Abramowitz and John McGlennon, (eds), *The Life of the Parties* (University of Kentucky Press, Lexington, 1986).
44. Tesh, 'In support of "single-issue" politics', pp. 32–8.
45. Maurice Duverger, *Les Partis Politiques* (Armond Colin, Paris, 1951).
46. Leon D. Epstein, *Political Parties in Western Democracies* (Pall Mall, London, 1967).
47. Ware, *The Breakdown of Democratic Party Organization, 1940–1980*, pp. 188–9.
48. See Alan Ware, 'Parties under electoral competition' in Alan Ware, (ed.), *Political Parties* (Basil Blackwell, Oxford, 1987), pp. 6–12.
49. Epstein, *Political Parties in Western Democracies*' Revised edn (Transaction, New Brunswick, 1980), pp. 369–70.
50. John McCarthy and Mayer Zald, 'Resource mobilization and social movements', *American Journal of Sociology*, 82 (1977), p. 1223.
51. See, for example, Ronald Inglehart, 'Political action: the impact of values, cognitive level and social background', in Samuel H. Barnes and Max Kaase, (eds.), *Political Action* (Sage, Beverly Hills and London, 1979).
52. Herbert H. Haines, 'Black radicalization and the funding of civil rights', *Social Problems*, 32 (1984), pp. 31–43.
53. J. Craig Jenkins and Craig M. Eckert, 'Channeling black insurgency: elite patronage and professional SMOs in the development of the civil rights movement', *PONPO Working Paper No. 115* (Institution for Social and Policy Studies, Yale University, New Haven, 1986), p. 28.
54. Walker, 'The origins and maintenance of interest groups in America', p. 398.
55. Ibid., p. 401.
56. Gerard, *Charities in Britain*, p. 113.

Chapter 6 Dangerous Areas of State Involvement?

1. S. L. Jenkinson, 'Church and state', in David Miller et al.; (eds.), *The Blackwell Encyclopaedia of Political Thought* (Basil Blackwell, Oxford, 1987), p. 71.
2. Lucian W. Pye, 'The legitimacy crisis', in Leonard Binder et al., *Crisis and Sequences in Political Development* (Princeton University Press, Princeton, 1971), p. 139.
3. In connection with scientific research in Britain the idea that scientists should have independence in conducting their work came to be known in the twentieth century as the Haldane-Addison principle.
4. Thomas S. Kuhn, *The Structure of Scientific Revolutions*, 2nd edn (University of Chicago Press, Chicago, 1970).
5. It was precisely such fears of political interference that underlay much of the opposition by artists and artistic performers to Section 28 of the Local Government Bill introduced by the British government in the 1987–8 parliamentary session. The Section prohibits local authorities from promoting homosexuality.
6. Joyce Youings, *Sixteenth Century England* (Penguin, Harmondsworth, 1984), p. 191.
7. R. K. Webb, *Modern England* (Allen and Unwin, London, 1969), p. 227.
8. Michael Chesterman, *Charities, Trusts and Social Welfare* (Weidenfeld and Nicolson, London, 1979), p. 157.
9. Ibid., pp. 160–1.
10. Leonard Joblove, 'Special treatment of churches under the Internal Revenue code', *PONPO Working Paper No. 21* (Institution for Social and Policy Studies, Yale University, New Haven, 1980), pp. 6–7.
11. Ibid., p. 8.
12. Howard L. Oleck, *Nonprofit Corporations, Organizations and Associations*, 3rd edn (Prentice-Hall, Englewood Cliffs, NJ, 1974), p. 44.
13. Ibid., p. 54.
14. John Copeland and Gabriel Rudney, 'Business income of nonprofits and competitive advantage – II', *Tax Notes*, 33 (1986), p. 1232.
15. Joblove, 'Special treatment of churches under the Internal Revenue code', p. 21.
16. Oleck, *Nonprofit Corporations, Organizations and Associations*, p. 686.
17. In 1984–5 discretionary rate relief amounted to more than 17 per cent of total rate relief by local authorities in England and Wales; *Charity Statistics 1985–6* (Charities Aid Foundation, Tonbridge, 1986), p. 65.
18. Joblove, 'Special treatment of churches under the Internal Revenue code', p. 3.
19. Paul J. Weber and Dennis A. Gilbert, *Private Churches and Public Money* (Greenwood, Westport, Conn., 1981), ch. 2.
20. *New York Times*, 24 January 1987.
21. Robert O. Berdahl, *British Universities and the State* (Cambridge University

Press, Cambridge, 1959), p. 11.

22. On the early years of the UGC see Christine Shinn, *Paying the Piper: the development of the UGC 1919–1946* (Falmer Press, Lewes, 1986) as well as Berdahl, *British Universities and the State*.
23. Berdahl, *British Universities and the State*, app. IV.
24. Ibid., ch. 8.
25. See Michael Shattock and Robert O. Berdahl, 'The British University Grants Committee 1919–1983: changing relationships with government and the universities', *Higher Education*, 13 (1984), pp. 471–99.
26. Roger Geiger, 'After the emergence: voluntary support and the building of American research universities', *PONPO Working Paper No. 87* (Institution for Social and Policy Studies, Yale University, New Haven, 1985), p. 24.
27. Michael O'Brien, *McCarthy and McCarthyism in Wisconsin* (University of Missouri Press, Columbia and London, 1980), p. 194.
28. *New York Times*, 2 September 1987.
29. *New York Times*, 6 September 1986. On the relationship between the US Congress and colleges in the earlier period, see Lawrence E. Gladieux and Thomas R. Wolanin, *Congress and the Colleges* (Lexington Books, Lexington, Mass., 1976).
30. *New York Times*, 8 September 1986.
31. In response to these developments, a new university college (at Buckingham) was established by disaffected academics in the 1970s. On principle, this college would not accept government funds and it has remained a small and peripheral institution.
32. On the British state's role in subsidizing the arts up to the end of the 1960s, see John S. Harris, *Government Patronage of the Arts in Britain* (University of Chicago Press, Chicago, 1970).
33. F. F. Ridley, 'State patronage of the arts in Britain: the political culture of cultural politics', *Social Science Information*, 17 (1978), p. 454.
34. 'Our first major museums – were decisively for-profit. Yet they exhibited fine art, produced theatre of high quality . . . and hosted touring European classical vocalists and fine-arts dancers. The first American orchestras were for-profit, sometimes musicians co-operatives, sometimes established by entrepreneurs' Paul DiMaggio, 'Can culture survive the marketplace?', *PONPO Working Paper No. 62* (Institution for Social and Policy Studies, Yale University, New Haven, 1983), pp. 30–1.
35. Paul DiMaggio, 'Non-profit organizations in the production and distribution of culture', in Walter W. Powell, (ed.), *The Nonprofit Sector* (Yale University Press, New Haven, 1987), p. 204.
36. Paul DiMaggio, 'Cultural entrepreneurship in nineteenth-century Boston: the creation of an organizational base for high culture in America', *Media, Culture and Society*, 4 (1982), pp. 33–50.
37. F. F. Ridley, 'State patronage of the arts in Britain', p. 481.
38. However, 'Most of the political and conceptual groundwork for state patronage of the arts was laid between 1960, when Governor Rockefeller established a prototype agency, the New York State Council on the Arts

(NYSCA) and 1965, when Congress voted to establish the National Endowment for the Arts and Humanities.' Sharon Zukin, 'Art in the arms of power: market relations and collective patronage in the capitalist state', *Theory and Society*, 11 (1982), p. 439.

39. Zukin, 'Art in the Arms of Power', p. 441.
40. J. Michael Montias, 'Public support for the performing arts in western Europe and the United States: history and analysis', *PONPO Working Paper No. 45* (Institution for Social and Policy Studies, Yale University, New Haven, 1982).
41. Michael Useem, 'Corporate philanthropy', in Powell, (ed.), *The Nonprofit Sector*, p. 342.
42. See, for example, *International Herald Tribune*, 26–7 March 1977.
43. *New York Times*, 24 January 1987.
44. Berdahl, *British Universities and the State*, p. 83.
45. *New York Times*, 8 September 1986. It has also been argued that the SDI itself is an 'indirect' policy, in that essentially it is a response to the absence of civilian industrial policies in the US. See, for example, G. Jan Colijn, 'Non-strategic aspects of SDI', *Politics Working Papers No. 45* (University of Warwick, Coventry, 1987), pp. 17–25.

Chapter 7 The Regulation of Intermediate Organizations

1. National Audit Office, *Monitoring and Control of Charities in England and Wales* (HMSO, London, 1987), p. 3.
2. Michael Chesterman, *Charities, Trusts and Social Welfare* (Weidenfeld and Nicholson, London, 1979), p. 24.
3. Ibid., p. 38.
4. In fact, it is far from clear that *laissez-faire* views were widespread among the British political elite at this time. In the largely 'partyless' politics of the 1850s most Conservatives were hostile to this creed, and the bourgeois (Liberal) wing of what had been the Whig party was far less strong than it was to become at the end of the nineteenth century.
5. National Audit Office, *Monitoring and Control of Charities in England and Wales*. This illustrates one of the disadvantages of splitting the supervision of charities between two bodies – the Charity Commission and the Inland Revenue. In Canada, where there is only one supervisorial agency, Revenue Canada, charities must submit tax returns annually. Because it is a tax-collecting agency, Revenue Canada has the resources to check thoroughly any failure by charities to make such returns. Its computer indicates which charities have not done so and automatically sends out further notices to them. Failure to submit returns, and to provide a satisfactory account for this, can result eventually in deregistration. In Britain the resources of the Inland Revenue are only involved in the regular scrutiny of those charities which make claims for the recovery of tax deducted at source. On this role of the Inland Revenue, see *Efficiency Scrutiny of the Supervision of Charities* (HMSO, London, 1987), p. 67.

6. P. H. J. H. Gosden, *Self-Help* (Batsford, London, 1973), p. 64.
7. Ibid., p. 84.
8. In spite of widespread corruption for decades in the Teamsters, it was not until the mid 1980s that the US Department of Justice prepared a civil lawsuit aimed at removing all the members of the union's executive board and placing the union under the control of a court-appointed trustee. *New York Times*, 3 January 1988.
9. This situation differs from that in Canada, where each year Revenue Canada audits a small random sample of tax returns by charities to check on the spread of abuses by registered charities.
10. Chesterman, *Charities, Trusts and Social Welfare*, pp. 369–73. During an investigation by the Inland Revenue, though, the assets of a charity would normally be frozen.
11. Ibid. p. 373.
12. National Audit Office, *Monitoring and Control of Charities in England and Wales*, pp. 7–8. As in many American states, there is a minimum proportion of their income which charities in Canada must dispose of each year – in the Canadian case it is 90 per cent. For the effects of this on medical research charities, see Tom Deans, 'Charity-state relations in Britain and Canada: the case of medical research', PhD thesis, University of Warwick (in preparation).
13. In the Canadian case the leaflet distributed by the Philanthropic Advisory Service of the Canadian Council of Better Business Bureaus ('Give But Give Wisely') failed to distinguish between charities that did not meet the standards of the Bureaus and those for which the Bureaus lacked information. Consequently, a number of reputable charities, including the Diabetes Trust Fund, found themselves placed on the same list as a variety of disreputable organizations. Although the leaflet stated that the list should be interpreted as implying neither approval nor disapproval by the Bureaus, the image of some charities was probably harmed by the way in which information was presented. I am grateful to Tom Deans for pointing out this example to me.
14. David C. Wilson and Richard J. Butler, 'Corporatism in the British voluntary sector', in W. Streeck and P. Schmitter, *Private Interest Government* (Sage, London and Beverly Hills, 1985), pp. 85–6.
15. Gosden, *Self-Help*, p. 32.
16. John Copeland and Gabriel Rudney, 'Business income of nonprofits and competitive advantage – II', *Tax Notes*, 33 (1986), p. 1228.
17. E. W. Brabrook cited in Gosden, *Self-Help*, p. 259.
18. Copeland and Rudney, 'Business income of nonprofits and competitive advantage – II', p. 1229.
19. John Copeland and Gabriel Rudney, 'Business income of nonprofits and competitive advantage', *Tax Notes*, 33 (1986), pp. 749–50.
20. Ibid. p. 750.
21. Regina E. Herzlinger and William S. Krasker, 'Who profits from nonprofits?', *Harvard Business Review*, 65 (1987), pp. 93–106.

22. The non-entrepreneurial spirit which pervaded British universities for many years meant that generally their income-earning ventures were treated by the Inland Revenue as being part of their educational purposes. Even income from sales in university-owned bookshops has remained untaxed. It is quite possible that the great expansion of commercial enterprise by universities in the 1980s may eventually lead to the Inland Revenue taking a rather more restrictive view of the justifiability of sales to outsiders in terms of their advancement of charitable purposes.
23. If an income-generating organization merely had to provide benefit to a charity through its activities, then virtually any business activity could be carried out under the cover of charitable status. This, indeed, would be a consequence of a decision in the Canadian Federal Court of Appeal in 1987 (*Alberta Institute on Mental Retardation v. The Queen*); the far-reaching implications of this decision are such that it is likely to be appealed further.
24. See, for example, *Unfair Competition by Nonprofit Organizations with Small Businesses* (US Small Business Administration, Washington DC, 1984).
25. Ibid.
26. *Chicago Tribune*, 19 February 1987.
27. Similar complaints about YMCAs have also been made to Revenue Canada.
28. On the use of charity in the US to promote the self-interest of those soliciting for funds, see Carl Bakal, *Charity USA* (Times Books, New York, 1979), chs 8 and 17.
29. *Sunday Times*, 23 March 1986.
30. *The Provision of Alcohol on Charity Premises* (Charity Commission, London, 1986), p. 4.
31. The Canadian experience also helps to illuminate this contrast between Britain and the US. Revenue Canada has received complaints from some, but not all, of the industries that have been making complaints about 'unfair competition' in the US; this has occurred despite its policy of looking at possible profit motives when considering the registration of a charity. However, in Canada these industries have lacked a 'sponsoring' government department to help them coalesce, so that political pressure for the issue to be given greater priority has been non-existent.
32. Chesterman, *Charities, Trusts and Social Welfare*, pp. 78–9.
33. Edith L. Fisch, Doris Jonas Freed and Esther R. Schachter, *Charities and Charitable Foundations* (Lond, Pomona, NY, 1974), p. 298.
34. Francis Gladstone, *Charity, Law and Social Justice* (Bedford Square Press/NVCO, London, 1982), p. 98.
35. Robert L. Holbert, *Tax Law and Political Access: the bias of pluralism revisited* (Sage, Beverly Hills and London, 1975), p. 25.
36. *Observer* Colour Supplement, 20 October 1985.
37. Chesterman, *Charities, Trusts and Social Welfare*, p. 364.
38. Ibid., p. 360.
39. Paul N. Ylvisaker, 'Foundations and nonprofit organizations', in Walter W. Powell (ed.), *The Nonprofit Sector* (Yale University Press, New Haven, 1987), p. 375.

40. J. Craig Jenkins, 'Nonprofit organizations and policy advocacy', in Powell, (ed.), *The Nonprofit Sector*, p. 299.
41. Jack L. Walker, 'The origins and maintenance of interest groups in America', *American Political Science Review*, 77 (1983), p. 399.
42. Paul B. Downing and Gordon L. Brady, 'The role of citizen interest groups in environmental policy formation', in Michelle J. White, (ed.), *Non-profit Firms in a Three-Sector Economy* (Urban Institute, Washington DC, 1981), p. 77.
43. *New York Times* Educational Supplement, 12 April 1987, p. 57. See also *New York Times*, 26 March 1987.
44. Gladstone, *Charity, Law and Social Justice*, pp. 116–17.
45. David Gerard, *Charities in Britain* (Bedford Square Press/NCVO, London, 1983), p. 105.
46. This survey data is discussed in Gerard, *Charities in Britain*, pp. 104–5.
47. *New York Times*, 9 April 1987 and 12 April 1987.
48. *New York Times*, 10 April 1985.
49. 'Registered charities – ancillary and incidental political activities', *Information Circular 87–1* (Revenue Canada, Ottawa, 1987). Italics added.
50. *Report of the Charity Commissioners for England and Wales for the Year 1986* (HMSO, London, 1987).

Chapter 8 Intermediate Organizations and Democracy

1. Both its adherents and opponents have been responsible for this. One consequence of the ambiguity was the decision by Dahl to change the title of his book, *Pluralist Democracy in the United States*, to *Democracy in the United States* for its second edition. He said of 'pluralism': 'Among political scientists the word now seems to mean whatever any writer chooses it to mean.' Robert A. Dahl, *Democracy in the United States*, 2nd edn (Rand McNally, Chicago, 1972), p. vii.
2. Grant McConnell, 'The public values of the private association', in J. Roland Pennock and John W. Chapman, *Voluntary Associations* (Atherton Press, New York, 1969), p. 155.
3. David Truman, *The Governmental Process* (Knopf, New York, 1951).
4. Patrick Dunleavy and Brendan O'Leary, *Theories of the State* (Macmillan, London, 1987), p. 17.
5. Robert A. Dahl and Charles E. Lindblom, *Politics, Economics and Welfare* (Harper and Row, New York, 1953), pp. 284–5.
6. Dunleavy and O'Leary, *Theories of the State*, p. 17.
7. Interestingly, there is often resistance to political activities among volunteers in those medical research charities which provide services for disease sufferers in addition to raising funds for research. I am grateful to Tom Deans for pointing this out to me.
8. For an analysis of the problems in maintaining democratic control within political parties, see Alan Ware, *Citizens, Parties and the State* (Polity Press, Cambridge, 1987), ch. 6.

9. James Douglas, 'Political theories of nonprofit organization', in Walter W. Powell, (ed.), *The Nonprofit Sector* (Yale University Press, New Haven, 1987), p. 53.
10. David Hine, 'Italy: parties and party government under pressure', in Alan Ware, (ed.), *Political Parties* (Basil Blackwell, Oxford, 1987), p. 74.
11. Michael Sosin, *Private Benefits* (Academic Press, Orlando, Fla., 1986).
12. Among the many universities to have engaged in lobbying Congress for funds are Brown, Columbia, Eastern Michigan and Northwestern.
13. *New York Times*, 9 April 1987.
14. Arthur F. Bentley, *The Process of Government* (University of Chicago Press, Chicago, 1908) and David Truman, *The Governmental Process*.
15. The term 'Book of the Month Club members' came to prominence in Britain after the 1987 general election. Strains in the Alliance parties emerged after their poor electoral performance, and Liberal party members now spoke of their allies in the Social Democratic party as being members of this kind.
16. See, for example, Martin Wattenberg, *The Decline of American Political Parties, 1952–1980* (Harvard University Press, Cambridge, Mass., 1984) and M. N. Franklin, *The Decline of Class Voting in Britain* (Clarendon Press, Oxford, 1985).
17. W. Lance Bennett, *Public Opinion in American Politics* (Harcourt, Brace, Jovanovich, New York, 1980), p. 232.
18. The classic study of the deployment of ambiguous policy positions in election campaigns in the US is Benjamin I. Page, *Choices and Echoes in Presidential Elections* (University of Chicago Press, Chicago, 1978), ch. 6. See also Benjamin I. Page, 'The theory of political ambiguity', *American Political Science Review*, 70 (1976), pp. 742–52, Mary Ellen Leary, *Phantom Politics* (Public Affairs Press, Washington DC, 1977) and Alan Ware, *The Logic of Party Democracy* (Macmillan, London, 1979).
19. On the distinction between 'arbiter' and 'arena' versions of pluralism, see Jack Lively, 'Pluralism and consensus', in Pierre Birnbaum, Jack Lively and Geraint Parry, (eds), *Democracy, Consensus and Social Contract* (Sage, London and Beverly Hills, 1978).
20. Jack L. Walker, 'The origins and maintenance of interest groups in America', *American Political Science Review*, 77 (1983), p. 399.
21. E. E. Schattschneider, *The Semisovereign People* (Holt, Rinehart and Winston, New York, 1960); see also William Gamson, 'Stable unrepresentation in American politics', *American Behavioral Scientist*, 12 (1968), pp. 15–21.
22. Kay Lehman Scholzman, 'What accent the heavenly chorus? Political equality and the American pressure system', *Journal of Politics*, 46 (1984), p. 1021.
23. *Observer* Colour Supplement, 20 October 1985, p. 37.
24. Dahl and Lindblom, *Politics, Economics and Welfare*, p. 313.
25. Ibid. p. 302.
26. Ibid. p. 304.
27. Carole Pateman, *Participation and Democratic Theory* (Cambridge University Press, Cambridge, 1970), pp. 42–3.

28. *Financial Times*, 22 June 1987.
29. George Sayers Bain and Robert Price, *Profiles of Union Growth* (Basil Blackwell, Oxford, 1980), ch. 3.
30. Data on union density supplied by Professor George Bain, School of Industrial and Business Studies, University of Warwick.
31. Keith Bradley and Alan Gelb, 'The replication and sustainability of the Mondragon experiment', *British Journal of Industrial Relations*, 20 (1982), p. 31.
32. The main study in the 1970s of the rise of these values was Ronald Inglehart, *The Silent Revolution* (Princeton University Press, Princeton, 1977).
33. Scott Keeter, 'Public opinion in 1984', in Gerald M. Pomper et al., *The Election of 1984* (Chatham House, Chatham, NJ, 1985), p. 98.
34. Douglas, 'Political theories of nonprofit organization', p. 49.
35. Ralph M. Kramer, *Voluntary Agencies in the Welfare State* (University of California Press, Berkeley, 1981), p. 159.
36. Ibid. pp. 159–60.
37. Ibid. p. 162.
38. Nevertheless, there are many instances which can be cited of these institutions taking stances on issues which clearly do reflect an impartial approach or a commitment to principle. An obvious example is the 1985 Report by the Church of England, 'Faith in the city', which was highly critical of the policies of the Conservative government.
39. See, for example, Douglas A. Hibbs Jr, 'Political parties and macro-economic policy', *American Political Science Review*, 71 (1977), pp. 1467–87, Edward T. Jennings Jr, 'Competition, constituencies and welfare policies', *American Political Science Review*, 73 (1979), pp. 414–29 and L. J. Sharpe and K. Newton, *Does Politics Matter? the determinants of public policy* (Oxford University Press, Oxford, 1984). For a brief discussion of the 'do parties matter?' controversy, see also Ware, *Citizens, Parties and the State*, ch. 7.
40. This view is developed in Desmond S. King, 'The state and the social structures of welfare in advanced industrial democracies', *Theory and Society*, forthcoming.
41. Robert A. Dahl, 'Comment on Manley', *American Political Science Review*, 77 (1983), p. 387.
42. Robert Michels, *Political Parties* (Free Press, New York, 1962). On the weakness of the electoral mechanism as an instrument of popular control, and on the difficulties involved in democratizing political parties, see Ware, *Citizens, Parties and the State*, chs 3 and 6.
43. John Manley, 'Neopluralism: a class analysis of pluralism I and pluralism II', *American Political Science Review*, 77 (1983), p. 370.
44. Robert A. Dahl, *Modern Political Analysis* (Prentice-Hall, Engelwood Cliffs, NJ., 1963), pp. 8–9.
45. Robert A. Dahl, *A Preface to Economic Democracy* (Polity Press, Cambridge, 1985).

Bibliography

Books

All England Law Reports (Butterworth, London, 1973).

Allardt, Erik, et al., *Nordic Democracy* (Det Danske Selskab, Copenhagen, 1981).

Archbishop of Canterbury's Commission on Urban Priority Areas, *Faith in the City* (Church House, London, 1985).

Bain, George Sayers, and Robert Price, *Profiles of Union Growth* (Basil Blackwell, Oxford, 1980).

Bakal, Carl, *Charity USA* (Times Books, New York, 1979).

Balk, Alfred, *The Free List* (Russell Sage, New York, 1971).

Banfield, Edward C., and James Q. Wilson, *City Politics* (Vintage Books, New York, 1966).

Barker, Anthony, (ed.), *Quangos in Britain* (Macmillan, London, 1982).

Barnes, Paul, *Building Societies: the myth of mutuality* (Pluto, London, 1984).

Barnes, Samuel, H., and Max Kaase, (eds), *Political Action* (Sage, Beverly Hills and London, 1979).

Bennett, W. Lance, *Public Opinion in American Politics* (Harcourt, Brace, Jovanovich, New York, 1980).

Bentley, Arthur F., *The Process of Government* (University of Chicago Press, Chicago, 1908).

Berdahl, Robert, O., *British Universities and the State* (Cambridge University Press, Cambridge, 1959).

Binder, Leonard, et al., *Crisis and Sequences in Political Development* (Princeton University Press, Princeton, 1971).

Birnbaum, Pierre, Jack Lively and Geraint Parry, (eds), *Democracy, Consensus and Social Contract* (Sage, Beverly Hills and London, 1978).

Black, Antony, *Guilds and Civil Society in European Political Thought from the Twelfth Century to the Present* (Methuen, London, 1984).

Boddy, Martin, *The Building Societies* (Macmillan, London, 1980).

Boléat, Mark, *The Building Society Industry* (Allen and Unwin, London, 1981).

Brenton, Maria, *The Voluntary Sector in British Social Services* (Longman, London, 1985).

Bridges, Amy, *A City in the Republic* (Cambridge University Press, Cambridge, 1984).

Charity Statistics 1982–83 (Charities Aid Foundation, Tonbridge, 1983).

Charity Statistics 1983–84 (Charities Aid Foundation, Tonbridge, 1984).

Charity Statistics 1984–85 (Charities Aid Foundation, Tonbridge, 1985).

Charity Statistics 1985–86 (Charities Aid Foundation, Tonbridge, 1986).

Charity Trends 1986–87 (Charities Aid Foundation, Tonbridge, 1987).

Ch'en, Kenneth, *Buddhism in China* (Princeton University Press, Princeton, 1964).

Chesterman, Michael, *Charities, Trusts and Social Welfare* (Weidenfeld and Nicolson, 1979).

Clarkson, Kenneth, and Donald Martin, *The Economics of Nonproprietary Organizations* (JAI Press, Greenwich, Conn., 1980).

Cole, G. D. H., *Self-government in Industry* (G. Bell and Sons, London, 1919).

Cole. G. D. H., *Social Theory* (Methuen, London, 1920).

Cole, G. D. H., *Guild Socialism Restated* (Leonard Parsons, London, 1920).

Cole. G. D. H., *Chaos and Order in Industry* (Methuen, London, 1920).

Connolly, William E., *The Terms of Political Discourse* (D. C. Heath, Lexington, Mass., 1974).

Crook, David Paul, *American Democracy in English Politics 1815–1850* (Clarendon Press, Oxford, 1965).

Dahl, Robert A., *Modern Political Analysis* (Prentice-Hall, Englewood Cliffs, NJ, 1963).

Dahl, Robert A., *Democracy in the United States*, 2nd edn (Rand-McNally, Chicago, 1972).

Dahl, Robert A., *A Preface to Economic Democracy* (Polity Press, Cambridge, 1985).

Dahl, Robert A., and Charles E. Lindblom, *Politics, Economics and Welfare* (Harper and Row, New York, 1953).

Dore, Ronald, *British Factory – Japanese Factory* (Allen and Unwin, London, 1973).

Douglas, James, *Why Charity?* (Sage, Beverly Hills and London, 1983).

Dunleavy, Patrick, and Brendan O'Leary, *Theories of the State* (Macmillan, London, 1987).

Duverger, Maurice, *Les Partis Politiques* (Armond Colin, Paris, 1951).

Efficient Scrutiny of the Supervision of Charities (HMSO, London, 1987).

Epstein, Leon D., *Political Parties in Western Democracies* (Pall Mall, London, 1967), revised edn (Transaction, New Brunswick, 1980).

Figgis, John Neville, *Studies of Political Thought from Gerson to Grotius, 1414–1625*, 2nd edn (Cambridge University Press, Cambridge, 1923).

Fisch, Edith L., Doris Jonas Freed and Esther R. Schachter, *Charities and Charitable Foundations* (Lond, Pomona, NY, 1974).

Fox, Daniel M., *Health Policies, Health Politics: the British and American experience, 1911–1965* (Princeton University Press, Princeton, 1986).

Franklin, M. N., *The Decline of Class Voting in Britain* (Clarendon Press, Oxford, 1985).

Fraser, Derek, *The Evolution of the British Welfare State*, 2nd edn (Macmillan, London, 1984).

Geldof, Bob, *Is That It?* (Penguin, Harmondsworth, 1986).

General Accounting Office, *Tax Policy: Competition Between Taxable Businesses and Tax-Exempt Organizations* (General Accounting Office, Washington, D.C., 1987).

Gerard, David, *Charities in Britain* (Bedford Square Press/NCVO, London, 1983).

Gladieux, Lawrence E., and Thomas R. Wolanin, *Congress and the Colleges* (Lexington Books, Lexington, Mass., 1976).

Gladstone, Francis, *Charity, Law and Social Justice* (Bedford Square Press/ NCVO, London, 1982).

Gorman, Robert F., (ed.), *Private Voluntary Organizations as Agents of Development* (Westview, Boulder, Colo., 1984).

Gosden, P. H. J. H., *Self-Help* (Batsford, London, 1973).

Gray, Bradford H., (ed.), *The New Health Care for Profit* (National Academy Press, Washington DC, 1983).

Grossmith, George and Weedon, *The Diary of a Nobody*, 5th edn (J. W. Arrowsmith, Bristol, 1910).

Hague, D. C., and W. J. M. Mackenzie and A. Barker, (eds), *Public Policy and Private Interests* (Macmillan, London, 1975).

Hall, Peter Dobkin, *The Organization of American Culture, 1700–1900* (New York University Press, New York, 1982).

Handel, Gerald, *Social Welfare in Western Societies* (Random House, New York, 1982).

Hansard, Parliamentary Debates.

Harris, John S., *Government Patronage of the Arts in Britain* (University of Chicago Press, Chicago, 1970).

Hirsch, Fred, *Social Limits to Growth* (Routledge and Kegan Paul, London, 1977).

Hirschman, Albert O., *Shifting Involvements* (Martin Robertson, Oxford, 1982).

Hobbes, Thomas, *Leviathan,* Everyman edn (Dent, London, 1914).

Holbert, Robert L., *Tax Law and Political Access: the bias of pluralism revisited* (Sage, Beverly Hills and London, 1975).

Inglehart, Ronald, *The Silent Revolution* (Princeton University Press, Princeton, 1977).

Kendall, Leon T., *The Savings and Loan Business* (Prentice-Hall, Englewood Cliffs, NJ, 1962).

King, Anthony, (ed.), *The New American Political System* (American Enterprise Institute, Washington DC, 1987).

Kramer, Ralph M., *Voluntary Agencies in the Welfare State* (University of California Press, Berkeley, 1981).

Kuhn, Thomas S., *The Structure of Scientific Revolutions*, 2nd edn (University of Chicago Press, Chicago, 1970).

Lane, Jan-Erik, (ed.), *State and Market* (Sage, Beverly Hills and London, 1985).

Larson, Gary O., *The Reluctant Patron* (University of Pennsylvania Press, Philadelphia, 1983).

Laski, Harold, *The Grammar of Politics* (Allen and Unwin, London, 1948).

Leary, Mary Ellen, *Phantom Politics* (Public Affairs Press, Washington DC, 1977).

Lijphart, A., *The Politics of Accommodation* (University of California Press, Berkeley, 1968).

Lindblom, Charles E., and Robert A. Dahl, *Politics, Economics and Welfare* (Harper and Row, New York, 1953).

Lipsey, Richard G., *An Introduction to Positive Economics*, 2nd edn (Weidenfeld and Nicolson, London, 1963).

Lissner, J., *The Politics of Altruism* (Lutheran World Foundation, Geneva, 1976).

Liu, Hui-chen Wang, *The Traditional Chinese Clan Rules* (J. J. Augustin, Locust Valley, NY, 1959).

Lubenow, William C., *The Politics of Government Growth* (David and Charles, Newton Abbot, 1971).

Lubove, Roy, *The Professional Altruist* (Harvard University Press, Cambridge, Mass., 1965).

McKay, David, *American Politics and Society* (Martin Robertson, Oxford, 1983).

Margolis, Howard, *Selfishness, Altruism and Rationality* (Cambridge University Press, Cambridge, 1982).

Mellor, Hugh W., *The Role of Voluntary Organizations in Social Welfare* (Croom Helm, London, 1985).

Mendelson, Mary Adelaide, *Tender Loving Greed* (Knopf, New York, 1974).

Michels, Robert, *Political Parties* (Free Press, New York, 1962).

Mill, John Stuart, *On Liberty*, Everyman edn (Dent, London, 1910).

Miller, David, et al., (eds), *The Blackwell Encyclopaedia of Political Thought* (Basil Blackwell, Oxford, 1987).

Monthly Digest of Statistics (HMSO, London).

National Audit Office, *Monitoring and Control of Charities in England and Wales* (HMSO, London, 1987).

Nicholls, David, *The Pluralist State* (Macmillan, London, 1975).

Nie, Norman H., Sidney Verba and John R. Petrocik, *The Changing American Voter* (Harvard University Press, Cambridge, Mass., 1976).

Nielsen, Waldemar A., *The Endangered Sector* (Columbia University Press, New York, 1979).

Nightingale, Benedict, *Charities* (Allen Lane, London, 1973).

Nisbet, Robert A., *Community and Power* (Oxford University Press, Oxford, 1962).

Norman, E. D., *Church and Society in England, 1770–1970* (Clarendon Press, Oxford, 1976).

Norton, William D., *The Cooperative Movement in Social Work* (Macmillan,

London, 1927).

O'Brien, Michael, *McCarthy and McCarthyism in Wisconsin* (University of Missouri Press, Columbia and London, 1980).

Oleck, Howard L., *Nonprofit Corporations, Organizations and Associations*, 3rd edn (Prentice-Hall, Englewood Cliffs, NJ, 1974).

Olson, Mancur, *The Logic of Collective Action* (Harvard University Press, Cambridge, Mass., 1965).

Owen, David, *English Philanthrophy 1660–1960* (Belknap Press of Harvard University, Cambridge, Mass., 1965).

Page, Benjamin I., *Choices and Echoes in Presidential Elections* (University of Chicago Press, Chicago, 1978).

Pateman, Carole, *Participation and Democratic Theory* (Cambridge University Press, Cambridge, 1970).

Pennock, J. Roland, and John W. Chapman, (eds), *Voluntary Associations* (Atherton Press, New York, 1969).

Phelps, Edmund S., (ed.), *Altruism, Morality and Economic Theory* (Russell Sage, New York, 1974).

Pifer, Alan, *Philanthropy in an Age of Transition* (Foundation Center, New York, 1984).

Plamenatz, John, *Democracy and Illusion* (Longman, London, 1973).

Pomper, Gerald M., *The Election of 1984* (Chatham House, Chatham, NJ, 1985).

Powell, Walter W., (ed.), *The Nonprofit Sector* (Yale University Press, New Haven, 1987).

The Provision of Alcohol on Charity Premises (Charity Commission, London, 1986).

Rapoport, Ronald B., Alan I. Abramowitz and John McGlennon, (eds), *The Life of the Parties* (University of Kentucky Press, Lexington, 1986).

Report of the Charity Commissioners for England and Wales for the Year 1970 (HMSO, London, 1971).

Report of the Charity Commissioners for England and Wales for the Year 1978 (HMSO, London, 1979).

Report of the Charity Commissioners for England and Wales for the Year 1980 (HMSO, London, 1981).

Report of the Charity Commissioners for England and Wales for the Year 1985 (HMSO, London, 1986).

Report of the Charity Commissioners for England and Wales for the Year 1986 (HMSO, London, 1987).

Report of the Chief Registrar of Friendly Societies for 1981–1982 (HMSO, London, 1983).

Report of the Chief Registrar of Friendly Societies for 1983–1984 (HMSO, London, 1985).

Research Papers of the Commission on Private Philanthropy and Public Needs (Department of the Treasury, Washington DC, 1977).

Royal Commission on the Taxation of Profits and Income Cmnd 9474 (HMSO, London, 1955).

Schattschneider, E. E., *The Semisovereign People* (Holt, Rinehart and Winston, New York, 1960).

Schumpeter, Joseph A., *Capitalism, Socialism and Democracy* (Allen and Unwin, London, 1943).

Sharpe, L. J., and K. Newton, *Does Politics Matter? the determinants of public policy* (Oxford University Press, Oxford, 1984).

Shinn, Christine, *Paying the Piper: the development of the UGC 1919–1946* (Falmer Press, Lewes, 1986).

Smith, Gordon, *Politics in Western Europe*, 4th edn (Heinemann, London, 1983).

Sosin, Michael, *Private Benefits* (Academic Press, Orlando, Fla., 1986).

Starr, Paul, *The Social Transformation of American Medicine* (Basic Books, New York, 1982).

Statistical Abstracts of the United States 1985 (Department of Commerce, Washington DC, 1985).

Streeck, W., and P. Schmitter, *Private Interest Government* (Sage, London and Beverly Hills, 1985).

Taylor, Michael, *Anarchy and Cooperation* (John Wiley, London and New York, 1976).

Thompson, E. P., *The Making of the English Working Class* (Vintage Books, New York, 1966).

Titmuss, Richard, *The Gift Relationship* (Pantheon, New York, 1971).

Tönnies, Ferdinand, *Community and Society* trans. Charles P. Loomis, (ed.), (Harper and Row, New York, 1963).

Townsend, Sue, *The Secret Diary of Adrian Mole, Aged 13¾* (Methuen, London, 1982).

Trattner, Walter I., *From Poor Law to Welfare State*, 3rd edn (Free Press, New York, 1984).

Truman, David, *The Governmental Process* (Knopf, New York, 1951).

Unfair Competition by Nonprofit Organizations with Small Businesses (US Small Business Administration, Washington DC, 1984).

Verba, Sidney, and Norman H. Nie, *Participation in America* (University of Chicago Press, Chicago, 1972).

Ware, Alan, *The Logic of Party Democracy* (Macmillan, London, 1979).

Ware, Alan, *The Breakdown of Democratic Party Organization, 1940–1980* (Clarendon Press, Oxford, 1985).

Ware, Alan, *Citizens, Parties and the State* (Polity Press, Cambridge, 1987).

Ware, Alan, (ed.), *Political Parties* (Basil Blackwell, Oxford, 1987).

Wattenberg, Martin, *The Decline of American Political Parties, 1952–1980* (Harvard University Press, Cambridge, Mass, 1984).

Weale, Albert, *Political Theory and Social Policy* (Macmillan, London, 1983).

Webb, R. K., *Modern England* (Allen and Unwin, London, 1969).

Weber, Paul J., and Dennis A. Gilbert, *Private Churches and Public Money* (Greenwood, Westport, Conn., 1981).

Weisbrod, Burton, A., *The Voluntary Nonprofit Sector* (D. C. Heath, Lexington, Mass., 1977).

Wells, Nicholas, *Crisis in Research* (Office of Health Economics, London, 1987).

White, Michelle J., (ed.), *Non-profit Firms in a Three-Sector Economy* (Urban Institute, Washington DC, 1981).

Whiteman, Peter G., and David C. Milne, *Whiteman and Wheatcroft on Income Tax,* 2nd edn (Sweet and Maxwell, London, 1976).

Wilson, Graham K., *Unions in American National Politics* (Macmillan, London, 1979).

Wilson, James Q., *The Amateur Democrat* (University of Chicago Press, Chicago, 1962).

Wolfenden Committee Report, *The Future of Voluntary Organizations* (Croom Helm, London, 1978).

Youings, Joyce, *Sixteenth Century England* (Penguin, Harmondsworth, 1984).

Young, Dennis, R., and Richard R. Nelson, (eds), *Public Policy for Day Care of Young Children* (D. C. Heath, Lexington, Mass., 1973).

Articles, Essays and Papers

Ackerman, Bruce, 'Neo-federalism? the contemporary relevance of the Federalist Papers', paper presented at the *Political Thought Seminar*, Columbia University, New York, 1987.

Ashworth, Mark, 'Individual donations to charity', in *Charity Statistics 1982–83*.

Baggott, I. R., 'The politics of public health: alcohol, politics and social policy', PhD Thesis, University of Hull, 1987.

Beer, Samuel H., 'In search of a new public philosophy', in King, (ed.), *The New American Political System.*

Ben-Ner, Avner, 'Non-Profit organizations: why do they exist in market economies?', *PONPO Working Paper No. 51* (Institution for Social and Policy Studies, Yale University, New Haven, 1983).

Bittker, Boris I., and G. K. Rahdert, 'The exemption of non-profit organizations from federal income tax', *Yale Law Journal,* 85 (1976), pp. 299–359.

Bradley, Keith, and Alan Gelb, 'The political economy of "radical" change: an analysis of the Scottish Daily News worker co-operative', *British Journal of Political Science*, 9 (1979), pp. 1–20.

Bradley, Keith, and Alan Gelb, 'The replication and sustainability of the Mondragon experiment', *British Journal of Industrial Relations*, 20 (1982), pp. 20–33.

Buck, Peter, and Barbara Gutmann Rosenkrantz, 'The social ecology of small foundations', paper presented at *Davis Center Colloquium on Medical and Welfare Policy in the United States, 1860–1980*, Princeton University, 1985.

Bulpitt, Jim, 'English local politics: the collapse of the *ancien régime?*', paper presented at the *Annual Conference of the Political Studies Association*, England, 1976.

Burnell, Peter, 'Third world charities in Britain and official funding', *Politics Working Papers No. 46* (University of Warwick, Coventry, 1987).

Colijn, G. Jan, 'Non-strategic aspects of SDI', *Politics Working Papers No. 45* (University of Warwick, Coventry, 1987).

Copeland, John, and Gabriel Rudney, 'Business income of nonprofits and competitive advantage', *Tax Notes*, 33 (1986), pp. 747–56.

Copeland, John, and Gabriel Rudney, 'Business income of nonprofits and competitive advantage – II', *Tax Notes*, 33 (1986), pp. 1227–36.

Cousins, Paul F., 'Quasi-official bodies in local government', in Barker, (ed.), *Quangos in Britain*.

Dahl, Robert A., 'Comment on Manley', *American Political Science Review*, 77 (1983), pp. 386–9.

Deans, Tom, 'Charity-state relations in Britain and Canada: The case of medical research', PhD thesis, University of Warwick (in preparation).

Deans, Tom, and Alan Ware, 'Charity-state relations: a conceptual analysis', *Journal of Public Policy*, 6 (1986), pp. 121–35.

DiMaggio, Paul, 'Cultural entrepreneurship in nineteenth-century Boston: the creation of an organizational base for high culture in America', *Media, Culture and Society*, 4 (1982), pp. 33–50.

DiMaggio, Paul, 'Can culture survive the marketplace?, *PONPO Working Paper No. 62* (Institution for Social and Policy Studies, Yale University, New Haven, 1983).

DiMaggio, Paul, 'Nonprofit organizations in the production and distribution of culture', in Powell, (ed.), *The Nonprofit Sector*.

Douglas, James, 'Political theories of nonprofit organization', in Powell, (ed.), *The Nonprofit Sector*.

Downing, Paul B., and Gordon L. Brady, 'The role of citizen interest groups in environmental policy formation', in White, (ed.), *Non-Profit Firms in a Three Sector Economy*.

Downs, Anthony, 'Why the government budget in a democracy is too small', *World Politics*, 12 (1960), pp. 541–63.

Easley, David and Maureen O'Hara, 'The economic role of the non-profit firm', *Bell Journal of Economics*, 14 (1983), pp. 531–8.

Ellman, Ira, 'Another theory of nonprofit corporations', *Michigan Law Review*, 80 (1982), pp. 999–1050.

Gamson, William, 'Stable unrepresentation in American politics', *American Behavioral Scientist*, 12 (1968), pp. 15–21.

Geiger, Roger, 'After the emergence: voluntary support and the building of American research universities', *PONPO Working Paper No. 87* (Institution of Social and Policy Studies, Yale University, New Haven, 1985).

Grant, Wyn, 'Corporatism and the public–private distinction', in Lane, (ed.), *State and Market*.

Gray, Bradford H., 'The new entrepreneurialism in health care – overview: origins and trends', *Bulletin of the New York Academy of Medicine*, 61 (1985), pp. 7–22.

Haines, Herbert H., 'Black radicalization and the funding of civil rights', *Social Problems*, 32 (1984), pp. 31–43.

Hall, Peter Dobkin, 'A historical overview of the private nonprofit sector', in Powell, (ed.), *The Nonprofit Sector*.

Handlin Smith, Joanna F., 'Benevolent societies: the reshaping of charity during the late Ming and early Ch'ing', *Journal of Asian Studies*, 46 (1987), pp. 309–37.

Hansmann, Henry B., 'The role of nonprofit enterprise', *Yale Law Journal*, 89 (1980), pp. 835–901.

Hansman, Henry B., 'The rationale for exempting nonprofit organizations from corporate income taxation', *Yale Law Journal*, 91 (1981), pp. 54–100.

Hansmann, Henry B., 'Mutual insurance companies and the theory of nonprofit and cooperative enterprise', *PONPO Working Paper No. 89* (Institution for Social and Policy Studies, Yale University, New Haven, 1985).

Hansmann, Henry B., 'Economic theories of nonprofit organization', in Powell, ed., *The Nonprofit Sector*.

Hawes, Catherine, 'Nursing home reform and the politics of long-term care', *PS*, 20 (1987), pp. 232–41.

Haynes, Douglas, E., 'From tribute to philanthropy: the politics of gift giving in a western Indian city', *Journal of Asian Studies*, 46 (1987), pp. 339–60.

Heidenheimer, Arnold J., 'Secularization patterns and the westward spread of the welfare state', 1883–1983', *Comparative Social Research*, 6 (1983), pp. 3–38.

Herzlinger, Regina E., and William S. Krasker, 'Who profits from nonprofits?', *Harvard Business Review*, 65 (1987), pp. 93–106.

Hibbs, Douglas A., Jr, 'Political parties and macro-economic policy', *American Political Science Review*, 71 (1977), pp. 1467–87.

Hine, David, 'Italy: parties and party government under pressure', in Ware, (ed.), *Political Parties*.

Hood, C., and W. J. M. Mackenzie, 'The problem of classifying institutions', in Hague, Mackenzie and Barker, (eds), *Public Policy and Private Interests*.

Inglehart, Ronald, 'Political action: the impact of values, cognitive level and social background', in Barnes and Kaase, (eds), *Political Action*.

Jacobs, Brian D., 'Nonprofits in the US private sector and their role in community development (with reference to the Local Initiative Support Corporation', paper presented at the *Annual Conference of the American Politics Group of the Political Studies Association*, Durham, 1984.

James, Estelle, 'The nonprofit sector in comparative perspective', in Powell, (ed.), *The Nonprofit Sector*.

James, Estelle, and Susan Rose-Ackerman, 'The nonprofit enterprise in market economies', *PONPO Working Paper No. 95* (Institution for Social and Policy Studies, Yale University, New Haven, 1985).

Jencks, Christopher, 'Who gives to what?', in Powell, (ed.), *The Nonprofit Sector*.

Jenkins, J. Craig, 'Nonprofit organizations and policy advocacy', in Powell, (ed.), *The Nonprofit Sector*.

Jenkins, J. Craig, and Craig M. Eckert, 'Channelling black insurgency: elite patronage and professional SMOs in the development of the civil rights movement', *PONPO Working Paper No. 115* (Institution for Social and Policy Studies, Yale University, New Haven, 1986).

Jenkinson, S. L., 'Church and state', in Miller, et al., *The Blackwell Encyclopaedia of Political Thought*.

Jennings, Edward T., Jr, 'Competition, constituencies and welfare policies', *American Political Science Review*, 73 (1979), pp. 414–29.

Jennings, M. Kent, Klaus R. Allerbeck and Leopold Rosenmayer, 'Generations and families: general orientations', in Barnes and Kaase, (eds), *Political Action*.

Joblove, Leonard, 'Special treatment of churches under the Internal Revenue code', *PONPO Working Paper No. 21* (Institution for Social and Policy Studies, Yale University, New Haven, 1980).

Johansen, L., 'The bargaining society and the inefficiency of bargaining', *Kyklos*, 32 (1979), pp. 479–522.

Karl, Barry D., and Stanley N. Katz, 'The American private philanthropic foundation and the public sphere, 1890–1930', *Minerva*, 19 (1981), pp. 236–70.

Keeter Scott, 'Public opinion in 1984', in Pomper, et al., *The Election of 1984*.

Kenyon, Timothy, 'The politics and morality of "Live Aid"', *Politics*, 5 (1985), pp. 3–8.

King, Desmond S., 'The state and the social structures of welfare in advanced industrial democracies', *Theory and Society* (forthcoming).

Kramer, Ralph M., 'The voluntary agency in a mixed economy: dilemmas of entrepreneurialism and vendorism', *PONPO Working Paper No. 85* (Institution for Social and Policy Studies, Yale University, New Haven, 1985).

Krashinsky, Michael, 'Transaction costs and a theory of the non-profit organization', *PONPO Working Paper No. 84* (Institution for Social and Policy Studies, Yale University, New Haven, 1984).

Lane, Jan-Erik, 'Introduction: public policy or markets? The demarcation problem', in Lane, (ed.), *State and Market*.

Lively, Jack, 'Pluralism and consensus', in Birnbaum, Lively and Parry, (eds), *Democracy, Consensus and Social Contract*.

McCarthy, John, and Mayer Zald, 'Resource mobilization and social movements', *American Journal of Sociology*, 82 (1977), pp. 1212–41.

McConnell, Grant, 'The public values of the private association', in Pennock and Chapman, (eds), *Voluntary Associations*.

Major, Eric, and Mark Ashworth, 'Local authority support of charitable bodies', in *Charity Statistics*, 1984–85.

Manley, John, 'Neopluralism: a class analysis of pluralism I and pluralism II', *American Political Science Review*, 77 (1983), pp. 368–83.

Marmor, Theodore R., Mark Schlesinger and Richard W. Smithey, 'Nonprofit organizations and health care', in Powell, (ed.), *The Nonprofit Sector*.

Montias, J. Michael, 'Public support for the performing arts in western Europe and the United States: history and analysis', *PONPO Working Paper No. 45* (Institution for Social and Policy Studies, Yale University, New Haven, 1982).

Nelson, Richard, and Michael Krashinsky, 'Two major issues of public policy: public subsidy and organization of supply', in Young and Nelson, (eds), *Public Policy for Day Care of Young Children*.

'Nonprofit corporations – Definition', *Vanderbilt Law Review*, 17 (1963), pp. 336–42.

Obler, Jeffrey, 'Private giving in the welfare state', *British Journal of Political Science*, 11 (1981), pp. 17–48.

Page, Benjamin I., 'The theory of political ambiguity', *American Political Science Review*, 70 (1976), pp. 742–52.

Permutt, Steven E., 'Consumer perceptions of nonprofit enterprise: a comment on Hansmann', *Yale Law Journal*, 90 (1981),. pp. 1623–32.

Polivy, Deborah Kaplan, 'A study of the admissions policies and practices of eight local United Way organizations', *PONPO Working Paper No. 49* (Institution for Social and Policy Studies, Yale University, New Haven, 1982).

Posnett, John, 'A profile of the charity sector', in *Charity Statistics 1983–84*.

Posnett, John, 'Trends in the income of registered charities, 1980–1985', in *Charity Trends 1986–87*.

Posnett, John, and Jim Chase, 'Independent schools in England and Wales', *Charity Statistics 1984–85*.

Pye, Lucian W., 'The legitimacy crisis', in Binder, et al., *Crisis and Sequences in Political Development*.

Rajan, Linda, 'Donations to charity by individuals: a comparison between 1980 and 1984', in *Charity Statistics 1985–86*.

'Registered Charities – Ancillary and Incidental Political Activity', *Information Circular 87–1* (Revenue Canada, Ottawa, 1987).

Ridley, F. F., 'State patronage of the arts in Britain: the political culture of cultural politics', *Social Science Information*, 17 (1978), pp. 449–86.

Roberts, Hibbert, R., 'The domestic environment of AID-registered PVOs: characteristics and impact', in Gorman, (ed.), *Private Voluntary Organizations as Agents of Development*.

Rose, Richard, 'The state's contribution to the welfare mix', *Centre for the Study of Public Policy Paper No. 140* (University of Strathclyde, Glasgow, 1985).

Ruderman, F., 'Child care and working mothers', (Child Welfare League of America, 1958).

Rudney, Gabriel, 'A quantitative profile of the nonprofit sector', *PONPO Working Paper No. 40* (Institution for Social and Policy Studies, Yale University, New Haven, 1981).

Rudney, Gabriel, 'The scope and dimensions of nonprofit activity', in Powell, (ed.), *The Nonprofit Sector*.

Salamon, Lester M., 'Rethinking public management: third party government and the changing forms of public action', *Public Policy*, 29 (1981), pp. 255–75.

Salamon, Lester M., 'Government and the voluntary sector in an era of retrenchment: the American experience', paper presented at *The International Conference of Philanthropy*, Venice, 1985.

Salamon, Lester M., 'Partners in public service: the scope and theory of government-nonprofit relations', in Powell, (ed.), *The Nonprofit Sector*.

Saxon-Harrold, Susan, 'Patterns and attitudes to charitable giving: a household survey 1985–86', in *Charity Statistics 1985–86*.

Saxon-Harrold, Susan, 'Patterns and attitudes to charitable giving: a household survey 1987', in *Charity Trends 1986–87*.

Schill, Michael H., 'The participation of charities in limited partnerships', *Yale Law Journal*, 93 (1984), pp. 1355–74.

Schlesinger, Mark, and Robert Dorwart, 'Ownership and mental-health services', *New England Journal of Medicine*, 311 (1984), pp. 959–65.

Schlozman, Kay Lehman, 'What accent the heavenly chorus? Political equality and the American pressure system', *Journal of Politics*, 46 (1984), pp. 1006–32.

Schuster, J. Mark Davidson, 'Tax incentives as arts policy in western Europe', *PONPO Working Paper No. 90* (Institution for Social and Policy Studies, Yale University, New Haven, 1985).

Shattock, Michael, and Robert O. Berdahl, 'The British University Grants Committee 1919–83: changing relationships with government and the universities', *Higher Education*, 13 (1984), pp. 471–99.

Simon, Herbert A., 'Rationality as a process and as product of thought', *Papers and Proceedings of the American Economic Association*, 68 (1978), pp. 1–16.

Simon, John G., 'The tax treatment of nonprofit organizations: a review of federal and state policies', in Powell, (ed.), *The Nonprofit Sector*.

Smith, Brian H., 'US and Canadian nonprofit organizations (PVOs) as transnational development institutions', *PONPO Working Paper No. 70* (Institution for Social and Policy Studies, Yale University, New Haven, 1983).

Smith, Brian H., 'US and Canadian PVOs as transnational development institutions', in Gorman, (ed.), *Private Voluntary Organizations as Agents of Development*.

Steinberg, Richard, 'Nonprofit organizations and the market', in Powell, (ed.), *The Nonprofit Sector*.

Stolpe, Herman, 'The cooperative movements', in Allardt, et al., *Nordic Democracy*.

Tendler, Judith, 'Turning private voluntary organizations into developing agencies', *AID Program Evaluation Discussion Paper No. 12* (US Agency for International Development, Washington DC, 1982).

Tesh, Sylvia, 'In support of "single issue" politics', *Political Science Quarterly*, 99 (1984), pp. 27–44.

Thränhardt, Dietrich, 'Established charity organizations, self-help groups and new social movements in Germany', *Discussion Papers in Political and Administrative Science No. 3* (Institut für Politikwissenschaft der Westfälischen Wilhelms-Universität Münster, Münster, 1987).

Useem, Michael, 'Corporate philanthropy', in Powell, (ed.), *The Nonprofit Sector*.

Walker, Jack L., 'The origins and maintenance of interest groups in America', *American Political Science Review*, 77 (1983), pp. 390–406.

Ware, Alan, 'Parties under electoral competition', in Ware, (ed.), *Political Parties*.

Weisbrod, Burton A., 'Toward a theory of the voluntary non-profit sector in a three-sector economy', in Phelps, (ed.), *Altruism, Morality and Economic Theory*.

Weisbrod, Burton A., 'Private goods, collective goods: the role of the nonprofit sector', in Clarkson and Martin, (eds), *The Economics of Nonproprietary*

Organizations.
White, Michelle J., 'An introduction to the nonprofit sector', in Michelle J. White, (ed.), *Nonprofit Firms in a Three-Sector Economy*.
Whiteley, P., and S. Winyard, 'The origins of the "new poverty lobby"', *Political Studies*, 32 (1984), pp. 32–54.
Wildavsky, Aaron B., 'The Goldwater phenomenon: purists, politicians and the two-party system', *Review of Politics*, 27 (1965), pp. 386–413.
Wilson, David C., and Richard J. Butler, 'Corporatism in the British voluntary sector', in Streeck and Schmitter, *Private Interest Government*.
Ylvisaker, Paul N., 'Foundations and nonprofit organizations', in Powell, (ed.), *The Nonprofit Sector*.
Zukin, Sharon, 'Art in the arms of power: market relations and collective patronage in the capitalist state', *Theory and Society*, 11 (1982), pp. 423–51.

Index

This book is about the many organizations in Britain and the United States which are neither legally part of the state nor permitted to distribute any profits they earn. These 'intermediate organizations' include charities, churches, famine relief agencies, non-state universities, credit unions and social clubs.

In a unique study of this area of the British and the American economy, Alan Ware provides a rigorously analytical and historical account of the relationship of intermediate organizations to both the state and the 'for-profit sector'. Among other issues, the author considers the disappearance of nineteenth-century working class 'mutual' organizations, the growth of profit-making activities by non-profit distributing bodies and the growth and change in voluntarism. He argues that the boundaries between intermediate organizations and the other two 'sectors' are becoming more blurred in a variety of ways and that intermediate organizations do not constitute a separate 'sector' of society.

The book also examines the problems of regulating such organizations and explains the consequences of the British and American practice of having relatively little state intervention in the affairs of such organizations. Finally the author discusses the activities of these organizations in relation to pluralist accounts of the working of liberal democratic states.